Postdigital Positionality

Postdigital Positionality

Developing Powerful Inclusive Narratives for Learning, Teaching, Research and Policy in Higher Education

By

Sarah Hayes

BRILL

LEIDEN | BOSTON

All chapters in this book have undergone peer review.

The Library of Congress Cataloging-in-Publication Data is available online at http://catalog.loc.gov

Typeface for the Latin, Greek, and Cyrillic scripts: "Brill". See and download: brill.com/brill-typeface.

ISBN 978-90-04-43025-9 (paperback)
ISBN 978-90-04-43026-6 (hardback)
ISBN 978-90-04-46602-9 (e-book)

Copyright 2021 by Koninklijke Brill NV, Leiden, The Netherlands.
Koninklijke Brill NV incorporates the imprints Brill, Brill Nijhoff, Brill Hotei, Brill Schöningh, Brill Fink, Brill mentis, Vandenhoeck & Ruprecht, Böhlau Verlag and V&R Unipress.
All rights reserved. No part of this publication may be reproduced, translated, stored in a retrieval system, or transmitted in any form or by any means, electronic, mechanical, photocopying, recording or otherwise, without prior written permission from the publisher. Requests for re-use and/or translations must be addressed to Koninklijke Brill NV via brill.com or copyright.com.

This book is printed on acid-free paper and produced in a sustainable manner.

Contents

Acknowledgements   VII
List of Figures   VIII
Author's Positionality Statement   X

Prologue: Opening the Airing Cupboard from All Sides   1
1   Virtual Airing Cupboards   2
2   Postdigital Airing Cupboards   4
3   Airing New Postdigital Policy Discourse   5
4   Viral Discourse in the Virtual Airing Cupboard   7
5   The Construction of Language   7
6   Positionalities   9
7   Cancel Culture   11
8   Inclusivity   12
9   Inclusion in Policy Discourse and a Need for Postdigital Dialogue   13
10   Inclusion in Decisions about Our Data Requires Some 'Re-plumbing'   15
11   McDonaldisation of a Virus   17
12   Postdigital Inclusivity   18
13   Can Universities Really 'Capture', 'Measure' or 'Deliver' Inclusivity?   19
14   Inclusivity Is Not a Static Concept That Institutions Can Control   21
15   New Ethics and Ownership Questions   22

Introduction   24
1   Postdigital Positionality   24
2   Covid-19   25
3   Covid-19 Positionalities   27
4   A 'New Normal' for Institutions, Different 'New Normals' for Each of Us, or Both?   32
5   HE Policies That Self-Isolate   35
6   Precarity, Disadvantage and the Rationalisation of Academic Labour   35
7   Politics, Ethics and Human Attributes in the Virtual Airing Cupboard   39
8   Inclusive Practice for Algorithmic Identities   40
9   Rationality or Positionality   41
10   New Postdigital Understandings of Interpersonal Relations and Inclusivity   43
11   The Debate to Come   45

1 **Positionality in a Postdigital Context**   49
   1   Why Is Postdigital Positionality a Matter for Everyone?   49
   2   Positionality in a Traditional Sense   66
   3   Postdigital Positionality in a Pandemic   89

2 **Rationalisation of Higher Education and the Postdigital Context**   109
   1   The Shared Political Economic Spaces of Technology and Culture   109
   2   Airing Debate on Postdigital Positionality   143

3 **Postdigital Positionality as a Learner**   161
   1   Learning, Experience and Inclusion as Personal and Embodied, Not
       Rationally Audited   161
   2   Resisting the Iron Cage of 'the Student Experience'   169

4 **Postdigital Positionality as a Teacher**   191
   1   Measuring What Exactly, and Why?   191
   2   Finding New, Personal and Plural Starting Points from Which to
       Teach   204

5 **Postdigital Positionality as a Researcher**   211
   1   The McPolicy of Research Excellence   211
   2   Scientific Research, Crises and Convergences   219

6 **Postdigital Positionality as a Leader and Policy Maker**   227
   1   What Is Shaping the University and What Might the University Now
       Shape?   227
   2   Ecological Approaches towards Policy That Begin from Positionality
       Not Rationality   245

7 **Conclusions on Postdigital Futures**   252
   1   When Biological Environments Change, Social Arrangements Need to
       Alter Too   252

   Glossary   271
   References   274
   Index   309

Acknowledgements

I extend my ongoing love and thanks to my family: David, Calum and Joe Hayes, Jasmine our cat and to my brother Gary Strong, for always supporting my work (in Jasmine's case sleeping on it) and for sharing their ideas on it. To my partner, David, I give particular thanks for his commitment to always reading and reviewing my writing and for his honest feedback. I express my ongoing thanks and appreciation also to Petar Jandrić for his close friendship and co-authorship with me of so many enjoyable works that helped to also inspire this one. I am very grateful to Christine Sinclair for her powerful insights, detailed feedback and valued friendship. I thank Michael Peters for the really enjoyable and engaging collaborative writing projects that he and Petar Jandrić have invited me to participate in, the articles from which I have also cited here. I acknowledge too, the warm support from my colleagues in the Education Observatory, at University of Wolverhampton who are also critically and creatively developing, interpreting and contributing to 'postdigital dialogues' (Jandrić et al., 2018) via local and international research projects. To all authors who write for the Springer journal *Postdigital Science and Education*, I recognise each of your valuable contributions and I thank you all for the many articles from this community which have helped to develop my ideas. Also, to George Ritzer, I express my appreciation for his accessible, adaptable, McDonaldisation theory that I continue to explore. With much thanks to Dennis Hayes too, for his friendship, lively, critical, debates and insights into McDonaldisation, academic freedom and therapeutic culture in the Higher Education (HE) sector. Whilst I have not personally met Blanca Torres-Olave or Jenny J. Lee, I wish to thank them for their inspiring 2019 article on *Shifting positionalities across international locations: embodied knowledge, time-geography, and the polyvalence of privilege*. Thanks to James Ball too, for his brilliant insights in *The system: who owns the internet and how it owns us* (Ball, 2020) and to Sir Anthony Seldon for his exploration of artificial intelligence and its impact on education (Seldon, 2020). To all who placed symbols of hope outside their homes and in their windows during the long periods of pandemic lockdown, thank you for the inspiration these provided as photographs to include. Finally, this book is dedicated wholeheartedly to all who experience any form of exclusion, prejudice or marginalisation, whether intended or not, and via whatever postdigital means it may occur, human or beyond.

Figures

1   Airing cupboard.   1

2   A dry mortar silo attributed with its own form of constructive thinking.   8

3   A 'cash only' notification.   26

4   A vape store selling hand sanitiser.   27

5   A box of free books outside a home.   29

6   Ice was dumped outside the Scottish Parliament in protest.   30

7   A construction site notice advises workers to socially distance.   31

8   Footway works are cancelled due to Covid-19.   32

9   Love locks on a bridge are joined by a face mask.   54

10   A Black Lives Matter sign displayed on a van.   81

11   Healthcare workers identify their own positionality in their car window.   83

12   Student nurses urge people to 'stay home' on a sign in their window.   83

13   A sign offering medical staff 'a well-earned drink on us'.   84

14   A sign on a gate thanking key workers.   85

15   Supermarket shelves running low on stocks.   90

16   A sign urges people to 'give way to social distancing'.   92

17   A teddy bear is left hanging in a plastic bag on a gate post as a symbol of lockdown.   94

18   A campervan in a driveway displays a 'stay safe' and 'smile' poster.   94

19   Children's rainbow drawings placed outside a pub.   95

20   A child's rainbow drawing displayed on a gate post.   95

21   A pilot draws an emoticon of a smiley face in the sky above a UK city.   96

22   A householder urges people not to stroke their pet dog.   101

23   A lecture theatre where I taught in Ghana in 2019.   122

24   A university window displays the word 'IMPACT'.   129

25   A university window displays the word 'AMBITION'.   129

26   A university window displays the word 'PASSION'.   130

27   The word 'HUMILITY' is displayed on a banner outside a cricket ground.   131

28   The word 'TEAMWORK' is displayed on a banner outside a cricket ground.   132

29   An airing cupboard hot water tank infrastructure.   150

30   An airing cupboard water tank specifications.   150

31   My laptop showing the Internet of Tanks opportunity.   151

32   Covid-19 government guidance to 'stop the spread' whilst in a children's play area.   157

33   Covid-19 list of rules displayed in a children's play area.   157

34   A 'shield our city' sign proclaiming that: 'distance makes us stronger'.   165

35   A sign with a rainbow thanking all key workers.   176

FIGURES   IX

36   A staying Covid-19 secure sign detailing five steps to safer working together.   178
37   A 'stay safe' sign as part of a Rainbow Trail.   178
38   A 'keep your social distance' sign.   182
39   An 'only travel if you need to' sign.   195
40   A sign reminding people to use sanitiser.   201
41   University iconography where a window is inscribed with the word 'EXCELLENCE'.   205
42   A sign asking those with Covid-19 symptoms not to enter a building.   222
43   A sign listing a set of rules for visitors to an office to observe if their visit is essential.   224
44   A reminder to 'put on your mask' before entering the office.   228
45   A reminder to download the SmartShop app to help avoid checkout queues.   230
46   A sign indicating that due to Covid-19 an online booking system has been set up for appointments.   230
47   A sign reminding people that 'only orders placed online are available at this store'.   231
48   A sign instructing people to please stay apart from each other.   241
49   A local business details its policy for operating as 'normal' during the Covid-19 pandemic.   248
50   A reminder of government regulations during the pandemic.   253
51   Reminders of the 'hands, face, space' hygiene routine.   259
52   Reminders of the requirement to wear face coverings in all shops.   260
53   A snowman sports a face mask alongside the more traditional carrot during Winter 2020.   268

Author's Positionality Statement

It may seem unorthodox to begin a book on positionality, in a postdigital university context, with a reference to a *Terminator* movie, but do hear me out, if you will. My own route though HE during the last twenty-two years has often felt rather like a series of fragments. I could just move on from each of my diverse past roles, cancel them from memory even, or I could retain these experiences and reflexively bring them into a critical dialogue with my present positionality. This reminds me of the scene with the shattered Terminator in the second movie, re-attracting pools of liquid metal to re-form in its latest appearance. Postdigital contexts seem to me to be fluid and organic like this, with what is cultural or technological converging in this manner, appearing sometimes human, sometimes machine, a blend of both bringing new perceptions to us of who we are. Positionality theory offers one way to anchor ourselves in everchanging postdigital situations, and to bring our individual experiences (past, present and future) into both personal and collective dialogues. The virtual airing cupboard of the Internet has placed many fragments of each of us in multiple locations. If you will permit me a further analogy, rather like the horcruxes in *Harry Potter,* these are hidden and possibly just as difficult to eradicate. We cannot individually retrieve these fragments because they have moved and changed shape as data, but we can seek to reclaim our own individual postdigital positionalities. To do so, provides a strong resistance to the rationalised policy choices made by others, on what they perceive our experience is. I have sought to include varied cross-disciplinary, academic, cross-sector, media and popular culture sources, to present the case for a debate, rather than to overtly take sides on the many emotive issues that I have referenced. It has felt messy and incomplete, as I have written these references in, often in real time as they emerged, but postdigital existence has this effect, compounded too by the bewilderment wrought by the Covid-19 global pandemic. Writing in this way has been exhilarating, with moments of panic about how much to include about unfolding events, mixed with pleasure in photographing people's material expressions of their positionality during the crisis. Most of the images in the book were photographed in the UK due to travel restrictions, but the diverse sources the book draws on are from across the globe. I am fully conscious of changes in myself and those I care for too, during lockdown after lockdown, and so I reflexively recognise my own positioning as a university researcher, sociologist, educator, partner, parent, carer and a mature, white female. I refer to my own work alongside the work of many others (acknowledging too of course the labour of my humble airing cupboard)

AUTHOR'S POSITIONALITY STATEMENT

throughout the book. In choosing the examples that I have shared, there will be others I have not included (so apologies to my dishwasher, if it did not get a mention this time). I hope though, that readers wherever they are in the world, will explore their own perspectives on the matters raised. Do share your own research, fill in inevitable gaps, get in touch and help to collectively extend this open debate on postdigital positionality, inclusivity and implications for how HE policy is framed, as we look ahead towards the future. Always though, keeping one eye on the past.

PROLOGUE

Opening the Airing Cupboard from All Sides

To say in a sentence what this book is about, I would venture that it is: *an intention to explore positionality in the postdigital context that Higher Education (HE) now inhabits, to raise open debate on the implications for individuals and for HE inclusivity policies.* As such, this preface sets the scene by discussing some assumptions and challenges this book will explore. However, as odd as it may sound, I begin this debate by opening up the airing cupboard...

Airing broad and varied viewpoints to contribute to ideas on inclusivity is not an easy thing to do in our current cultural climate. Some debates can, speaking metaphorically, resemble pulling out the same old sheets from an airing cupboard.

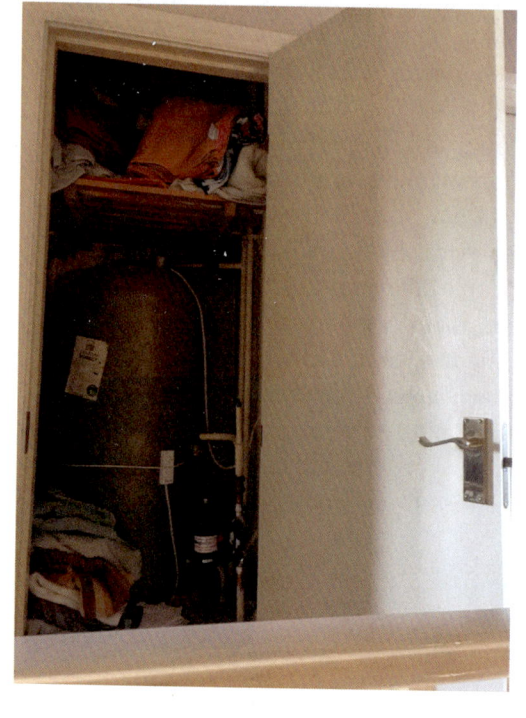

FIGURE 1
Airing cupboard

The arguments that seem to get aired and re-aired are the more popular, recent and easy-to-reach ones, just like the comfortable, well-worn sheets that fall out on you, as you open the airing cupboard door. In a very full airing cupboard, the tank and pipes inside are concealed by all that is happening up

© KONINKLIJKE BRILL NV, LEIDEN, 2021 | DOI: 10.1163/9789004466029_001

front. It would be easy to forget that these mechanisms are there in the background, to ensure the warm air continues to circulate. Then there is also a risk that, whilst I am searching towards the back of the cupboard, a discovery of some dirty laundry brings to mind the old adage: *how much of this should be aired anyway?*

The saying 'don't air your dirty laundry in public' originates from physical situations where dirty laundry (really an analogy for unpleasant or inconvenient secrets) was supposed to remain hidden when visitors called, in case any revelations led to embarrassment for a family. If I place my scruffy linen on a washing line outside though, it will only be noticed by people passing by and perhaps the odd drone circling overhead. If I sit in a room with family and share a few dirty secrets, then these too are only passed between those who are present.

These days though, across virtual news and social media websites on the Internet, personal stories abound alongside expressions of offence taken by others to opinions, values or events described. These are not only tales of an occasion and related reactions and experiences, however. These are also data. This may be data I do not realise has been gathered when I spoke to a news channel, posted a tweet or a photo, interacted with classmates on a data-driven system for my university studies, or taught a class online. Data is collected with all kinds of potential re-use in mind, but unlike scruffy laundry items, data can travel quickly and simultaneously into many other systems. It can cross fluid boundaries that are human, technological, biological, political, economic and linguistic with new, far-reaching implications for human ontologies (Peters, 2019, Peters, Jandrić & Hayes, 2021a, 2021b). Perhaps in the past the so-called dirty laundry led to families refusing to speak to, or to visit each other. Such snubs can now be achieved with much larger public audiences on online platforms, via the 'virtual airing cupboard' of the Internet. We might think of it as rather like a massive airing cupboard, where the physical 'tank and pipes' (and who and what is powering these) are easily overlooked in the entanglements up front.

1   **Virtual Airing Cupboards**

One way to play with such a metaphor for links between online communications across data-driven systems and issues of inclusivity is to imagine that, rather than opening the door of the physical airing cupboard at the top of your stairs (should your home have any stairs) you are typing into your preferred Internet browser which takes you into the virtual airing cupboard. The sheets of information before you, in the form of web pages, are not so unlike the old sheets picked out from the airing cupboard in the hallway, as they fall out from the front. Maybe you consciously saved and bookmarked some searches, or maybe a device you are using decided on your behalf to present you with topics and items you have recently browsed or purchased.

These online activities are evolving into 'onto-platforms' that know us and our 'hourly fluctuations of the self – better than we can know ourselves' (Peters, 2019). Such a situation has ongoing implications too for how each of us finds ourselves positioned as a human being, for our perceptions of personal opportunities, identity and inclusion. For example, it is worth reflecting on just how often some form of verification is expected from each of us in our activities online. As Braidotti points out in *Posthuman Knowledge* (2019), the process of confirming that you are 'not a robot' has now become a routine aspect of transactions across the Internet. It is much harder to raise questions ourselves of the systems we access such as 'do you plan to sell my data?' or 'what commercial interests and economic partnerships lie behind this system that I am writing my most intimate details into?' The imperative to verify our human identity effects a shift where the central point of reference is now 'the algorithmic culture of computational networks – not the human' (Braidotti, 2019a: 1).

Algorithmic activity of this nature, despite the complex programming behind it, has slipped quietly (and often unnoticed) into the daily activities of many humans. It did not though arrive accidentally. Programmers were trained in universities, companies hired them and the hardware and software we use, and that uses us as data, was designed and distributed. Yet the universities where so much scientific and technological research and innovation originates, are also ideally positioned to lead critical debate on related societal knowledge and new potential to reduce or exacerbate inequalities. What complicates this is that universities, within global political economy, have become closely interlinked with corporate businesses with strong economic interests in the data driven systems and analytics that operate across the virtual airing cupboard of the Internet (Ball, 2020, Ramge, 2020, Williamson, 2019a, 2019b, 2020a, 2020b, 2020c). Universities are therefore entangled in a situation where 'software code, algorithms, data analytics and infrastructures have become inseparable from policy processes and modes of governance' (Williamson, 2019a: 1).

Yet in HE policy, despite the widespread digitalisation of university activities, a coherent and transparent approach towards the implications this has for inclusivity has yet to be demonstrated. Whilst one part of the university is busy generating policy for areas that digital technologies might enhance, not far across the campus, a different set of strategies to address equality, diversity, inclusivity, or measure student participation, retention and success are also being churned out for audit and regulation. There is little dialogue (if any) between HE policy for inclusivity concerning people, and university policy relating to cutting edge research and impact across a broad digitalisation of science and efforts towards a circular bioeconomy (OECD, 2020, Aguilar, Twardowski & Wohlgemuth, 2020). Yet such research now has far reaching implications for shifts in human identity, and indeed in how existence itself, is understood (Peters, Jandrić & Hayes, 2021a, 2021b).

2   Postdigital Airing Cupboards

In a postdigital conception of HE, all of these dimensions are perceived to be interconnected. A growing body of literature is offering deeply contextual interpretations of what it means to be 'postdigital' (Pepperell & Punt, 2000, Cramer, 2015, Jandrić, Knox, Besley, Ryberg, Suoranta & Hayes, 2018). For some, this entails rejection of an implied conceptual shift of the 'digital revolution', a shift apparently as abrupt as the 'on/off' logic of the machines now pervading people's daily lives (Pepperell & Punt, 2000: 2). Boellstorff (2016) draws attention to: 'a key sticking point in contemporary theories of technology' that holds direct relevance for this book: 'the false opposition of the digital and the real'. Calling this a fundamental misrepresentation, Boellstorff raises the issue of the language we use when we talk of the physical as 'real' and compare this with terms like 'digital', 'online', or 'virtual', to infer that these are somehow less real. Firstly, such 'conflations of physical with real, and digital with unreal, even in rhetorical passing, have devastating consequences for addressing the reality of the digital'. Secondly, this presumptive gap reflects 'deep-seated assumptions about value, legitimacy, and consequence' (Boellstorff, 2016: 387). This brings concerns for equality and inclusivity, as it 'forecloses comprehensively examining world makings and social constructions of reality in a digital age' (Boellstorff, 2016: 388).

This means that a discussion of the postdigital context we now occupy is a feminist issue too, when it concerns education that is analogue, digital, or postdigital in on/offline worlds (Deepwell, 2020). Pointing to the 'reality of flawed, broken, and partial coverage of subjects, identities, and visibilities online – particularly for women', Deepwell cites a 'failure to record or capture so much of feminist knowledge production or women's experiences of the world'. She contrasts rhetoric surrounding the Internet and its promised capacity for change with the reality of 'overload' and she asks whether feminist knowledge has ever fully had a digital paradigm? A good question, given that a look at 'the systems

OPENING THE AIRING CUPBOARD FROM ALL SIDES

that distribute power and money in the internet era' reveal that 'the winners are overwhelmingly white, overwhelmingly male, and overwhelmingly from the kind of background that was doing pretty much fine before the Internet too' (Ball, 2020: 225). When Deepwell reflects on whether this is 'a problem for a postdigital education or for humanity', I would suggest that we need to interrogate both.

In a postdigital society there are no hard boundaries separating what takes place for individuals across the virtual airing cupboard of the Internet and their arrival to study, teach, research or hold a leadership role in HE. They bring with them a unique positionality, but one that is now subject to much fragmentation due to blurs in what is considered natural or organic, digital, engineered, or synthetic (Peters, Jandrić & Hayes, 2021a). Whilst in some interpretations a postdigital context could simply mean accepting that digital is now in the background and just part of the fabric of our society, there are reasons to examine digitalisation as fundamentally much more. Even in the process of adapting to digital ways of being, rapid developments have brought new technological convergences that are shifting science itself into new fields of disciplinary knowledge. Rather than perceive these subjects as discrete, or in isolation from each other, they might be understood as 'new knowledge ecologies', rapidly emerging in a postdigital landscape where technological ability now shapes science (Peters, Jandrić & Hayes, 2021a).

In this context, biology as digital information, and digital information as biology, are now dialectically interconnected (Peters, Jandrić & Hayes, 2021a) which in turn requires new conceptions in policy, and extensions to traditional and contemporary theories.

3 Airing New Postdigital Policy Discourse

Now that new scientific activities are driven primarily through what can be digitised, data has become a very valuable commodity. This takes us deeply into 'a world where a mining of the psyche takes place within bio-informational capitalist networks that require the surrender of autonomy for a full integration into the circuitry' (Peters, 2019). Ramge (2020) suggests that Artificial Intelligence (AI) abuse is increasing in three main ways in the digital economy: (1) via a *monopolisation of data* by large Information Technology (IT) companies and Internet platforms, (2) through *manipulation of the individual* in the commercial space where the interests of companies rather than users are advanced and (3) in the *abuse by political actors and regimes* through surveillance, incentives and repressive measures. Raising the question: *what do we actually want the future to resemble?* (Ramge, 2020) therefore cuts to the chase on the 'hot air' surrounding inclusivity agendas. There are futures where AI systems can 'relieve us of tedious tasks', or 'improve health and education' or bring about 'sustainable development to increase prosperity for all' and 'strengthen democratic discourse instead of undermining it in the echo chambers of social media' (Ramge, 2020). New postdigital policy discourse is therefore necessary to determine ways to 'achieve a successful synthesis of the analog and the digital', to 'use intelligent machines intelligently'. Ramge argues that 'postdigital citizens workers and consumers' should no longer 'fall for the big tech corporations promises of salvation' (Ramge, 2020). Furthermore, amid recent biodigital innovations, where biology and technology merge, there is now a use of biology to make products which takes us down a potentially new economic and disciplinary trajectory. This is a route where human philosophical goals of inclusivity and equality might be furthered via the principles of bioeconomy, environmental self-renewal and new synthetic enhancements. Such a biologisation of digital processes may reflect a very different kind of political economy (Peters, Jandrić & Hayes, 2021a, 2021b).

Human habits in a virtual environment may seem different, but such perceptions then have a tendency to mislead approaches towards policy in universities concerning digital change. Rather than rationalise about what digital technology is 'enhancing' or 'driving' in education, more nuanced understandings are required. This means a shift to how we construct policy and write related strategies in HE, if implications for inclusivity and disadvantage are really to be addressed. The overlap and parallels across physical and virtual environments, as well as across space and time, are more aptly observable now in the notion of a postdigital society that all of us inhabit, rather than simply to discuss digital drivers. In taking a postdigital perspective towards policy a continuity is recognised across online and offline experiences, knowledge and cultural theory prior to digital advances, and our anticipated futures.

Interdisciplinary theories about the mutually constitutive relationship of technologies in individual human lives (Mackenzie & Wajcman, 1999, Braidotti, 2019a) recognise that people shape, and are shaped by, technology and culture. They make postdigital choices, as they connect with old and new media, with predigital artefacts like my airing cupboard of bricks and mortar, with digital systems and postdigital entireties. As Feenberg has commented: 'the postdigital no longer opposes the virtual or cyber world to the world of face-to-face experience. The digital is integrated and imbricated with our everyday actions and interactions' (Feenberg, 2019: 8). A postdigital perspective on inclusivity requires attention to be paid to the technological 'plumbing' of the Internet and of our institutions, to who and what is controlling such infrastructures and to the risks of not connecting people, activities and objects.

OPENING THE AIRING CUPBOARD FROM ALL SIDES

There is a need to review uses of language and effects of datafication. Thus, debate might be aired on what a postdigital inclusivity policy discourse might look like, as universities endeavour to respond.

4   Viral Discourse in the Virtual Airing Cupboard

Rather than refusing to speak to someone in the family who has aired some 'dirty laundry' about me in some manner, I can now 'unfriend' them effortlessly on Facebook, discuss them over Twitter, or avoid their LinkedIn invitation, as well as close my front door in their face. Unlike ignoring their knock on my door though, or their phone calls which are one-to-one encounters, my activities in the virtual airing cupboard have a much wider reach. What links the online and offline 'airing' of opinion is a use of natural language, which of course I have applied in my chosen analogy to airing cupboards. Annika Mann (2018) has pointed out the 'contagious' aspects of language that have long interested theorists concerning how ideas in general spread, but she also notes the intersection between contagion and language. When a biological threat strikes, such as Aids or the Covid-19 pandemic, there is a contagion both from the 'communicable disease and its means of communication' (Mann, 2018). New words and phrases find their way into circulation, alongside the ideas that they are transmitting. It can then almost appear as if our language is mutating rapidly before us, rather like a virus itself. One example can be noticed in the term *covidiot* which blends together covid and idiot to describe those who don't keep a distance from others to avoid catching and spreading the Covid-19 virus, or who refuse to undertake quarantine, once infected with it.

In terms of government policy, the notion that the fight against the Covid-19 virus entails *'following the science'* has been a much-used phrase during 2020 and 2021. As vaccines for Covid-19 have been developed, the behaviour of countries with regard to global distribution has been discussed as *'vaccine nationalism'* or *'vaccine diplomacy'.* Such words and ideas take the form of cultural truths that are moulded and then spread within discourse. They may also get treated as if they are universal representations of reality, where one dominant set of values overrides others.

5   The Construction of Language

However, perhaps a little controversially, Frank Van Splunder (2020) argues that languages do not exist anyway. In *Language is Politics*, he describes languages as constructions. We may speak of natural languages, as opposed to computer generated codes perhaps, but even so-called 'natural' languages are in fact artificial constructions too. On this basis, language has a strength in acting rather like a fluid form of mortar to develop and construct our human thinking, but also to apply ideas to objects and commodities. In our consumer culture many goods, services and products are injected with human qualities and acts of thought, labour or feelings (Hayes, 2019a), as demonstrated in the advert on the silo pictured in Figure 2.

FIGURE 2   A dry mortar silo attributed with its own form of constructive thinking

Yet sometimes something so obviously commercial, as in this photo I took of a dry mortar silo on a local building site, as it professes to be undertaking 'constructive thinking', can (in its own way) contribute to further theory and debate. It might even help us to avoid the silos of theory that can occur in HE, leaving disciplines sitting apart from each other, when they might instead engage in constructive thinking about areas of convergence.

Firstly, languages enacted as discourse can construct one particular world view (when others may exist), even lies can sound as if they may be true. Secondly, languages are used to construct identities. Van Splunder (2020) gives the example of identities of nations, groups or individuals that can be defined by who they are, or against who they believe they are not. Then there is the actual linguistic construction that takes the form of grammar, vocabulary and

OPENING THE AIRING CUPBOARD FROM ALL SIDES

spelling. The order of words and the patterns in which these are placed can manipulate, differentiate and control meanings to serve certain needs and ideologies (Van Splunder, 2020, Hayes, 2019a).

In postdigital society, the close associations between many contributing forces to such 'truths' are recognised. These include technology, culture, biology, language and information, all as causal and inseparable contributors to what is transmitted in discourse. As these and other political and economic forces intermingle with human values and viruses, cultural evolution in postdigital society is driven through 'bioinformationalism', via a 'viral modernity' (Peters, Jandrić & McLaren, 2020). Therefore, recognising positionality in postdigital contexts helps to indicate too that 'knowledge and voice are always located in time, space and social power. The concept of positionality refers us to the who, where, when and why of speaking, judgement and comprehension' (Barker & Jane, 2016: 643). On this basis, the virtual airing cupboard of the Internet might also be aptly described as a *viral* airing cupboard. If a physical airing cupboard is a warm ecosystem where I might be able to grow something, the online airing cupboard may be virtual, but it has a vast potential to germinate, grow and rapidly spread ideas. Whilst such comments about the Internet are hardly new, many more devices now connect online environments with our physical and natural living circumstances. This is never more so than during the lockdown periods aiming to reduce the Covid-19 infection, which saw a huge surge in online activity of all kinds, even if this did not include everyone globally, in terms of access. Furthermore, in a postdigital context (Jandrić, Knox, Besley, Ryberg, Suoranta & Hayes, 2018) personal positionalities on the most intimate of topics are now shared publicly across multiple platforms and forums. Unlike a whispered secret though, these narratives remain active and independent of the human who first shared them. Each posting, comment or response becomes detached from the location, personal viewpoint and original positionality of the person to whom these words once belonged. Free of context, words and ideas can travel and modify as this data is picked up by others. In this way a 'super-spreader' of misinformation online can appear to resemble a 'super-spreader' of an infectious virus. A close association between viral biology on the one hand, and information science on the other, can lead to further analogies between viral 'epidemics and infodemics' (Peters, Jandrić & McLaren, 2020).

6 Positionalities

However, despite all kinds of mutation of communications, what gets stated, uploaded, captured or shared still has an originator. A topic communicated can be revealing in content, but it also says something about those who shared it (whether they are human or not). As such, positionality theory, where identity is fluid, dynamic and contextual, is one way to examine individual experiences in postdigital society and to discuss implications for assumptions about inclusivity in HE policy.

Positionality is understood as the intimate and ever-changing social, technological and political contexts that intermingle with, create and continue to influence, a person's values, identity and opportunities. This could include impacts on their gender, race, sexuality, class, location, ability, prospects and many other factors, and so identity remains fluid within relations of power. Through examining positionality, a critical analysis of self-understandings becomes possible, via reflexivity. In short, reflexivity provides our individual route towards unpacking our postdigital positionality and considering the positionality of others. Given all that now happens in the virtual airing cupboard, and its interconnection too with everything outside of it, reflexively engaging with our postdigital positionality can help us to retain some sense of agency. As a point of anchor, it can provide a resistance to being objectified as data alone. It enables each of us to subjectively provide our own fluid narratives, as people who are both cultural and technological citizens in postdigital society.

The ways in which a person's identity is also shaped by new cultural, technological and biological influences (depending on their positionality) brings additional challenges for inclusivity agendas. Furthermore, potential bias or discrimination experienced by individuals can now be shaped by multiple combined factors (Morris, 2020a) that remain 'real' across online and offline locations. The virtual airing cupboard of the Internet can seem like a warm familiar environment for me to share my 'dirty laundry', as I sit in my physical (or virtual) room on my laptop choosing what language I will use to comment in an online forum. What I write there is not though simply picked up by a human hand, like the laundry from the hall cupboard. A letter I might once have sent through the post via a post box went to a specific addressee. Data that I share now can be categorised by a computer without my knowledge and according to parameters that I am unaware of. It can be reused, as well as read, re-read, downloaded, edited and forwarded, along with any images I have aired too. The content can be internalised by many other humans and devices, edited and shared again. This carries the constant risk of reactions to any values that I may have expressed virtually: there could be legal implications too. I may find that I have become 'unfriended' or that 'dirty laundry' has been posted online about me too. Strangers may have urged others to cut me off or to appropriate aspects of my identity, in ways I had not anticipated, when I first began to type.

Whilst much of this may sound like familiar territory, a further debate now emerges with the convergence between biology and information that is now

OPENING THE AIRING CUPBOARD FROM ALL SIDES

flowing through the virtual airing cupboard. The scenarios described above take place in a paradigm of 'bioinformationalism', which draws a close association between viral biology on the one hand, and information science on the other, to critically discuss how communications 'mutate' across our political economy (Peters, Jandrić & McLaren, 2020). A new paradigm, 'biodigitalism', also refers to the mutual interaction and integration of information and biology, but this manipulation of biological systems in computational biology is beginning to fundamentally reconfigure all levels of theory and practice (Peters, Jandrić & Hayes, 2021a). There are new implications for human agency, if critical reason itself starts to require a biodigital interpretation, rather than the other way around. This could shift for example assumptions concerning cognitive processes and the disciplinary traditions from which these positions have emerged over centuries. With a new constellation of forces shaping the future of what humans might become in postdigital society, we encounter too a new biopolitics of identity which brings philosophies of race, class, gender and intelligence, into new compelling dialogue with genomics and information. (Peters, Jandrić & Hayes, 2021a). There are many non-human positionalities to notice now and to be conscious of the fluid postdigital boundaries they can also cross.

7   Cancel Culture

Dubbed as 'cancel culture', this is where an opinion shared by someone online but deemed to be unpopular by someone else, leads to a boycott of them as a person. Whether in the name of social justice or social judgement, the person is 'cancelled' by those who feel unhappy about the views that they aired. Cancel culture is one of many socially constructed nicknames for what humans do to others and has become widely 'aired' across online forums. Others such as 'ghosting' (where a person is dropped without a word by someone whom they believed that they were dating online) or 'zombieing' (where the 'ghoster' gets back in touch) reveal similar trends. Yet the notion that a human opinion aired can simply be switched off, or that they themselves might be 'cancelled' – like the next online shopping order that I place, or the sheets that I choose to overlook at the rear of the cupboard – has implications for a person's positionality. Furthermore, the broader implications of accepting (or otherwise) a person or a particular culture's supposed attitudes, can alter each individual's mental wellbeing, access to others, opportunities, participation and their sense of inclusion. People are placed, and replaced, through power relationships that interplay both online and offline. These pass between different digital systems as well as through humans.

As a result, there are implications for *what*, and not only *who* gets to be 'included' these days, in inclusion policies. This requires an underpinning debate about the stance which is taken by each university and those in it towards algorithmic activity and new biodigital knowledge ecologies that are both individual and collective. Universities cannot meaningfully be concerned with inclusivity between humans in isolation from a widespread digitalisation of life taking place all around us. In postdigital society, what is digital is now also closely intermingled with all other aspects of human life, values and emotion and the expression of these, through language (Jandrić, Knox, Besley, Ryberg, Suoranta & Hayes, 2018). So, whilst my airing cupboard analogy is a figurative one, it helps to illustrate an interplay across physical and virtual circumstances surrounding humans that postdigital theory encapsulates. It is argued that all technological, cultural and biological changes remain with us, whether or not the machines, theories or the practices themselves are still actively in use. Whatever form virtual airing cupboards may now take, in terms of the many devices and online platforms used to express opinions via the Internet, there are now new implications for the construction of inclusivity policies in education, just as there are new postdigital participants and partnerships to be considered.

8 Inclusivity

The term 'inclusivity' is now widely adopted in organisations and companies across the globe. In HE policy discourse it is frequently interpreted in terms of fairness and equality of opportunity for all citizens to access education as a basic human right, throughout life. Further emphasis may be placed in university *equality, diversity* and *inclusion* policies on respecting all identities and cultures of learners, and on institutions adjusting their core values and plans to support such principles. So far so good, but these values expressed in existing policy discourse tend to be based on interactions between human beings alone. Little seems to be 'included' in HE inclusion policies on how principles of inclusivity, diversity and human rights are now subject to a complex interplay of data, software and communications, via the role that technological platforms and devices play (or don't play) in individual lives. Yet, 'we live in a digital age where the relations between online and offline can have positive impacts on everything from inequality and belonging to climate change but can also have negative impacts in these domains' (Boellstorff, 2016: 397).

In what has been discussed as a 'knowledge society' (Delanty, 2001), where digital technologies increasingly shape knowledge across multiple forums,

OPENING THE AIRING CUPBOARD FROM ALL SIDES

concerns over fake news in an era of post-truth have gripped global society. An inclusive and empowering approach is to see valid knowledge as that which 'includes an acknowledgement of the knower's specific position in any context, because changing contextual and relational factors are crucial for defining identities and our knowledge in any given situation' (Maher & Tetreault, 1993). Furthermore, whilst gender, race, class and other aspects of our identities may be perceived by some people as rather fixed in nature, to understand these features of each of us, as markers of relational *positions,* rather than essential qualities (Alcoff, 1988) enables a clearer understanding of how technologies constantly intermingle with the facets of who each of us are. This is a powerful route too, towards maintaining our own agency in whatever situations we encounter online and offline and in determining what knowledge can be treated as valid.

Throughout 2020 and 2021, the Covid-19 pandemic and related lockdown policies contributed to a dramatic increase in the use of online systems to support learning, health and welfare. Some people were better positioned than others, in terms of their access to digital devices and their skills to interact through these, depending on the levels of existing disadvantage that they faced. A realisation of these disparities has led to wider discussions about digital inclusion and concerns over digital poverty, but much of this focuses around the simple task of supplying laptops to those without them. The complexities in relation to skills, data, ethics, shared or inappropriate learning spaces, disabilities, motivations and many other deeply contextual factors remain unaddressed. Amid these rapid changes, and on the back of huge amounts of work on inclusivity in HE in recent years, a common assumption remains also that 'the principles of inclusive practice are well established' (Department for Education, 2017). However, this does not explicitly say which 'principles', what forms of 'practice', or by whom these were in fact 'established'. It is necessary therefore to review such suppositions and reconsider both what might constitute inclusivity, and what we can now feasibly include, in our HE policies for inclusive practice.

9   Inclusion in Policy Discourse and a Need for Postdigital Dialogue

It is not my intention in this book to undertake extensive critical linguistic analysis of policy statements like the one above on inclusive practice, as was the case in *The Labour of Words in Higher Education* (Hayes, 2019a). When I drew attention then, to what I referred to as McPolicy, it was to demonstrate a lack of inclusivity in HE policy texts in themselves, via a sustained pattern of omitting direct references to the actual people who enact teaching, research and other related professional activities. I pointed out that, via nominalisation, 'things', such as technologies, strategies or buzz phrases are frequently attributed with having accomplished particular outcomes, instead of attributing those outcomes to the labour that has generally been performed by human beings. This is a more subtle linguistic form of cancel culture, but it is one with profound effects on how 'included' different groups might feel in HE policy-making. I argued too, with reference to George Ritzer's McDonaldisation thesis (Ritzer, 1993, 2018), that: 'strong levels of repetition and standardised statements in HE policy begin to resemble any menu in a global catering chain' and:

> A similar logic to marketing a regular cappuccino or a gingerbread latte seems to have been adopted in writing HE strategies regardless of which organisation these may relate to. (Hayes, 2019b)

There is something of an irony then, that in adverts for drinks or cars, human qualities are regularly attributed to consumer products, yet in HE policies, ascribing noticeable credit to people for their labour is curiously absent. As HE has responded to a world structured to meet the needs of capitalism and global markets, policy discourse has rationally reflected this in a narrow form of reasoning that prioritises productivity and homogenisation for efficiency. Just as Ritzer noticed a 'fast food' model of efficiency, calculability, predictability and control had become repeated across companies and organisations, their policy language has come to mirror this. However, Ritzer also observed that such rationalities can eventually become irrational (Ritzer, 1993, 2018). What has happened in HE is an irrational separation between two rational policy discourses. On the one hand, the discourse that argues technology is driving change, enhancing learning and employability, tends not to reference human labour in these processes. On the other hand, the policy discourse for social welfare, human rights and inclusivity in HE, tends not to refer to technology. These observations build on a disconnect already observed by Delanty (2001) some twenty years ago. He argued that:

> the challenge facing the university today is to link cultural reproduction and technological reproduction. (Delanty, 2001: 157)

Delanty discussed a market-driven capitalism 'shaping the university in the image of technoscience', as disengaged from 'battles of cultural identity' (Delanty, 2001: 157). What is needed instead is for universities to be the location 'where these discourses intersect' (Delanty, 2001: 158). Rather than an exclusive

OPENING THE AIRING CUPBOARD FROM ALL SIDES

intellectual exchange that remains inside the walls of an institution, it needs to be an inclusive, cross-sector debate led by the university:

> linking the requirements of industry, technology and market forces with the demands of citizenship. (Delanty, 2001: 158)

Postdigital positionality offers a powerful route towards re-engaging the separate terrains of culture and technology with citizenship in an ongoing, inclusive, 'postdigital dialogue' (Jandrić, Ryberg, Knox, Lacković, Hayes, Suoranta, Smith, Steketee, Peters, McLaren, Ford, Asher, McGregor, Stewart, Williamson & Gibbons, 2018). This is a community dialogue which universities can and should take a lead on, in collaboration with schools, human rights agencies, charities, legal and technical experts and individuals (UPP Foundation, 2018, Hambleton, 2020, Hayes et al., 2020). This is not least because an innocent sounding term like 'data' now brings acute risks to those most vulnerable in society (The State of Data, 2020: 5). Daily breaches of human rights are clinically discussed as 'data'. However, data becomes a form of shorthand, a proxy for what is frequently intimate human information and activities undertaken by our young children, through to our elderly citizens. This is a reality that leaves the vulnerable unprotected and our children: 'creating a resource that for-profit companies gain from' (The State of Data, 2020: 5). As both a personal and interpersonal dialogue, this is currently an incomplete and pressing societal exchange that, if led by universities, to include schools through from early years and across lifelong learning, would help to more inclusively inform our 'inclusivity frameworks'.

10   Inclusion in Decisions about Our Data Requires Some 'Re-plumbing'

Outside of the university, the territories of cultural reproduction and technological reproduction are deeply interconnected across the virtual airing cupboard of the Internet. Not only does the Internet connect 'people in vast numbers' it 'allows inanimate *objects*' to connect too (Seldon, 2020: 160). Known as the Internet of Things (IoT), this 'facilitates the collection of big data on a scale we are still unable fully to access or exploit, as the sheer volume can mitigate against sifting the quality from the unreliable evidence and forming solid conclusions' (Seldon, 2020: 161). A danger arises though for HE as a sector if it potentially joins the existing 'smart schools', by the creation of 'smart universities'. These are now developing akin to 'smart cities' with institutions 'working to connect online services which are currently separate' (Seldon, 2020: 161). Yet it is also an uncertain time to be investing heavily in physical educational spaces when the pandemic has propelled so much of our HE activity online. That aside, as inclusive as these virtually linked campus environments may sound, we are failing (metaphorically speaking) to connect some vital plumbing underneath.

Treating such developments as simply technological efficiencies, leaves universities vulnerable. If we do not take time to reconnect old pipes with new digital wires and linguistic communications, so to speak, we will continue to perpetuate inequalities and to exclude citizens from vital knowledge about what their 'data is up to' when it's out on its own. We need to metaphorically undertake the 'plumbing' that enables us to see how cultural reproduction and technological reproduction are intertwined. When these are treated separately, Internet giants and big businesses are free to further inequality reproduction (Ball, 2020). Therefore, to recognise the realities of what data-driven technologies are driving apart between culture and technology, provides insights to act quickly to preserve human rights.

Omitting such concerns from our university inclusivity strategies, via nominalised McPolicy statements, where entities other than humans are said to 'act', displaces people (Hayes, 2019a: 148). In urging readers to observe persistent configurations of McPolicy, I noted, in parallel, some of the ways in which rapid patterns of technological change in wider global society can disempower, as well as empower people. In particular, the data-driven systems, robotics, and unseen algorithmic activities that cannot easily be contested, leave users with little control over their own data, or its utilisation. When things and statements, rather than people, accomplish particular outcomes this leaves all of us acutely vulnerable, with our labours unattributed, and 'things' of all kinds free to act. Later I will demonstrate how even my humble airing cupboard in the hallway might be harbouring its own 'aspirations' to become more connected. If we fail to reflect on an interconnection between technoscience and cultural identity though in our HE policy discourse for inclusivity, then instead of catching up, universities (and the people within and around them) now risk being cancelled.

Related issues have been raised by scholars of Human Data Interaction (HDI) who have called for greater inclusivity for people in decisions concerning their personal data. They argue that each of us needs to understand what is happening to the data that is being gathered about us as individuals (legibility) and to be able to change relevant digital systems. We will then be in accord with our own wishes (agency) and will be able to work with those who are processing our data (negotiability). As such, there is a need for analytics algorithms to be more transparent and comprehensible to people and for those systems that process data to give people more capacity to control, inform and correct their data. Support is called for too, to help people re-evaluate their decisions about their data held within commercial systems as their circumstances change (Mortier, Haddadi, Henderson, McAuley & Crowcroft, 2014).

11 McDonaldisation of a Virus

This has become ever more pressing during the Covid-19 pandemic, that has through necessity, accelerated the scope of people to work and study from home and dramatically increased the use of computing to teach, learn and research online. This has implications for how HE responds to equality, diversity and inclusion matters under these new circumstances, when this situation is unlikely to reverse significantly into the future. Increased necessity to access the Internet has taken university business wholesale online. Just like many other forms of work currently being conducted from peoples' homes, this leaves scope for viral forms of McDonaldisation (Ritzer, 1993, 2018) of workplaces and workspaces to take hold. Remote methods for controlling the efficiency of employees working in their homes provide new ways to calculate and control productivity. Covid-19 has taken many of us much deeper into the virtual airing cupboard than before, but we don't all arrive there with equal support or capabilities. This wholesale change has not though, placed the Internet business model of aggressive advertising, commercial techniques for transfer of data or concerns over cyber security and anonymous manipulation of user activity inside the university for more scrutiny.

Universities do not control the World Wide Web. This means there is more scope now for students and staff to be tracked, their data to be breached and manipulated, their comments to be trolled or cancelled, their privacy to be violated, alongside any positive developments in terms of increased digital skills, flexibility and wider communication opportunities. As James Ball (2020) has pointed out:

> Browsing the internet feels like something safe and private. The intrusion is invisible. (Ball, 2020: 204)

Whilst universities engage mostly with the social and cultural aspects of inclusivity policymaking, the technical ones often go unnoticed. However, the technical aspects are closely interlinked to enormous commercial and government powers and human rights violations via the Internet (Mozilla Manifesto,

2003). Universities now need to connect their support for inclusivity with raising awareness of people's digital (and postdigital) rights; given that these are now further impacted in numerous ways due to Covid-19 (EFF, 2020). In the UK, consultation has begun on a national data strategy, further demonstrating the strong role that data now plays in anticipated futures (GOV.UK, 2020a). This very sudden situation of shifting so much online due to the pandemic has played out very differently in each individual human context. Guest editors for a special issue of the Journal of Literacy and Technology have entitled this collection: The eLearning Literacy for Suddenly Online (2020). In this 'suddenly online' situation (Wallace, Burton, Chandler & Darby, 2020) there are also many data-related precarities that can be encountered. Whilst HE regulators and journalists are keen for universities to tell their 'inclusivity stories' supported by selective data, it is necessary for inclusivity frameworks to be cognisant of ethics and human rights in relation to data-driven systems. This is difficult to do though, if inclusivity policy continues to treat cultural issues as separate from technological ones.

12   Postdigital Inclusivity

Whether observing an absence of references to human labour in policy, or noticing the rise of autonomous machines, algorithms and opaque data agreements, this does not mean that people are not still present in the background, writing policy, programming, coding, making judgements in the design of systems, or deleting each other from social media accounts. That the instruments we use to write with have implications for what we write, has perhaps always been true to some extent. Now, new networks of information, systems, images, video, coding, apps and data are integral to all of our human processes across life. As the need for social distancing has been evident during this pandemic: 'large global companies such as Google, Microsoft, Facebook and international organisations including the Organisation for Economic Co-operation and Development (OECD) and UNESCO, as well as a global education industry of edu-businesses, consultancies, investors and technology providers, are coming together to define how education systems should respond to the crisis' (Selwyn, Macgilchrist & Williamson, 2020). The data-driven nature of such alliances brings privacy and surveillance concerns, alongside disquiet at the swift adoption of commercial platforms at scale, without significant vetting procedures. Despite aspirations towards addressing inequalities remotely, the profound longer-term implications for systems of public education need to be considered too (Selwyn, Macgilchrist & Williamson, 2020). This postdigital

OPENING THE AIRING CUPBOARD FROM ALL SIDES

context or fusion of human and digital activity, brings both emancipation and new forms of bias, ethical issues and impact on existing systemic inequalities. How these intimate connections interplay to affect each individual as a global citizen, I argue, has wide-reaching implications for the inclusivity debate in HE, for how we write policy, and for what universities can, or cannot claim to be able to control.

13   Can Universities Really 'Capture', 'Measure' or 'Deliver' Inclusivity?

Universities are required to respond to legislation such as the Equality Act (2010) and the Public Sector Equality Duty (2011). This includes the annual publication of information and measurable objectives which focus on the elimination of discrimination, the advancement of equality of opportunity for people from different groups and good relations between them. Under the Equality Act (2010) human characteristics are protected from discrimination through law (Equality and Human Rights Commission, 2019). The recognised 'protected characteristics' include: *age, disability, gender reassignment, marriage and civil partnership, pregnancy and maternity, race, religion or belief, sex* and *sexual orientation*. Public sector organisations are expected to meet the needs of people with protected characteristics and encourage them to participate across public life, including education. These important legal obligations can though, become rationally interpreted in policy discourse in ways that simply focus on the compliance of people around certain individual topics. This approach may be efficient in publishing information and objectives, but it overlooks broader interconnections.

In a recent campaign, a review of the Equality Act has the 'aim of amending this landmark anti-discrimination legislation' (The Equality Act Review, 2020). There are calls for new factors to be taken into account, such as homelessness or immigration status, but then there are also questions of which of the most vulnerable should receive a Covid-19 vaccine in terms of priority. Decisions are complex where there is an intersection with existing protected characteristics, and new potential characteristics as these emerge. There are also more hidden forms of bias that have surfaced. These include questions concerning the compliance of data-driven digital systems that may have integral forms of bias (Mortier, Haddadi, Henderson, McAuley, Crowcroft & Crabtree, 2020) yet are part of decision processes concerning humans. There are bioinformational and biodigital developments too that could fundamentally affect how inclusivity is experienced by individuals in the near future (Peters & Jandrić, 2019, Peters, 2020a, 2020b).

How people are positioned in relation to combinations of protected characteristics, access to services and their perceptions of inclusivity are no longer formed through human interactions alone. Devices that generate data change context as they are shared between individuals or other devices, and individuals change context as they move around in space and time (Mortier, Haddadi, Henderson, McAuley, Crowcroft & Crabtree, 2020: 34). Now that so many communications and other activities are conducted across virtual and physical spaces (together), new cultural interpretations of what is understood by inclusivity are bringing complex arguments to this arena. The role of 'bioinformation' (Peters, Jandrić & McLaren, 2020) is one of these. The 'biological' information generated about individuals in healthcare, health-related research, screening, or testing services may concern an individual's past or present physical or mental health, future health risks, and even bodily constitution. The personal value of bioinformation has gained much interest, including for example 'the role it could play as a predictive, explanatory, descriptive, or relational tool in an individual's construction of the narrative that constitutes her identity' (Postan, 2016: 148). These are new dimensions to individual positionality and are not necessarily visible, unlike the media stories that bring various perspectives on marginalised groups to our attention, or indeed the social media systems that provide ways for people to share these, include, exclude, discriminate against, or even cancel others. Depending on the positionality of those involved, different forms of discrimination can quickly acquire new angles (and audiences) that do not necessarily help those affected. For example, Mirzaei (2019) cautions against a recent dilution of meaning in relation to the term 'woke', which first arose in the 1940s to symbolise 'awareness of social issues and movement against injustice, inequality, and prejudice'. Woke was 'originally associated with black Americans fighting racism, but has recently been appropriated by other activist groups', even now being 'cynically applied to everything from soft drink to razors' (Mirzaei, 2019).

Ritzer (2018) has pointed to all manner of augmented forms of McDonaldisation that have arisen as digital systems have merged with physical life. His ongoing adaptation from Weber's theory of rationalisation (Weber, 1930) that has taken new forms in our postdigital global culture is helpful in noting the many irrationalities that can occur (Ritzer, Jandrić & Hayes, 2018). One example is the rational approach we have adopted in the UK to support us in measuring inclusivity and diversity in universities. Based on capturing and benchmarking data against certain indicators (Office for Students, 2018–2022) this may, at the same time, be overlooking hidden forms of bias. These can be running through the data-driven systems themselves that are silently furthering the disadvantage of some people over others (Mortier et al., 2014, Mortier,

OPENING THE AIRING CUPBOARD FROM ALL SIDES

Haddadi, Henderson, McAuley, Crowcroft & Crabtree, 2020). It is now necessary to question exactly what counts as 'data' in relation to inclusivity. If we are asked to measure any data then we can question, is it static or fluid? As such, who and what we are measuring, via which systems, and whether these have been designed with inclusivity, equality and diversity values at the centre are all important considerations.

14   Inclusivity Is Not a Static Concept That Institutions Can Control

These and many other complexities arising from human technological relations mean that inclusivity, like identity, is not a static concept that might be applied in relation to humans alone. However, if university policymaking begins only from the concept of human-to-human interactions, where 'the principles of inclusive practice are well established', then it is hardly surprising to find institutions making claims like these:

> The Strategy aims to deliver measurable equality and inclusion outcomes for both students and staff. (University of Greenwich, 2019–2022)

> The University will proactively mainstream equality and diversity into all areas of decision making, leadership development, committee representation and policy review. (Keele University, 2018–2022)

The statements above fit with what is required under the legal Acts already mentioned, but following the patterns of McPolicy that I have outlined above, the linguistic structures also claim that 'the strategy' or 'the university' (rather than human beings) 'aim to deliver' or will 'proactively mainstream' equality, diversity and inclusion. The 'measurable equality and inclusion outcomes' in Equality, Diversity and Inclusion Strategies like these are worth reflecting on too. Can 'equality and inclusion outcomes for both students and staff' be 'delivered' at all when there are so many unseen aspects at play? How are such outcomes to be defined for diverse individual students and staff, with or without declared, protected characteristics? Who measures these, in what ways and what else might be intersecting with what people perceive as their identity, or indeed define as inclusivity? Such statements also presuppose that equality and inclusion outcomes (and related data) remain fixed for these to be measurable or mainstreamed. Taking on very broad inclusivity agendas to suggest that they might be addressed in this rational way, raises questions concerning exactly what universities can, or cannot, meaningfully control. They can provide information, but whether university web pages providing advice on topics like 'how to be a white ally' (University of York, 2020) contributes to sustained systemic change in relation to discrimination, is open to debate. Many institutions are responding in similar ways to each other, but there are also questions of whether imposing a uniformity of institutional response to agendas of race, gender or disability is in fact the same as being inclusive.

15   New Ethics and Ownership Questions

There are now though further urgent ethical questions to bring to the ones already outlined above. These include interrogation of a proliferation of new technological platforms and advances in the ways to gather data on students (Williamson, 2017). Scientific efforts to aid the better understanding of human learning and achievement have broadened across many academic disciplines, as new digital technologies have enabled re-examination of existing educational issues (Kuhl, Lim, Guerriero & Van Damme, 2019). Ben Williamson has drawn attention to movements by education data scientists and learning engineers towards making students themselves 'machine readable' by gathering data on their living bodies. He argues that artificial intelligence (AI) systems are being combined with learning science in 'digital laboratories' where 'ownership over data, and power and authority over educational knowledge production, are being redistributed'. This is leading to 'highly contested understandings of biological learning bodies' and 'creating new data objects as ways of conceptualizing learning and educational outcomes' (Williamson, 2020c).

In a recent report for UNESCO, the challenges of 'datafication' (Mayer-Schönberger & Cukier, 2014a, 2014b) are also balanced against 'a world of possibilities in terms of individualising learning and education governance' in the developing world (Pedro, Subosa, Rivas & Valverde, 2019). Such broader developments, challenges and possibilities also impact on inclusivity policies as universities adopt these commercial systems. The ethics of these need to be considered also alongside the personal choices made by people using their own devices. Whilst one mobile phone user may wish to have dynamic content aggregated for them based on their personal activities and movements, their commute to work, or their patterns of consumption, others may not. In HE, learning analytics welcomed by one student, may be intrusive for others.

Applications of tangible human data and other rapid digital developments have implications for how universities continue to construct equality, diversity and inclusion policies and frameworks. There are consequences too for how institutions seek to eliminate attainment gaps, how they discuss groups

OPENING THE AIRING CUPBOARD FROM ALL SIDES

who they hope to target, to improve these figures and the actions that they might take. Yet in a recent report addressing this topic (UUK and NUS, 2019), there was no mention throughout of the role that such technological developments now play. Nor was digital technology referred to in relation to equality and diversity objectives in the strategy for the Office for Students (Office for Students, 2018–2022). If these changes are overlooked, policies will remain focused on ingrained inequalities, bias and disadvantage at only human-to-human levels. It is now necessary to also consider and explore the complex and dialectical human-technological relations that are currently missing from university inclusivity frameworks. How these intersect with each individual's levels of digital skills and their various forms of disadvantage, can lead to profound marginalisation rather than empowerment to enter and succeed, in education and the workplace. Whilst there are many angles that might be taken, my aim in this book is to gather together a collection of current arguments from recent literature with implications for re-establishing how inclusivity policy is perceived in HE. This is intended to aid the discussion about how to reform current styles of writing HE policy documents that, presently, not only isolate humans from technology, but also isolate many interconnected issues from each other. I will draw sources together through a fusion of two academic theories that are not currently brought into active dialogue with each other. In so doing, I will introduce the concept: 'postdigital positionality', as a potentially productive way of furthering this debate.

Introduction

1 Postdigital Positionality

This then is a debate that firstly, needs to acknowledge how multiple and diverse 'actors' (that are not all human) are now altering much of what may once have been described as 'established' or 'inclusive' practices in HE. Secondly, it is a debate that once recognised, can be explored across all of the key activities of HE, in order to notice how educational access, inclusivity and opportunities for individual people can now be altered in new ways depending on how each of us are positioned in postdigital society.

I refer to this discussion in terms of 'postdigital positionality' because 'postdigital' theory helps to capture the first point about the broader context in which HE now operates, where a digitalisation across all areas of life has intermingled with all that went before and is about to come. Postdigital refers in general terms to the conditions surrounding humans, where: 'we are increasingly no longer in a world where digital technology and media is separate, virtual, 'other' to a 'natural' human and social life (Jandrić et al., 2018). This means that on an individual basis, the people who we are, the places we are in, the technological, social, historical, cultural, economic, biological and political contexts that surround each of us are interconnected. This has implications for what we discuss in HE as principles of inclusivity, access and participation. Such principles cannot simply be 'plugged in' to universities, when much of the complex ecosystem they now operate in, is external, commercial, data-driven and thus not directly under any institution's control (Mortier, Haddadi, Henderson, McAuley, Crowcroft & Crabtree, 2020). It is also deeply personal in that humans and machines are interacting on an individual, as well as an institutional and societal level, concerning how things ought to be done. The digital platform, as Ben Williamson has observed, is now 'a key participant in HE reforms that are intended to align the public mission of universities with the private interests of digital capitalism' (Williamson, 2020b). Universities also have knowledge exchange frameworks to encourage many local and international partnerships with commercial agents. It is therefore time to include in this debate, all of the implications of these rapid digital developments, and their relevance for HE inclusivity frameworks, alongside many other factors that affect how humans experience 'digital inclusion' (Park, Freeman & Middleton, 2019).

Regarding the second point, 'positionality' theory (England, 1994, Cousin, 2010, Bourke, 2014, Torres-Olave & Lee, 2019) provides a productive route into

© KONINKLIJKE BRILL NV, LEIDEN, 2021 | DOI: 10.1163/9789004466029_002

INTRODUCTION 25

exploring how these recent technological, cultural and biological changes, interlinked with our political economy, support both educational and employment opportunities, for some people. By the same token, they can further marginalise others. How people understand and relate to their own diversity and that of their peers is also partly shaped across technological, as well as human networks. Neither remains static, or free from bias and they are deeply intertwined as intricate and fluid complexities that connect with our identity creation, biological composition, power relations and personal contexts. By drawing attention to positionality, the unique experiences of individuals in their varied cultural, postdigital surroundings comes to the surface. This is important when much of what is reported in the media and across social networks rationally captures only fragments, 'products' even, of peoples' identities, without the fuller personal narrative. It is important too when policy statements concern generalised constructs that omit subjectivity.

Having previously raised the concerns that HE policy texts lack inclusivity in their linguistic construction, I demonstrate now why a broader understanding of 'the principles of inclusive practice' in a postdigital context needs to be discussed and established across HE institutions and reflected in new policies and practices. The multi-layered cultural and technological challenges and disruption wrought by the Covid-19 pandemic makes this an even more pressing debate:

> Covid 19 presents us with a real challenge and a real responsibility. These ideas invite debate, engagement and action by governments, international organizations, civil society, educational professionals, as well as learners and stakeholders at all levels. (International Commission on the Futures of Education, 2020)

2 Covid-19

The personal individual contexts surrounding each of us have come to the forefront more than ever when (at the time of writing) nations across the world are either still in lockdown, emerging from lockdown policies introduced in response to the 2020 Covid-19 pandemic, or re-entering further lockdowns. Therefore, many of the examples provided in this book reflect these unusual and uncertain times. Both the uniformity and diversity of national approaches towards a highly infectious virus and the measures to confront it have been reported globally. For me, the pandemic has shone a light into many places and personal spaces that rational, neoliberal policy discourse frequently conceals.

Each time blanket policies or measures are introduced there are also exceptional circumstances revealed. The diversity of positionality of those who are affected, or those who need to implement the rules, is demonstrated. One-size-fits-all approaches seem to either further disadvantage those already marginalised or reveal acts of entitlement from those in positions of privilege. From carers who have lost support or respite that they previously had, to Members of Parliament urging compliance, but then acting in a self-interested manner to break quarantine, each rational Covid-19 discourse also exposes how rationalities can become irrational (Ritzer, 1993, 2018). Furthermore, this also reveals numerous situations that are not easily controlled, either online or offline.

FIGURE 3
A 'cash only' notification

As illustrated in Figure 3, as protective measures, such as the use of credit and debit cards rather than cash to pay for goods was introduced, other businesses insisted on cash only, as limited opening times were imposed. Balancing the risk of infection from cash with a need to avoid fraud is a decision that will differ, when some companies are better placed than others to withstand economic upheaval.

INTRODUCTION

FIGURE 4
A vape store selling hand
sanitiser

Some businesses such as the one pictured in Figure 4 added the sale of hand
sanitiser to their stock (often at inflated prices) even when this seemed oddly
out of place with the usual identity and range of goods sold. Opportunities for
profit were also balanced with thoughtful gestures of targeted opening hours
for the more vulnerable, key workers and carers.

3 Covid-19 Positionalities

As more has been learned from research into Covid-19, this seems to have demonstrated too, just how differently people's bodies are reacting. From being
unaware of any symptoms, to becoming seriously ill or, in an increasing number of cases, experiencing longer term Covid-19 problems that have been popu-
larly labelled as 'Long Covid' or 'Long Haul Covid'. A recent research report
(NIHR, 2020) has flagged up the dangers though of applying terms that lead to
assumptions that what each patient is experiencing is the same set of symptoms. They have therefore opted to refer to phrases such as 'ongoing Covid-
19' and 'living with Covid-19'. Drawing on the experience of epidemiologists,

researchers, policy makers, professionals and patients, they also explain their decision to retain (not synthesise) different perspectives that emerge from each specialist area on the longer-term effects of the virus for individuals. This is an illustration of how positionality can inform research and also impact on policy.

As new strains of Covid-19 emerged from different parts of the globe we were learning that even the virus itself was able to demonstrate diversity in how it behaved, who it infected and to what severity. Such approaches to health can also be helpful in considering how inclusivity policy more broadly might be better understood. Rather than take one synthesised rational opinion that a set of inclusive practices have been firmly established for universities, a more holistic view means that, as things change, policy discourse might adapt as well, to encompass multiple positionalities. As the authors of 'Living with Covid-19' point out:

> Covid 19 has a disproportionate effect on certain parts of the population, including care home residents. Black and Asian communities have seen high death rates and there are concerns about other minority groups and the socially disadvantaged. These people are already seldom heard in research as well as travellers, the homeless, those in prisons, people with mental health problems or learning difficulties; each having particular and distinct needs in relation to ongoing Covid19 that need to be understood. (NIHR, 2020)

Throughout the pandemic a key challenge has been for governments and leaders to balance health and economics. Variations between countries, and across regions of countries in the numbers of cases reported, have complicated things further. Choices are constantly being made by leaders balancing control of the virus (to save human lives) with the demands of productivity and profit (to maintain our unequal neoliberal political economy). Essentially Covid-19 has urged uncomfortable decisions concerning who and what we choose to protect. This is not a context where the rationality of McDonaldisation fares as well as usual either. Efficiency, calculability, predictability and control (the features that Ritzer argued that global chains of fast food and coffee shops survive on) all become a challenge, if individuals demonstrate their own positionalities in stepping away from waste and mindless consumption, towards a culture of sharing, re-use and sustainability.

As illustrated in Figure 5 many households are now placing items for others to re-use outside their homes instead of throwing things away. There is an

INTRODUCTION

FIGURE 5
A box of free books outside a home

irony in seeing the box from a leading coffee machine brand being recycled in this way. There is also the unfortunate trolling by librarians of a book lover who built a swap box outside her home during lockdown. When she tweeted about it to encourage others to swap and share, amid thousands of 'likes', she was accused of doing 'such a middle-class thing' and told the books would spread Covid. Others called her 'stupid' and 'misguided' and slammed her for having 'no real understanding of the role of libraries'. A further troll said: 'So, take home a used book and maybe take home the virus that kills your mother' (Metro News Reporter, 2021).

It is poignant too at a time when the hospitality industry is also being crippled by the requirement for social distancing. In a striking video online, bar workers can be seen physically dumping huge quantities of ice outside the Scottish Parliament in protest at being forced to close by the Covid-19 restrictions imposed by their government (BBC, 2020f).

The consumer culture that has thrived for decades is currently looking unwell and displaying its own set of symptoms from the pandemic. These are emerging as irrational inconsistencies when McDonaldisation requires

FIGURE 6   Ice was dumped outside the Scottish Parliament in protest

rational, predictable behaviours of consumption from us all. Furthermore, if social welfare, human rights and inclusivity gain cultural domination, we will be forced to re-examine the technological platforms on which the case for this is being 'aired': namely, to look more closely at the corporate ownership of the Internet itself and who can still claim to have any level of control (Ball, 2020). The neutral positionality that we have for so long assigned to digital technologies in the neoliberal economy may begin to reveal these as politically interested 'actors' alongside humans in this context (Winner, 1980).

In academia an underpinning economic emphasis on productivity has in recent decades replaced 'open intellectual enquiry' (Olssen & Peters, 2005). In terms of university policy, this has in turn encouraged an instrumental, problem-solving approach where individual strategies are produced to address each issue (Harman, 1984). However, this form of rationality then neglects the broader 'socio-cultural dynamism of policy processes' (Nudzor, 2009: 503). These are tensions that I discussed in *The Labour of Words in HE* which concern whether policy is understood as a dynamic process (one that recognises the constant changes around each person, their cultural context and the technologies that they interact with) or simply as a means to solve problems, which yields more static isolated models, documents and 'established' principles aimed at meeting a set of performance standards. The latter tends to be accompanied by a belief that following these models will bring about the changes required, but such documents sit apart from the processes that actually effect institutional change (Hayes, 2019: 58). The disruption from the

INTRODUCTION

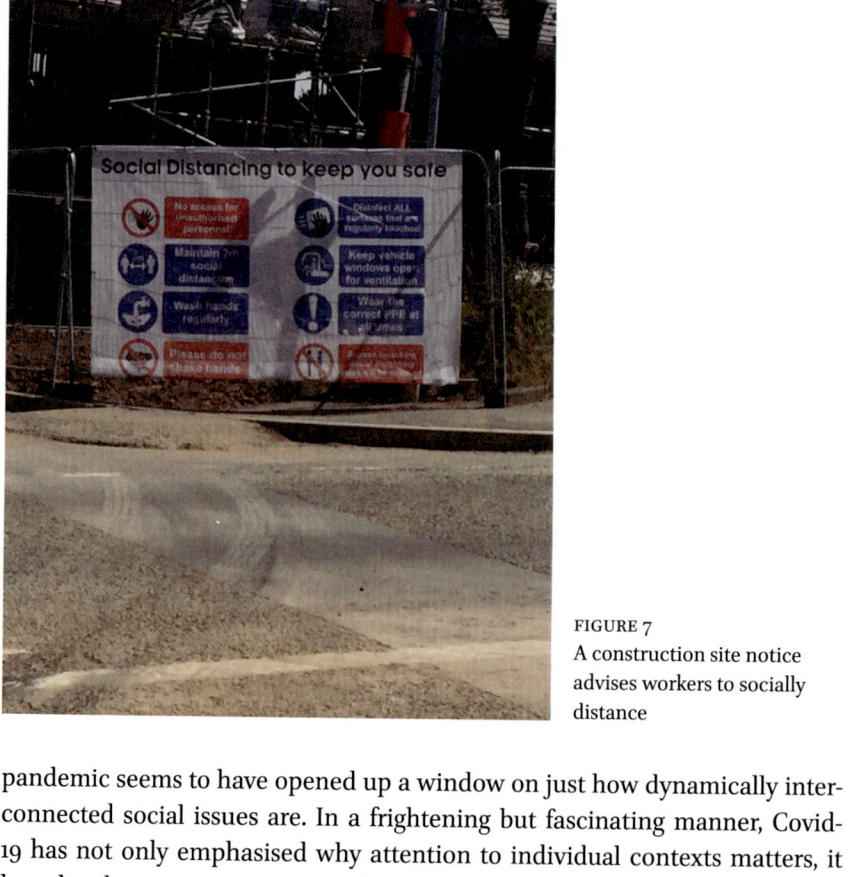

FIGURE 7
A construction site notice
advises workers to socially
distance

pandemic seems to have opened up a window on just how dynamically inter-connected social issues are. In a frightening but fascinating manner, Covid-19 has not only emphasised why attention to individual contexts matters, it has also drawn attention to a rich array of postdigital examples. These have emerged as emergency measures have been put in place for education, work, social care, lockdown and social distancing. In Figure 7 a construction site displays detailed advice on social distancing to keep workers safe.

In Figure 8 a highways sign advises that footway works are cancelled due to Covid-19. The biological and physiological circumstances that have made some people more likely to die, have intermingled with the social positioning that they occupy, risks in work or living spaces and their levels of access to advice and care via technology.

The stark reports of loss of lives, livelihoods, homes, relationships and human grief occupy web pages alongside incongruous attempts to recreate life as it was before lockdown, like creating 'Mumdonalds' Happy Meals to replace routine, family fast food experiences (Abernethy, 2020) and creating 'social distancing logos' (Valinsky, 2020).

FIGURE 8
Footway works are cancelled
due to Covid-19

4   A 'New Normal' for Institutions, Different 'New Normals' for Each of Us, or Both?

As lockdowns came into place around the world during 2020, universities understandably had little existing policy for such circumstances. Even as they scrambled Gold Command-style committees to write temporary statements, those involved were adapting also to a need to discuss and write policy across online systems, rather than around a table on campus. With the main focus on continuity, references to a 'new normal' have focused since then mostly on the teaching context. What a 'new normal' might look like for HE policymaking has received less attention, as will be explored later. The rapid movement of so many HE activities into online platforms during successive lockdowns has implications for universities in terms of a larger 'shift in authority to private actors' (Hogan & Williamson, 2020: 67). The pandemic has brought governments and educational institutions into new alliances with commercial technologies, but over time this also has potential to undermine democratic control of public education (Hogan & Williamson, 2020: 67). This is because

INTRODUCTION

such coalitions have different values. They are bringing 'new kinds of multi-sector public-private partnerships and policy networks in relation to edtech expansion, and the enhanced role of the private sector in educational delivery and governance' (Hogan & Williamson, 2020: 2). As time allows, this requires closer scrutiny from universities in terms of ethics, and alongside their strategies for inclusive practices.

A discourse of 'new normals' though, is not conducive to recognising what needs to change across the whole ecosystem of university policymaking. It is not helpful for noticing firstly, the problem that arises when educational technology policy is framed separately from inclusivity and diversity policy. Secondly, it is worth noticing the ease with which phrases like 'new normal' become routinely adopted, in a similar way to 'best practice' and other problematic buzz phrases (Hayes, 2019a: 1). Long before we become critically aware of it, such constructs start shaping academic practices. However, 'new normal' is a risky form of language, when little remains 'normal' presently in many academics' or students' lives.

In the shorter term for individual staff and students, we have each been subject to our own private merger between online platforms, our diverse home environments, our personal health and family circumstances, capabilities and responsibilities. Across the globe these individual positionalities differed enormously in terms of personal or family 'capital' to cope with what successive lockdowns thrust upon them (United Nations, 2020). Studies like Moving to Online Teaching and Homeworking (MOTH, 2020) were conducted to examine how people were adapting to the challenges posed by Covid-19 on their professional and personal lives. The researchers are considering findings alongside studies which have already identified the 'emotional' nature of academic labour, teaching and burnout before the pandemic brought new complexities to these relationships (Bodenheimer & Shuster, 2020). Research studies that have captured diverse academic lived experience from the start of the pandemic reveal inequities in how each of us was positioned to run with this situation at the point when the crisis struck (Peters et al., 2020, Jandrić & Hayes, 2020a, Jandrić & Hayes et al., 2020b, Watermeyer et al., 2020). This documentation of human academic subjectivities from across the globe is not easily captured in policy statements from the 'old normal' like these:

> The student engagement framework represents our approach to engagement by, with and for students. (Hayes, 2019a: 123)

> Packaging, marketing and communicating student engagement to applicants, current students and staff. (Hayes, 2019a: 122)

Frameworks do not represent how individuals engage, diverse people do. No amount of McPolicy statements that are 'packaging, marketing and communicating student engagement' will alter this. Many students took on roles as key workers alongside or in lieu of their studies, with much uncertainty as to when they might further their own goals once more in education and future employment. As reported recently, research published by women plummeted during the lockdown whilst articles written by men were alleged to have increased. Whilst 'anyone with a family will be slowed down by lockdown' it is 'women who will probably be disadvantaged more strongly' (Fazackerley, 2020a).

Following years of Technology Enhanced Learning policies, it was a biological virus in the end that took just days to whisk academia online wholesale, alongside a reduced footfall for the environment, in terms of travel. At the same time 'the hidden labour of domesticity that is part of many academics' real lives' (Fazackerley, 2020a), visibly surfaced. These and other examples have implications for reviewing how policy is planned and phrased, in the future. After all, the buzz phrases that were previously attributed with our human labour of teaching and research in McPolicy don't seem about to offer to home school our children (BBC, 2020e) or to care for our elderly relatives, any time soon.

It quickly became apparent too, that Covid-19 itself did not respect equality, diversity and inclusion values, as the figures of cases, hospitalisation and death by race and ethnicity were published (CDC, 2020). The Color of Coronavirus project (APM, 2020) monitors such statistics. Wide disparities by race seem to be due to numerous cultural, economic and technological reinforcing factors, including: workplace exposures, inability to work from home, no access to sick days, geographic areas where people reside, dependence on public transport where the virus is more easily spread, less access to testing, a higher presence of underlying health conditions, receiving delayed medical care, no access to online healthcare, or merely distrusting health providers. Thus, racial disparities from compounding, elevated risks termed as *systemic racism* (APM, 2020) have been further illuminated by the pandemic alongside challenges of gender and disability. In these circumstances it is worth reflecting on what passes for 'normal' (Fuller & Jandrić, 2019). How we might move from an 'old normal' to a 'new normal' in HE may simply be the wrong question to ask, if this is concerned with established principles and meeting generic standards, post-pandemic. A discussion on more dynamic 'new normals' that have befallen each of us, and an examination of their place in the inclusivity debate may be more useful in shedding light on each of our diverse, postdigital contexts.

INTRODUCTION   35

5   HE Policies That Self-Isolate

In the context of educational opportunities, these interconnected issues illustrate why HE policies that self-isolate from each other, are a problem and not
a solution. Rather than addressing single issues in strategies written and filed
separately from each other, it is worth considering all of the factors together
that now affect inclusive practices. There is a valuable opportunity to cast fresh
eyes on these reading through the diverse accounts of postdigital positionalities that students and staff are voicing (Peters et al., 2020, Jandrić & Hayes,
2020a, Jandrić & Hayes et al., 2020b, Watermeyer et al., 2020, MOTH, 2020). The
Covid-19 crisis has revealed too why the many research papers written in the
Global North about the pandemic should not be read in isolation from those
bearing insights on crises from the Global South. Whilst approaches towards
social distancing, face masks, travel, social care, mental health and ingrained
inequalities of all kinds may differ between nations, Covid-19 has also presented many similar challenges to those that were already being tackled in
the developing world. Steps to improve access and continuity of education for
marginalised groups through technologies in Low to Middle Income Countries
(LMIC) may now hold just as much relevance for disadvantaged groups living
in local regions of developed countries in Europe or the United States (Traxler, Smith, Scott & Hayes, 2020). The starkly uneven human access to digital
devices, skills and services revealed is a reminder that in postdigital society
there are also huge numbers of humans and communities who remain pre-
digital or semi-digital too.

6   Precarity, Disadvantage and the Rationalisation of Academic
         Labour

Despite the different challenges and experience that designing and teaching
for online and distance learning requires, in comparison with teaching face-
to-face, universities will often employ tutors for these courses on short-term
contracts. This can be the case on collaborative international programmes,
where teaching takes place in partner institutions as well as in the university
that is hosting the course. As the pandemic took hold, for those university staff
on precarious or flexible contracts life instantly became even more insecure
(Collini, 2020, Ivancheva, 2020). Simultaneously, Covid-19 'empowered technology vendors to position themselves as frontline emergency response providers' (Williamson, 2020a, Hogan & Williamson, 2020). In HE there has also
been a growing situation where many new scholars carry large debts into their

first academic appointments. On top of this, they meet intense pressures to perform in research, teaching, management and administration, yet their roles may also be fixed term.

I have worked with and taught many staff in this situation, when I have led teaching or research training programmes in the UK and abroad. Precarious or casual contracts are increasingly common (Hunsinger, 2020: 2). The expectation is for mobility from these staff too, who frequently need to seek employment far from where they live, leaving their family and any established networks that might have helped their career progression. This can leave them exposed and given the sudden conditions of lockdown keeping people at home, even more so, if they are unable to travel for work (Ivancheva, 2020). The postdigital positionality of a casual academic can thus differ enormously from that of senior, established academics. Whilst conditions will fluctuate between institutions and countries, staff on precarious contracts may be working full time for years but seeing very few of the benefits. They can find themselves expected to publish but without funding for conference fees, travel, or any form of professional development. If they need to attend meetings it may come at personal expense (Cantrell & Palmer, 2019).

Whilst the flexibility of the academic gig economy may work well for some people, for others it leaves them at risk and potentially omitted from the channels into inclusivity policy where they might have been able to input, to effect change. Meanwhile, Ovetz (2020: 1) argues that the turn to remote working, to stem the spread of the virus has added to an existing 'epidemic – the digital automation and deskilling of teaching in higher education' because the pandemic has now created ideal conditions for educational technology venture capitalists to support the outsourcing and rationalisation of academic labour (Ovetz, 2020: 2). Ivancheva (2020) refers to an 'unbundling' of content in universities that could have led to 'shorter, low-cost, flexible unbundled curricular units' that might have been:

> made available online and used by previously 'atypical' and systematically disadvantaged students: women, people with caring responsibilities and disabilities, and mature full-time working students. Employers and communities could become more involved with universities, demanding need-based content. (Ivancheva, 2020)

Unfortunately, unbundling has instead 'developed mostly as public-private partnership between universities and education technology' (Ivancheva, 2020, Verger, Fontdevila & Zancajo, 2016). How education more globally is becoming

INTRODUCTION

rationalised through partnerships with commercial providers, has considerable implications for inclusivity policies. These connections are currently
under-explored. Verger, Fontdevila and Zancajo (2016) have questioned why so
many countries with such different cultural, political and economic contexts
are engaging in processes of education privatisation reform and who resists
this situation. Additionally, now that the Covid-19 pandemic has brought such
reliance on technology and forms of monitoring and controlling human activity, other authors are questioning what resistance these are meeting (Taylor,
Sharma, Martin & Jameson, 2020).

There is now a strong rationality that surrounds the gaining of digital
skills which are widely deemed by governments and educational agencies to
improve opportunities for those in disadvantaged situations. There are many
complexities though, that need to be surfaced in this arena. This requires multi-
agency, cross-sector discourse and contextual, community-based understandings to inform initiatives. Whilst local areas develop all manner of schemes
to support citizens to gain digital skills, or to re-skill following displacement
from work during the pandemic, there are many larger powerful commercial players participating. For example, Holon IQ argue on their website that
they are:

> Powering decisions that matter at the world's smartest institutions.
> (Holon IQ, 2020)

Hogan and Williamson (2020: 37) highlight the way in which Holon IQ is
assuming a powerful position to both 'catalogue and catalyse' global edtech
market activity but also to frame what is offered as more 'affordable and equitable' in an 'education economy' (Hogan & Williamson, 2020: 38). Holon IQ
have their own Higher Education Digital Capability Framework which is billed
as 'an open-source capability framework for higher education. 4 dimensions,
16 domains and 70+ capabilities' (Holon IQ, 2020). I have argued before that
in university employability strategies, students are frequently referred to in
terms of 'graduate attributes', 'skills', 'assets' and 'components' with academics
urged to develop 'best practices' to deliver such capabilities (Hayes, 2019a: 2). I
pointed to Employability McPolicy which appears to follow the patterns of the
McDonaldisation principles of *efficiency, predictability, control* and *calculability* based on a simple, rational exchange value where: 'student learning = gain-
ful employment' (Hayes, 2019a: 129).

The issues that follow such approaches include education becoming framed
'through market logics' and 'the narrowing of education goals, privileging

certain types of knowledge and information over others, such as subjects that can be easily tracked and translated into data (Hogan & Williamson, 2020: 62). Furthermore, there are now new players jumping in to help education institutions when they find that 'packaging, marketing and communicating student engagement' isn't enough. Companies like Noodle will package a whole lot more for universities under the mission of 'building online capacity':

> Building online capacity means integrating technology, learning design, marketing, recruiting, support, placement, and financial services. And doing so with flexibility, transparency, and efficiency. (Noodle Partners, 2020)

Such 'packaging' changes the nature of academic labour bringing questions to the surface about what narratives and values universities now wish to retain. Hunsinger (2020) has argued that:

> Universities are meaning-making machines, much like everything else in the knowledge ecologies of late capitalism. They are full of people and things, creating a plurality of meanings and interpretations, and eventually developing knowledge. With that in mind, each university signifies a plurality of purposes to many different public and private interests. (Hunsinger, 2020: 1)

However, he points to the problem that these ideas and interests are caught now in an acceleration that 'complicates their capacity to be meaningful knowledge systems to many possible participants because the speed erases the possibility of the distributed cognition needed for knowledge' (Hunsinger, 2020: 1). I would argue that this is important in the case of university policy frameworks too, particularly in relation to the challenges of writing meaningful inclusivity policy that does not immediately lose its relevance. Policymaking and civic engagement in the writing of policy is something that does not sit aside from either the cognition or compassion that is needed for developing knowledge. These are intertwined with the rapid technological and biological developments that we are immersed in and consequently in this postdigital landscape we have interconnected ethical challenges to tackle. We cannot inhabit only the parts of 'the cloud' we choose to or keep data to ourselves, any more than we can pick and choose what we take out from the virtual airing cupboard. If reaching into my hall cupboard I pull down more than I bargained for, I can replace it unseen. In the virtual version of this scenario, what I am about to download, is already anticipated.

INTRODUCTION

7 Politics, Ethics and Human Attributes in the Virtual Airing Cupboard

I have previously argued that the discourse of university McPolicy is:

> Deeply implicated in maintaining a particular organisation of academic labour. As human attributes become discussed objectively in strategy documents, in terms of exchange value, this risks alienating people from their more tacit understandings (or use values) in terms of what they do'. (Hayes, 2019a: 52)

Thinking about ourselves subjectively in terms of personal attributes is one thing, but a rational breaking down of each of us into a recognised objective set of attributes is a different matter. It is though, an approach that serves algorithms very well (Amoore, 2020, Alpaydin, 2020, Jandrić, Knox, Macleod & Sinclair, 2017, Beattie & Hayes, 2020). Of course, if I describe some of my perceived personal attributes to readers of this book, I am likely to share them from my own individual positionality, to reflexively give them context, explain where these have sometimes been of help (or hindrance) to me in certain situations. Amoore (2020) points out why such positionality and context does not hold relevance for an algorithm:

> At the level of the algorithm, it scarcely matters whether the clustered attributes are used to define the propensities of consumers, voters, DNA sequences, financial borrowers, or people gathering in public space to make a political claim. (Amoore, 2020: 4)

Amoore (2020) describes as an example a case where algorithms were trained to recognise what a human protest is. This was based on 'the attributes of urban public life, the norms and anomalies latent in the data streams extracted from multiple sources, from Twitter and Facebook to government databases' (Amoore, 2020: 1). Amoore's concern though, is that such algorithms 'condense multiple potential futures to a single output' and therefore:

> machine learning algorithms that anticipate our future propensities are seriously threatening the chances that we have to make possible alternative political futures. (Amoore, 2020: 1)

Alpaydin (2020) describes machine learning as: 'programming computers to optimise a performance criterion using example data or past experience'.

As Amoore points out, it is this example data and the algorithmic decisions based on it that have been the main focus of critique, with arguments concerning 'removing the bias' or the 'value judgements' being the dominant ones (Amoore, 2020). This is the perspective raised earlier where HDI scholars present the case for greater agency, legibility and negotiability concerning the data on which algorithmic decisions are made (Mortier, Haddadi, Henderson, McAuley & Crowcroft, 2014).

Amoore takes a somewhat different perspective to the assumption that:

> there is an outside to the algorithm – an accountable human subject who is the locus of responsibility, the source of a code of conduct with which algorithms must comply. To call for the opening of the black box, for transparency and accountability, then, is to seek to institute arrangements that are good, ethical, and normal, and to prevent the transgression of societal norms by the algorithm. (Amoore, 2020)

Instead, for Amoore:

> What matters is not primarily the identification and regulation of algorithmic wrongs, but more significantly how algorithms are implicated in new regimes of verification, new forms of identifying a wrong or of truth telling in the world. (Amoore, 2020)

In these terms, Amoore believes that we have 'no need to look beyond the algorithm for an outside' as such, where humans are underwriting its conduct. Instead she proposes 'a different way of thinking about the ethicopolitics of algorithms'. She refers to this as a *cloud ethics* which is concerned with the political formation of relations to oneself and to others that is taking place, increasingly, in and through algorithms (Amoore, 2020). These are important considerations in relation to each of our postdigital positionalities. Rather than humans as underwriters of algorithmic conduct, they concern instead the analysis of humans as literally made 'of data' (Cheney-Lippold, 2018).

8   Inclusive Practice for Algorithmic Identities

Based on these ideas, it not easy to see how any university inclusivity framework or policy could feasibly write and enact policy founded on a claim that 'the principles of inclusive practice are well established' (Department for Education, 2017). These are constantly being re-worked in the cloud, as our

INTRODUCTION 41

'algorithmic identities' shape and reshape, based on data each of us continually produce inside and outside of universities:

> Algorithmic interpretations about data of our web surfing, data of our faces, and even data about our friendships set new, distinct terms for identity online. And it is through these terms that our algorithmic identities are crafted – terms in which race is described by ones and zeros and emotions defined by templates of data. (Cheney-Lippold, 2018)

The case for claiming and developing our own postdigital positionalities has never been stronger, unless we want the only account of ourselves to be the algorithmic version:

> Algorithms assemble, and control, our datafied selves and our algorithmic futures. It's about how algorithms make our data speak as if it were a man, woman, Santa Claus, citizen, Asian, and/or wealthy. And it's also about how these algorithmically produced categories replace the politicised language of race, gender and class with a proprietary vocabulary that speaks *for* us – to marketers, political campaigns, government dragnets, and others – whether we know about it, like it, or not. (Cheney-Lippold, 2018)

This then is the virtual airing cupboard producing knowledge: 'that shapes both the world and ourselves online' via 'algorithms, data and the logics therein' (Cheney-Lippold, 2018). How universities might respond, as centres of knowledge themselves, is now a pressing question. As Hunsinger (2020: 12) puts it: 'corporations and governments with neoliberal agendas are taking strategic aim at universities in this pandemic'. If bureaucratic imperatives undermine 'the relationships, research, shared governance, and learning that we seek to develop in university' (Hunsinger, 2020: 12) we can still rationally point to a growing stockpile of data. Whether we will still be able to identify any of us as individuals within it though, 'as the existential core of the university' (Hunsinger, 2020: 12), remains currently in the balance

9 Rationality or Positionality

The Labour of Words in Higher Education was concerned then with a rationality in HE policy that has seen universities addressing a 'menu' of issues such as *student engagement, employability,* and *Technology Enhanced Learning*

one-by-one, in discrete strategy documents. This approach towards 'solving' each of these topics reflects the means-to-an-end logic of neoliberalism where 'quick fixes' tend to predominate. Students from recent generations have been viewed instrumentally as if they were a 'problem' in relation to each perceived 'issue' (Partington, 2020). They have been stereotyped as 'snowflakes' or 'careerists' in the media, or said to prioritise value-for-money above the 'love of learning' when they do not fit the 'ideal' student who 'would enable HE to continue to deliver the same curricula in the same way' (Partington, 2020). Even though many universities have now produced equality, diversity and inclusion policies and frameworks which acknowledge their varied communities and state their commitments, still a rational policy discourse persists which suggests that such values can simply be 'embedded' (Hayes, 2018, Partington, 2020). Here are just a few examples:

> Through this strategy, we will embed a University-wide culture of inclusion. (University of Leicester, 2017–2021: 2)

> Embed equality into all aspects of University life. (University of Leeds, 2014–2019: 7)

> Our teaching and learning strategy will embed policies and processes that ensure no group with protected characteristics is systematically disadvantaged at any stage from admission to graduation and into employment. (Brunel University London, 2015–2020)

I argue that this form of rationality in HE policy discourse needs to change because equality and inclusion are experienced differently by each individual. As illustrated above, the many factors that now influence these experiential positionings in postdigital society are not under the control of any university to simply be embedded.

Indeed, for diversity to be thoroughly explored, examining more individual postdigital experiences is necessary. There are now many new disciplinary and cross-disciplinary research fields that are contributing to postdigital insights. Some authors have drawn close links between the effects of Covid-19 on the cultural infrastructure of societies across the globe, including education. They point to the need to fundamentally rethink the transactional approach where education has tied itself so closely to economic markets and to look more closely at relationships that cut across learning, biology and technology. For example, to consider insights from 'epigenetics', the study of the interaction between environmental conditions and organic development. In education therefore, to examine links between learning, human cells and technologies:

INTRODUCTION   43

> The relationship between nature and culture in education requires a
> deep level analysis of the biological and physical substrate of human
> learning. Only with a sufficiently fundamental level of analysis can soci-
> ety reorganise its systems of learning and scientific inquiry to this rapidly
> changing environment. (Johnson, Maitland & Torday, 2020: 1)

By exploring the individual, diverse positionalities of those who study and
work in the postdigital context that HE now operates in, a more honest dialogue about the dynamic nature of inclusive practices can take place. Extending what is meant by inclusivity to include all key participants is now even
more pressing when the global pandemic has also thrust so much of education
into commercial online platforms. This has exposed related data and ethics
concerns requiring new attention to avoid underprivileged groups becoming
further disadvantaged. A striking example at the time of writing is the rational
use of an algorithm to replace A level results for thousands of UK students unable to sit exams (Sodha, 2020). This situation discussed as 'inequalities exacerbated by an algorithm' (Powell, 2020) was followed by an even more striking U
turn, as attempts to avoid damage limitation for individual students has led to
new practical problems for universities and anxieties about retention (Fazackerley, 2020c). These interactions back and forth across humans and technical
processes have played out before our eyes revealing the individual postdigital
situations of students, teachers, researchers, politicians and algorithmic platforms, in an astonishing set of circumstances, that I will return to discuss in
rather more detail a little later.

10   New Postdigital Understandings of Interpersonal Relations and
Inclusivity

Postdigital positionality then is a new perspective towards inclusivity through
which such cases might be examined to further broaden debate on HE policy
reform. This original concept is established by extending ideas on the well-
theorised topic of positionality in research practices but re-examining and
applying these through a 'postdigital' lens across academia as a whole. This
dual focus enables alternative routes into contemporary debates on inclusive
practices in HE. In particular, ways that highlight the many new means through
which a blend of human, technological, biological, economic 'actors' (such as
individuals, groups, digital devices, ecological systems, platforms and data)
are now dialectically influencing policy discourse and social practice in seen,
and unseen, ways. This is important in order to demonstrate issues of empowerment or discrimination that can be overlooked when HE policy still treats

digital technologies as instruments alone, to simply 'enhance' the core activities of academia (Hayes & Jandrić, 2014, Hayes, 2015, Hayes & Bartholomew, 2015, Hayes, 2019c). This narrow discourse has furthered a generalised, universal view which unfortunately masks the deeply individual, contextual nature of human technological encounters in learning and research (Jandrić & Hayes, 2020c).

Therefore, a key part of this debate concerns the powerful positional and fluid nature of the individual interactions we each experience in postdigital society and educational encounters. How postdigital positionality translates into interpersonal relations has profound but often veiled relevance for inclusivity agendas. Inclusivity policies currently remain at the level of measuring pre-defined categories of disadvantage and seeking to educationalise sets of actions into strategies to address these within the boundaries of universities. This approach may purport to aspire to 'excellence', but it lumps together aspects of individual identity under the generalised banner of phrases like 'the student experience'. As such it assumes a 'macho consumerist identity' (Bartram, 2020) that overrides individual positionalities within a broader 'audit culture' (Slaughter & Leslie, 1997, Shore & Wright, 1999, Ball, 2003, Olssen & Peters, 2005, Biesta, 2009, Rudd, 2017). Given the complex intersections that we each encounter across the virtual airing cupboard, I raise the question as to whether we can even refer to 'interpersonal' now, without some acknowledgement that the 'inter' of human interactions is no longer with 'persons' alone (Fuller & Jandrić, 2018, Braidotti, 2019a, 2019b, Savin-Baden, 2021).

In summary, this book will act as a significant source of reference by signposting much that has been written so far about the new postdigital context and ecosystem in and around HE. In bringing these perspectives together with a body of literature on positionality, I propose a counter response to the narrow, dehumanising discourse of McPolicy, as discussed in *The Labour of Words in Higher Education* (Hayes, 2019a) by opening this broader debate. Interventions accompanying Covid-19 may have distanced us all from our campuses across the globe but this has also flooded cyberspace with human voices expressing their personal contexts via digital platforms (Jandrić & Hayes, 2020a, Jandrić & Hayes et al., 2020b). As such, the pandemic is a dreadful reality but also a stimulus that illuminates how important biological matters have become in our postdigital era, as we contemplate what shape a post pandemic HE might look like. It is now time to collectively disrupt redundant, rational agendas that seek only to 'embed' generic, static principles of inclusive practice, supported by opaque data and metrics. This is because these have little bearing on individual and dynamic postdigital experiences of inclusivity. If the best that our HE policies can do is to repeatedly give agency to inanimate statements, then we can only expect (at best) to preserve a status quo of inequalities, rather than to further social justice and equal opportunities.

INTRODUCTION

11   The Debate to Come

Examining positionality in the postdigital context of HE enables new diverse perspectives to be heard on the constitutive role that technological platforms, biodigital science, data and human activity now play in people's lives. This post-digital context has implications for inclusivity, bringing both visible and invisible effects to bear, providing new opportunities but also exacerbating disadvantage. Debate needs to follow on how to 'unlearn' former approaches towards policy that focus on humans, but then proceed to write McPolicy statements that miss them out in the discourse. New methods that are more cognizant of a 'postdigital gathering between humans and machines' (Jandrić & Hayes, 2020c) could help to write a more honest account of diversity and inclusivity. This is necessary within a broader global context where sustainability and collaborative movements towards a bioeconomy will provide a new focus for education. The shift from a knowledge-based economy to more of a bio-based economy (Saachi, Lotti & Branduardi, 2020) is likely to yield new cooperation that cuts across subjects such as science, economics, education, law and social science. A recent move by international lawyers to draft plans to criminalise ecosystem destruction is one such example. The new legal definition of 'ecocide' will soon be a complement to other existing international offences such as crimes against humanity, war crimes and genocide (Bowcott, 2020). Such changes will in turn impact on disciplines that are taught in universities and on the positionality of students, teachers, researchers and policy makers. As we contemplate a post-pandemic university (Carrigan, 2020a) there are new 'postdigital ecopedagogies' that might be imagined (Jandrić & Ford, 2020). As technological and scientific convergences lead to new globally agreed ecopolicies, a more organic approach to these shifts in HE policy could go further towards addressing the many systemic inequalities that the pandemic has revealed. Whatever new discourse eventually replaces McPolicy, it will have more chance of being effective for inclusivity if it reflects a twofold and converged debate:

1.   To acknowledge a new 'postdigital' context in HE where multiple and diverse 'actors' (that are not all human) are now altering much of what may once have been described as 'established' or 'inclusive' practices in universities.
2.   To recognise and explore what this means across all key activities of HE, to notice how educational access, inclusivity and opportunities for individuals are now altered in new ways depending on their positionality and yielding new interpersonal relations.

Therefore, in the chapters to come the role of positionality in a postdigital context will be examined firstly in Chapter 1, to inquire as to why this is a matter for everyone. Considering when human identity becomes data, or data becomes identity is central to this debate, as rapid new biodigital developments (Peters, Jandrić & Hayes, 2021a) and 'precision education' (Williamson, 2019a) bring new intensive scientific advances in the biological sciences into the lives, bodies and brains of learners. The possibilities or potential alienation from such developments depends on how values and educational purposes are conceived within policy. This leads into a reflexive look at some tenets of positionality that are omitted in McPolicy but relate to subjective ideas of individuals about their identity and who they might become. It requires personal reflexivity for each of us to choose our positionality before this is chosen for us via human and technological systems. The disruption wrought by the pandemic has been documented by viral viewpoints that do not sit outside of HE. These have intertwined with existing social, political and technological reactions and responses to inequalities, including vaccine distribution. Yet some believe that Covid-19 could also act as a portal through which alternative approaches in HE might now start to be realised.

In the first half of Chapter 2, the background to McPolicy claims is reviewed to shed light on a problematic, unrealistic separation of two broad policy areas: technology and inclusivity, and their associated forms of discourse. HE policies for digital research, scientific progress and Technology Enhanced Learning (TEL) sit apart from strategies and regulatory frameworks seeking to address inclusivity for students. Policy for TEL has mostly ignored the intersection of digital learning with diversity and inclusivity strategy documents. Meanwhile, inclusivity policies focus on recruitment, participation and other social issues, with little critical attention paid to rapid, widespread digital and scientific change (OECD, 2020) and the inequities, possibilities and ethical issues that accompany this. The second half of Chapter 2 looks at why shared political economic spaces of technology and culture are important for airing varied debates on what inclusivity means for individual positionality in postdigital society. Without this, contradictory policy statements around social justice risk cancelling each other out and social mobility stalls (Sandel, 2020). Widening participation policy discourse therefore now needs to widen much further. There is an urgency to include intimate and fluid linkages between commercial data-driven platforms, digitalisation of biology, artificial intelligence and all human characteristics and endeavours. There is a need also to reflect this fluid, emerging context in which I write, where Covid-19 is a biological actor contributing to altering existing political economic spaces of technology and culture.

In Chapter 3, alternatives to the increasingly irrelevant discourse of 'the student experience' in HE policy are contemplated. This has perpetuated a myth

INTRODUCTION

that all societal issues might be educationalised into policy and delivered back to students as a package deal. This reductive discourse drives a wedge between teachers and students. It metaphorically 'cages' students, and as Covid-19 so graphically demonstrated, it can physically restrict their movements too. The pandemic revealed digital poverty and exclusion, issues of connectivity, a lack of skills, confidence and spaces where students and staff might work, as well as consequences from an algorithmic calculation of grades. Meanwhile promises and profound ethical challenges accompany rapid digital convergence across disciplines and innovations in AI. The lives of learners and teachers are now digitised and datafied, with implications for lifelong learning, human wellbeing and personalised education. As such, HE policy cannot meaningfully sit apart from news and social media or corporate data driven platforms that universities have adopted. HE needs to develop a new unifying role that spans these areas. A positionality that is less insular and controlling, and more able to take the lead on these critical postdigital debates, as they intersect with technological, ecological and societal change.

In Chapter 4, the tired culture of 'measuring excellence' in HE is met with questions concerning what is included, and what gets excluded, in this rational consumer focused approach towards teaching. This form of McPolicy seems to originate from the government mantras that sought competitive advantage in a so-called 'information age' driven by technology. Now that political economic focus seems to be shifting, as a global sustainability agenda is looking towards more ecological approaches (UNESCO, 2020d). The Knowledge-Based Economy (KBE) focus is giving way then to a more circular bio-based economy, reinforced by biodigital progress, where education flexibly and organically supports new interdisciplinary liaisons to help meet sustainability goals (Aguilar, Twardowski & Wohlgemuth, 2020, Saachi, Lotti & Branduardi, 2020). For teachers, who have experienced a loss of identity, with their academic labour invisible in policy, yet with selected aspects of their roles incessantly 'measured', there are new opportunities to assert their positionality and develop 'postdigital ecopedagogies' (Jandrić & Ford, 2020).

In Chapter 5, the McPolicy discourse of measuring research in terms of impact assessment is discussed initially, to show why positionality is important to academics. Neoliberal forms of discourse, as opposed to classical liberal discourse have altered the positionality of academics and divided different (but connected) academic activities in universities. Individualised incentives and performance targets are a model of accountability for research that sits at odds with both the 'idea of the public good' and with new cutting-edge scientific research in support of sustainable futures (Peters, Jandrić & Hayes, 2021a, 2021b, 2021c). Therefore, if we are intent on working towards inclusive practices in universities, why do our HE policies exclude so many aspects of society that now impact on inclusivity for individuals? The 'industrialised' nature of science and implications for quality are discussed alongside the need for new merged and inclusive policies that reflect the postdigital positionality of the university itself and the local context it occupies.

In Chapter 6, rational conceptions of leadership in HE are reviewed, to consider how marketised McPolicy discourse and related practices have culturally distanced students and staff from their institutions. As universities have made rational edtech alliances to manage activities during the pandemic, this has irrationally created new challenges. The student data that institutions sought to gather, measure and control has increasingly merged with new cloud-based systems and commercial interests. This creates new ethical challenges that make it harder for universities to embed inclusivity agendas, as if these existed apart from global digital advances. As technology consortiums seek to influence HE policies based on values of investment and profit, this places less emphasis on emancipatory education for those on the margins, in terms of inclusivity, widening participation and levelling up. HE now has new responsibilities in this context, amid a global focus on education for sustainability, supported by digital technologies and biological systems (Peters, Jandrić & Hayes, 2021a, 2021b, 2021c) Given the disruption this brings to former assumptions about society, the economy, and human existence, McPolicy discourse on inclusivity has new participants to include.

In Chapter 7, the book concludes by revisiting the key arguments surrounding our changed postdigital positionalities in this new landscape of digitalisation and biodigital convergence. There are opportunities for sustainable development using natural and synthetic materials but there are also ethical and political implications that will change our assumptions concerning 'established inclusive practices'. The university now has an opportunity and a responsibility to reconnect the broad cultural and technological spheres that neoliberal political economic McPolicy rhetoric separates. We can permit instead a new political bioeconomic policy discourse to develop, as we encourage open debate on the inclusive, ecological routes HE policy might now take (Peters, Jandrić & Hayes, 2021a, 2021b, 2021c).

CHAPTER 1

Positionality in a Postdigital Context

1 Why Is Postdigital Positionality a Matter for Everyone?

From isolation to online exhibitionism. From fluid identities to protected and unprotected characteristics. From technological dependence, inclusion, exclusion and indifference. From emancipation to exploitation. From medical attention to lack of healthcare. From opportunity to marginalisation. From free speech to censorship. From inviting to cancelling. These are just a few of the very broad dimensions that connect with individual positionality, in relation to digital devices, data and platforms, as they interact with each of our socioeconomic and sociocultural, as well sociomaterial and biological circumstances. Whilst referring to this landscape as postdigital, it is immediately accepted that such terminology is imperfect, but also useful, as it provides a basis for critical and open dialogue (Jandrić et al., 2018). More people than ever before are interacting across the virtual airing cupboard of the Internet, and all that it now connects with, as the pandemic has contributed to further altering this scene. It leaves individuals positioned differently to each other, but with collective questions too.

As humans have become routinely subject to rational forms of computer processing, data compilation, extraction and related deterministic discourse in many aspects of their lives, who they perceive themselves to be as subjective beings, can become either diminished, or extended. For Steve Fuller, 'human' is a normative category concerning what 'self-described' humans decide to include, or exclude (Fuller & Jandrić, 2018). Fuller suggests that we might reach an agreement about the performance standards that a putative 'human' should meet that a 'non-human' does not meet. Braidotti in *Posthuman Ecologies* (2019) refers to the 'falsely universal' notion of the 'human' and 'of the system of moral values and human rights that rest upon it'. Braidotti applies a 'posthuman paradigm as an analytical tool for understanding the perspectival nature of knowledge and for drawing attention to the primacy of non-human influences in formative processes' (Braidotti, 2019). This has direct relevance for how a so-called non-human might be suitably acknowledged as a participant alongside humans in an inclusivity strategy, given that human data now passes between technological devices, as well as between humans and their own devices.

© KONINKLIJKE BRILL NV, LEIDEN, 2021 | DOI: 10.1163/9789004466029_003

However, other authors have pointed to how the identity of a human is constructed differently across different disciplinary fields too. As Mark Poster (1990) has observed, the discipline of computer science is identified through its relationship to the computer: 'identity remains part of the disciplinary protocol of the field, even if the actual object, the computer, changes significantly, even unrecognisably, in the course of the years' (Poster, 1990: 147). On this basis, it could be said that in the humanities, the subjective human content is emphasised, even if what it means to be human has changed alongside new, intimate digital and biological interactions with computers that we might debate via biodigital philosophy (Peters, Jandrić & Hayes, 2021a). There are further questions too concerning the place of our human vitality amid global steps towards a circular bioeconomy (Peters, Jandrić & Hayes, 2021b). These intermingle currently with public health and the effects of a global pandemic across society (Dingwall, Hoffman & Staniland, 2013).

Gary Hall (2013) suggests that what has come to be called the digital humanities should not though, simply be perceived as a bringing together of computing and humanities, as if these were 'equivalent'. He suggests that it is necessary instead to maintain a distinction between digital computing and the humanities. More emphasis has been placed on 'direct, practical uses computer science can be put to in the humanities' to improve processes and operations. This is a one-way flow that imposes a particular rational logic from computer science on the humanities. There has been less discussion on what 'the humanities themselves bring to the understanding of computing' (Hall, 2013: 782). This argument has connection too with the treatment of technology on the one hand, as an efficient way to fix processes or enhance teaching in some HE policies, but the omission of the consequences of digital technologies on the other hand. It is no longer adequate to simply generate sets of policies that are isolated from each other, when there are complex implications for equality, diversity and inclusion.

1.1 McDonaldisation Values Humans as Rational Objects Not Postdigital Subjects

George Ritzer's (1993/2018) McDonaldisation thesis is one route towards placing the tensions between humanities and computing within a more global overview of recent political economic change and wider cultural activity. Adapted from Weber's theory of rationalisation (Weber, 1930) McDonaldisation demonstrates how humans came to be valued objectively, in a model that mimics the basic criteria on which fast food restaurants have become profitable. Digital developments simply become applied in rational, predictable, commercial agendas in this model, to increase efficiency and exercise greater control over

POSITIONALITY IN A POSTDIGITAL CONTEXT 51

employees. Computing capabilities then are merely tools adopted to improve performance standards for humans. New examples of McDonaldisation can be noticed as processes of globalisation and automation through technology have brought many forms of large-scale rationalisation into play in physical, online and augmented situations. However, the rationality underpinning the more traditional predigital examples of McDonaldisation appear to be meeting new tensions in postdigital society that can yield unexpected, irrational outcomes (Ritzer, Jandrić & Hayes, 2018). These were particularly apparent in the analysis of McPolicy statements that began to lose meaning as linguistic constructions, not people, were repeatedly attributed with human tasks (Hayes, 2019). Reflecting on biodigital philosophy (Peters, Jandrić & Hayes, 2021a), we might also debate possible shifts to come from former models simply based on technology to support rational, human production and consumption.

I have previously discussed how a persistent tendency in recent decades to reorganise and reform education through what sounds like a 'common sense' logic in policy discourse (McPolicy) has effectively seen humans writing themselves out of their own roles (Hayes, 2019a). Given predictions of a 4th Industrial Revolution (Schwab, 2017, Peters, Jandrić & Hayes, 2018, WEF, 2019) that threatens people with mass unemployment, I pointed out a curious pattern of assigning human characteristics to technologies in policy language and irrationally attributing human labour to machines and not to people (Hayes & Bartholomew, 2015). Alongside much reform and disorientation concerning the purposes of education, as well as a rising 'therapy culture' (Furedi, 2004) the potential for humans to be diminished by Artificial Intelligence (AI) presents a real threat (Seldon, 2020: 1).

1.2 Evolutionary Technological and Cultural Shifts and the Role of Education

If in education we have treated digital technology as a simple enhancement to learning, but have largely ignored its implications for equality, diversity and inclusion policy, the same could be said of the omission of critical, emancipatory educational theory from development of new artificial intelligences. Now though is a pressing time to examine ethical tensions, bias and discrimination that can occur at various stages in computing design, development and application, and what this means for inclusivity policy. We are living with real impacts and inequalities in people lives that have emerged through disciplinary divides between digital computing, the humanities and social sciences. Many studies in human computer interaction (HCI) are now examining the intersections across disciplines that might better inform more ethical computing design and algorithmic activity. There are postdigital complexities too that encompass more than simply design. Very broadly, there has been a developing need for us to reconnect cultural and technological developments (Delanty, 2001: 157) through education. This is becoming more apparent, as recent global green agendas pin hopes for sustainable futures on bioeconomic developments based on biodigital technologies, but also place education as central to the global Sustainable Development Goals (SDGs) being achieved (UNESCO, 2020d).

Now that an evolutionary shift presents itself in the form of biodigitalism, our natural and cultural environment is converging with digital advances. This brings new ways to reduce our emissions and develop renewable energy and resources (Peters, Jandrić & Hayes, 2021b). Fundamental changes to how humans perceive themselves and their roles will follow. The concept of being postdigital offers a productive (but not perfect) route that enables human subjectivities, rather than objective rationalities alone, to be explored in this context:

> The postdigital is hard to define; messy; unpredictable; digital and analog; technological and non-technological; biological and informational. The postdigital is both a rupture in our existing theories and their continuation. (Jandrić, Knox, Besley, Ryberg, Suoranta & Hayes, 2018: 895)

The Springer journal *Postdigital Science and Education* was formed in 2018 for exploratory and inclusive purposes. It has enabled the adaptable concept of being postdigital to be shaped, extended and applied in multiple situations to reveal subjective and collective experiences. Just as McDonaldisation has been adapted to be explored in different contexts to demonstrate all manner of large-scale global rationalisation based on production and consumption, the postdigital can be owned and varied positionalities on it shared. I chose the title of postdigital positionality to enable counter arguments to neoliberal rationalities and generalisations about inclusive practices, as these play out in McPolicy across HE. There will be opinions too on whether linking the post-digital perspective with positionality theory does shed any light on new ways into inclusivity policy in universities. It provides a talking point though, that aims to be inclusive in inviting those opinions.

1.3 Postdigital Positionality Avoids Digital Bureaucratisation of Meaning

Therefore, postdigital positionality is a concept under development, and rather like a beta phase of testing in computing, there could be some known or unknown bugs for readers to find. In the process we may arrive at something better, but for now it gives us something to work with and refine. Computing techniques are applied in all manner of human activities across organisations, along with objective goals that seek greater quantitative efficiency. Insights from the humanities applied to better understand computing and data activities instead lean towards a more qualitative, subjective analysis. Currently inclusion policies and rational digital skills agendas are overlooking many ethical implications that emerge from such analysis. There should not be separate agendas that pick and choose some issues of student or staff wellbeing and not others because humans have never been more subject to rational forms of computer processing with related impacts on their emotions and health.

The Covid-19 pandemic, and the need for humans to distance from each other and work online, has also added numerous biological and informational complexities to the postdigital contexts that humans now occupy (Jandrić, Knox, Besley, Ryberg, Suoranta & Hayes, 2018). Massimo Leone (2020) has explored the issue that 'insignificance' is seeping into our everyday lives. He suggests that the progressive digitalisation of our very ways of being 'is turning the relation between subjects and objects, as well as that among individuals, into empty stereotypes' (Leone, 2020: 1). This is leading to contemporary 'obsessions' and therefore we require 'strategies to resist the alienating effects of the digital bureaucratisation of meaning' (Leone, 2020: 1). Material and digital reactions to this situation can be observed, from a desire to personally make a mark of some kind, such as tattooing the body, placing placards in windows during lockdown, taking part in a physical demonstration, trolling others or oversharing, across an online forum.

Additionally, a 'therapeutic' ethos that has diffused across society and into education, points to further examples of a human need to be noticed, such as 'presenteeism' (Ecclestone & Hayes, 2019: 108), as does a desire to be 'memorable' as a person, in the form of a 'selfie' (Leone, 2018: 44). There are others who attach padlocks to bridges to signify their presence and regard for a lover in the form of 'love locks' (Hayes, 2019: xi), as shown in Figure 9, where a stray face mask has been included. Further individual forms of expression have taken the form of protests against the enforcement of facemasks, lockdowns and general infringements of liberty.

Ultimately, whether we know it or not, we are now in a zone of being human where we need to choose whether we become postdigital objects alone or learn who we might become also as postdigital subjects, each with our own unique positioning. Postdigital positionality recognises human autonomy within each of our individual contexts. This subjective stance places each of us in a stronger position for emancipatory forms of collaboration in education where individual diversity is recognised as a strength over rational objective statements of excellence that render each of us as insignificant.

FIGURE 9   Love locks on a bridge are joined by a face mask

A lot of rational computer processing and data collection taking place around us currently goes unnoticed. Some authors have suggested that the term postdigital refers to just this. Thus, the Internet and digital capacity, just like electricity, will only be noticed now through its absence, or when things go wrong (Negroponte, 1998, Cramer, 2015, Jandrić et al., 2018). This in itself though is still only part of the picture, when there are still many people globally and locally who are not able to access digital services for many different reasons (Traxler, Smith, Scott & Hayes, 2020). Yet, a lack of personal access to digital activity does not necessarily exclude people from other forms of physical surveillance, having data collected about them, or others discussing them during online conversations and sharing their images across social media. Whilst this book focuses on the context of inclusivity, in relation to HE policy, many of the ideas that are explored are applicable to all of us, in whatever location around the globe. The pandemic has forced new human dependencies on digital means of communication, online working, virtual health and social services appointments and has also drawn attention to disparities of many kinds.

1.4   Unconscious Bias from Humans Encounters Conscious Bias from Machines

Problems with the divide between policies that aim to address equality, diversity and inclusion, and those that discuss technology as a separate driver of change to rationally support market-driven economic aims, can be noticed with regard to the treatment of bias. Returning briefly to the analogy of the airing cupboard, it is easier to respond with a bias towards what is spilling out at the front, when I open the door. This means little attention is paid to the items closer to the pipes and the hot water tank further back, well at least until something goes wrong with this technology. In the virtual airing cupboard of online opinion, the devices and technological platforms through which so many comments are expressed are given little consideration, as they operate in the background. They gather and distribute data through computer programming that reflects their purpose, but also generate and contribute to bias, alongside humans. All manner of preconceptions, presumptions, partiality or prejudice can be at work out of sight due to opaque operations that users are largely unaware of. The present focus remains on human bias of the type involved when humans express opinions in the moment (or act accordingly), that are quickly cancelled by others. This demonstrates the disconnect between 'cultural reproduction and technological reproduction' (Delanty, 2001: 157). A postdigital perspective is one route towards connecting the two. Whilst individuals are 'cancelling' each other online over different isolated gestures and comments, there are deep and multifaceted inequities that play out across institutions, structures and the programming of technologies. Online or offline, 'battles of cultural identity' (Delanty, 2001: 157) are both cultural and technological, in terms of bias.

As an illustration, for some time now many organisations and companies have required their staff to undertake unconscious bias training. This is said to address issues of implicit bias, sometimes discussed as prejudice, or unsubstantiated judgments either supporting, or discriminating against one thing, person or group in comparison with others, in ways that might be deemed unfair. Amidst a recent row where some UK Members of Parliament (MPs) who were urged to undertake unconscious bias training, instead rejected it (Murphy & Walker, 2020), some people argued that the training might be viewed by employees 'as something which should enable them to better do their job'. Others commented over Twitter that such training is 'patronising' and that a form of 'snowflake' training should be offered to the providers of unconscious bias training themselves, in retaliation. There were comments too that suggested that by refusing to do this training, the MPs 'say something unpleasant about themselves' (Whitaker, 2020).

There are others who air alternative perspectives on this topic, arguing that (rather than cancel each other) people and organisations should cancel the unconscious bias training itself. They point out that organisations are simply 'rushing to tick the box of unconscious bias training' in response to recent 'civil unrest over systemic racism' (Liesch, 2020). This is based firstly, on a claim that unconscious bias training was not actually created as a solution for systemic bias, prejudice and discrimination. Instead it was 'designed as a risk-mitigation and compliance tool'. Furthermore, 'it was not designed by people who experienced and understood discrimination, but by corporate lawyers who were intent on protecting their organisations from litigation' (Liesch, 2020). Whilst this comment on design may be so, a key argument for holding open debate about postdigital positionality as a concept, is to avoid assumptions of what others may or may not have 'experienced'. In the virtual airing cupboard, there is a great deal of voicing of what others are expected to 'feel', perhaps connected too with a widespread preoccupation with emotional difficulties and popular therapy (Ecclestone & Hayes, 2019: 5).

Further issues raised concerning the training itself, are that many features that could help to foster 'less biased, more equitable, and lasting behaviour change' have not been included. For example, 'voluntary participation, a focus on the system as opposed to the individual and practising equitable behaviour over time'. Instead, training is 'mandatory, targeted at the individual and conceptually disconnected from day-to-day work' (Liesch, 2020). There are also numerous ways in which cognitive bias affects each of our actions.

> We cannot count the number of ways that dimensions of identity intersect in a given person at a given point in time. The world is waking up to the fact that we cannot train the bias out of anyone. (Liesch, 2020)

Wherever readers of this book choose to position themselves on the topic of unconscious bias training, there is a discussion to be had about not only the design approach for staff sessions but also the design and potential ingrained bias of technological platforms that deliver such training. Furthermore, the arguments expressed by Liesch (2020) are made from a position with a commercial interest, appearing on the *Tidal Equality* website, which seeks people to trial their alternative form of training, called *Equity Sequence*. This illustrates the varied and vested interests that positionality theory can help reveal. Thus, exploring the postdigital positionalities of individuals calls into question the objectivity or neutrality of any actor (human or not), effectively arguing that usually someone's interests are at stake. How that 'someone' is now perceived in a postdigital context requires new thinking in relation to inclusivity policies. To write these without full acknowledgement of the role that technological change now plays in people's lives and in universities, could be said to be an act of exclusion in itself.

POSITIONALITY IN A POSTDIGITAL CONTEXT 57

This is because, firstly, the numerous facets of people's identities are no longer constructed via human and social means alone. We are all now (whether we ourselves use technology, or not) partly constituted through data created by us, or about us. Data-driven systems are a part of all of our lives, monitoring, evaluating and reconstituting different aspects of human existence. Whilst some of this activity is more recognisable than other aspects, we are now partially formed by the mobile, communicative, wearable, implantable, programmable, transportable, connectable, invasive and disposable devices and data, that organise and co-construct how individuals perceive daily life. Thus, the positionality of individual humans, which was traditionally discussed by qualitative researchers to explain how their ontological or epistemological values may have influenced a project outcome, is worth extending. The lens of positionality offers one way to examine the web of complexities humans and technologies bring to inclusive policy and practices.

Secondly, I suggest that the positionality of non-human actors (in terms of their political context, potential bias, origins, development, ethics, accessibility, legibility, negotiability and accountability) increasingly need to be taken into account, alongside discussions about the positioning of humans. These are not merely interesting questions, they also have deep ramifications for inclusivity in education and across wider society, if they are overlooked.

Therefore, in the rest of this chapter, following further examples that illustrate the first point, I will then describe how positionality has been understood more traditionally in a research context. I will explain why exploring positionality in a postdigital context offers new insights for HE inclusivity agendas and I will discuss some examples of postdigital positionality during the pandemic. It is important not to view these instances in isolation from what might be learned for future directions in HE. In terms of the second point, I will share technological examples that illustrate ramifications for positionality and inclusivity in education and across wider society, to show why inclusivity policy discourse would benefit from a reboot.

1.5 Living with Technology and Diversity as Fluid Not Static

New arrangements now define human relationships in society, given that intelligent computer systems and algorithms are daily residents in many of our lives (Jandrić, Knox, Macleod & Sinclair, 2017). This though requires a different way of 'thinking of technology which does not decide upon its status in advance' (Dawson, 2019: 463). The same could be said of diversity. Simply stating words like technology or diversity in policy as if these were simple solutions (like unconscious bias training), misses out on the fluidity of lived experience. In her book *On Being Included*, Sara Ahmed (2012) discusses diversity as an ordinary, even unremarkable, feature of institutional life, but one that manifests as multiple embodied realities. So it is with embodied experiences of technology, as these intermingle with fluid experiences of diversity. Ahmed emphasises a need to ask what diversity does and what we are actually doing when we use the language of diversity. To ask the same questions about technology and data (as part of the conversations on diversity and inclusion) would be a powerful connection.

The problem in HE policy is that we have, for some years now, ascribed a status to words and buzz phrases that has hidden from sight the related facets of human labour, technology and relations with diverse individual subjectivities (Mautner, 2005). Static forms of policy discourse have shaped the identity of students as a faceless 'body' via statements like 'the student experience' (Hayes & Jandrić, 2018). This phrase linguistically conceals the diverse routes that students take through HE, including how each person may experience successes, challenges and inclusion in unique ways, depending on their positionality.

As individuals and institutions, an array of online and social media identities, as well as data-driven computing devices now participate with us (and for us), both in, and outside of, academia. Technologies harvest and curate both products and people who might interest us, based on close surveillance of our online actions on Amazon, LinkedIn, Facebook and many other platforms. Yet, in many local and global contexts these interactions vary too, in terms of who has access to digital ways of living and learning and how these are enacted culturally (Traxler, Smith, Scott & Hayes, 2020). Then there are others in society who by choice still seek to avoid digital technology, where possible. Examining social theory concerning technology, oppressive and liberating forms of power, politics and language surrounding education and individual positionality through a postdigital lens, can address our current environment of rapid socio-technical change. This includes attention to what existed before digital and what may exist beyond:

> Instead of assuming as a starting point a dichotomy between analog and digital educational forms of life, it assumes that they are *always already* plugged into one another: a flesh electric. (Lewis, 2020: 265)

This colourful idea also helps to avoid a situation where policy discourse is critically analysed in isolation from cultural and technological context. Plugging these into one another as a 'flesh electric' would power up the inclusivity policies with dynamic enactments of diversity and technology. Our policies need a recharge, and a regular installation of updates.

POSITIONALITY IN A POSTDIGITAL CONTEXT   59

So, whilst some research studies challenge hegemonic policy language, and others address a flow of platform capitalism into HE, few draw out perspectives on the fluidity of technology and diversity in individual lives and what this means for institutional inclusivity policies. How this fluidity plays out in each of our postdigital, academic lives requires a reflexive appreciation of these connections and possibilities. Tyson E Lewis has summarised where such discussions might lead, if only we had the courage to 'ask a vampire squid' for some sound advice on moving forward:

> To invent new kinds of postdigital, diabolical fables that enable us to acknowledge the other in ourselves and ourselves in others across any purported digital or species divide in such a way that the uncanny space of mirroring produces joyous encounters rather than merely destructive ones. (Lewis, 2020: 266)

1.6   *Postdigital Spaces Where Human Identity Is Enacted*

The key thesis put forward in this book is that people each have a 'postdigital positionality' that has a 'dialectic relationship' (Freire, 2000: 50) with other key elements of their individual identity and experience. This is because there are new postdigital spaces in which human identity is now enacted, reduced, evaluated, challenged, threatened, empowered or reconceived. Thus, I suggest that developing postdigital positionality theory offers a fruitful route towards stronger individual and collective agency and narratives in HE, where it is fully acknowledged that humans are inextricably intertwined with both digital and predigital technologies. This means that a person's beliefs, political stance, cultural context, location, gender, race, class, socioeconomic status and educational background are all variables and experiences that are not only framed in socio-cultural circumstances, but now in complex socio-technical ones too. As such, they have a postdigital positionality that is unique to them.

Once such a debate is explored, this provides a powerful argument against empty policy or media rhetoric that mindlessly imposes broad categorisations on human beings, that they may not choose for themselves. There is space too, for people to change how they perceive themselves and their positioning within an ever-changing postdigital context. This is important when the placing of people into any kind of grouping risks objectifying human qualities, which can swiftly turn into linguistic constructions that attribute actions to this group, or even state (on their behalf) how they should live or what they should feel. If 'within positionality theory, it is acknowledged that people have multiple overlapping identities' (Kezar, 2002: 96), then postdigital positionality theory is inclusive of how both the digital and analogue now merge with many other aspects of personal identity to develop a person's positionality. As Crenshaw (1989) has pointed out, identity-based politics has enabling aspects for people of different gender, race or those with a disability, but it can also cause individuals to become labelled within one group, when they may identify with other groups in society too. In the case of violence against women there are intersections between, for example, race, gender, and politics, but there may also be points where these cross-cutting experiences further intersect with disability, or mental illness. However, as human cases are increasingly discussed online in the news and via social media, or classified in a database, or the person involved feels excluded from parts of life, their identity is also being shaped by these digital platforms.

1.7   *When Does Human Identity Become Data, or Data Become Identity?*
Exploring one's own postdigital positionality offers an insight into the recognition of broader factors that may be contributing to potential isolation, self-worth or discrimination. There are examples to be noticed in the apps we choose ourselves, but we may not be aware of (or even care about) the data these gather on us. Yet, an app intended to raise confidence, or help with weight loss, or wearable exercise devices, are not just simple tools or additions to people's lifestyles. The ways in which they have been programmed, marketed and how they operate with an individual's perceived identity, helps to demonstrate how what is digital, is closely associated with what is not, and both become blurred as data is collected and used.

Then there is the question of surveillance technologies such as facial recognition that gather data in public spaces. Recent backlash on these controversial technologies has now resulted in some US cities banning their use, citing 'the risk of biases against Black people, women and older people' (Hatmaker, 2020b). Such decisions are significant in terms of data privacy, given that some facial recognition software even 'allows clients to upload a photo of anyone to cross reference it against a massive database full of photos scraped from online sources, including social networks' (Hatmaker, 2020a). In a recent landmark case in the UK, the use of AFR Locate was argued to have breached human rights when biometric data was analysed without the knowledge or consent of the individual concerned. The court upheld that there was 'no clear guidance on where AFR Locate could be used and who could be put on a watchlist, a data protection impact assessment was deficient and the force did not take reasonable steps to find out if the software had a racial or gender bias' (Rees, 2020).

Yet, in a somewhat irrational twist, Covid-19 has now led to the demand for an increase in tracking and surveillance. This includes 'webcams to enable customers to check online to see how busy the high streets are, in a bid

POSITIONALITY IN A POSTDIGITAL CONTEXT 61

to help with social distancing' (Beardmore, 2020). Track-and-trace apps have been enlisted despite concern over invasion of privacy (Amnesty International, 2020). Alongside humans adapting to working online more autonomously, 'tattleware' software, such as Interguard and Sneek are being bought by companies to increase surveillance on their employees, taking photos of workers as often as once a minute (Gabrielle, 2020). Such examples help to show how data privacy takes on a life of its own across platforms, demonstrating a multidirectional flow of how human identity might be appropriated into data, and in turn, human data (such as photos or bioinformation) might be sold or used in potentially discriminatory ways. Developments in neuroscience and neurotechnology have been analysed in relation to human rights to identify:

> Four new rights that may become of great relevance in the coming decades: the right to cognitive liberty, the right to mental privacy, the right to mental integrity, and the right to psychological continuity. (Ienca & Andorno, 2017)

It therefore becomes important for universities to avoid inclusivity policies that home in specifically on issues related to the human body but that overlook issues related to the mind, or vice versa:

> While the body can easily be subject to domination and control by others, our mind, along with our thoughts, beliefs and convictions, are to a large extent beyond external constraint. Yet, with advances in neural engineering, brain imaging and pervasive neurotechnology, the mind might no longer be such an unassailable fortress. (Ienca & Andorno, 2017)

Many social media platforms are now routinely used by people 'to raise awareness 'for the racial, civic, and social causes they care about' (Dickey, 2020). This has led to Instagram 'building a product equity team and hiring a director of diversity and inclusion' and thereby taking responsibility for what they build into their system (Dickey, 2020). In the context of marketised education, the use of many commercial platforms sits alongside aspirations for inclusive practices. Is there not a need now for universities to bring in their own response to product equity scrutiny? This would be a small step towards acknowledging that technologies carry more than just a perceived efficiency into universities. They have earned their right to be scrutinised by inclusivity committees along with the data they gather, because the use of such commercial platforms has wide reaching implications beyond enhanced efficiency.

1.8   *Were You Abused by a Human or a Computer Program?*

Just when it seemed as if the questions that humans were grappling with concerning 'political correctness' (Lea, 2010) were complex enough, examples of algorithmic activity, such as 'keep calm and rape t-shirts' were autogenerated by a 'scripted computer process' (McVeigh, 2013). A more recent study from the United Nations Educational, Scientific and Cultural Organisation (UNESCO) highlighted the way in which AI generated female voices can also generate bias in companies such as Apple and Amazon. The report questions 'the male engineering teams who have built AI systems that cause their feminised digital assistants to greet verbal abuse with catch-me-if-you-can flirtation' which can send a signal that women are docile helpers with no agency, available at the touch of a button to honour commands regardless of their tone or hostility. 'In many communities, this reinforces commonly held gender biases that women are subservient and tolerant of poor treatment' (West, Kraut & Ei Chew, 2019). Without sounding too facetious, such programming issues could be heading into a university or college near you, ready to quietly reinforce inequalities that inclusivity policies have been seeking to address.

A lot written about academia in recent years is of a cautionary nature, with many articles describing academic oppression, anxiety and despair (Gill, 2010, Hall & Bowles, 2016, Hall, 2018). These papers reflect personal stories of pain felt by those on short-term, precarious contracts, victims of bullying, inequalities, mental health issues and overwork. Where once rational lines of bureaucracy, and indeed academic autonomy, were more obvious to spot, it is now harder to tell where many rules, instructions, data and judgements are actually coming from, or going to. It has also become trickier to distinguish between the acts of humans and those of computer code, between government and media interest in universities and strategic institutional or political decision making. This raises questions about the role of fake news in a post truth era (Flood, 2016). On a personal and institutional level, there are emerging issues concerning trust, disillusionment, ethics, reliability and bias, bringing complexity and obscurity into education, welfare and health.

Hearing from individuals in their own voices about their positionality in HE is helpful in distinguishing what might be seen as authentic knowledge in an era of fake news. Questions can be asked about who the 'knower' is and from what position they are speaking, writing or gathering data. There are links here to human trust, emotions and generosity, when 'kindness is a seriously under-rated virtue in a marketised higher education sector' (Welch, 2020). This has implications for new critically reflexive understandings of leadership and policymaking, as well as for learning, teaching and research. For example, if an author seeks to examine how either racial or gendered identities might inform leadership development and challenge hegemonic discourses, it is now expedient to also consider the postdigital context in which these discourses are constructed and distributed, as well as deconstructed or reconfigured. Therefore, postdigital positionality ought to be personal, collective and inclusive of all, because everyone can contribute to what this means as lived experience in their context.

1.9   Civic Dimensions to Postdigital Academic Lives

Human and computer systems are interwoven with neoliberal forms of organisation in universities and colleges. Yet they fuse seamlessly too, with opinions given all too generously, on social platforms, in the virtual airing cupboard. They fuse too, as pre-digital elements of society and civic life. This means that our status as individual hybrid, postdigital beings brings implications for learning, research, university strategy and work in wider civil society, even as we experience globally and locally emerging effects of a Fourth Industrial Revolution (Schwab, 2017, Peters, Jandrić & Hayes, 2018, WEF, 2019, Connor, Mahoney & Lewis, 2019, Hayes, 2019c). Nurturing a vision beyond formal courses, clear connections to civic education that values democratic voices and recognises regional and global changes is important. The pandemic has augmented many fundamental changes that were already happening in terms of automation, with implications for all citizens. For example, there are signs that the Covid-19 crisis has speeded up the process of robots replacing humans. This gives rise to questions on where matters of identity, diversity and value for humans and technologies will sit in the coming years. If some predictions are correct, then we could see humans settling into the back seats in academia (just as they might do in a self-driving car):

> People usually say they want a human element to their interactions but Covid-19 has changed that, says Martin Ford, a futurist who has written about the ways robots will be integrated into the economy in the coming decades. (Thomas, 2020)

From robot cleaners for institutions and offices, to fast-food chains like McDonald's testing robots as cooks and servers, Covid-19 has accelerated a shift away from humans and toward machines. Aspects of this automation are warmly welcomed to keep critical services running and spare us from disease (Thomas, 2020). There are also aspects of human loneliness being met by 'Chatbot girlfriends' and other practices of seeking romance or friendship from artificial intelligence (AI), thus removing human partnerships and replacing these with computing alternatives (Olson, 2020). There are changes to transport as autonomous means of delivery receive a boost helping 'customers reduce physical contact and address labour shortages caused by lingering quarantines and travel restrictions' (Bloomberg News, 2020).

Universities are not immune to these commercial changes and consumer preferences induced by self-isolation and 4IR, now working in tandem. A march of digital platforms into HE to cater for online interactions during lockdown has been followed by the usual 'migration' of students back onto university campuses during the autumn of 2020. Their return has received more interest than usual though, with diverse online commentary on the risks that students may pose to the citizens in the cities they are travelling to in order to study (BBC, 2020c).

As automation competes with the need for human activity there are also curious postdigital examples where pre-digital scenes have returned that might have been thought unlikely just a year ago. The notion of milk floats and milk men and women returning to deliver milk to homes might have been considered as being 'consigned to the history books by the rise of the supermarkets'. However, 'thanks to the coronavirus pandemic, these dairy deliverers on their electric floats are busier than ever as they try to keep up with newfound demand for their services' as 'shoppers try to reduce, or forgo, their trips to supermarkets' (Parveen, 2020). Then again who would have imagined that drive-in movies would have found a renaissance either, as New York attempted to provide 'family-friendly, socially distant fun' (Rein, 2020).

Examples then that provoke a glance backwards, as well as forwards, when contemplating the future of life, learning and what constitutes inclusive practices beyond the pandemic. With this in mind, although it is necessary to expose the problems of our current state, it is worth considering what other reactions, besides panic, may be open to us in this context:

> At moments of radical social and cultural change such as literary studies is experiencing now, we need not panic. We need to avoid the pessimistic and dystopian thinking that dominates much of the contemporary popular literature on the supposedly detrimental impact on attention and education of digital media and technology, and avoid the technological determinism which accompanies such thinking, as if digital media and technology might have some inherent traits and affordances that exist before or beyond their use by the user, reducing us to mere actors without agency, let alone hope – but an intra-active posthuman agency is much more powerful than that. (Ablitt, 2019: 105)

Writing with reference to a postdigital paradigm in literary studies, Ablitt argues above that there is no crisis, because the postdigital 'doesn't negate but instead enhances that which came before' (Ablitt, 2019: 105).

POSITIONALITY IN A POSTDIGITAL CONTEXT   65

Many publications and conferences now call for radical change away from marketised universities and colleges where learning and learners themselves, are commodified. Some suggest that a new 'vision' is required to 'shift the way education workers, students and the general public think about the politics of education' (Gamsu & Hall, 2019: 83). Others point to the profoundly political nature of adult education that historically has enabled access for those who would otherwise have been excluded, calling for broader conceptions of civic education envisioned by the 1919 government Report on Adult Education (Clancy, 2019) and the Adult Education 100 Campaign (WEA, 2019).

Certainly, as people have become displaced from workplaces of all kinds, there is a need for inclusivity in HE to operate in the broadest possible sense. Therefore, dialogue concerning the postdigital context surrounding those of us in HE needs to connect with overlapping civic concerns in the regions surrounding institutions. Postdigital positionality requires a broader approach than university regulatory bodies have been used to so far. Therefore, agencies such as the Office for Students in the UK and similar quality control bodies elsewhere can no longer treat 'data' as isolated from the interconnected cultural and technological spheres of civic life.

1.10 *Filling the Void of Excellence with Data*

HE now has multiple regulatory frameworks for excellence, yet as Readings pointed out in 1996, 'today, all departments of the University can be urged to strive for excellence, since the general applicability of the notion is in direct relation to its emptiness' (Readings, 1996: 23). A quarter of a century later, we now seek to fill this emptiness with data. Data-driven university access and participation policies make reference to fairness, morality and transparency, as they seek to address concerns over progression and attainment gaps for different social groups and ethnicities (Office for Students, 2018). However, such concerns are now also part of a much larger picture that can no longer be overlooked. Those writing university policy based on 'human' values, now need to consider how these are also infused by Artificial Intelligence (AI) algorithms, whose reasoning on exam results, recruitment, actions and ethics act both digitally and physically in people's lives (Hemment, Belle, Aylett, Murray-Rust, Pschetz & Broz, 2019). This new hybrid context includes concerns about the 'platform university' (Means, 2018, Williamson, 2019b) and effects on how students and staff are 'positioned', and on how they come to view this positioning, in relation to their aspirations in or for education.

Fawns Aitken and Jones (2020) have raised concerns about a datafication of 'teaching quality' that now takes place, where digital traces of educational activity are increasingly generated, harvested, analysed, and mobilised in ways that foreground instrumental understandings, not only of evaluation but of education itself (Fawns, Aitken & Jones, 2020). As such, they argue that valuation must take account of those aspects of teaching, learning, and educational context that are missing from digital data. They are not alone in arguing against the measurement of teaching quality through selective data.

In a Special Issue entitled 'Measuring Excellence' in Higher Education (Hayes et al., 2021), a group of authors explore the concept of 'measuring excellence' and 'the dilemmas it raises in the postdigital context now surrounding universities, including the complexities thrown into the mix by Covid-19' (Hayes, 2021). Postdigital positionality is one way to uncover and to better understand these complex and often hidden aspects of academia. It offers a route for exploring how facets of our identities as teachers, researchers and leaders are also infused with digital, pre-digital and post-digital elements. A postdigital debate can help draw attention as to why educational activity cannot simply be 'skewed towards generating favourable data' where outcome measures concerning grades and retention alone are 'taken as isolated proxies for quality' (Fawns, Aitken & Jones, 2020).

Such entanglements with data-driven technological and human systems have diminished the levels of control that humans can exercise over their own situations. This has links too, with a 'wider therapeutic turn in popular culture, politics, personal and institutional life' (Ecclestone & Hayes, 2019: ix).

These aspects of postdigital life manifest themselves within universities in the form of wellbeing agendas, counselling, moves to combat loneliness, policies to increase a sense of belonging and in the physical shape of safe spaces and therapy animals to reduce anxiety. According to Berg, Huijbens and Larsen (2016), 'a rise in anxiety must be seen, in part at least, as the result of the neoliberalisation of the university'. Yet, when digital change and automation have ridden in tandem with the political economic changes wrought by neoliberal forms of capitalism, these aspects of societal change need to be examined together. Whether societal progress is based on physical tools or virtual instruments, human labour and values remain a constant amid technical and cultural change (Hayes, 2019a: 147). The difference now, is that human choices are becoming indistinguishable from those taken by machines that act as proxies for humans. We are therefore at a crossroads where we each need to choose our positionality, before this is decided for us.

2 Positionality in a Traditional Sense

Positionality has a dual meaning traditionally where it refers firstly, to the social and political context that creates a person's identity, in terms of, for example,

POSITIONALITY IN A POSTDIGITAL CONTEXT

their gender, race, class, location and ability. Secondly positionality involves how a person's identity influences, and also potentially may bias their understanding and outlook on the world. Such discussions have been conventionally important in relation to researchers and the research process (in particular for qualitative researchers, although I argue that postdigital positionality now has an increasing importance for people universally) in explaining their part or influence in any research or indeed other activities that they have undertaken. This dual meaning of positionality is core to the topic of this book and to the twofold debate discussed at the end of the introduction. Firstly, that it is necessary to acknowledge a new postdigital context in HE where multiple and diverse 'actors' (that are not all human) are now altering much of what may once have been described as 'established' or 'inclusive' practices in universities. Secondly, exploring what this means across all of the key activities of HE is necessary in order to notice how educational access, inclusivity and opportunities for any individual person may now be altered in complex ways, depending on their 'positionality'. So, I will provide an overview of how positionality has traditionally been understood, in relation to the role of a researcher in connection to their research methodology and outcomes. I will then bring this into the twofold debate this book raises to help to explain a relevance for all of us.

Part of each research study habitually involves explaining how a researcher or a research team's 'position', as they understand it in terms of their human identity and context, has implications for the research choices that they have made. Position is inclusive of many considerations, such as a person's location, their status, gender, ethnicity and their point of view, values and opinions. The researcher themselves must reflexively interpret which aspects of 'who they are' should be disclosed and explained in relation to their research focus and its outcomes. As an example, if you are a white researcher seeking to understand how students of diverse ethnicities may be experiencing aspects of university, then it is important to be cognisant of one's own positionality: as a white person in a particular setting, drawing conclusions on the experiences of others, whose ethnicity is different from your own (Bourke, 2014). To genuinely acknowledge the assumptions that could be influencing the research choices made in this situation, is to appreciate that undertaking research to better understand something about others, is a messy business. Any illusions of objectivity need to be challenged because research is an 'ongoing dialogue with different social worlds' (Holliday, 2016: 7).

2.1   Tenets of Positionality in Postdigital Society

On this note, Torres-Olave and Lee (2019) suggest that positionality is constructed around three main tenets: (1) identities are complex and fluid, (2) they are enmeshed in power relations and (3) they are contextually bound. As well as recognising the importance of intersectional factors such as race, ethnicity, class, gender, age, nationality and sexuality in shaping human experience, they argue that other areas such as what positionality means for scholars whose work (and lives) crosses different national boundaries are under researched. They point also to the need for a reflexivity that goes beyond the mere acknowledgment of social identity as static and towards a need for a better accounting for people's dynamic situational context. Included in this is the worldliness, or fleshliness of experience, and the dynamic role that time and space play (Torres-Olave & Lee, 2019). I would argue then that how these three tenets, around which human positionality is said to be constructed now intersect too with people's postdigital situational contexts, is particularly relevant for inclusivity agendas. They cannot ignore the 'flesh electric' (Lewis, 2020: 265) aspects of people's lives. It is not only researchers who find themselves in 'ongoing dialogue with different social worlds' (Holliday, 2016: 7), this is something that affects us all. In other words, there are countless subjective variables at play in such dialogues, in terms of individual positionality, as this now plays out across postdigital society.

The arguments put forward by Torres-Olave and Lee (2019: 4) are made in the particular context of research in international locations, where they point out why researchers themselves cannot be treated as 'disembodied' from what is being studied. They explain why researcher identities cannot be presented as 'impervious to change and neatly telegraphed in the requisite methods section, not to be re-examined again in the remainder of the text' (Torres-Olave & Lee, 2019: 4). The shifting nature of human subjectivity, as this then moves into a different place and time zone, is said to also bring with it, certain effects. The physical bodies of those of us engaging in research abroad 'may be in a very different "space" than our minds, including our beliefs and assumptions' and what is 'marginalised in one country or region may be marginalised differently in others, or not at all' (Torres-Olave & Lee, 2019: 4, Traxler, Smith, Scott & Hayes, 2020).

As someone who has taught and undertaken research in different parts of the world (including such varied locations as: Italy, Vietnam, Ghana, Singapore, Muscat, Australia, Greece and Denmark) this is a lived experience that I can echo. The very nature of travelling to another nation, eating different food, participating in local cultural activities and talking with local people there, alters my perspective. As a white female teaching in some locations it has been necessary for me to dress differently, to show respect in particular ways that are accepted in that region for certain beliefs, values, items or physical places. As a sociologist, educator and researcher, I have found that being physically present in a different country to teach also changes how I write a research paper.

POSITIONALITY IN A POSTDIGITAL CONTEXT   69

It is possible to plan teaching and research activities in detail before travelling somewhere, but it is then a process of flexible adaptation as I internalise both the unfamiliar context and the ideas that my hosts and participants share:

> We were given a formal introduction to the Assistant Director, Internationalising HE (India), who facilitates internationalisation activities on behalf of the British Council in India and to our hosts and details of the programme our workshop would be delivered within. Day 1 would be a conference, where government officials would lay out expectations, and a local e-learning expert would be present. In Vietnam, we participated in a local quality conference, which followed our taught programme. In Hyderabad, we could absorb the unfamiliar context on Day 1, tweak our approach to support local aspirations and notice cultural nuances not visible through email. (Lamb, Bartholomew & Hayes, 2017: 214)

Here I am describing my own processes of adjusting to undertaking several days of teaching in locations in India (2016) and in Vietnam (2015). Whilst this brief account gives some insight into these formal contexts and preparations, the teaching rooms, facilities, access to Internet and living accommodation where I stayed were completely different. Expectations, customs, attire and political contexts were also diverse:

> After anticipating as much as possible, there is a need for an ongoing reflexivity within a UK teaching team abroad to integrate local, culturally important aspects and political agendas that it would be hard to be aware of before teaching in the host institution begins. (Lamb, Bartholomew & Hayes, 2017: 216)

Whilst Torres-Olave and Lee (2019) were discussing positionality in research, many researchers are also teachers. Paying attention to identity, location and power relations in terms of our own positionality and that of others helps to avoid a rational, disembodied or instrumental approach towards the complexities of inclusivity.

2.2   *Positionality Goes Public, Global and Viral*
What I didn't share in the excerpts above, is the personal emotion that I carried with me as I prepared to teach in India in 2016. I was missing the funeral of a close family member back in the UK who passed away just days before I was due to fly. There are some decisions that researchers have to make in terms of just how personal a statement of positionality they will record in relation to

the study they have undertaken. This will depend too on the topic and how intimately involved they are with it, their choices they made in their collection and analysis of data, as well as how this is eventually summarised as results for publication.

This is interesting to reflect on when digital platforms have now enabled extensive sharing of intimate personal details to global audiences. There are many news websites where, alongside breaking news tragedies, personal narratives and experiences of every aspect of life's minutiae are featured. These are specific, personal positionality accounts that have gone public. They place an individual's circumstances, plight, decisions, dilemmas, appearance, happiness, achievements or experiences of discrimination, injustice or pain onto the phone screens of others who are clicking their way through the news. Those who read these details are forming opinions wherever they are located and linked to their own values. Therefore, how certain technologies and indeed social and cultural movements and related data are disseminated is having a cumulative effect on how we each understand the concepts and any related principles for *equality, diversity* and *inclusion.*

What is publicly aired in terms of positionality across the virtual airing cupboard of the Internet is meeting in turn with mixed responses towards inclusivity, depending on the positionality of each reader. If we consider a rational approach to statements concerning embedding inclusive practice in HE then 'embedding inclusive practice' is treated as an objective. This approach overlooks the deeply subjective and dynamic aspects of inclusivity, as it is constantly being performed in each of our lives as 'flesh electric'. As such, in later chapters that examine some different roles in HE, through postdigital positionality, the three tenets noted by Torres-Olave and Lee (2019), that: (1) identities are complex and fluid, (2) they are enmeshed in power relations and (3) they are contextually bound, will be considered as dimensions of subjectivity, deeply intertwined with technology and culture, with variable impact on what can be conceived as inclusivity.

2.3 *Where Objectivity Meets with Subjectivity*

One of the problems raised in *The Labour of Words in Higher Education* (Hayes, 2019a), was that rational policy discourse (McPolicy) assumes an objectivity that is difficult to question. The policy statements sound as if everyone should believe that this is how the world works, so to speak. Yet the attribution of human academic activities to non-human actors, such as institutions, buzz phrases and technologies is still written by someone, even if the identity of that someone is concealed. The same could be said of the programming, coding and design of data-driven systems where there is human involvement, but

POSITIONALITY IN A POSTDIGITAL CONTEXT

there are differences between the natural written language through which a human being expresses intentions and the activities of a computer interacting with data. The problem with describing what people do (and what they do with technology) as buzz phrases and even acronyms of those buzz phrases (e.g. TEL) is that this objectifies aspects of human labour and behaviour. Human subjectivity, creativity, emotion and reflexivity are rendered into a marketable item that might also be objectively measured and evaluated. Thus, people become referred to as if they were objects, not human subjects, through 'reification' (Lukács, 1971). Certain terms can gain a life of their own as they become adopted and imbued with particular qualities.

The idea of a 'circuit breaker' lockdown is an example that has been frequently discussed by politicians (as a more radical alternative to Covid-19 lockdown policies that focus only on regions). Now widely reported by the media too, people are being asked to believe in the circuit breaker, on the basis of how many lives may be saved (Gallagher, 2020). Thus, a phrase that once applied to an electric switch designed to protect a system from excess electrical current, overload or short circuit, has taken an emotive shape. Those who are unsure of its value in the longer term can be accused of letting more people die. This risk though depends on other factors including the trajectory the virus takes, as well as the vulnerability of those who come into contact with it.

A reification of language is not unlike algorithmic activity by a computer when people become referred to as objects. Recalling observations on computers from Mark Poster (1990), where 'identity remains part of the disciplinary protocol of the field' an important part of this debate is to question what humans hope to preserve in terms of their subjective human content. This is a pressing consideration amid increasingly intimate digital interactions between data-driven computing systems and their role in our private and public health arrangements and interactions. Academic work is often deeply personal and self-defining with individuals committing many unpaid hours to develop what they do with their students, colleagues, external collaborators and in administrative and leadership roles. If such labour is discussed as disembodied activity in HE policy, it becomes alien to the individuals concerned. Such a rationality becomes irrational if it then limits the scope of these endeavours. If agency is also given to terms (and not to people) this moves HE policymaking further away from genuine conversations on positionality. Hall argues that 'there's no enunciation without positionality. You have to position yourself somewhere in order to say anything at all' (Hall, 1990: 18). On this basis, Bourke suggests that 'positionality represents a space in which objectivism and subjectivism meet' (Bourke, 2014: 3). Each of us could 'strive to remain objective but must be ever mindful of our subjectivities. Such is positionality, the acknowledgement of who we are as individuals, and as members of groups, 'and as resting in and moving within social positions' (Bourke, 2014: 3). This requires reflexivity regarding how as individuals we each relate to an interplay of wider culture and technology, how we shape it and are shaped by it, in a postdigital age.

2.4 Practicing Reflexivity Could Be Tricky for an Algorithm

The challenge then is for HE institutions to find routes that move away from McPolicy and towards a reflexivity where new discourses concerning diverse postdigital subjectivities might be critically explored in relation to inclusivity policy. It is important to self-test one's own stance and assumptions and to consider when subjective 'self-descriptions' from those being discussed, may be more appropriate to include as narratives, than to write objective rationalities that ascribe an 'experience' to them (Argenton, 2015: 921, Hayes & Jandrić, 2018: 127). Then there is the question of how such human critical reflexivity applied by people to the choices of language that they use might ever be enacted similarly by an algorithm? Eran Fisher (2020) in her chapter: *Can algorithmic knowledge about the self be critical?* raises the point that it is natural language that 'allows reflexivity' and the reasoning 'to reflect and examine the self and in turn transform the conditions of possibility of observed behaviour'. Humans can behave anxiously and identify hurtful behaviour through language, interpretation and reflexivity, but:

> The algorithmic episteme represents a collapse of that constructive space between theory of the self and the performative, actually existing self, as well as an impossibility to communicate in natural language. (Fisher, 2020: 117)

Fisher (2020) places this reasoning within the subjectivities that have characterised different forms of capitalism, where:
- industrial capitalism moulded a subjectivity that realizes itself by means of hard work, obedience, diligence and frugality (Gramsci, 1971).
- consumer capitalism moulded a subjectivity that realizes itself by means of consumption, hedonism and individualism (Bell, 1976).
- we might now ask how informational, digital, network capitalism moulds a subjectivity that realizes itself through publicity, exposure, communication, sharing and surveillance (Fuchs, 2011, van Dijck, 2013, John, 2016) (practices that create the raw material to produce algorithmic knowledge: data), and through delegating the understanding of the self to technological systems, the underlying rationale of which remains completely opaque and inaccessible for auditing through natural language (Fisher, 2020: 118).

POSITIONALITY IN A POSTDIGITAL CONTEXT 73

The new algorithmic self in this conceptualisation is rendered into 'data patterns':

> The algorithmic episteme suggests that we cannot say what is similar between individuals except that they show a similar data pattern in a given context. Two people showing similar data patterns on Amazon, for example, might be sociologically very different. (Fisher, 2020: 118)

Thus, we have a point of connection here between George Ritzer's description of our lives as con(pro)sumers, where we are exploited for our labour as we produce copious data and feedback for companies and agencies (such as Amazon, Facebook and news channels) all free of charge (Ritzer, Jandrić & Hayes, 2018). This is repeated across all manner of data-driven platforms when we are busy commenting on, and cancelling, what others are saying as we reinforce echo chambers across the virtual airing cupboard. How can we even know what proportions of our human activities have been captured, sorted and classified for use by others elsewhere? Regardless of how each of us may perceive ourselves, in terms of personal identity, we can find ourselves being branded and pigeon-holed (through opaque processes) by the online activities we undertake. As Fisher points out:

> During the 20th century, a person might feel that she is part of the working class, or part of a gender group. Such ascription to a social category did not imply that everyone belonging to that group is identical in every way, but rather that anyone belonging to that group perceives herself as identical in aspects that are *politically significant*, for example, suffering from similar forms of discrimination, or sharing economic interests. (Fisher, 2020: 118)

Rendered into data 'promoted by the algorithmic episteme', not only do 'we have no way of knowing ourselves by ascription to a social category' this also 'threatens to undermine and deconstruct the foundations of political action' (Fisher, 2020: 118).

Therefore, where before:

> mass media created categories of identity that could be spoken of with natural language, understood theoretically, be subjected to critique and resisted through political action. (Fisher, 2020: 118)

Now we seem to be in territory where:

74   CHAPTER 1

> Digital media, in contrast, categorizes individuals based on data patterns
> which cannot be understood with natural language, spoken about or cri-
> tiqued. (Fisher, 2020: 118)

Alongside these observations, in HE policy there seems to be a passive rein-
forcement of these troubling trends. It's time then to open up the institutional
airing cupboards that store data on inclusivity and to critically connect university 'established' practices with the many implications arising across 'the entire
ecosystem of connective media' (Fuchs, 2011).

2.5   *Making Associations of One Kind Can Risk Missing out Others*
The problem of institutional airing cupboards that gather data in isolation
from the arguments above is realised when policy for inclusive practice is
based on some associations about people's characteristics, but not on others.
Taking as an example an experimental official statistic introduced in 2019 by
the UK Office for Students (OfS) called Associations Between Characteristics
of Students (ABCS), this set of analyses seeks to better understand how outcomes (including access to HE, continuation in HE, degree attainment and
employment outcomes) vary for groups of students 'holding different sets of
characteristics' (Office for Students, 2019).

> We define groups of students by looking at a set of characteristics so that
> we can determine the effect of not just one characteristic on an outcome,
> but the effect of multiple characteristics. (Office for Students, 2019)

Recalling earlier discussion surrounding bias, (Liesch, 2020) argued that: 'we
cannot count the number of ways that dimensions of identity intersect in a
given person at a given point in time. The world is waking up to the fact that
we cannot train the bias out of anyone'. Based on such arguments can we really
count the 'characteristics' about anyone then either, or indeed 'define groups
of students by looking at a set of characteristics'?
    Whilst making associations of this kind may inform some general trends,
it risks overlooking many other aspects of each individual student's postdigital positionality that are important or defining for them, rather than rationally determined via pre-defined generic characteristics. In HE, students are
encouraged to work with critical and interpretive processes, to make ethics
applications for the research studies that they undertake involving human participants, and to be reflexively responsive as to how their personal values and
bias may influence their dissertation outcomes. The rational approach of ABCS
seems a somewhat irrational way to be objectively measuring the 'multiple

characteristics' of these diverse students, when as teachers and researchers we are actively encouraging each of our students to do the opposite in their own studies, i.e. to be critical, self-reflexive, subjective practitioners in their discipline. As Collini (2018) has questioned: 'does marketisation threaten to destroy what we most value about education?' and 'does this new era of accountability distort what it purports to measure?'

Another interesting connection to throw into this debate concerns the interpretations that are made by humans or machines concerning 'fairness'. The next example illustrates rather well the importance of taking into account how human subjectivities, and indeed student futures, now intersect with both technology and culture, with implications for inclusivity agendas. How any technology is introduced into any existing culture requires careful thought, yet the furore caused by use of an algorithm in the UK in the Summer of 2020 to grade A-level examination results indicates that multiple considerations were not taken into account. This is a topic that I will return to a little later in this chapter, but it is worth noticing here that there are similarities between adopting a methodology such as ABCS as laid out by the OfS, and the problem of the 'algorithmic episteme' (Fisher, 2020) that was let loose to determine grades, but then quickly 'scrapped after almost 40% of A-level results were downgraded from school teachers' predictions'. The UK Prime Minister, Boris Johnson, explained to schoolchildren affected that 'their grades were almost derailed by a mutant algorithm', whilst Stian Westlake, the CEO of the Royal Statistical Society (RSS) said that:

> the 'colourful phrase' did reflect the fact that ministers, officials and students 'were surprised by the results that it generated'. But, he said, 'the algorithm wasn't a mutant or a freak of nature. This was something that could have been foreseen'. Mr Westlake, a former adviser to the Universities Minister, said the results were 'a predictable surprise' because of the demand that it reduce grade inflation. 'The fact that this could have produced a lot of inaccuracy, which translates into unfair grades for individuals, that was known', he said. (Manthorpe, 2020)

Ofqual, the exam regulator said that there were instructions from ministers to them 'to keep grade inflation down, which meant students' results would have to be downgraded from teachers' predicted grades, which tend to be higher than actual results' (Manthorpe, 2020).

There were further comments from Mr Westlake on 'the need for transparency in the creation of algorithms, not only because it helped prevent errors, but also because it allowed a public debate about their aims':

I think the really important lesson from this is that we can't treat statistics as a holy grail, he said. We need to prepare them with transparency, we need to make sure we understand the assumptions that are going into them and we need to make sure that we use them in the right way. If you've got statistics that only have a certain degree of accuracy, as for example the A-level adjustments did, we can't pretend they are more accurate than they really are. (Manthorpe, 2020)

Fisher (2020: 119) has argued then that 'the algorithmic episteme' is problematic because it undercuts the critical faculties inherent in narrative, speech and inter-subjectivity'. As can be observed so readily through cancel culture, people use these faculties to greater or lesser effect, as they post opinions in the virtual airing cupboard. Drawing on Habermas (1972), Fisher (2020: 119) points to the reflexive experience that 'is the core of the practice which emancipates individuals from being an object and allows them to develop a subjectivity'. As such, this is a practice that has to be controlled and done by the subject. This in turn has implications for how university inclusivity policies discuss human characteristics, digital technologies and what can, or cannot be controlled now within HE institutions.

2.6 *Visible and Invisible Processes of Interpellation in the Postdigital Airing Cupboard*

Postdigital positionality recognises that dimensions of identity intersect in endlessly fluid ways for any given person, at any given point in time. If, as Torres-Olave and Lee (2019) point out, positionality is constructed around: complex and fluid identities, enmeshed in power relations and contextually bound, then as intersectional factors (such as gender, race, ethnicity, class, age, nationality and sexuality) come into play across the digital mechanisms discussed above, the 'flesh electric' is bringing countless, subjective variables into play.

The selecting of objective characteristics about any individual (defined by either humans, or algorithms) to base recommendations on, can therefore be a risky approach. If I sit browsing on my iPad and I find that on YouTube I am offered music suggestions based on what I have already listened to, then I can take these or leave them. If unseen data is gathered without my knowledge and an algorithm entrusted with decisions that alter my healthcare, employment prospects, or my child's route into university, then these are different matters. It could be time for me to leave my laptop and join the students taking to the streets to protest. The use of data on a school's historical performance to inform algorithmically determined grades saw the work of individual students become 'lost in the statistics'. The disproportionate effect for high-performing students at under-performing schools in poorer areas caused much anger with many people arguing that this reflected the 'wider biases of the UK's education system' (Porter, 2020). However, using teachers' predictions can bring problems too, including potential racial bias. Therefore, rather than using data about school performance alone to head off grade inflation, use of data about hidden bias to counteract societal injustice, alongside lots of different techniques could help to counter the bias present in teacher assessment too.

Ultimately, there is the issue too that 'exams were never a great metric for learning or success anyway' (Katwala, 2020).

There are countless different postdigital scenarios like this, where human and technological power relations are at play, as characteristics of humans are rendered into data and ascribed to a social category. As Fisher has pointed out, there is no way of knowing ourselves in this opaque process and as such it 'threatens to undermine and deconstruct the foundations of political action' (Fisher, 2020: 118). One of the problems that data-driven digital platforms present us with (alongside the many opportunities that they bring too) is that, as digital media interacts with wider culture (both online and offline) we are each continually confronted with ideas for us to either accept or reject. As I am browsing different websites, some perspectives may matter more to me or to other people – depending on individual postdigital positionality. However, this can lead into both visible and invisible processes of interpellation that human subjects (who bring their own personal embodiment of power relations and personal values) can find that they either wish or need to respond to. As I have selected examples to refer to in this book, I am aware that I have found these through online searches that often pick up stories from popular news media, but I have also added my own search terms. Alongside browser activity that I cannot fully see in terms of programming, my searches written in natural language were chosen by me. Therefore, postdigital activities bring collective and performative forms of bias and preferences.

Interpellation, understood as processes of encountering cultural values and internalising these, includes ideologies that 'address' people and offer them a particular identity which they are encouraged to accept (Althusser, Louis. 1971). The ways in which certain attitudes are presented and the routes through which these values can now travel into our inboxes or browsers are many. The process of accepting or not accepting a particular culture's given attitudes can quickly alter a person's standing or positioning, placing them in certain power relationships. To give a brief example, author J K Rowling has experienced huge success through the Harry Potter works, via her books, the movies and huge online followings, but she has also recently experienced backlash and cancel culture for expressing personal beliefs. Her letters and comments 'on transgender rights, including examples of where she thought demands by transgender activists were dangerous to women' have been 'criticised by LGBTQ+ advocacy groups as divisive and transphobic'. The reactions online have meant 'two of the biggest Harry Potter fan sites have distanced themselves' from her saying that her views are 'at odds with the message of empowerment in her best-selling books' (The Guardian, 2020a). For those reading this book, reactions to the J K Rowling example will vary, depending on personal lived experience and positionality in relation to gender, but there could be other factors too that influence whether or not to 'cancel' someone, or something. There is a multi-directional fluidity to notice around this example, as people take varied stances concerning transgender rights, but also tweeting opinions on broader dimensions, such as generational factors:

> 'In terms of awareness and language, there is definitely a generational shift going on', says Finn Mackay, a sociology lecturer at the University of the West of England and author of a forthcoming book on female masculinities and the gender wars. 'We know that Generation Z, a marketing term used to define those born roughly between 1995 and 2003, are most likely to use different pronouns like they/them, or to identify as non-binary, and they see these terms as a lot more fluid'. (Brooks, 2020)

Others, such as 'Lucy Hunter Blackburn, of the policy analyst collective Murray Blackburn Mackenzie', argue that 'talk of a generational divide must also confront the ageism inherent in much online discussion', adding:

> This debate has become an excuse to parade some pretty ugly attitudes about the right of women over a certain age to have a public voice, and the value of older women's political views. An unflattering veil has been drawn back on attitudes towards older women, particularly it appears among younger men, despite the fact that polling shows that at all ages it's men who have views based more strongly on physical sex. (Brooks, 2020)

There will be other individuals and organisations who will be more reluctant to comment, but this may reflect different postdigital positionings concerning the risks that they perceive of falling prey themselves to cancel culture, or taking into account 'libel chill', reflecting an unease to speak publicly on some topics, if there is a risk of litigation.

POSITIONALITY IN A POSTDIGITAL CONTEXT   79

2.7   *Positionalities on 'Taking the Knee', Removing Statues and 'Clapping*
       for Carers'

Further examples of positionalities can be noticed in much recent media
coverage of social movements like Black Lives Matter (BLM). The question of
whether people 'take the knee' as a form of physical protest against racism and
incidents of police brutality has been under debate. An action undertaken by
American Football quarterback, Colin Kaepernick, who remained seated on
the bench during the US national anthem on 26 August 2016 has led to a range
of responses. Kaepernick said at the time: 'I am not going to stand up to show
pride in a flag for a country that oppresses black people and people of colour'
and later in the same year Kaepernick switched from sitting to kneeling on one
knee (BBC, 2020b). Recently a rather different approach was taken by US basketball player, Jonathan Isaac, a forward with Orlando Magic and an ordained
minister. He became the first National Basketball Association (NBA) player not
to wear a Black Lives Matter shirt during the rendition of The Star-Spangled
Banner and remained standing while his teammates knelt around him. He
explained this contrasting decision to that of Kaepernick 'by saying that kneeling or wearing a Black Lives Matter T-shirt 'don't go hand in hand in supporting
Black Lives Matter' and added: 'Black lives are supported through the Gospel'
(Gillespie, 2020). The UK Home Secretary, Priti Patel has since expressed disa-
greement with the BLM protests, describing them as 'dreadful' and saying that
'she did not agree with the gesture of taking the knee'. She argues that there are
other ways 'people can express their opinions' (Parveen, 2021).

These different interpretations of BLM reveal just some of the complex
human differences and viewpoints that manifest across matters of racism,
religion and sport, both online and offline, and become influential in broader
public education on matters of discrimination.

Whilst recent BLM protests around the globe have raised a broader awareness of matters of racial discrimination, they have revealed further positionalities from authors who comment on complexities that are less 'aired' in the
media. Gittos (2020b) points out that whilst 'the BLM culture war rages on,
knife-crime victims continue to pile up'. Bringing to mind my analogy of the
airing cupboard's most popular, easy-to-reach sheets, he adds that:

> we only ever hear predictable arguments on two sides of a culture war.
> One side blames absentee fathers and other 'cultural factors' like violent
> music. The other side blames economic degradation and cuts to youth
> services. The men and boys who die in these incidents simply fall into the
> background. (Gittos, 2020b)

Drawing on the work of Stuart Hall (Hall et al., 1978/2013), Gittos questions whether racialising these issues is actually the best way to help us understand them:

> Where Hall understood race to be one in a complex web of factors influencing the police too many today narrowly focus on racial disparity in the justice system and its supposed roots in individual prejudice. This can obscure rather than clarify the issues at stake. (Gittos, 2020a)

Referring to the Macpherson Report (1999) that stated, in the case of the Stephen Lawrence murder in the UK, that the police investigation was 'marred by a combination of professional incompetence, institutional racism and a failure of leadership', Gittos emphasises that this interpretation of 'institutional racism' was based on 'unthinking assumptions held by individual police officers'. However, as a definition, it was a departure from the 'institutional racism' described in Hall's analysis in *Policing the Crisis* (Hall et al., 1978/2013). Hall's argument was that the institution of the police had been weaponised in the course of class conflict, which disproportionately affected the black working class. This important change in the meaning of 'institutional racism' sets the context for the fixation on racial disparities in policing (Gittos, 2020a).

This suggests therefore that, whilst individuals are 'cancelling' each other online over different isolated gestures and comments of all kinds, there are also deep and multifaceted inequities that play out across institutions, historical structures and cultures and the programming of technologies alongside. The 'online sheets' in the virtual airing cupboard reveal current and popular arguments underpinned by the opaque platforms and data that deliver these to our browsers and phones. These intermingle too with content in newspapers and what is broadcast through our televisions, like an episode of Britain's Got Talent (BGT) when dance group Diversity performed a routine inspired by Black Lives Matter:

> It depicted a white police officer kneeling on the Diversity star and temporary BGT judge Ashley Banjo, echoing the killing of the unarmed black man George Floyd in the US. The group all took the knee before the start of the song Black Lives Matter by Dax, which includes the lyric 'I can't breathe', the last words uttered by Floyd. (The Guardian, 2020b)

Amid many complaints, criticism and the praise for the performance, a response to the backlash, was posted on Instagram by Banjo:

POSITIONALITY IN A POSTDIGITAL CONTEXT 81

In the present moment though there is still so much to say... But I will just let this performance say it for me. For the thousands of supportive messages of love and inclusion – thank you. And for the thousands of messages of hate and ignorance I've received – thank you... You highlight exactly what needs to change and why this was so important to me and the rest of [Diversity].

Others, such as Historian David Olusoga, have raised the problem of the platform of television itself and of the TV industry failing to promote people from minority-ethnic backgrounds to positions of power (Hirsch, 2020). Different personal expressions therefore cut across a range of digital platforms and broadcasting media, they receive a lot of attention in the virtual airing cupboard in relation to cancel culture but there also many links to physical expressions of support for BLM as well as examples of cancel culture. As illustrated by a postdigital example below, messages over mobile technologies mean different things to different people. Here in Figure 10 the occupants of this van parked on a hillside in Wales have chosen to display their support for Black Lives Matter by writing the words on a sign in the window of their vehicle. At least this is a form of communication they can drive to locations themselves. Once messages travel through the virtual airing cupboard we simply lose this control.

FIGURE 10   A Black Lives Matter sign displayed on a van

Postdigital perspectives are valuable in that they draw attention to intersectional arguments and complexities that could be missed amongst the sheets of the virtual airing cupboard. As Chang (2020) observes, 'trending social media has indicated that there are currently two pandemics: Covid-19 and racism'. These are 'key concerns in various parts of the world, particularly in nation states that experienced European colonisation and imperialism' (Chang, 2020). However, Chang highlights the 'deeper calls for systemic change, from policy to ideology to everyday practice' and also discusses critiques that have been 'directed at the privilege, positionality, and participation of Asian communities not only with #BLM-oriented activism, but also in education and general society' (Chang, 2020). In raising complexities like these, Chang 'seeks to contribute to this critical discourse through a brief discussion of historical solidarity between Black and Asian activists and social movements' arguing that 'larger collaborations and legacies are often muddled amidst simplified Black/White binaries'. It is therefore important to 'explore some of the ways that historical Black-Asian solidarity can inform more intersectional and transnational analyses and pedagogies of Asian students, educators, and activists' (Chang, 2020).

The pandemic has seen further campaigns rapidly gather momentum, as people have sought to express solidarity with those healthcare professionals and key workers who have continued to remain active during the lockdowns.

The Clap for our Carers campaign, launched by Annemarie Plas during the first pandemic lockdown of 2020, was intended for UK citizens to express their gratitude for the contributions of essential workers, by clapping, cheering, banging pots and pans or raising applause from windows or doorsteps at 8 pm each Thursday (Williams, 2020).

Whilst huge numbers of people stayed at home to work or found themselves furloughed during the lockdowns, key workers were thanked for continuing to leave the house. Messages of appreciation appeared in windows of businesses and homes alongside declarations from key workers themselves in their windows or on their cars, as can be seen in Figures 11 and 12. Unfortunately, what began as a voluntary gesture was accompanied by a rationality urging the public to express physical signs of appreciation. This quickly gained an angle that was less celebratory and more judgmental, as people started to be 'named and shamed' online for not clapping.

In another form of pointing out the 'dirty laundry' so to speak, this self-positioning of some people as online critics to expose others that they perceived not to be demonstrating gratitude in this particular way, was evidenced through postings made to website Mumsnet. The woman who was criticised for not clapping from her doorway said: 'I just feel like I'm a total outcast on my previously friendly street now even though only one person posted it and only two others agreed' (Williams, 2020).

POSITIONALITY IN A POSTDIGITAL CONTEXT 83

FIGURE 11
Healthcare workers identify
their own positionality in
their car window

FIGURE 12
Student nurses urge people to 'stay
home' on a sign in their window

FIGURE 13
A sign offering medical staff 'a well-earned drink on us'

One should not overlook the irrationality of this rationality in this case, given that Mumsnet usually operates as an Internet forum to share mutual advice and support for parents. This seems to demonstrate how quickly a rationality (McClapping, if you will) became played out more irrationally, across augmented forums, as criticism via a website claiming to provide mutual parental support. Whilst some coffee shops were able to extend the offer of free drinks to key workers, as in Figure 13, others in the hospitality industry were forced to close if they were in districts with high infection rates. Some signs were broadly inclusive too of the key workers beyond medicine, such as teachers and shelf stackers (Figure 14).

2.8   Reflexive Re-interpretation or Retrospective Re-alignment of Historical Culture

Postdigital theory is concerned with identity norms of new contexts and those of old ones, as these now span both virtual and physical activities. The positionalities discussed above share dimensions of human identity that are enacted

POSITIONALITY IN A POSTDIGITAL CONTEXT   85

FIGURE 14
A sign on a gate thanking
key workers

to sometimes include physical gestures or expressions made by the body, personal calls of judgment that are spoken or written, either online or offline, and material items, such as T shirts or stances on the toppling of statues.

Such interactions can clearly be noticed in calls during 2020 to remove statues where these may be linked to proponents of slavery or racist views. Some of the opinions seems to suggest that all manner of 'retrospective realignment' of aspects of the history of nations and institutions are needed where links to discrimination can be observed. Questions are raised about how far this can go, when history itself cannot be erased and museums and books remain. There are further debates about what then replaces statues that have been 'cancelled' from these former national cultures, such as an empty plinth. Or different arguments that 'confident forward-looking nations don't erase their history' (Hirsch, 2020). Other perspectives bring lifelong learning into this realm, to suggest that statues 'are an important educational tool that give those who don't read history books a reason to start thinking about the past'. Re-interpretation rather than removal is suggested to provide: 'a far more nuanced and complete version of their history' (Shearing, 2020). The National Trust in the UK commissioned a report aimed at illuminating the connections between colonialism and their properties, which opens with a pledge to honestly and openly share lesser heard stories that reveal the complexity of past, present and future:

> Commitment to research, interpret and share the histories of slavery and the legacies of colonialism at the places we care for. Those histories are deeply interwoven into the material fabric of the British Isles; a significant number of the collections, houses, gardens and parklands in our care were created or remodelled as expressions of the taste and wealth, as well as power and privilege, that derived from colonial connections and in some cases from the trade in enslaved people. We believe that only by honestly and openly acknowledging and sharing those stories can we do justice to the true complexity of past, present and future, and the sometimes-uncomfortable role that Britain, and Britons, have played in global history since the sixteenth century or even earlier. (Huxtable, Fowler, Kefalas & Slocombe, 2020)

As such, the National Trust has suggested reflexive re-interpretation can take place for individuals, as they visit these historic properties. Though what cannot be heard is the lived positionality voiced by those from the past who experienced discrimination, research like this is among many varied responses from institutions and museums to debates on equality, diversity and inclusivity. Examining these examples from different cultural institutions through postdigital positionality presents an opportunity for each of us to internalise many different perspectives and thus to disrupt the virtual airing cupboard of cancel culture.

Since the 'Colonial Countryside' review of the links between the National Trust and historic slavery, it has though come to light that £150,000 of public and lottery money was used to pay for this review. Concern has now been raised that, alongside threats to free speech in universities, heritage institutions are trying to 'airbrush' history (Hope, 2021). Plans to fine universities where peoples' views are 'cancelled' are to be accompanied with the introduction of a 'free speech champion' linked to the Office for Students regulator. Steps will also be taken to ensure that heritage groups do not use public funds for political purposes in an attempt to defend the attempted rewriting of Britain's history (Gant, 2021).

As these cultural dilemmas continue to play out though, it is necessary to bring any new measures into dialogue with the technological problems raised earlier concerning disparities that arise through Human Data Interaction

POSITIONALITY IN A POSTDIGITAL CONTEXT   87

(HDI). There is an intersection where ethical examinations undertaken in the humanities to re-interpret reflexively human culture, need to inform us of ways that opaque data-driven platforms that conceal bias from view, might be reflexively re-interpreted also, to support not hinder, human emancipatory agendas.

At the start of this chapter Fuller described 'human' as a normative category concerning what 'self-described' humans decide to include, or exclude (Fuller & Jandrić, 2018). Now that the performance standards of humans through history are receiving reflexive attention, it is time to include our non-humans in this endeavour. Computing systems as well as cultural artefacts are now active participants in our recent history, but they were never neutral nor unbiased because their actions passed through humans. Now a fluidity exists where human data passes seamlessly between technological devices, as well as via humans, yet identity is different (Poster, 1990: 147). Subjective human content is not the same as rational objective logic, despite how things may look on the surface. Maintaining distinctions between digital computing and the humanities as discussed by Gary Hall (2013) should not prevent active dialogue, at this intersection informing inclusive practices. This is now particularly important, at a time when museums, universities and all manner of organisations are making ethical, cultural changes to encourage greater inclusivity. The computer platforms and data participating in these processes needs to be subject to the same scrutiny that is being applied to humans. This is because the changing technologies that humans have both designed and developed have shared our political economic culture of capitalist values, which have also altered how universities are now perceived. HE has experienced a reduced autonomy over knowledge (Delanty, 2001) amid new forms of accountability (Power, 1997) and rationality (Ritzer, 1993). Human academic labour has become integrated both into global markets (Slaughter & Leslie, 1997) and also the related technologies that support these.

2.9 *We Are Never Alone in (Self) Knowledge Creation*

These different positionalities reveal and require what Torres-Olave and Lee (2019: 5) describe as 'a constant renegotiation between self and setting'. They also argue that 'learning the identity norms of the new context, whilst still beholden to those of the old, requires a constant renegotiation between self and setting. This is an essential aspect of (self) knowledge creation' (Torres-Olave & Lee, 2019: 5).

The constant renegotiation between self and setting discussed by Torres-Olave and Lee (2019) in an international researcher context, is applicable to these forms of interactions, as they take place for people between human physical experiences (such as disability) and virtual platforms with hidden aspects associated with them. When Torres-Olave and Lee (2019) argue that positionality is constructed around the three main tenets mentioned earlier, these complex and fluid complexities of identity creation, power relations and context can be noticed in the following example of TikTok. Here a clear interplay across self and setting in new data and politics driven online international contexts can be observed.

TikTok originated in 2014 as an app called Musical.ly, where youngsters 'would post short videos of themselves miming to pop songs. In 2017, Musical.ly was bought by the Chinese Internet company ByteDance and relaunched as TikTok with an already impressive number of around 680 million monthly active users (Fabiani, 2020). Since then it has become a defining social media app for young people to use in all manner of ways.

For example, in the case of 20 year old India Atkinson, who used TikTok to educate others about her disability, a rare condition meaning she was born without fingers on her left hand (McGarvey, 2020). Her videos explain humorously all the things that she is able to do, such as apply makeup, plait her hair and attend university. She has thus used a creative format to share her self-knowledge with society, and in so doing, she seems to have inspired millions of others to discuss disability. Yet the technological platform on which she is airing her positionality towards personal challenges and receiving much positive feedback, is at the same time the subject of controversy around censorship. Whilst TikTok is owned by a Chinese company called ByteDance, and not by the Chinese government, the app has been accused of censoring content that mentioned topics sensitive to the Communist Party of China, revealed in leaked documents (Fabiani, 2020). Whilst TikTok responded with a statement concerning their content moderation and data security practices (TikTok, 2019), there remains an absence of political content on the social media app.

Only two months later, Tiktok suspended the account of student Feroza Aziz for posting videos about the Chinese oppression of its Uighur Muslim population. 'TikTok claimed it did not suspend Aziz's account for its content but said instead her videos were removed due to a human moderation error' (Fabiani, 2020). Yet since then Netzpolitik.org have demonstrated how TikTok work behind the scenes to label political content as either 'not recommended' or 'not for feed', making it difficult to search, even to the extent of hiding videos of people with disabilities (Köver & Reuter, 2019).

Thinking about moving within postdigital positions is now necessary so that each of us can acknowledge and find routes to resist the silent actors out there. *In The Labour of Words in HE* (Hayes, 2019a) I argued that the textual constructions written in natural language by humans can still alter how academic labour is perceived, when buzz words such as 'employability' are given agency linguistically to perform human tasks. It is no longer possible to separate out what is also constructed by algorithms and data-driven systems in conjunction with human decisions. Fisher (2020) raised the issue that algorithmic knowledge about the self will struggle when it comes to reflexivity, and the ability to be self-critical. This requires new levels of human subjectivity to be explored in relation to how we interact inclusivity in conjunction with data-driven systems, in these rapidly changing circumstances.

3 Postdigital Positionality in a Pandemic

This is quite a context to introduce further challenges into, but the pandemic has done just this during 2020. Before our eyes (as we look out over the top of our face masks) a global biological threat has played out differently in each of our individual lives, demonstrating the importance of paying attention to positionality in a postdigital context. This rupture to human existence and our existing political economy has provided (perhaps only briefly) something of a pause for reflection, with some authors suggesting this could be a potential 'portal' (Roy, 2020) and others arguing that 'the real world cannot be switched off or rewound like the German television drama, *Dark* (Suoranta, 2020) when 'reality *violently breaks in*' (Coeckelbergh, 2020). The danger is that the pandemic could produce 'a hypnotic paralysis which makes the crowd follow to its extreme every leading, suggestive impulse' (Simmel, 1950: 228, Suoranta, 2020).

The speed in which quarantine measures were enforced, led (again perhaps only temporarily) to some neoliberal rationalities being abandoned, such as the physical places that we once occupied before the lockdown. Many of the bastions of McDonaldisation could be found deserted across the globe. At the same time, there were reminders of the basic goods that mattered to people, as supermarkets ran low on stocks of toilet paper and other essentials (Figure 15) and people were asked not to bulk buy or limits would be placed on certain items.

Those people self-isolating were re-thinking aspects of their lives, as evidenced via their images, videos and comments across social media. All of these personal accounts from this historic situation should not sit in isolation from what might be learned for future directions in HE and beyond.

However, David Beer (2020) observes that this is also a challenging time to be writing. The combination of 'a weird mixture of lethargy and restlessness' makes it 'hard to concentrate on something for long enough to get into the depths of the issue'. Then there is the 'sheer speed that things are moving'

FIGURE 15
Supermarket shelves running
low on stocks

where it is easy to 'get stuck describing a moment that suddenly, even a few days later, feels long-gone'. Finally, a 'sense that the thing I'd normally be analysing – society – will not be the same'. Beer comments further that 'unknowable differences are currently populating an imagined horizon':

> It could be that increased networking, heightened and more visual social media connections, video links, mobile tracking and other features will persist, these will need to be thought through in detail. (Beer, 2020)

As I read this blog, I felt that I could closely identify with this honest account of postdigital positionality in a pandemic from a writer trying to make sense of changes in relation to technology and culture. Currently the Covid-19 pandemic and related lockdown policies have dramatically increased the use of online systems to support learning, health, welfare and entertainment. Some people were better positioned than others to access these digital devices, platforms, services and to employ the skills to interact through these. Globally and locally in different parts of the world, digital access, services, skills and opportunities are not evenly distributed (Traxler, Smith, Scott & Hayes, 2020, Roy, 2020). Then there is an individual's choice not to use technology too.

Such choices have tended to be 'framed using the rather binary concept of the digital divide where non-use is conceptualized as stemming from lack or deficit, drawing a line in the sand between digital haves and have-nots' (Thoren, Edenius, Eriksson Lundstrom & Kitzmann, 2019: 325). Postdigital positionality challenges such simplified, techno-deterministic policy logic where 'individuals who do not use a particular technology (such as a computer or the Internet) tend to be portrayed as deficient in terms of a skill set, ability or socio-economic potential' (Thoren et al., 2019).

The pandemic has revealed disparities in developed, as well as less developed parts of the world, with the so-called 'digital divide' not only worsened through Covid-19 (Lem, 2020) but now connecting with many other forms of existing disadvantage across society. Whilst social distancing has, for some, involved home-based work, for others it has meant a loss of work. For some it has brought a break from travel, for others more desperate forms of travel (Roy, 2020, Jandrić et al., 2020). Therefore, arguments like this one can apply only to some, but not all of the global population:

> The shift to a locked-in world has accelerated the acceptance of identity as distinct from physical body or place. We still want to communicate, socialize and play during this time, but have only a digital version to offer. Those constraints are forcing new expressions of selfhood, from the Zoom background used to express a personal interest or make a joke, to the avatars roaming rich, interactive metaverses. (Gabrielle, 2020)

It is interesting to contemplate though, that for some people, their sustained online presence may be developing into an identity that is overshadowing their physical identity:

> In stark contrast to the masked, distant, de-individuated person we show outside our homes, something a little less than human. There are indications that this redacted version of ourselves is becoming something of a style. (Gabrielle, 2020)

Such arguments suggest that we may have 'pivoted', not just in how we conduct the work that we do online, but as people who are now more vibrant virtually than we were as physical humans. Yet for others who decide instead to adopt hoodies with built in masks, or even full hazmat suits for face-to-face socialising, such as Micrashell 'a socially responsible solution to safely allow people to interact in close proximity' (Micrashell, 2020) they may want to disagree. Even as commuting into physical workplaces and study spaces was abandoned (for a while) and people became their own technical support engineers, if they could

92   CHAPTER 1

continue working online, there was the question of trust alongside opportunities for employers to undertake surveillance. Therapy animals needed to be our own pets (if we had them), with dogs and cats taking their own part in our new home-based gig economy as they wandered across our screens or lay sleeping across our ever-warm laptops.

3.1   McSocial Distancing

In early 2020, when 'social distancing' and 'self-isolation' first made their way into our daily language and practices, a group of companies responded to these Covid-19 health guidelines by producing socially-distancing logos for their global marketing campaigns (Valinsky, 2020). McDonaldisation (Ritzer, 1993, 2018), where sections of society appear to embody a similar rationality to that of global fast food chains, seemed at this point to be alive and well. Nor was this move particularly surprising. Predictability is after all, one of the key principles of McDonaldisation theory, alongside efficiency, calculability, control and the 'irrationality of rationality' (Ritzer, Jandrić & Hayes, 2018).

Humorous, distancing signs like the icons produced by McDonald's, Coca-Cola, Audi and Volkswagen offered a diversion to what (for some people) was

FIGURE 16
A sign urges people to 'give way to social distancing'

POSITIONALITY IN A POSTDIGITAL CONTEXT 93

already proving to be a tedious process. Public opinion on the logos was though divided. Were these images assisting the global effort by reminding people to distance from each other, or just making light of a serious matter? (Valinsky, 2020). Whichever of these viewpoints appeals, the production of static logos still plays its part in reinforcing a generalisation. It takes on a form of authority as a social construction when it is placed into phrases like 'give way to social distancing', as can be seen in Figure 16. Why not say, 'give way to other people'? As such, the process of social distancing becomes reified, to infer that it is experienced by everyone in a similar, predictable way. The many more individual aspects of social distancing and self-isolation, including the varied national lockdown timelines, separation from loved ones, personal grief, loss, quarantine, migration, and/or economic hardships experienced by so many people across the globe are rendered less visible (Jandrić et al., 2020).

3.2 Symbols of Lockdown Positionality

Yet a different form of imagery has provided us with a reminder of the more individual experiences of self-isolation.

Soon after lockdown was imposed, people began placing rainbows, teddy bears (Figure 17) and other personal, creative responses to social distancing in the windows of their houses or their campervans (Figure 18). Others encouraged their children to chalk messages on the walls of their homes or on the pavement outside.

Whether in support of key workers, health services, the Black Lives Matter movement, or simply to mark this unprecedented time in some way, images, statements and other items were placed within public view, outside pubs and on fences. Such symbols of lockdown simultaneously appeared through peoples' social media accounts, in newspapers and on television. This is but one illustration of what it means to live in postdigital times, where digital technologies, media and virtual relations of all kinds are inextricably intertwined with our physical human and social lives (Jandrić et al., 2018). Maybe it is also an example of how humans are not yet ready to be rendered invisible by digital advances, even when staying at home for their own protection from a highly infectious virus. However, whether they represent others, or draw attention to personal circumstances, the symbols of lockdown described above, have been chosen and placed on display in people's homes and personal contexts by individual people.

Even if some items were manufactured for others to buy and display, such as the rainbow posters praising workers in the health service, others chose to draw, knit or craft rainbows and place them in their windows, outside pubs (Figure 19), on gate posts (Figure 20) or share these symbols online.

FIGURE 17
A teddy bear is left hanging in a plastic bag on a gate post as a symbol of lockdown

FIGURE 18   A campervan in a driveway displays a 'stay safe' and 'smile' poster

POSITIONALITY IN A POSTDIGITAL CONTEXT

FIGURE 19   Children's rainbow drawings placed outside a pub

FIGURE 20   A child's rainbow drawing displayed on a gate post

Some went further still taking advantage of the empty skies to draw a message of hope in the form of an emoticon using an aircraft (Figure 21).

3.3   *Documenting the Voices of Covid-19*

The need to document the human voices of Covid-19 from all locations (on land or in the skies) and from all circumstances is a powerful route into appreciating

FIGURE 21   A pilot draws an emoticon of a smiley face in the sky above a UK city

the importance of positionality in a postdigital society. Research Councils are currently funding many scientific and social scientific research projects at the time of writing. One of these in the UK is the 'NHS Voices of Covid-19'. Funded by the Arts and Humanities Research Council (AHRC). 'It is supported by a diverse group of stakeholders including the National Health Service (NHS), the Trade Union Council (TUC), Age UK, the Stroke Association and many other health, community and heritage organisations. Other participants in the project include patients, policymakers, frontline NHS staff, young people and individuals with high-risk conditions' (AHRC, 2020). This blending of cross-sector stakeholders and the hundreds of volunteers who have undertaken the actual recording of these interviews demonstrates a strong interest in how diverse individuals are positioned during this historic crisis.

3.4   *Writing the History of the Present*

It is these deeply personal human narratives that are 'writing the history of the present' (Jandrić & Hayes, 2020a). They are providing us all with deep insights into how postdigital change is experienced on an individual basis and through a global and local crisis. This process is powerfully illustrated through the broad collection of personal accounts shared by those working

POSITIONALITY IN A POSTDIGITAL CONTEXT 97

and studying in universities across the world as lockdown took hold between March–May 2020. In 'Teaching in The Age of Covid-19' (Jandrić & Hayes et al., 2020b), the written responses to a Call for Testimonies sent out by Professor Petar Jandrić, to be published in the Springer journal *Postdigital Science and Education* was quickly retweeted across social network sites demonstrating the swift realtime response (Ryberg, 2020). Petar Jandrić, himself, describes his own positionality as he embarked on gathering accounts for this experimental collective article:

> This general vision, without a clear idea of what I was doing, paved a bumpy road for the development of this collection. On 17 March 2020, I shared the Call for Testimonies on *Postdigital Science and Education* social network sites and I emailed it to the journal's mailing list. Based on my previous experience with similar calls, I expected to receive 10 to 15 contributions and produce a standard-length collective article aiming at postdigital dialogue (Jandrić et al., 2018) about the pandemic. Yet my call went 'viral', at least for academic standards, and a couple of weeks later, I had more than 50,000 words written by more than 80 authors. So how do I make sense of all that material? (Jandrić & Hayes, 2020a)

'Teaching in the Age of Covid-19' is distinctive also because the request by Petar Jandrić for workspace photos from each author's home, if people wished to share them (and most did), has provided further dimensions from which to view this history of the present. Transitioning teaching and learning to be conducted entirely from home spaces over virtual platforms has though brought new complex considerations to examine in the balance between health, education, technology, diversity of individual circumstances and equality of opportunity.

3.5 *Pledging Open Sharing in Support of Learning*

Earlier, the pledge from the National Trust in the UK described a 'commitment to research, interpret and share the histories of slavery and the legacies of colonialism at the places we care for (Huxtable, Fowler, Kefalas & Slocombe, 2020). The values of honest and open acknowledgement were mentioned to do justice to the complexity of past, present and future, including sometimes the confrontation of what is uncomfortable to admit. A human pledge refers to a solemn promise or undertaking to at least do something. Whilst not necessarily binding, it nevertheless can draw communities together and help further a common cause.

In terms of business and marketing, the word 'pledge' has been adopted as a brand name for a popular furniture polish which is advertised globally under phrases like: 'impress yourself, when it glistens, you glisten', alongside connotations that the act of polishing will 'renew' whatever you clean in this way and thus ourselves too (Pledge.com). In *The Labour of Words in HE* (Hayes, 2019a: 8) I pointed out the irrationality of rational HE policy statements by contrasting these with the discourse used in the marketing of products. Non-human products are 'humanised' in a manner that closely connects the properties of the product to the person using it. This intimate discourse of marketing sits in contrast with a linguistic tendency in HE policy documents, where teachers and students find themselves detached from their own skills, attributes and labour, which has been delegated to buzz phrases and technologies. This has impact on how included, or not, academics and students may feel in policymaking.

Pledge is a product manufactured by SC Johnson who describe themselves as 'a family company at work for a better world' and like many companies at this time they are detailing their support of initiatives linked to public health during the Covid-19 crisis (SC Johnson, 2020). My reason for mentioning such dimensions concerning use of the word pledge, is to draw attention to complex intersections of culture, technology, language and political economy. The breadth of such interconnections impact on diversity and inclusion in postdigital society. For example, companies are also changing packaging and wording of products, if these appear to be derived from colonial connections or racial stereotyping. The change of name of Uncle Ben's Rice to Bens Original is one such example (Smithers, 2020).

Global companies and commercial platforms now have links to education at all levels. They have brought with them profitable interests, background culture and technology. They may have entered silently the academy through routes to support learning, research and marketing but it is important to recognise where these then align the public mission of universities with the private interests of digital capitalism' (Williamson, 2020b). McDonaldisation has already highlighted how rationalities that emerge around consumers and producers of products and knowledge both online and offline can lead into irrationalities. Alliances between HE and digital capitalism bring an interplay that impacts on what is written and what can feasibly be enacted through HE equality, diversity and inclusion policies.

Whilst postdigital is not a perfect term (Jandrić et al., 2018), it encapsulates this landscape of multiple and diverse 'actors' (that are not all human) that are now altering much of what may once have been described as 'established' or 'inclusive' practices in universities. People as individuals are now flesh electric (Lewis, 2020: 265) in that they embody and internalise values and ideologies from across the ecological landscape of digital capitalism. Whilst a can of Pledge can be attributed in marketing discourse with features closely linked to

POSITIONALITY IN A POSTDIGITAL CONTEXT 99

humans and that help them sanitise their homes in a time of crisis, it cannot itself demonstrate the personal self-reflexivity to undertake a solemn promise to contribute to collective change.

Responses within the global scientific community to share health and scientific research openly, has emphasised a widespread understanding of a need to respond collectively and also at many levels to the Covid-19 global crisis. This has further strengthened the existing alliances between commercial interests, science and education. The Open Covid Pledge was founded by scientists, lawyers, entrepreneurs, companies including Amazon, Facebook, Microsoft, IBM, Uber and other individuals in 2020 'to promote the removal of obstacles involving intellectual property in the fight against Covid-19' (Open Covid Pledge, 2020). In August 2020 the Creative Commons took over leadership and stewardship of the Open Covid Pledge to work with the steering committee with the hope too that continuation of this model might help to address other crises such as climate change. These are powerful global connections and aspirations that universities have connections with, but it is hard to observe where these are reflected in HE policy.

Inspired by the Open Covid Pledge, alongside recognition of the wholesale movement of education online during lockdown, the Open Covid Pledge for Research in Education has been formed. This growing community of educators and researchers are pledging to:

- Make our intellectual property openly and freely available to the world to support educators, students and decision-makers, to help educational organisations survive and thrive, and to build a fairer and more resilient education system.
- Where possible, openly license or dedicate to the public domain our intellectual property (Open Covid Pledge for Research in Education, 2020).

This is a promise that is made inclusively, with respect to the whole enterprise of education, despite lacking clarity on what the future may hold. The emphasis is on opportunities to learn, which despite the crisis, are perceived as constant, if not heighted presently. The instigators of this pledge point to the many 'new research programmes that have sprung into being' as 'established researchers have refocused their efforts' and argue that 'new evidence is emerging all the time about the impact on teaching practice, student participation and working lives' (Open Covid Pledge for Research in Education, 2020). This pledge then draws crucial connections together that are not, as yet, reflected in the policies that universities write concerning educational inclusivity: namely that our culture, politics, technologies, data, resources, health and education are interlinked, as we seek to address potential bias and inequalities post-Covid-19.

As universities seek to tackle inclusivity at an institutional level, there are also opportunities to learn from each other at a global level (UNESCO, 2020b).

Such learning can begin with open sharing of research and teaching resources, but this then requires an honest description in policy to reflect the diverse, postdigital positionalities of each of us. The principles of inclusivity cannot simply be 'plugged in' to universities, as the complex ecosystem that they now operate in, sits outside of institutions. It is driven by global aspirations alongside commercial, data-driven interests, but we cannot afford to overlook individual positionings within this picture, or this moves the whole endeavour in the direction of rational objectives, rather than human subjectivities.

Writing all of these implications into HE inclusivity frameworks may not, though, be too daunting a prospect, given that we would no longer be claiming to 'embed' so much into HE under the pretence of control. Rather we would be accepting that HE institutions now need to be plugged into these pledges of open sharing, in support of inclusive opportunities to learn.

3.6   Viral Viewpoints and Inclusive Practices

The relevance of these examples to this book on postdigital positionality in HE arrives via the many complexities that are now prompting people to act in terms of inclusivity. Where once access and participation in education was discussed at a largely social level, there are now more factors (and actors) to consider than interactions between people and their institutions of study alone. This has implications for understanding what influences inclusive practices in universities and what institutions can (and cannot) claim to be enacting, or indeed providing. It also has implications for how individuals experience what they believe to be inclusion.

Rational policy statements about what governments and educational institutions intend to *do*, frequently overlook the agency of individuals and groups to *act*. The outcry over the A level algorithm in the UK is one such example. There is also the danger pointed out by Suoranta (2020), that amid the current levels of global confusion that we find ourselves in 'a hypnotic paralysis which makes the crowd follow to its extreme every leading, suggestive impulse' (Simmel, 1950: 228, Suoranta, 2020). Impressions can be given in the news media, and indeed in HE policy, that certain moral statements, feelings and actions are undertaken on behalf of all of us (Simpson & Mayr, 2010). Indeed, many news websites have augmented news coverage, with deeply personal and emotive snippets of people's daily lives shared alongside breaking stories of disaster and events in different parts of the world.

In a postdigital society it is increasingly difficult to separate who (or what) is contributing to the 'viral' viewpoints that can be seen to spread rapidly across

POSITIONALITY IN A POSTDIGITAL CONTEXT   101

multiple platforms. Peters, Jandrić and McLaren (2020: 3) have referred to
'viral modernity', pointing to the association between viral biology on the one
hand and information science on the other. They argue that this applies to
'viral technologies, codes and ecosystems in information, publishing, education and emerging knowledge (journal) systems'. The complex relationships
between epidemics, quarantine, and public health management during the
Covid-19 pandemic have further revealed this 'fusion of living and technological systems' (Peters, Jandrić & McLaren, 2020: 3). During the Covid-19 crisis,
moral judgements have intermingled with public health advice and misinformation 'infodemics' (Peters, Jandrić & McLaren, 2020, Gregory, 2020, Peters
& Besley, 2020). Much has been written too, concerning post-truth and fake
news in postdigital society which is transmitted virtually across multiple forms
of media as well as in physical spaces (Peters, Rider, Hyvonen & Besley, 2018).

After online headlines emerged stating that people's pets may carry the Coronovirus, further reports and images quickly emerged to claim this information had resulted in animals being physically thrown to their deaths (7News,
2020). In less dramatic images, homeowners displayed signs requesting that
those passing by refrain from petting their animals in view of potential dangers
of transmission through fur (Figure 22).

FIGURE 22   A householder urges people not to stroke their pet dog

If this appears bizarre, it is worth reflecting, that some surprising viral ideas
have gripped society historically, well before the digital age and during times
when diseases were rife. One example, 'the great book scare' was 'a frantic

panic during the late 19th and early 20th centuries that contaminated books – particularly from lending libraries – could spread deadly diseases'. Arising partly 'from a combination of new theories about infection and a distaste for the concept of public libraries themselves, Americans and Britons feared the library's easy access to what was seen as obscene or subversive books'. Legislation followed in the UK, with 'the law updated in 1907 with explicit reference to the dangers of spreading disease via book lending, and those suspected of having an infectious disease were forbidden to borrow, lend or return library books, with fines of up to 40 shillings for such crimes, equivalent to roughly $200 today'. Thus 'the perceived danger of public access to reading material, it seems, can take as much of a physical as an intellectual form. (Hayes, J., 2019). For those of us still cleaning our shopping trollies with sanitiser, or teaching having been provided with face visors and disinfectant wipes for the books and the photocopier, this could now sound all too familiar. Annika Mann (2018) describes contagion as:

> Both a communicable disease *and* its means of communication, a means that is transformed by the disease in turn. Contagion has been of particular interest to literary scholars and theorists because the term provides such an apt model for how language itself works, how meaning is transformed by its communication. (Mann, 2018)

At a time when humans were already grappling with an overflowing virtual airing cupboard, the physical communicable virus of Covid-19 has reminded us of the intimate relations between our physical bodies and our means of communication. Scientific remedies to aid us in defeating the pandemic may need a controlled temperature, rather like the physical airing cupboard, but there is a need to keep an eye too, on how this environment is connecting with the virtual cupboard. When on 8 February 2020 Adam Kucharski, an epidemiologist and author, wrote in the Guardian that: 'misinformation on the coronavirus might be the most contagious thing about it' (Kucharski, 2020) this was picked up the same day and quoted in a media briefing by the Director General of the World Health Organisation. Kucharski advises:

> The best way to tackle these online rumours? Treat them like a real-life virus. (Kucharski, 2020)

They are also postdigital rumours because they do not remain online alone. Thanks to the contagion of language they take the form of any media of conversation. The human decisions to place an image of a rainbow in a window, tweet

POSITIONALITY IN A POSTDIGITAL CONTEXT

support for others, or 'clap for carers' (Williams, 2020) are personal motivations but are also interlinked with 'bioinformation' (Peters, Jandrić & McLaren, 2020). This is information generated by multiple and diverse 'actors' (that are not all human) but may still influence how humans respond physically or virtually with empathy towards others, or indeed how they present their own positionality on all manner of issues across various postdigital platforms.

The warning of 'Don't Kill Granny' is one such example. Swiftly reported worldwide, this blunt slogan was aimed at young people in Preston, Lancashire in the UK. It was intended to warn them 'about the consequences of ignoring coronavirus social distancing rules – unwittingly taking the virus back home to vulnerable relatives and friends' (Day, 2020). It proved popular with Grandmothers but less so with others such as Callum Taylor who tweeted that: 'Many young people have lost elderly grandparents during this pandemic and are still grieving. Using the slogan #DontKillGranny is utterly vile and insensitive! I would have expected better from a Labour run council!' (Taylor, 2020). There are also differences between the acts of empathy undertaken by individuals (however these might be influenced) and those rationally undertaken by either journalists, profit-making companies and government agencies, on behalf of others. Despite these distinctions, the voices and opinions from different sectors (with different vested interests) are now merging into a swirling mass of postdigital commentary, requiring some additional ventilation, perhaps.

3.7   McInclusivity or Genuine Activism?

Issues arise in terms of who (or what) speaks on behalf of other individuals and groups in crisis. The plight of migrants crossing the Channel between France and the UK is one such illustration. The ice cream giant Ben and Jerry's posted a response on Twitter to the UK Home Office plans to 'stem the latest surge in Channel crossings' by invoking tougher border controls and returning migrants seeking refuge in the UK to France. In tweets addressed to the Home Secretary, they wrote: 'Hey @Priti Patel we think the real crisis is our lack of humanity for people fleeing war, climate change and torture' adding that 'people cannot be illegal' (Brewis, 2020). The Home Office responded by calling Ben and Jerry's ice cream 'overpriced junk food' and as these posts were rapidly shared, the story played out to reveal different viewpoints within the public domain. At the same time, as 'scores of Twitter users praised the US company for speaking out', one person wrote 'Ben and Jerry: not all political heroes wear capes, some simply make amazing ice-cream and just seek to make the world a better place' (Brewis, 2020). However, other Twitter users revealed a different positionality, as they condemned Ben and Jerry's for their 'large scoop' of 'virtue signaling' served with 'grossly overpriced ice cream' (Swinford, 2020), for political 'pontificating' and alleged hypocrisy' (Brewis, 2020). Further Twitter users pointed out that not only do Ben and Jerry's not have to deal personally with the consequences of immigration, they are owned by Unilever, against whom 'a group of 218 Kenyan tea plantation workers have filed a complaint with the UN' (Brewis, 2020). At the same time, multiple suggestions for new flavours of ice cream were also posted, including 'Social Justice' flavor (HRH the saboteur, 2020).

Not unlike the 'McSocial Distancing' logos, this example has played out to reveal a form of 'McInclusivity' that has both raised attention on the plights of migrants as a group and also trivialised the issue. What it hasn't done is explore how migration and inclusivity is being experienced through the individual perspectives of each migrant. Instead it has altered the discourse about migrants in different ways even to include discussions on how people shop for ice cream. It becomes necessary to ask *whose* rationality or logic is at play in anything we now read or view, bearing in mind that even a form of rationality itself must be theorised as fluid, regardless of where it originated from. In a global context where neoliberal forms of capitalism have come to dominate so much of how we live, this is experienced differently in developed and developing countries as well as in individual lives. Across television, print and virtual media, journalists deploy techniques to humanise the cases they report and to evoke empathy from readers, but not necessarily to enact solidarity at a political level (Varma, 2020). Varma contrasts this approach with 'radical inclusion' that actually 'begins with marginalized people's analytical perspectives' (Varma, 2020: 1) which reveal a personal positionality, rather than an institutional or company stance.

3.8   *McVaccination Programmes or Vaccine Alliances*

Examples like the COVAX vaccination programme help to illustrate the difference between a personal positionality and a media, institutional or company stance, but also how these are mutually constitutive:

> The relative obscurity of this vaccine program belies its critical role in the global battle against Covid-19. Indeed, COVAX may well be the most important acronym of 2021. As vaccine nationalism rears its ugly head, it's the best – perhaps the only – bet on getting billions of doses to lower- and middle-income countries. (Lister, 2021)

In order to avoid a McDonaldised consumer culture and discourse dominating the distribution of vaccines only to those who can afford to buy them across the globe, coalitions are seeking 'to buy coronavirus vaccines in bulk and send

POSITIONALITY IN A POSTDIGITAL CONTEXT   105

them to poorer nations that can't compete with wealthy countries in securing contracts with the major drug companies' (Lister, 2021). COVAX includes the Vaccine Alliance known as Gavi and the World Health Organization (WHO) and is funded by donations from governments, foundations and multilateral institutions. However, as this report points out, *secured* does not mean *obtained.*

There are many more contextual aspects and hurdles too, such as capacity, logistics, funding, country and individual readiness, cultural and educational factors, to enable doses of vaccine to reach the individual human bodies of those who require them. The vaccine is after all a product making its way through a global consumer-based society where 'vaccine panic' has taken hold and:

> The greatest challenge to global coverage is a 'me-first' attitude that's been criticized by global health officials. (Lister, 2021)

In terms of positionality and inclusivity, the spread of the virus itself has broad effects across different communities, now that vaccines have been developed. Individuals and countries across the globe find themselves confronted with new moral dilemmas. These require reflexivity to recall where serious delays in anti-retroviral treatments reaching continents like Africa for example led to catastrophic death rates from HIV and AIDS. Therefore an urgency to work towards the safety of all is competing also with national, economic, cultural, political and logistical priorities, and with the emergence of new variants that do not respect borders.

3.9   *Could the Pandemic Be a Portal?*

In terms of a more hopeful outlook there are other positions being taken on the potential responses that humanity might make, with regard to the pandemic. As nations entered lockdown, amid traffic ceasing, businesses closing and wildlife returning, some authors speculated on the 'work' of the virus in 'bringing the engine of capitalism to a juddering halt' (Roy, 2020). Certainly, it holds some appeal to envisage Covid-19 could be also 'distancing' humanity from the excesses of capitalism, ingrained forms of neoliberal rationality and inequalities. Yet whether 'the pandemic is a portal' that we might now choose to walk through 'ready to imagine another world' (Roy, 2020) is still up for wider discussion. Could humans be ready to undertake a 'global reset of education' to move away from the global conditions we have created 'that are hostile to our best interests and counterproductive to our collective wellbeing (Robinson, 2020: 7)? If so, then 'the battle of the decade', with respect to public education systems, may be upon us (Fullen, 2020). Fullen argues that 'since the 1980s, education has become part of a system of stagnation' and one in which many students show a 'dramatic loss of interest'. He points to the significance of the pandemic in de-skilling each of us:

> the pandemic brings a new context to us virtually every week. Thus, we are all de-skilled in this prolonged period of non-linear ambiguity. We are in a more complex world compared to any time in the past. From a change perspective, there is nothing so complex to solve than the situation we have at present times, and there is no indication that conditions will get better. (Fullen, 2020: 26)

In a collection of testimonies from academics and students from around the world, captured at the start of the lockdown (Jandrić et al., 2020), speculation of this nature was also on many peoples' minds. Authors suggested that 'this is a time when universities could embrace and offer something more emergent, sustainable and healthy', that 'the critical voice from the university might be crucial', but then again, a 'critical question is, will we be allowed by society to take that role?' In the struggle ahead, this is still unclear. At the time of writing, many school pupils have returned to their classrooms and playgrounds and these are very different in appearance to the ones that they left 6 months ago. Almost as soon as the new autumn term began though, schools were shutting again due to a rise in Covid-19 cases. In the UK Government, guidance for the return to schools emerged only days before lessons resumed, with this being described as 'insulting' to staff (Stubley, 2020).

Meanwhile universities were dubbed to be particularly 'unhealthy' as they proceeded to reopen their campuses as planned (UCU, 2020). Universities that ordinarily offer potentially life transforming changes to peoples' lives were being argued instead to risk 'doing untold damage to people's health and exacerbating the worst health crisis of our lifetimes' if the migration of over a million students across the UK should proceed as it usually would at this time of year (UCU, 2020). The argument that this movement of people following the 'A levels fiasco' (BBC, 2020b) and removal of the cap on the number of students that universities can recruit (Fazackerley, 2020b) now risks 'overwhelming some institutions and turning universities into the care homes of a second wave' (UCU, 2020). Since these comments, students have returned to universities across the UK. Within days of freshers' week, there are reports of thousands of students now entering campus lockdowns, and even feasibly being asked to remain on campus over the Christmas break. The students are being discussed as 'trapped' by a 'shambolic return to university' and questions being asked by

POSITIONALITY IN A POSTDIGITAL CONTEXT

students themselves as to why they were told to attend in the first place (BBC, 2020d). Such an emerging context, as Beer (2020) has commented, is hard for writers to keep up with. Given the direction that HE had been moving, in terms of measuring excellence across various areas, prior to Covid-19, it is hard to imagine what would currently be being 'measured'. There will however be much to compare in time and the rich qualitative data will be important to respond to. Meanwhile, speculation on a post-Covid-19 normal will continue.

An author from the collection of Covid-19 testimonies pointed out, though, that universities do need to 'invent new stories, new purposes and new identities – ones which can address the concerns of local communities and the global society' (Jandrić et al., 2020). Covid-19 has yielded vast numbers of research publications. In education, these currently range from practical advice on moving teaching online (referred to by some as a 'pivot'), sharing materials and tips, commentaries on mental health, the effects of working virtually from home and speculation as to what the 'new normal' means, amid the broader context that HE now needs to respond to. Prior to the lockdown, universities had left themselves little room for such debates (Hayes, Jopling, Hayes, Westwood, Tuckett & Barnett, 2020). Strategies can be located for each new regulatory issue, but less so the ongoing authentic dialogues (Hayes, 2019a) that would avoid these, and the technologies or inclusion that they refer to, simply being 'free-floating' (Rikowski, 2003: 140). Detached issues may be perceived to enable an ease of measurement, but the nature of what HE is being asked to measure for regulation (Office for Students, 2018) has postdigital dimensions that currently remain overlooked.

3.10   *Circulating What Is Included in the Contents of the University Airing Cupboard*

Inclusivity in HE has long been perceived as a practice, culture or set of values by which diverse learners are admitted into a context where they can achieve their potential to succeed. The inference is that such achievements are 'driven' by universities to support social mobility:

> Universities driving social mobility: we aim to create a future in which anyone with the will and potential to succeed, regardless of their background, has the opportunity to transform their lives through accessing an outstanding learning experience at a UK university. (UUK, 2020)

What universities are actually in a position to be able to 'drive' now, in terms of inclusion, is a key part of the postdigital positionality debate. Reflecting on this context, Traxler has argued that due to an:

onset of pervasive and ubiquitous connectivity and mobility, profoundly transforming the production, ownership, distribution and nature of learning and knowing and problematising the role and status of universities and lecturers. (Traxler, 2020)

This is not so much about:

Inclusion of people from the outside world selectively invited into the higher education system but the inclusion of the higher education system into the world outside. (Traxler, 2020)

However, he has argued further that for the UK, Brexit has now intervened and been swiftly joined by the Covid-19 pandemic with 'both of these threatening to overturn a world of steady change and stable argument' (Traxler, 2020). Therefore, we have an opportunity for circulating the contents of the university airing cupboard, by opening it from all sides. The pandemic has intimately exposed the diverse contexts of students and staff, revealing differences and inequities in academic lives that cannot be contained within buzz phrases like 'the student experience' (Hayes & Jandrić, 2018). These personal narratives bear little resemblance to the rational McPolicy statements analysed in *The Labour of Words in Higher Education* (Hayes, 2019a). Therefore, in the post Covid-19 HE context we need to revisit this language.

CHAPTER 2

Rationalisation of Higher Education and the Postdigital Context

1 The Shared Political Economic Spaces of Technology and Culture

As anyone who has read *The Labour of Words in Higher Education* will be aware, I adopted the label of *McPolicy* to compare a rational method of writing HE policies (that has become widespread across universities) with humorous examples from consumer goods marketing:

> I have noticed with interest though, that I can visit the supermarket and purchase a bottle of wine that has more 'body' attributed to it than a student or a lecturer within an HE policy. (Hayes, 2019: 7)

I argued too that:

> Frivolous though that may sound, in a book that explores rationality and irrationality through nominalisation in university policy documents, cultural texts of different kinds are not separate from each other. What we read from a label on a commodity may have no obvious connection to a university strategy, yet both exist within a shared political economic culture. (Hayes, 2019: 7)

Building on Weber's theory of how bureaucracy once exemplified modern rationality, by coordinating the activities of large organisations towards a single objective, Ritzer has shown since that such rationalisation can spread from government and manufacturing processes into consumption and consumer services. My analysis of *McPolicy* was intended to show that such arguments might be extended even to written university strategy texts, that appear to also reflect the key principles of McDonaldisation that Ritzer discussed (Hayes, 2019).

As I introduce this chapter, I will pick up from where *The Labour of Words in Higher Education* left off in arguing that:

> The concept of widening participation in HE has been adopted within narrow margins which can be broadened. (Hayes, 2019: 150)

© KONINKLIJKE BRILL NV, LEIDEN, 2021 | DOI: 10.1163/9789004466029_004

Strategic and practical work in relation to inclusivity, equality, diversity and participation in universities cannot sit apart from how digital technologies now relate to human life, risks, intelligence, opportunities and communications. Our shared political economy means there are points of interplay at every turn. Therefore, after initially setting up the context for this chapter, I will explain what the first and second halves of the chapter will address.

The language we use and the commercial platforms on which ideas are expressed are deeply intertwined with the data about each of us. As discussed earlier, we can think of language as intersecting across any number of situations (from communicable disease to communication over the Internet) where ideas spread due to 'contagious' aspects of language (Mann, 2018). Humans do though have the ability to query rational statements built on assumptions about the diverse positionalities and circumstances of others.

Questioning the reasoning behind any rationality and why a discourse is structured as it is, or how it could be otherwise, involves critically reflexive thought that draws on human experience. Humans imagine different futures and they express their ideas about these in natural language. This is a different form of processing of ideas to the quantification of human properties or attributes expressed as a number or written within a form of computer coding. Yet we have this shared problem too, that we have now literally 'become data'. As Cheney-Lippold (2018) points out, the data we have generated is the 'making of our digital selves' and it can be manipulated algorithmically to bring about futures where 'cloud ethics' (Amoore, 2020), rather than people, are deciding what it means to critically protest anything.

Even in recent novels, Sudjic (2021) points out that the 'personality' we think of as our own is being determined by algorithms and then harvested for data. As such, individuality is a 'stream-of-consciousness that is not entirely your own, that you participate in but also acts upon you' (Sudjic, 2021). Perhaps it is time then to bring this situation into critical dialogue with our 'postdigital selves' (Jandrić et al., 2018). To do so is to make connections with what it means to be postdigital, from our own positionality as a human with our own perceived identity. Such personal considerations need not be confined within anyone else's deterministic discourse about technology, or inclusivity. If our personal postdigital positionalities are shared, they can also support resistance to McPolicy and endeavours instead towards 'knowledge socialism' via 'collegiality, collaboration and collective intelligence' (Peters, Besley, Jandrić & Zhu, 2020).

It can be helpful to recall that intelligence matters to each of us and that there are points of connection when we examine the roots of human and computer interactions and their links with philosophy (Russell & Norvig, 2016).

RATIONALISATION OF HIGHER EDUCATION 111

Universities exist around and for intelligence, but universities now also need to connect inclusivity strategies with stronger understandings of what it means for diversity and equality when we actually *build* intelligent entities (Russell & Norvig, 2016). It is necessary to also consider what it means for inclusivity, diversity and equality when we build partnerships with the commercial providers whose platforms are now being 'powered' by new intelligent entities.

Our increasingly autonomous data-driven systems and all manner of new technologies come under the branch of computer science referred to as Artificial Intelligence (AI). Russell and Norvig (2016) discuss eight definitions of AI that they lay out across the four categories of *thinking humanly and thinking rationally* (concerned with thought processes and reasoning) and *acting humanly and acting rationally* (concerned with behaviour). Russell and Norvig (2016) suggest that *thinking* and *acting humanly* are concerned with success based on human performance. Whereas, *thinking* and *acting rationally* are concerned with measuring against an ideal performance measure, called: rationality. Whilst considering these categories, it is worth reflecting once more on the ideas from Steve Fuller, where 'human' is a normative category concerning what 'self-described' humans decide to include, or exclude (Fuller & Jandrić, 2018). Fuller suggested reaching an agreement about the performance standards that a putative 'human' should meet that a 'non-human' does not. Then there were arguments that the identity of a human is constructed differently across the different disciplinary fields of computing and humanities (Poster, 1990) and suggestions that even as we explore the flow of digital humanities in our lives, we should not treat computing and humanities as 'equivalent' (Hall, 2013). We cannot afford to allow a one-way flow to impose a particular rational logic from computer science on the humanities: we need to bring new understandings of computing through humanities too (Hall, 2013: 782). This is a valuable 'postdigital dialogue' (Jandrić et al., 2018) that avoids the tired McPolicy rhetoric of a quick technological 'fix' and provides space to also examine the implications for equality, diversity and inclusion.

Often discussed as if this were a very recent phenomenon, the science of AI has been around for decades, with the term first attributed to John McCarthy in 1955 (Hyacinth, 2017: 15). To go back considerably further in terms of 'machine intelligence', Anthony Seldon (2020: 99) points to computational or counting devices such as 'the abacus in use in Babylonia as early as 2400 BC'. Tracing developments since, he discusses 'the earliest analogue computer designed to calculate astronomical positions', attributed to 'the Greeks in 100 BC' and adds that 'the slide rule was developed in the 1620's following the discovery of the concept of the algorithm [sic] by John Napier. In the early nineteenth century 'the first mechanical computer was devised by Charles Babbage' using punch cards and an integrated memory, with 'analogue computers using a mechanical or electrical model' following on in the 1920s, and digital computers by the late 1930s (Seldon, 2020: 100). Perhaps we have been postdigital for longer than we realise.

Integral to this chapter though, is a recognition that underlying a rational discourse about any technology, or a rant on social media, are power relations linking wires, routers, data, software, systems, opportunities and inequities, with people, both online and offline. AI emphasises 'the creation of intelligent machines or programs that think, learn, and react like human beings' (Hyacinth, 2017: 15). It is the combination of hardware, software, data, methods, algorithms and technologies that make software 'smart' in a way 'that may seem human-like to an outside observer' (Hyacinth, 2017: 15). In more recent developments, wearable devices, household appliances and sensors connected to the Internet, that can be recognised by other devices to collect and process data, are referred to as the Internet of Things (IoT). When AI is added to the Internet of Things, these devices can analyse data, make decisions and act on that data without the involvement of humans, as the Artificial Intelligence of Things (AIoT) (Marr, 2019). Yet despite these apparently new developments, and a rational policy discourse that frequently places technology (rather than people) at the forefront of an ability to transform, James Ball reminds us that:

Systems don't build themselves. (Ball, 2020)

Discussing the promises of all that the Internet was once expected to bring for humanity, Ball explains how, rather than a democratising force, power has been concentrated and remains, in the places where it already existed. Discussing the hopes of the early 1990s, the movement of the business world into the Internet, the WikiLeaks interventions to shift power and the Arab Spring protests against corrupt governments, Ball argues that our former mood of celebration of the Internet has been replaced with mistrust. Citing the appearance of World Wide Web creator Tim Berners Lee in 2012 at the London Olympics and his 'this is for everyone' tweet (Berners Lee, 2012), Ball flags up the contrast between the exultant dance festivities of nearly a decade ago, that revelled in shared ownership, and the current situation:

The Internet giants are viewed with mistrust, accused of playing a role in spreading misinformation, enforcing censorship and avoiding tax. Its billionaires are scrutinised and condemned for their working practices. Residences around the palaces of Silicon Valley have come to resent their corporate neighbours. (Ball, 2020)

RATIONALISATION OF HIGHER EDUCATION

Ball makes some important distinctions though, between giants like Amazon, Facebook, Apple and Google, who are products of the Internet, and the structure of the Internet itself:

> Despite its lofty language – the use of words like the 'cloud', language which suggests something free and natural, beyond the control of people – the internet is a network of physical cables and connections. It's a web of wires enmeshing the world, connecting huge data centres to one another and to us, storing and sharing the innermost details of our lives. (Ball, 2020)

Fictional though they may be, movies like *The Net*, the *Terminator* series, *Enemy of the State* and recent *James Bond* films (that I have found myself re-watching with family sometimes during lockdown) have depicted such networks and power grabs. It seems that even in the movies we can get a better sense of the cultural implications of technological developments than we can in education and the policy we write for it. These tales (even if they date quickly) are often unsettlingly close to technological developments we subsequently see emerging before our eyes. Then there are groups that have formed to examine the sorts of existential risks we see portrayed in the movies. Amongst the experts and donators on the scientific board, are also celebrities who have featured in such movies, supporting a key aim:

> We humans should not ask what will happen in the future as if we were passive bystanders, when we in fact have the power to shape our own destiny. (Future of Life Institute, 2020)

The Future of Life Institute advocates education, research and intervention. It is necessary too to recall that our political economy is more advantageous for some people rather than others. We may all contribute to the enormous data pile, but people are positioned very differently in relation to it. As Ball points out:

> Each of those cables is owned by someone, as is each of those data centres – and every piece of that data is also owned by someone, and that someone is almost never the person who that data is about. (Ball, 2020)

To lift our heads further out of the 'cloud', so to speak, Ball adds that each data owner:

> Was backed and financed by someone, and each physical site lies in the jurisdiction of a government and a myriad of regulators. We refer to the

online world as if it's abstract from the reality we all occupy every day: this is a myth, and it's a myth that obscures where the real power lies. (Ball, 2020)

Important for postdigital connections to be made concerning how each of us sees ourselves as positioned in this landscape, is the argument too that:

Online power is offline power: the internet has handed more power, control and money to the people who already had plenty. (Ball, 2020)

Digital change and the networked society have not fundamentally altered societal inequities then. Looking at this issue through a postdigital lens helps to avoid digital determinism and a churning out of related, rational and objective McPolicy. Examining individual postdigital positionalities reveals the unique subjectivities that will otherwise remain hidden. Placing these observations into the broad inclusivity agendas that universities seek to address, requires a very thorough and honest housekeeping exercise. Not only is it necessary to notice, include and critically discuss in inclusivity policy frameworks, the role of the Internet and the networked, data-driven commercial platforms used by universities, the places where these systems are reinforcing existing inequalities needs acknowledgement too.

Recognising the commercial purposes for which Virtual Learning Environments (VLEs) and Learning Management Systems (LMS), as well as data analytics software were designed are a part of this, but there are now many more 'profit-oriented private organisations in education across the globe' (Verger, Lubienski & Steiner-Khamsi, 2016). The Global Education Industry (GEI) consists of a huge number of money-making services and actors who provide data-driven systems, curriculum packages, private tutoring, certification, teacher training, recruitment of students, student services and accommodation (Verger, Lubienski & Steiner-Khamsi, 2016). Powerful commercial coalitions (that have rapidly formed during the pandemic) now push for long term changes to education systems with serious risks for democratic public education to become irreversibly undermined (Selwyn, Macgilchrist & Williamson, 2020: 25).

The first half of this chapter therefore explores this shared political economic culture in relation to how digital technology has become articulated in a narrow way in HE policy, and as a separate agenda from policies for inclusive practices. It examines the changes that universities have experienced and the challenges to their status as autonomous sites of knowledge. This leads into how the principles of McDonaldisation, that George Ritzer referred to as globally dominating (Ritzer, 1993, 2018) have developed in HE institutions (Hayes, D. & Wynyard, 2002, Hayes, D., 2017). As universities have responded to the

RATIONALISATION OF HIGHER EDUCATION 115

wider consumer culture of physical shopping malls and theme parks, McU-niversities have followed suit (Ritzer, 2005, Hayes, D., 2017). There are many visible icons that demonstrate these patterns, but what is less visible are the commercial alliances behind the scenes of the McUniversity and the connections of these with the discourse of McPolicy (Hayes, 2019a). The McPolicy style of writing has framed a certain understanding of technology, by constructing it as a static, neutral set of tools to simply 'embed' in education and to automatically 'enhance' learning. For decades now, this rational assumption about digital platforms as something that educators can control has marginalised human positionality and people's individual, dialectical relations with technology in education. Strategies for Technology Enhanced Learning (TEL) have positioned academics and students in ways that have simply ignored diversity, with the intersection of these university strategy documents with inequality at an institutional level receiving little attention (Czerniewicz & Rother, 2018, Hayes, 2019: 135).

However, to simply bring all university strategies under one framework for equality, diversity and inclusion does not cure the problem. In postdigital society, like the analogy of the airing cupboard, not all inequities are visible or easily accessible to respond to with a quick fix. Therefore, inclusivity policies cannot begin from a shared understanding that 'the principles of inclusive practice are well established' (Department for Education, 2017). Where do these principles begin or end in universities? Do they sit within or outside of the disciplines that we teach and the buildings that we occupy? Do we seek, as senior managers, to address via the words of institutional policy, every aspect of global citizenship experienced and contributed to by our students and staff? If so, then generalisations will not do. Recent events during the pandemic have disrupted any illusion that inclusive practices are either established or fixed.

Rather than seek to maintain a form of 'analogue McPolicy' where each new challenge must be embedded in the site of the HE institution, we can instead begin a more productive debate concerning 'postdigital policy'. This needs to first be contextualised in a long history of how computing technology has been positioned in society in support of capitalist inequities and discrimination. Ball observes:

> The internet and the way it works were all human decisions, made by groups of men – its almost always men – in small rooms with their own particular ideologies, motivations and divisions. (Ball, 2020)

Ball calls the system behind the Internet 'overwhelmingly Western and overwhelmingly male' (Ball, 2020). It has been staring us in the face really, but the virtual airing cupboard has been so overflowing with our advertising, consumer temptations and cancel culture that (like the physical airing cupboard) we fail to see the underlying plumbing. However, if we really wish to address inclusive practices in our universities then we can no longer fail to engage with the inequities of what now powers all of our activities during a pandemic that is going nowhere fast.

If the Internet (used by more than three billion people in some form every day) has been shaped by Western males with their positionalities, ideologies and profit-making agendas underpinning its operation, then we have a major issue and a serious dichotomy. We use the Internet as our shared virtual airing cupboard. It is over the Internet that our debates about inclusivity and diversity themselves are raging every second of the day. If the Internet itself is fundamentally biased, then this is also shaping, to some extent, the online technologies and activities of staff, students and policymakers seeking to further and address inclusivity in HE. Ritzer might refer to this as another potential irrationality our rational, consumer-based (and also computer-based) approaches, have fuelled. If so, it is a big one and we are all implicated.

The recent data breaches experienced by universities, including Northumbria in the UK, provide further evidence that whilst HE may have joined the investors in commercial technology consortiums, this may not be as an equal partnership. Due to the amounts of data they amass, universities as well as charities are particularly susceptible to cyberattacks (Afifi-Sabet, 2020). They get targeted by ransomeware, phishing emails and malicious links:

> Universities typically have complex and porous digital systems so attackers can often find their way back in repeatedly to cause more harm. (Hellard, 2020)

This though, takes the form of harm to individual students and staff. It is a subjective matter and not an objective issue, when portals are closed and clearing systems halted. The future plans of students become halted too. To go on trying to rationally 'embed' everything but the kitchen sink into university policy, risks taking responsibility for many things like this that we cannot hope to control. Whilst precautions can be put in place for staff and students to comply with, this does not address the fundamental cause of security problems. Furthermore, making objective statements about deeply subjective matters in strategies means that staff and students remain disconnected from the very policies that concern their safety.

The Covid-19 pandemic has demonstrated globally just how interlinked different social, economic, political and cultural policies are. It has shown how rational approaches (such as the A Level algorithm in the UK) can lead to

RATIONALISATION OF HIGHER EDUCATION   117

irrationalities, if human positionalities are not considered. Take for example, the Covid-19 testing arrangements, as these are developing in the UK at the time of writing. There is a large human demand for testing and many drive-in testing locations have been set up to accommodate this. However, demand is not smooth, and it comes in surges. As people sought a test online, they were directed to testing locations hundreds of miles away from where they live, because in the system their local centre was shown to be at full capacity. Even as some attempted the long journey it turned out to be a longer one in practice, because the distances 'appear to have been calculated as the crow flies, rather than being a true reflection of how long it would take to drive' (Schraer & Triggle, 2020). Such issues arising from both human and technological factors are proving a disincentive to being tested, which may mean some local increases in cases of the virus end up being overlooked, leading to new outbreaks (Schraer & Triggle, 2020). Examples like this demonstrate how, depending on a person's situation, disadvantage can be further increased both through the design of digital platforms and the way that this plays out with physical circumstances during crises.

Complex cross-cultural connections, and how these intersect with digital systems, need therefore to be recognised as interlinked in policymaking for inclusivity. Continuing with the Covid-19 testing examples, there are postdigital dimensions to other technological errors. This can be seen in a recent data error in the UK where 15,841 positive tests were left off the figures reported because a daily test report in a CSV file was loaded into Microsoft Excel but the bottom rows of the spreadsheet were cut off (Hern, 2020).

> Microsoft's spreadsheet software is one of the world's most popular busi-
> ness tools, but it is regularly implicated in errors which can be costly, or
> even dangerous, because of the ease with which it can be used in situa-
> tions it was not designed for. (Hern, 2020)

Excel spreadsheets are easy, standalone applications that can be used by anyone, but this has become a regular problem now because the data input into these is not traceable and can be overtyped. As old technology encounters new systems, with human interventions along the way, it is not difficult to see how data errors can impact on human situations to cost lives, or alter individual health or work situations through error, bias, or discrimination. Policy discourse for inclusivity needs to reflect this postdigital positionality of individuals too, in order to move beyond rational and objective digital panaceas.

The second half of this chapter examines why recognition of shared political economic spaces of technology and culture are important for the airing of varied debates on what inclusivity means wherever individuals are positioned in postdigital society. In HE, many strategies continue to be produced in isolation from each other, addressing separate topics and omitting interactions where inclusivity and technology intersect:

> A first step is to review any lack of inclusivity present in the language in which these are written. (Hayes, 2019: 135)

This requires debates like the decolonising curriculum arguments to include a more critical examination of how all HE policy is linguistically constructed, and who and what is inputting into the policy process. HE policy language about inclusivity cannot be quarantined in some policies and not be present in others. Nor is it a separate discourse from government, media, business, marketing, public or theoretical discourse circulating in the virtual airing cupboard, on this very broad topic. Digital online communications systems and commercial platforms have made it easy for any dialogue to pick up traces from different institutional or personal positions, with implications for how inclusive practices in HE, and related policy, are now constructed and perceived. Inclusivity discourse and data are not controlled within walls and (not unlike a pandemic) this requires open discussion on how to adjust to this, make changes and develop more inclusive policy:

> Not least because contradictory statements around social justice risk cancelling each other out, if widening participation and student retention are enacted by generic statements, projects and technology, rather than diverse staff and students themselves. (Hayes, 2019a: 150)

Widening participation policy discourse now needs to widen further still. It needs to include, describe and acknowledge the activities, design, purposes and origins of data-driven digital platforms as these closely interlink with human endeavours:

> The concept of widening participation in HE has been adopted within narrow margins which can be broadened. (Hayes, 2019a: 150)

In order to do this, it is necessary to notice interconnections where, for example:

> Barriers to inclusivity, participation and social mobility can occur through the language of policy, as well as through the practices of recruitment. (Hayes, 2019a: 150)

Examples in Chapter 1 revealed the various stances made by companies and individuals on different topics. These exchanges have relevance too for university equality, diversity and inclusion policies that seek to respect the identities and cultures of learners from diverse backgrounds, minority and migrant communities. HE is now closely interconnected with commercial platforms, images, icons, devices and systems for teaching, research and marketing activities. To put it humorously, universities cannot have their cake (or ice cream, even) and eat it. These commercial connections and the wider activities of companies that universities are now partnered with, are no longer separate from the policy statements that HE institutions make. It cannot be rationally argued or inferred that these systems can be entirely administered by academic institutions, as if they alone were in control of this agenda. Each human interaction with a system and the data it collects, has unique implications for the positionality of the person concerned. Associations arising from this are not confined within systems as they flow between virtual and physical spaces. This new postdigital context means that sustained habits of writing HE policies require a re-think. Repetitive assumptions in policy of what technology will achieve (Hayes, 2019a: 3) must instead acknowledge that all postdigital encounters are different, reflecting the positionality of the individuals involved.

A complex combination of factors plays out differently for each of us. However, both humans and computers may become objectively categorised in policy discourse. Ritzer has described extensions of his original theory to reflect augmented situations where humans may metaphorically occupy varying 'cages' of consumption (Ritzer, Jandrić & Hayes, 2018). In Chapter 3 I will examine the situation of students in lockdown in relation to this analysis. However, in the second half of this chapter, I will consider how Ritzer's augmented cages may help to illustrate diverse postdigital positionalities. Humans who are now routinely subject to rational forms of computer processing and objective evaluation through McDonaldisation are also finding new ways to perceive their subjectivity. As Ritzer might put it, they are manipulating the bars of the rubber cages that they find themselves in (Ritzer, Jandrić & Hayes, 2018). Covid-19 is a biological actor that is contributing to altering existing political economic spaces of technology and culture. The postdigital nature of these dynamic experiences and their relevance for inclusivity are key debates in HE policy reform.

1.1 *Rational Presuppositions That Technology Will Always 'Enhance'*
The technologies discussed in the introduction above have developed over decades in a shared political economic culture of capitalist values which have also

altered how universities operate and are now perceived. Universities, which had more traditionally held an autonomy over knowledge (Delanty, 2001) have been subject to new forms of accountability (Power, 1997) rationality (Ritzer, 1993) and regulation. This has in turn had an impact on the academic labour of staff and students as universities have become increasingly incorporated into global markets (Slaughter & Leslie, 1997). The rationalities that I refer to in policy discourse, reinforce these changes and related values, to cast technology in a simple calculation: 'as a guarantee that the use of technology will enhance learning' for profit (Hayes & Bartholomew, 2015: 114). This is quite a presupposition given that technology means different things to different people in different situations and cannot simply be assumed to have inherent positive qualities where learning is always enhanced (Hayes & Jandrić, 2014: 198). This is important too for discussion on postdigital positionality and the twofold debate that this book is concerned with. A simple logic of digital enhancement for everyone is inadequate for inclusive policymaking, particularly when there are new consequences emerging from:

> The intelligence exhibited by machines by which it mimics cognitive functions that humans use, while interacting with other humans'. (Hyacinth, 2017: 15)

Whose cognitive functions does it mimic? Or whose body image are systems of identification based on? Bias that has crept into the programming of technological systems has impact on how students are able to access education. Passports are used to verify student and staff identity in university application processes, but recently the UK Passport application process itself was shown to demonstrate bias. The 'website uses an automated check to detect poor quality photos which do not meet Home Office rules. These include having a neutral expression, a closed mouth and looking straight at the camera' (Ahmed, 2020).

> Women with darker skin are more than twice as likely to be told their photos fail UK passport rules when they submit them online than lighter-skinned men. (Ahmed, 2020)

Recently a black student challenged this algorithmic process that is used by millions of people as 'she was wrongly told her mouth looked open each time she uploaded five different photos to the government website' (Ahmed, 2020). The issues had arisen within the software, rather than the student's photo and she managed to get the photo approved eventually by writing a note to say her

RATIONALISATION OF HIGHER EDUCATION   121

mouth was closed. This doesn't though solve the issue that such systems need
to work well for everyone, regardless of facial differences and that:

> The impact of automated systems on ethnic minority communities is
> regularly overlooked, with detrimental consequences. (Ahmed, 2020)

Furthermore, given that a freedom of information request in 2019 had already
revealed that the Home Office were aware of the problem but had decided
that the 'overall performance' was good enough to launch the online checker
(Ahmed, 2020), this illustrates how systemic inequalities can play out across
both computer and human bias. In another recent example, the already problematic UK contact-tracing app that had been sending out error messages
encountered a 'fat finger error' (Corona24 News, 2020). Whilst this was quickly
corrected it added to a number of reputational problems after 16 million people had already downloaded the app Such interactions, back and forth across
human bodies and machines in individual contexts, are increasingly significant
to any discussion about inclusivity in postdigital HE. In the passport example,
facial detection accuracy was dependent on the diversity of the data the system had been fed into the training programme that was intended to 'teach' the
computer what to search for. Linked discrimination occurs at human decision-
making levels:

> Discrimination can also be built into the way we categorise data and meas-
> ure the performance of these technologies. The labels we use to classify
> racial, ethnic and gender groups reflect cultural norms, and could lead to
> racism and prejudice being built into automated systems. (Leslie, 2020)

Multiple and diverse 'actors' (that are not all human, and not all machine) are
now altering much of what is still being described as 'established' or 'inclusive'
practices in universities. Furthermore, these interactions have implications
for human rights and equality (Equality and Human Rights Commission, 2017,
Hector, 2020) and also for human capabilities (Sen, 1992: 87) as these intersect
now with the powerful capabilities of digital platforms and data. Postdigital
debate focuses a broader recognition of these relations, communications and
exchanges that are now constantly passed between humans and intelligent
machines, within a shared political economic culture. Positionality places the
individual and their experiences as central. Perceptions of fairness are socially,
culturally and technologically intertwined and intersect too with each person's
identity and perceived capabilities. It is necessary then, to explore what this

122 CHAPTER 2

means across all of the key activities of HE (in relation to societal changes), to notice how educational access, inclusivity and opportunities for individual people are now altered in new, complex ways, depending on their positionality, in this dynamic context.

1.2 Rationalisation of HE in a Neoliberal Political Economy

Delanty (2001) has pointed out that: 'the history of western social and political systems of thought can be said to be the expression of a deeply rooted conflict between two kinds of knowledge: knowledge as science and knowledge as culture'. Writing two decades ago now, he argued that it is communication that is now transforming both knowledge and democracy. Through the age of modernity, 'from the Enlightenment to the postwar period, the institution of knowledge existed in a space outside the flow of communication. This place has been occupied mostly by the university. Knowledge has been seen as a site, a place that can be occupied by something called a university' (Delanty, 2001).

Delanty's insights on challenges to knowledge across recent decades are helpful in contextualising the twofold postdigital positionality debate. This is firstly, because the traditional role of a university as a knowledge provider is influential in circulating statements on the 'established' nature of inclusive practices. Assumptions like this come from a long tradition of being a site, or place, of knowledge. Decades of work in the areas of widening participation, lifelong learning and inclusivity for different groups across society have concerned the 'admittance' of individuals to this 'site'. It is a site that in many universities worldwide contains grand halls and theatres, like the large teaching room shown in Figure 23, where significant lectures, examinations, conferences and graduation ceremonies take place. Knowledge is imparted, assessed and celebrated, usually.

FIGURE 23
A lecture theatre where I taught in Ghana in 2019

RATIONALISATION OF HIGHER EDUCATION   123

Covid-19, however, swiftly removed us all from these university sites across the globe, where alongside the rooms built for consumption of learning, are buildings that have emerged intended for consumption of entertainment, food and consumer goods, counselling, sport, cultural and social activities, as Ritzer might say, an array of 'cathedrals of consumption' (Ritzer, 2005). For many months these architectures were silent in the main, except for the laboratories loaned for the manufacture of sanitisers and ventilation equipment to fight the virus. In the wake of such a scale of disruption, it is worth paying attention to what this means for all of our futures in HE in a postdigital context.

Secondly, all of our key activities that have traditionally taken place in relation to this 'site' of the university might be better conceived now through implications for our personal and collective positionalities. Positionality is enacted wherever our location. It does not depend on admittance to a physical or virtual site, but it does articulate with our individual notions of inclusion in any of these spaces. Educational access, inclusivity and opportunities for individual people are altered in new ways though, now that we are conducting so many of these in a virtual airing cupboard. The discourse of McPolicy is a rational response from the site of institutions. Strategic plans have traditionally been written from within the university buildings, even if they are then placed on web pages and sent via emails. Yet attempting to maintain managerial or entrepreneurial control over technologies, communications and a worldwide network cannot be contained in this manner. Many authors have discussed the implications of neoliberal policy as it has become enacted within universities as measured outputs, strategic planning, performance indicators, quality assurance measures and academic audits (Slaughter & Leslie, 1997; Shore & Wright, 1999; Ball, 2003; Olssen & Peters, 2005). 'University strategy discourse has provided a window on the rational arguments that support these measures. It is also a means to notice when these move towards irrationality' (Hayes, 2019a: 64).

Davies (2016) describes different phases and policy dynamics of neoliberalism over recent decades that have sought to 'prop up' a broken model of capitalist accumulation (Davies, 2016: 133). He argues that global capitalist development has become confounded by its own success, yielding irrational symptoms in an effort to preserve the status quo. He cites the recent reliance on digital technologies to yield solutions:

Increasingly, it is non-representational codes – of software, finance, human biology – that mediate between past, present and future, allowing society to cohere. Where, for example, employee engagement cannot be achieved via cultural or psychological means, increasingly business is looking to solutions such as wearable technology, that treat the worker

124   CHAPTER 2

as an item of fixed capital to be monitored physically, rather than human capital to be employed. (Davies, 2016: 133)

What remains as a problem is that such rational approaches omit the distinctive and varied aspects of whom we are, as individual people. They omit the communicative powers concerning knowledge that are now afforded to the wider population. Thus, they omit our global citizenship.

1.3 *Global Citizens and Semiotic Representations That Cross Academic Disciplines*

Where once the knowledge within a discipline appeared to be set within recognisable boundaries to communicate to students and to test their knowledge, now there are complex global entities that do not slot in so tidily into a room or lecture theatre where I might learn about science or history alone. Considerations of:

social justice, human rights, conflict resolution, environmental sustainability and diversity do not fall neatly into disciplines. (Ellis, 2019: 1)

Ellis (2019) points out an interconnectivity between 'the human life-world and its experiential strata and domains', as such:

meaning falls into a stable typology, including performative, epistemic, and affective modes, and both sign types and types of language use anchor these modes as semantic formats in the discourses shared by human beings. Discourse structures, including the narrative, the argumentative, and the descriptive formats, ground the possible forms of knowledge available to a global citizen. (Ellis, 2019: 19)

Such complexities can be noticed when arguments arising from one disciplinary field can be noticed to omit valuable insights from another. However, across our disciplines:

Ethics, aesthetics, and critical thinking must now converge, in view of the contemporary threats. (Ellis, 2019: 19)

Despite what it may say in the policies that I have analysed, technology cannot simply be used to address key challenges in HE or in wider society. HE no longer has the autonomy to meet these alone and there are threats that cut across all of our disciplinary areas. Recall, for example, the problems surrounding Covid-19

RATIONALISATION OF HIGHER EDUCATION

testing in the opening to this chapter. Some universities have their own testing programmes, but still these are connected to the national records and open to the issues already discussed. To put it bluntly then, even in these days of self-driving vehicles, no technology that I plug in will have a dialogue with me on how to address these dilemmas, or on what policy I should write. Instead, technologies are adding to the complexities that universities are encountering, as well as enabling new approaches to help us with tackling these collaboratively.

1.4   *McDonaldisation of HE and how McPolicy Frames Technology*
How people have become positioned in relation to digital technologies within rational policy texts about what these will 'enhance' for humans, has hampered more critical and inclusive dialogues (Hayes & Jandrić, 2014, Hayes & Jandrić, 2017, Hayes, 2019c). In HE, this policy discourse has repeatedly reinforced the idea that: 'in exchange for the use of technology there will be enhanced forms of learning' (Hayes & Bartholomew, 2015, Hayes, 2019a: 94). For decades, this dominant approach has inhibited 'questions being raised about the diverse ways students and their instructors really experience technology' (Hayes, 2019a: 94). It is these distinctive and varied aspects of who we are as people, and how we are individually placed, that are often omitted from all manner of McDonaldised rationalities (Ritzer, 1993, 2018). In recent years, for example, statements like this from educational institutions and government bodies have become commonplace. They illustrate how technology has also been closely linked to human achievement:

> Technology can close achievement gaps, improve learning. (Stanford Graduate School of Education, 2014)

This reinforces a positioning of technology where it has been established as a common good in the links between social justice and education. The principle that technology 'improves learning' becomes the starting point for any discussions. This is rather like stating that 'the principles of inclusive practice are well established' (Department for Education, 2017). Any revisions to such principles are then not up for debate. However, the postdigital positioning of each one of us means that we now need to reopen both the debate on technology and the debate on inclusivity. This should not consist of separate HE policy discussions, as these are inextricably linked and intertwined with human experiences in the processes of accessing and participating in education.

Since universities have been held accountable for how students enter and progress through education, for the diversity of their intake and for how they demonstrate inclusivity, the role that digital technologies play in all of these processes requires stronger acknowledgement. In reports that tackle inequities, if technology is mentioned at all, it remains at the level of tackling barriers to accessing it, rather than deeper explorations of human agency, legibility and negotiability in relation to data driven systems (Mortier, Haddadi, Henderson, McAuley, Crowcroft & Crabtree, 2020).

The different technological platforms by which many of us (but not all) exist, calls into question old interpretations of positionality based only on social positioning as a human. Now that so much of our lives is processed through digital systems, there are countless ways that those without devices, wifi or related skills to work online can fall through the cracks. Where once people received letters to home addresses, so much of this paperwork is now conducted through online systems. Yet many agencies continue to insist on proof of address. In a sense society never embraced the digital age entirely. The Covid-19 pandemic has revealed big disparities (BBC, 2020e) Therefore, to talk of a postdigital context is really to acknowledge the existence of digital, alongside and intertwined with, everything else.

1.5 *Inclusivity Policy Can Acknowledge, But Cannot Contain, Our 'Franchised Identities'*

Digital technologies have now enabled new complex forms of appropriation of individual identity and by association, positionality. This is a complex and messy situation, as old forms of media have become intertwined with new media technologies, programmes, devices, algorithms, politics and economics. New powerful hybrid forms, that are constituted by people, politics, economics and combinations of images, video, written and spoken text and programming code are influencing who, or what, people believe themselves to be or who they might become, 24/7. The concepts of personal identity and our own individual sense of belonging to anything in life, are no longer 'owned' by individuals alone. In the postdigital world, identity is constantly created and co-created for us, intersecting with our perceptions of who we are, or how included any of us may feel.

Private features of our existence that once sat apart from public gaze are available for reshaping, giving or selling back to us, across multiple physical and digital routes. Recalling the analogy of the airing cupboard, and the old adage of 'dirty laundry', click bait has provided us with virtual dirty secrets that keep us turning over the 'virtual sheets'. Headlines draw the eye and content marketers are the winners as people continue to click through the pages (Elliss, 2014). Click bait style headlines are a marketing tool deployed by many companies, but the willingness of people to overshare on social media has literally changed people themselves into click bait. Acting as what Ritzer would refer to as 'pro(con)sumers' (Ritzer, Jandrić & Hayes, 2018), people upload for free their photos, judgements and 'half-baked thoughts' that live on indefinitely as 'digital breadcrumbs of the lives we used to lead' (Charles, 2020). The addictive nature of producing and consuming the mass of content on social media has led us to 'franchise our identities across two to three social networking platforms at a time' (Charles, 2020). This leaves each of us vulnerable to surveillance and datamining, but also our 'involuntary behaviours are being manipulated by social networking apps and sold on to the highest bidder' (Charles, 2020). Ashley 'Dotty' Charles refers to social media as 'unquestionably an era-defining innovation', but argues that it is:

> Changing the way we come together, I worry that it has also made it easier for us to fall apart. So be sure that when you're using social media, it isn't actually using you. (Charles, 2020)

This apparently shared ownership of each person's identity in a postdigital context means that any aspects of who they are remain open to populist interpretations and virtuous signalling as well as to celebration, abuse and discrimination. I may be a female student of mixed race, or a white male with a disability, a parent, a traveller, a migrant or a refugee. Whatever combination of features I personally identify myself with, there are journalists, politicians, companies, educational leaders, policy makers, marketing experts and others, who will state across multiple forms of written and spoken media, who I am, what I require, who I should aspire to, or what I should become. Fake news and post-truth have become partners with each of us too, whether we welcome them or not (MacKenzie & Bhatt, 2020). It is therefore necessary to 'understand the workings of digital technologies and how they are used in deception' (MacKenzie, Rose & Bhatt, 2020). We don't have to be present on any digital platform for other people or things to invent or decide who any of us are and what we need. In terms of a wider therapeutic culture (Apperley, 2014, Furedi, 2016, Ecclestone & Hayes, 2019) we may also begin to believe it.

Therefore, the Internet, its structure and data centres, the companies and platforms that own that data and the governments seeking to manipulate it, need to be uppermost in each of our minds when we log in. The attributes and capabilities we may consider to be part of humans alone, are also mechanised and measured both online and offline. Data is taken from us and different data is presented back to us. This changes the cultural nature of our personal data and it rationally alters its original connection with our individual positionality. If I, as a human and an academic, were to breach data ethics in some manner I would be subject to related inquiries and penalties. We are all though, in a situation of ethical compromise now as 'digital selves' formed by data

(Cheney-Lippold, 2018) that is manipulated algorithmically in the 'cloud ethics' (Amoore, 2020). In earlier discussions concerning human attributes that are subject to such re-working, I made the distinction between a subjective awareness of our own personal attributes and a more objective set of attributes that an algorithm might repurpose in some way. Amoore's concern was that such algorithms 'condense multiple potential futures to a single output' and that this anticipation of our future propensities threatens the chances we have to make alternative political futures possible (Amoore, 2020: 1).

Examining this issue in the broader political economy where universities have become increasingly marketised is a useful way to draw online and offline parallels. These can help to inform postdigital dialogue that builds on ecological rather than isolated understandings. In McPolicy human possibilities are reduced through restrictive and controlling language that rationally presents one view on the world. As such, McPolicy, not unlike an algorithm, may also 'condense multiple potential futures to a single output'. By anticipating what students will encounter as 'the student experience' or presenting to students a set of objective attributes to attain, this controlling discourse cuts off possible alternative futures for both students and staff. As just one offline example, we can even find random attributes presented back to us in imagery around campus, making university premises (as well as online systems) indistinguishable from those of corporate business.

1.6   The Visible Icons of Higher Education

At the beginning of *The Labour of Words in Higher Education,* I commented that people appear to be facing multiple forms of displacement across society (whether via technological unemployment, automation or dehumanised statements in policy language). Yet human beings (it would seem) are still seeking to 'preserve something of themselves across both the digital and material worlds' (Hayes, 2019a). I pointed to different ways in which human attributes have been linguistically detached from their owners in many HE policy texts:

> This vision of student success, in the form of employability, appears to involve breaking down what constitutes a student, in terms of sets of attributes and assets. The body is not just alienated, it is dismantled. McPolicy discourse thus sets up the conditions for multiple routes towards marginalisation and fragmentation of human labour. (Hayes, 2019a: 128)

Iconography plays its role alongside such discourse in HE. Visual banners have become commonplace on university campuses and have been reproduced across institutional web pages.

RATIONALISATION OF HIGHER EDUCATION   129

During the pandemic lockdowns these will have gathered dust somewhat in the absence of many people to view them, but they are notable nonetheless for the way in which they reinforce generality, rather than individual, diverse forms of positionality.

One example is the way that, many universities have reproduced single words describing detached attributes or values on posters and banners.

Some of these are engraved these into windows of classrooms and study spaces (as in Figures 24, 25 and 26).

FIGURE 24   A university window displays the word 'IMPACT'

FIGURE 25   A university window displays the word 'AMBITION'

130   CHAPTER 2

FIGURE 26   A university window displays the word 'PASSION'

This form of iconography appears innocent enough, but it is also part of our shared political economic culture of capitalist values. The same approach is to be found across many other businesses and sports grounds (Figures 27 and 28). In isolating these single attributes away from personal context this tends to 'cancel' more individual and creative interpretations of what these values actually mean to diverse members of the population.

Given that we live in a world of 'overwhelming pictorial content', Lacković (2020a) argues that 'a turn to examining and understanding digital communication mediated by pictures can be beneficial for contemporary higher education (Lacković, 2020: 444). This has been argued to be overdue when some authors were pointing to a form of academic iconophobia (fear of images) in the early 1980s (Sless, 1981) and 'this situation still prevails' (Lacković, 2020: 444). Lacković and Olteanu (2020b) argue that HE needs to respond to 'an unprecedented profusion of visual information across digital media' and to 'counteract the uncritical consumption of images from the perspective of semiotics' (Lacković & Olteanu, 2020b).

Miltner and Highfield (2017) have discussed the popularity of the Graphics Interchange Format (GIF) across the Internet. They point out that while the GIF has certain technical affordances that make it highly versatile, this is not the sole reason for its ubiquity:

GIFs have become a key communication tool in contemporary digital cultures thanks to a combination of their features, constraints, and affordances. GIFs are polysemic, largely because they are isolated snippets of larger texts. This, combined with their endless, looping repetition, allows

RATIONALISATION OF HIGHER EDUCATION 131

FIGURE 27
The word 'HUMILITY' is displayed on a banner outside a cricket ground

them to relay multiple levels of meaning in a single GIF. This symbolic complexity makes them an ideal tool for enhancing two core aspects of digital communication: the performance of affect and the demonstration of cultural knowledge. (Miltner & Highfield, 2017: 2–3)

People are able to use GIFs to open and close down debate over social media, as powerful communication tools that carry cultural meaning to huge numbers of followers. GIFs impart quick, powerful messages, are multi-generational and are not confined within linguistic boundaries. They can add humour, draw people in and can be inclusive in enabling anyone join an online conversation. On a less inclusive note, Lauren Michelle Jackson (2017) has pointed to a recurring problem of 'digital blackface' where:

FIGURE 28
The word 'TEAMWORK'
is displayed on a banner
outside a cricket ground

the tenets of minstrel performance remain alive today in television, movies, music and, in its most advanced iteration, on the Internet. (Jackson, 2017)

Jackson raises this concern, citing many examples to show how non-black users tend to adopt GIFs with black people in them for emitting their most exaggerated emotions, arguing too that:

No digital behaviour exists in a deracialized vacuum. (Jackson, 2017)

Whilst those of us who have taught critical media and popular culture courses may discuss examples like this with our students, the implications of all kinds of digital discrimination need to be understood beyond the contexts of

RATIONALISATION OF HIGHER EDUCATION   133

teaching and research alone, in universities. Multi-level forms of discrimination, via images and videos as well as texts, need to be acknowledged alongside the data-driven platforms they appear on within university policymaking that seeks to promote inclusive practices. This is necessary given the biased meanings that pictures, digital photographs and material icons can both embody and project.

1.7   *Less Visible Aspects of Commercial Alliances in* HE

Universities are rapidly becoming 'powered by artificial intelligence' and performance metrics in an increasingly market-driven sector (Williamson, 2019b). Such agendas now also share platforms with 'life-changing decision-making algorithms' that are 'infected with biases' (McDonald, 2019). These changes give rise to new ethical considerations of who, or what, can be trusted when academic life is increasingly structured via commercial as well as political interests. Universities are no longer simply commodifying and selling their own services commercially. Private companies have become an essential constitutive part of the HE industry, raising questions about the 'consequences for university teaching, research and societal roles more broadly' (Komljenovic, 2018). The reliance on commercial systems during the pandemic has brought this further to light, alongside challenges too that demonstrate that our systems 'are only as good as the humans producing them' (Seldon, 2020: 2).

Meanwhile, AI and AIoT are not obviously reminding us of their presence, but examples in the remainder of this chapter reveal why the postdigital nature of their activities cannot be excluded from HE debate on inclusivity, inequalities, diversity, discrimination and cancel culture. Digital technologies are intimately meeting with us at every intersection of human identity (Crenshaw, 1989, McCall, 2005). A sector-wide (and cross-sector) debate is needed to focus on how people are positioned as unique individuals amid this complex interplay of data, software and media communications described above. This concerns the roles that technological platforms and devices play (or don't play) in peoples' individual lives, their biological and physical circumstances and their social, political and economic contexts. The individual experiences and postdigital circumstances surrounding humans have implications across all of the key activities of HE. Educational access, inclusivity and opportunities for individuals can now be altered in many new ways, depending on their positionality.

1.8   *Intersectional Adhesives*

Intersectionality has brought valuable theoretical perspectives to bear on the intricacies of identity, diversity and inequalities, but McCall (2005) has argued that the older fields in the social sciences 'still have yet to deal fully with the complexity inherent in intersectional studies' McCall (2005: 1795). Disciplinary and interdisciplinary boundaries tend to conceal all kinds of connections that might be noticed between valuable research that explores intersectionality from different perspectives. With so many recent digital developments, intersectional computing (Kumar & Karusala, 2019) is now using the concept of intersectionality to potentially act as a form of 'glue' to bring together disparate domains of computing, with the field of Human Computer Interaction (HCI) 'now finding its way into conversations around equity, diversity and social justice' (Kumar & Karusala, 2019: 51). Whilst this is an unfolding discourse, its focus has become concentrated on:

> populations marginalised in a few explicit ways, mainly around the constructs of race, gender and class. There are also less explicit marginalised aspects of identity that a deeper engagement with the lens of intersectionality might surface, such as nationality, domain of work and linguistic ability among others. (Kumar & Karusala, 2019: 51)

Any number of aspects of each of our identities now also intersects with the postdigital contexts we find ourselves in. Subjective discussions on how we interpret these interactions offer a valuable form of resistance to rational statements that impose categories on individuals. Such classifications make their way into inclusivity policies through socially constructed labels that become applied to different sections of society. It is worth each of us questioning though, is the world really like this? How can space be opened in our university inclusivity policies for individual interpretations, and not blanket suppositions, to be heard?

In contrast to generic labels placed on humans are the fluid and personal ways in which each of us understands ourselves. Taking the experience of bell hooks as an example, she describes a subordination of her own positionality when others represent her:

> Because so much of the work I have done within feminist theory and cultural studies interrogates the way images are constructed to perpetuate and maintain sexism and racism, I am utterly mindful of the way in which my own understanding of what it is to be a black woman insurgent/intellectual writer is increasingly subordinated to the way in which I am represented by various structures of that white supremacist capitalist patriarchy I have spent my adult life critiquing. (hooks, 1996: 814)

RATIONALISATION OF HIGHER EDUCATION 135

Asking questions about how the Internet has since maintained or disrupted such deeply personal understandings of identity cannot simply be concentrated at the level of culture wars across social media. In terms of computing and the design and construction of the technical platforms that we use to air our views on, intersections also influence the lives of the:

> Researchers designers and practitioners responsible for advancing the discipline overall, and the active and passive users whose lives are shaped by these advancements. (Kumar & Karusala, 2019: 52)

Thus, wherever we find ourselves in the virtual airing cupboard, complex intersections underpin both the people and the platforms. James Ball (2020: 233) points out that where the Internet is concerned 'we moved fast and we broke things, and we didn't act quickly enough to repair the damage as we did so' (Ball, 2020: 233). This sounds like we now need to hire a very talented plumber to attend to the many elite interests that have dominated our shared virtual airing cupboard if we are to turn threats to opportunities. Ball suggests though that we:

> Break it down into getting small things done, rather than trying to build the communications backbone of the world in one go. We know it can be done because it's been done before. It's the next step of the technological revolution, and it's in our hands. (Ball, 2020: 233)

Reflecting on such plans in postdigital terms is one way to disrupt a one size fits all approach to who, or what, gets included. It enables a refocusing of issues to include the past, present and future theories and technologies that remain in our social contexts. There is no reason why we can't bring some of our older technologies into the debate with the newer ones whilst we are seeking to reset education and inclusivity policies beyond Covid-19. So far, my airing cupboard has served only as an amusing analogy, but I am not yet ruling out its fuller participation in our plans for the future, when I hear of robots learning to knit.

1.9 Exploring Shared Activities between Humans and Computing to Progress Inclusivity

Treusch, Berger and Rosner (2020) take the 'messy and seemingly unproductive process' of teaching a commercial robot to knit as a way to examine technological limitations and tensions arising from a potential collaborative practice: 'the uselessness of the chosen task allows us to re-consider the idealization of robotic collaboration'. By 'drawing on performative explorations and critique, we show how knitting enlarges our capacity to visualize what might be a suitable use case for cobots' (Treusch, Berger & Rosner, 2020). The notion of human collaboration with robots is particularly important given their potential for involvement in most spheres of human activity now. This is discussed in the context of 'cobots' 'as powerful contributors to a workforce and as powerful cultural figures':

> Envisioned as a co-worker and not as a substitute worker, the cobot exposes the possibility of building new interfaces of proximity between humans and cobots. (Treusch, Berger & Rosner, 2020)

Could this novel approach enlighten us on future postdigital dialogue (Jandrić et al., 2018) between humanities and computing to progress inclusivity, and to begin to close the gaps highlighted by Delanty (2001) and address challenges raised earlier by Mark Poster (1990) and Gary Hall (2013)?

Before I get too carried away though, moving from the example of knitting in HCI to another involving condoms, demonstrates multiple intersecting agendas that can also hamper shared goals. In their paper examining sexual health workers 'talk' around a condom distribution scheme, and implementation of a digital system to support this, 'problematic ideologies around young people and sexuality were exercised and reproduced' (Wood, Garbett, Morrissey, Hopkins & Balaam, 2018). The authors of this study found that despite calls to develop more holistic models of sexual health in national guidelines and international sexual health strategies, when a digital system was introduced, dominant and controlling models of sexual health discourse and rational efficiencies to prevent disease prevailed over community development models.

The sociotechnical approach met with the socioeconomic setting of the sexual health service where the positionality of the young people was imposed upon them 'as potential deviants requiring management and control'. This omitted multiple cultural, legal, political and economic circumstances that studies have shown to influence sexual and reproductive health in young people. Not unlike educational settings, sexual health workers in the UK operate in a context of targets and responsibility for sexual health is positioned at the individual level rather than the collective. The digital service implemented served to prop up this agenda rather than to provide space for the diverse positionalities of the participants (Wood, Garbett, Morrissey, Hopkins & Balaam, 2018). For these researchers conducting this digital study, a framing of the users as potential deviants meant that they were unable to retain the values of user-centred design, participation, and community approaches to sexual health in

RATIONALISATION OF HIGHER EDUCATION 137

conducting applied, collaborative research. Thus, the role of digital technology was also problematised (Wood, Garbett, Morrissey, Hopkins & Balaam, 2018: 10).

Ultimately then, if McDonaldised models of efficiency, calculability predictability and control prevail to reinforce top-down assumptions, then this tends to pose considerable challenges to user-centred participation and design. There are implications for inclusivity policies in universities that omit sociotechnical concerns from their detailed frameworks. One of the strengths of examining positionality through a postdigital lens is that it helps to reveal how (in very different social and technological situations) rational exclusive McDonaldised models might be noticed and disrupted to promote more diverse and inclusive ones.

Clarke and Schoonmaker (2020: 1) examined the problem of metadata in relation to publishing and asked: 'who has the power to decide what is accurate?' Whilst materials by people from diverse communities that reflect their identities, stories, and experiences are vital to social equity and empowerment of marginalised people, these are not prominent in the searches undertaken by traditionally mainstream communities. They are needed though, in order to see the world from alternative and empathetic perspectives. Library metadata is generally treated as factual and authoritative. This excludes, rather than includes, many marginalised communities. The researchers created a prototype to intentionally promote U.S. library resources by authors from traditionally marginalised communities, such as ethnic minorities, women, people of non-cisgenders, indigenous peoples, people identifying as LGBTQIA+, and people with disabilities (Clarke & Schoonmaker, 2020: 1). Whilst their technical goal was to develop wider access, their process of creation drew on critical design principles intended to raise questions and debate, rather than a purely technical fix to address deeply social concerns. They employed 'tricksterism' in the design process which 'actively lays bare the problematic ethics of our metadata interventions' (Clarke & Schoonmaker, 2020: 9). By intentionally transgressing boundaries in library metadata practices, they called into question the ethics of those practices themselves, such as what constitutes 'good' practice and when does it become 'bad', if it is redirected to advance social justice causes? Applying an amoral tricksterism to the design process enabled the designers to work in 'an ethical grey area and provoke questions about what a tool for justice might look like'. Through different use cases and bibliographic records, they demonstrated ways to open pathways for new design decisions that might potentially incorporate and reflect complex intersectional identities (Clarke & Schoonmaker, 2020: 10).

The need for disruptive design is further upheld by Adamu (2020) who discusses what is missing from the Human-Computer Interaction for Development

(HCI4D) literature in terms of 'the African standpoint logic'. Adamu (2020: 6) argues that positional understandings of African values are necessary for transcultural technological design:

> Innovative practices can be envisioned when the complex and inter-weaving formation and orderliness of members' social life is placed centrally in technological discourse, which will help to understand, design, develop, evaluate and deploy technologies in an Africa context. (Adamu, 2020: 6)

Clarke and Schoonmaker (2020) and Adamu (2020) each highlight different but related postdigital challenges for representation and positionality. These can arise in the act of, for example, routinely retrieving literature from the same 'echo chambers which reflect the first five or ten pages of Google Scholar' (Jandrić, 2019) and thereby missing so many possible alternate sources, due to the way metadata has been set up. Or designing systems, or selecting these for use, in international development countries based on rational assumptions that omit cultural context (Traxler, Smith, Scott & Hayes, 2020). It is necessary though to disrupt our humanities theories as well as our computer design assumptions. For example, members of groups such as the 'critical pedagogy movement tend to read (and cite) other members of the critical pedagogy movement' (Jandrić, 2019). This is an accepted academic practice across many disciplines and knowledge communities but can also become an exclusive one. A dual acknowledgement of a need to disrupt both humanities and computing practices could be a powerful route forward, as these go hand-in-hand in our postdigital knowledge production:

> The process of publishing is a form of 'social production' that takes place across the economy, politics and culture, all of which are in turn accommodating both old and new technology in our postdigital age. Technologies such as software cannot be separated from human labour, academic centres cannot be looked at in isolation from their margins, and the necessity of transdisciplinary approaches does not imply the disappearance of traditional disciplines. (Jandrić & Hayes, 2019)

Therefore, if the identity of a human is constructed differently across different disciplinary fields, and as Mark Poster (1990) observed, the discipline of computer science is identified through its relationship to the computer, the distinction can remain (Hall, 2013). These HCI disruptions though are bringing the cultural concerns of the humanities to bear on computing in novel ways that

RATIONALISATION OF HIGHER EDUCATION   139

can bring the disciplines into powerful dialogue. A dialogue that now needs to be acknowledged in university policymaking for inclusivity, because equality, diversity and all manner of inequalities are intimately constructed, and reconstructed, via digital interactions with computers that can keep people on the margins:

> In the postdigital age, the concept of the margins has not disappeared, but it has become somewhat marginal in its own right. We need to develop a new language of describing what we mean by 'marginal voices' in the social relations between knowledge production and academic publication. Universities require new strategies for cohabitation of, and collaboration between, various socio-technological actors, and new postdigital politics and practice of knowledge production and academic publishing. (Jandrić & Hayes, 2019)

1.10 *Writing More Inclusive Postdigital Policy That Considers Positionality and 'Dataism'*

It is now vital (given the vast amount of academic publication during the pandemic) to raise awareness of the intimate flow of knowledge that is passing between the humanities and computing, and to critically and honestly represent this in university policy. If universities continue to treat technology on the one hand, as merely a rational way to fix processes or enhance teaching in some HE strategies, but omit the consequences of digital technologies on the other hand from strategies for equality, diversity and inclusion, the implications are stark. The university agendas or frameworks aimed at inclusion, will be biased themselves. This means they will remain flawed approaches towards addressing all manner of inequities and simply linger (on the shelf or the hard drive) as disconnected McPolicy (Hayes, 2019a).

In postdigital society, positionality matters. Whilst it is increasingly difficult to separate who (or what) is contributing to the 'viral' viewpoints that spread rapidly across the Internet, at the same time as the Covid-19 virus claims lives, each human being has a positionality. In our postdigital contexts, individual positionality no longer sits apart from a 'fusion of living and technological systems' (Peters, Jandrić & McLaren, 2020: 3) from biodiversity, or from sustainability (Jandrić et al., 2020). Each of our self-declared positionings are protected by the Equality Act (2010), the Public Sector Equality Duty (2011) and the Equality and Human Rights Commission (2019), amongst other legislation. In order for university policy to reflect and uphold social justice, the hidden design and programming processes that reinforce existing inequalities, alongside exclusionary policy language, need to be addressed. This is not least because:

Metadata and data have become a regular *currency* for citizens to pay for their communication services and security – a trade-off that has nestled into the comfort zone of most people. (Van Dijck, 2014)

What we often fail to notice, and has yet to be represented in HE policy, is the problem that:

Datafication is rooted in problematic ontological and epistemological claims. As part of a larger social media logic, it shows characteristics of a widespread secular belief. Dataism, as this conviction is called, is so successful because masses of people – naively or unwittingly – trust their personal information to corporate platforms. The notion of trust becomes more problematic because people's faith is extended to other public institutions (e.g. academic research and law enforcement) that handle their (meta)data. (Van Dijck, 2014)

Van Dijck points to an 'interlocking of government, business, and academia in the adaptation of this ideology' and recommends an approach that looks more critically at 'the entire ecosystem of connective media (Van Dijck, 2014). This is an ecosystem of connective media that includes HE policy. Policy therefore cannot meaningfully sit apart from social media, the corporate platforms universities have adopted, flawed approaches towards collecting (meta)data for research publications, or data for excellence frameworks, such as the Teaching Excellence and Student Outcomes Framework (TEF) (Office for Students, 2019), the Knowledge Exchange Framework (KEF) (2020) or the Research Excellence Framework (REF) (2021). Such claims of excellence in the policy discourse do not sit apart either, from the potentially flawed methodologies or platforms on which these are based.

1.11 Data-Driven Policy Frameworks of 'Excellence' Bring Risks to Inclusive Practices

There are irrational aspects to utilising 'various computational methods (usually associated with artificial intelligences, deep learning, and such) to help us manage large amounts of information' (Jandrić, 2019) when this information is actually critical theory or inclusivity policy. However, as it is necessary to adopt such techniques, reflexivity about what this means can help to acknowledge that potential bias and ethical issues prevail until these can be addressed. In critical research projects using certain software or technological interventions it is an important requirement for a researcher to do just this. To reflexively acknowledge, as part of their positionality statement, how the use of such systems might

RATIONALISATION OF HIGHER EDUCATION

affect their outcomes or influence what is reported from the data. It is necessary then to disrupt both design assumptions behind platforms and metadata, as the above examples demonstrate, but also to challenge critical theories and university inclusivity policies, if they fail to acknowledge that commercial software used in data collection and analysis can have bias and manipulation infused through it. This becomes particularly important if policy frameworks that regulate what universities do, via data, make bold claims of 'excellence'.

In UK universities, such claims are applied to both processes and people, which again broadly implicate both computing and the humanities, in terms of the critical analysis of what this means in practice. The award of National Teaching Fellowships and University Teaching Fellowships (Advance HE) is based on an assumed relationship between teaching fellows and excellent teaching. However, research conducted with recipients found that fellows did not change their practice after receiving their Fellowship, as they simply accepted that they were already 'excellent'. The most significant impact was 'affirmation': an acknowledgement that their work was excellent, giving them 'permission' to continue (Warnes, 2020). Irrationality is revealed then through the rational McPolicy of awarding 'excellence', if this manifests in an acceptance that we have 'done enough', rather than an ongoing striving to do better. I can attest to this somewhat myself, as a Principal Fellow of the HEA (PFHEA), since 2016. However, if such awards are establishing a level of attainment alone, this is not unlike accepting that 'the principles of inclusive practice are well established' (Department for Education, 2017). If these become static principles, they then defeat the object of inclusivity, which is ongoing and dynamic, as new challenges constantly arise.

Yet challenging what sounds like a common sense goal of 'excellence' is not an easy thing to do, as Bartram (2020) points out:

> Taken at face value, it may initially seem difficult to argue with the sentiments enshrined in the rhetoric that surrounds the TEF – raising the status of teaching in Higher Education, re-balancing its relationship with research, incentivising institutions to focus on the quality of teaching, and making them more accountable for 'how well they ensure excellent outcomes for their students in terms of graduate-level employment or further study'. (OfS, 2018: 1, Bartram, 2020)

Whilst these can sound like 'laudable aspirations', Bartram (2020) demonstrates through queer theory that the TEF is emerging not only 'as a landmark initiative that is designed to further embed a neoliberal audit and monitoring culture into Higher Education' (Rudd, 2017: 59) but as:

a constraining exercise that restrains diversity and limits potential. (Bartram, 2020)

This is because 'TEF operates to normalise a macho consumerist identity' (Bartram, 2020). Such an imposed identity is argued to be consistent with a neoliberal philosophy of 'closing off alternative approaches' (Saunders, 2015: 403). It does this by locating HE firmly within a masculinist business ontology, whereby institutions, lecturers and students are systematically conditioned into compliance with a consumerist vision of universities that redefines how we come to see their purpose, the ways in which we judge their worth, and indeed how we behave and engage (Bartram, 2020). Bartram cites Rudd (2017: 73) in explaining that such a vision has become embedded as compliance in a wider discourse of newly constructed 'realities', both through conscious resignation, and more efficiently, through unconscious compliance. A queer analysis would concur that the TEF has helped to perpetuate and privilege this vision. Therefore, 'cross-examining its essentialising assumptions and reductive effects in order to de-normativise its hegemonic control is part of queer theory's raison d'être (Bartram, 2020).

Finding points of connection via queer theory between these observations on TEF bias from Bartram and those of DeVito et al. (2020) on queer theory in HCI to support Lesbian, Gay, Bisexual, Transgender, Queer, Intersex, Asexual (LGBTQIA), are powerful in demonstrating a dual resistance from both humanities and computing, to totalising McPolicy agendas. For DeVito et al. (2020), a redefinition of Queer HCI is:

> Research in HCI by, for, or substantially shaped by the queer community itself and/or queering methods and theory, regardless of application subdomain. (DeVito et al., 2020)

These researchers argue that as Queer Human-Computer Interaction (HCI) becomes an established part of the larger field, both as research on, and with, queer populations and in terms of employing queering theories and methods, the role of queer researchers and their positionalities will benefit from support. Queer people are now doing HCI research not specific to queer populations, but it is necessary to ensure that their allied researcher partners beyond the queer community develop the appropriate sensitivity and background knowledge to approach queer topics productively and respectfully (DeVito et al., 2020: 2).

It is therefore important that such research informs inclusivity policy for universities. If metrics, statistics and datasets are being brought together to

RATIONALISATION OF HIGHER EDUCATION   143

endorse judgements of excellence (Shattock, 2018: 21) and applied in the context of inclusivity, then the diverse experiences from the queer community can
hold such rational objective assumptions to account. This becomes a stronger
account still when it is voiced across both the humanities and computing.
Postdigital positionality enables such a dialogue to include in this, all other
cross-disciplinary and individual perspectives. This shifts the focus in policy
discourse on inclusivity to be less about what 'the university' is doing. It helps
it move closer towards what the people of the university, together with those
in civic society, are doing, as postdigital individuals, but working collectively to
support all of us to feel included.

2   Airing Debate on Postdigital Positionality

Everyone in the virtual airing cupboard seems to have an opinion of some sort.
Then there are the voices that are not aired over the Internet belonging to people that universities still seek to reach. The second half of Chapter 2 examines
why recognition of shared political economic spaces of technology and culture
are important for airing varied debates on what inclusivity means. Such debate
needs to take the ethos of a university outwards (Hayes et al., 2020), not try
to bring 'inclusion and diversity' inside walls that no longer exist. Traxler has
argued for:

> The need for a higher education sector engaged and 'included' in its soci-
> ety. (Traxler, 2020)

The policy that universities write concerning inclusion needs to reflect a new
understanding of the unique fusion of culture and technology with individual
identity in each of us. As such looking outwards as well as inwards is necessary. Universities are not a separate set of walls, as empty campuses during the
pandemic have attested. The people from those campuses have been working
and studying out in the virtual airing cupboard. We have all been off learning
what it is like to be on the outside looking back into the campus, under the
most abnormal circumstances. Yet this is a situation that could actually be part
of what we each come to see as our own 'new normal'. The individual perspectives that staff and students bring back to share on this experience are vital to
the debate on postdigital positionality and indeed to the post-pandemic university (Carrigan, 2020a).
    When I made the analogy with the airing cupboard at the start of this book,
I reflected on Covid-19 and its close connection with the human need for

ventilation. The life-threatening virus has revealed in particular the fragility of life for anyone with underlying respiratory conditions. Early in the global crisis, the availability of the technology to breathe for them (ventilators) was dependent on the economies of supply and demand, levels of manufacturing capacity, politics concerning deliveries between countries and the skills and training of enough staff to operate this equipment (Kliff, Satariano, Silver-Greenberg & Kulish, 2020). There were physical ramifications for the positionality of people from different cultures with these health concerns and therefore close links with inclusivity and diversity agendas.

It was soon noted that different ethnic groups were displaying a greater chance of having complications from the virus, requiring access to ventilation, but not necessarily receiving it, with views on this situation aired widely across the Internet. During lockdown, protests across the globe have arisen in relation to racism, disadvantage and the wide disparities that occur between different groups. Calls for 'getting woke' in terms of being 'acutely aware of racial and social injustice' are concerned with an ongoing awareness and learning from a position of understanding systemic and institutional forms of racism. The dimensions of argument expressed on this topic can range from encouraging activism that might critically disrupt the system of racial oppression in education (Roy, 2018), analysing 'whiteness' in digital text (Matias, 2020), or arguing that activist scholarship has now 'made everything about race, gender and identity' (Pluckrose & Lindsay, 2020). There has been a move by politicians, officials and the media to adopt the now widely used term Black Asian Minority Ethnic (BAME) in discussion of ethnic minority groups. Questions have been asked though about whether anyone in real life 'would refer to themselves as BAME' (Sandhu, 2018). The current UK Home Secretary, Priti Patel, has been reported to have called the BAME label 'patronising', 'insulting' and 'totally unhelpful' and it has also become an 'arguably overused term' that 'leaves little room for individuality or distinction' (Barrett, 2018, Osamor, 2020). BAME emerged from the use of Black Minority Ethnic (BME) a term with roots in the idea of 'political blackness', which refers to various ethnic groups gathering to fight against discrimination. It was a term used by many in the anti-racist movement in the UK in the 1970s (Sandhu, 2018).

In the 1990s though 'it was argued that the umbrella term lumped different minorities together, which was not only confusing, but it also gave less prominence to the identity of British Asians. The 'A' for Asian in BAME was then included' (Dawson & Thompson, 2019). Two main arguments that crop up are, firstly, that the term BAME 'has negative connotations or that it is too heavy-handed to be used to describe extremely diverse groups of people'. Secondly,

RATIONALISATION OF HIGHER EDUCATION 145

by way of contrast, is that it is a useful term, that there needs to be an effective way of referring to people's heritage in official reports, and a term like BAME is useful when speaking out against racial inequality (Dawson & Thompson, 2019). Objectivity and subjectivity seem once again to be in debate here, with the rationality of the language of official reports potentially stated as a reason to retain a more generic term for a hugely diverse group. Whilst others argue for subjectivity stating that 'identity is a personal thing and shouldn't be described as a generic term' (Dawson & Thompson, 2019).

Wherever readers of this book sit, in terms of the positions that they take on these and many other topics of social justice, I argue that it is necessary to also 'include' in our policies the 'work' of intelligent digital technologies and data-driven systems across the World Wide Web. These are the platforms on which we are now 'airing' our views about equality, diversity and inclusivity. They are deeply implicated in how we form our views on current cultural dilemmas in society. As such, these are not neutral systems and devices. They co-shape the data we use and the identities we have both on and offline. They are seamlessly operating as layers between teachers, students, researchers and policymakers. For these reasons alone, getting to know who developed the systems we use, what their decisions are based on and the forms of changes to educational values they are now influencing are just some of the reasons to engage with developers. Anticipating who might become our future systems designers and programmers is also important so that they might be a part of debates on how data is classified and the role of their own positionalities in such decisions.

2.1 *Systems Linked to the Virtual Airing Cupboard and Their Living Developers*

It is not as difficult as it sounds to include data-driven digital technologies at the policy table. This is because they are so recently developed, are still developing, and their developers are still around to contact and invite into the postdigital positionality debate:

> internet has only just entered its sixth decade: there are 1.7 billion people alive on the planet who were born before its invention. It's only been a mass phenomenon for 20 years. Many of its biggest companies are still run by the people who founded them; much of its architecture was built by people who are still alive and looking into the effects of what they began. (Ball, 2020: 219)

James Ball (2020) also points out that:

146   CHAPTER 2

> The internet is the product of a long chain of human decisions and incentives. It is not some force imposed upon us. But what's striking is how much it feels like that. (Ball, 2020: 219)

Then despite the multitude of voices, arguments across social media and the cancel culture wars, as humans, we have this rather odd but valuable point of connection too. What links people using the virtual airing cupboard of the Internet is that 'almost none of them feel like they're in control' (Ball, 2020: 219).

It may sound pessimistic, but this is also a starting point for change. If even 'the people who built the internet's infrastructure say the huge global network today doesn't feel like the result of what they built' (Ball, 2020: 219) then we have some consensus to debate where we might go next. It is though, a pressing debate given the 'data-driven online ad model' that has made it so easy for the Internet giants to own and transfer people's data and to apply algorithms despite their systemic inequality or bias (Ball, 2020: 232). Ball points out that the physical infrastructure of the Internet is not fundamentally all that different from its early origins. The Internet we engage with now is still a network of cables and lines that grew from technology used by its predecessors (Ball, 2020: 220). However, the intelligent technologies and related data that now network through the Internet are different. New generation architecture has emerged, and new companies and nations are stepping in to manage these. Ball suggests this is a spur to action to avoid the norms and priorities that authoritarian regimes could bring to managing related security and privacy protections (Ball, 2020: 233).

As an example, the earlier concerns about facial recognition software and bias can be met with forms of resistance beyond those involving lawsuits against authorities. Scheuerman, Wade, Lustig and Brubaker (2020) looked into 'how identity is operationalized in new technical systems'. They focused on how race and gender are defined and annotated in image databases used for facial analysis. Their findings revealed that:

> The majority of image databases rarely contain underlying source material for how those identities are defined. Further, when they are annotated with race and gender information, database authors rarely describe the process of annotation. Instead, classifications of race and gender are portrayed as insignificant, indisputable, and apolitical. (Scheuerman, Wade, Lustig & Brubaker, 2020: 1)

Describing how literally within the last decade, facial analysis technology has 'transitioned from a theoretical research problem to commercial reality',

RATIONALISATION OF HIGHER EDUCATION   147

these researchers point to the many technologies in which facial recognition is already embedded. It is used in social media, for unlocking access to devices, by law enforcement and even to track consumer behaviour inside stores for future marketing campaigns targeting specific demographics. The use of human identity characteristics in machine learning databases have caused concern for some time over race and gender bias. However, attempts to mitigate this and to build more diverse databases with the aim of creating fairer outcomes remain simplistic and lacking in critical and social theories (Scheuerman, Wade, Lustig & Brubaker, 2020: 2).

Additional concerns are that 'machine learning and human-computer interaction (HCI) communities do not have an agreed upon approach to how diversity is being operationalized in training and evaluation databases'. Scheuerman, Wade, Lustig and Brubaker (2020) refer to unethical attempts to address this, such as Google reportedly targeting homeless people to use their images to improve their face unlock system (Hollister, 2019). The need to more meaningfully represent race and gender in databases is important to address the current opaque and inconsistent approaches. However, Scheuerman, Wade, Lustig and Brubaker (2020) took this further in seeking to understand underlying decisions that become embedded into the construction of training and evaluation databases. They examined these, alongside critical scholarship dealing with the complex realities of identity. Following their analysis of 92 image databases to look at why race and gender are included, what information is implicit or explicit and what sources and annotation practices are used to define categories of race and gender, they recommended that facial analysis researchers adopt a socio-historical perspective when making decisions around classifications of race and gender and that they embrace their own positionality in terms of embedding such classifications (Scheuerman, Wade, Lustig & Brubaker, 2020: 2).

Studies of this nature are valuable to cite against the problems of digital skills agendas that are taught, or learned, in a vacuum or treated as detached attributes. Instead, whatever levels of digital skills are being developed in trainees, there is a need for training and educational agencies who offer such programmes to understand the wider ecosystem that surrounds digital skills acquisition.

2.2   *Positionality Is a Key Consideration for All Digital Skills Agendas*
Positionality needs to be addressed both for those teaching and those who are learning, so that bias and ethics are discussed in digital skills and computer coding programmes and critical research on diversity is included. Moving beyond the decisions made by those programming systems, to the background and identity of developers and programmers themselves, there are considerations of representation from minority groups moving into these professions.

Codding Mouza, Rolón-Dow and Pollock (2019) describe an initiative which was intended to broaden the participation of minoritised youth in computer science and to offer culturally responsive computer science programming in informal settings. They undertook this work within a theoretical framework of positionality, in order to take into account the 'numerous shifting and intersecting identities of each individual' involved. They argue that 'educators are positioned by factors such as age, gender, race, and lived experiences'. As such, they declared a need to scrutinise the positionality of their own facilitators, to look at how their community affiliations, organisational roles, and personal identities might influence the process and findings of their community-based research and computer science programming.

In seeking to create programmes that would serve underrepresented minoritised and female youth they adopted strategies that included methods for engaging youth, and practices that build on the knowledge and assets of local communities, using undergraduate computer science students as facilitators and near-peer mentors, and encouraging culturally responsive interactions between facilitators and the young participants who were underrepresented in computer science (Codding, Mouza, Rolón-Dow & Pollock, 2019). Based on such approaches there is evidence for building many more coding programmes and digital skills training initiatives from within local communities, but with cross-sector representation and broad diversity amongst the facilitators. This approach addresses a shortage in skilled computer programmers from the point of their positionalities first. Furthermore, in recruiting from diverse local communities where there are already initiatives in place to support life chances for local minority and disadvantaged groups there is an ecological infrastructure already in place to support inclusive practices.

The role of positionality in the examples above is further endorsed by Kaeser-Chen, Dubois, Schüür and Moss (2020) who argue that:

> Being positionality-aware is key for machine learning practitioners to acknowledge and embrace the necessary choices embedded in machine learning by its creators. (Kaeser-Chen, Dubois, Schüür & Moss, 2020)

Shifting the focus now a little towards the networked devices on which so much of our postdigital positionalities are now enacted, there are new challenges and opportunities to reflect on as AI continues to develop and to be added to the Internet of Things (IoT). These include device updates, protocols and user awareness for example, now that IoT devices and applications are playing an increasing role in modern life. It may seem that the networking of household items to the Internet is not immediately the concern of a university inclusivity

RATIONALISATION OF HIGHER EDUCATION   149

policy, but the use of smart systems on campus or in university accommodation are being introduced in all sorts of ways.

From smart campuses that optimise power consumption to ones that enable students to use their phones to check if washing machines are free, there are new examples continually appearing. Some campuses are acting as test-beds to inform digital decisions for surrounding communities, thus there are new public-private commercial partnerships involved. Most universities already have the campus-wide wifi needed with the ability to link the personal devices of staff and students. This means they may well be able to utilise IoT to connect all manner of wearable and connectable devices and data which can be argued to benefit students. Yet as companies lobby universities to sign up for the IoT, it is worth doing some additional reading between the lines, when new interpretations of inclusion and equity accompany the glossy brochure. In Deloitte's (2019) Smart Campus document there are some bold claims on the benefits to 'foster inclusion and equity':

> Understanding the patterns around various activities and initiatives within a campus can help a school foster inclusion and drive equity. Dashboards designed around inclusion and diversity can provide valuable, actionable insight. The knowledge gained from education drives the economy and improving access to education will only foster a more inclusive community. (Deloitte, 2019)

The assumptions that 'equity' is something an institution can 'drive' is discussed in the context of dashboards that have been 'designed around inclusion and diversity' (Deloitte, 2019). Universities would need to explore such arguments concerning claims of inclusion in considerable depth, to avoid the problem of treating IoT as just another quick fix.

2.3   *Learning Lessons from My Airing Cupboard*
Perhaps though, given all of these developments, I might reflect on what could be in store for my airing cupboard in the hall and whether its architecture is heading for a revamp anytime soon. If I go out just now and I open the door of my airing cupboard to search behind the pile of towels and sheets I can just about see the machinery that sits at the back. I can spot some of the water tank and pipes (Figure 29) and a tatty label that at least clearly identifies what the specifications of the copper cylinder are (Figure 30). Searching my airing cupboard like this will not though cause me to be identified by those who live in a house further along my street, or in a different part of the world. No one holds data about what items I store in my hallway airing cupboard (which is just as well).

FIGURE 29
An airing cupboard
hot water tank
infrastructure

FIGURE 30
An airing cupboard water
tank specifications

No one tracks what I search for in there, what I download as the sheets topple down on top of me or captures evidence that the cat has managed to sneak in there for a warm sleep. My airing cupboard does not have a relationship

RATIONALISATION OF HIGHER EDUCATION   151

(that I am aware of at least) with any other airing cupboards in houses along my street. They do not share data with each other in the way that my phone, iPad and laptop do.

Sitting back in front of my laptop again then, I get little sense of what lies behind my Google searches for sources for this book, or where the 'likes' I have registered on Facebook might be stored, counted or passed on.

After my guilty glance at some click bait earlier to read someone else's dirty laundry story, I have no idea how often I will now be prompted to read related topics. Nor does the complexity of the architecture behind the Internet seem to be any particular issue to me right now. I have my active wifi and I can connect wherever I go. This is also a problem though, if I do not notice the ethical problems and security issues that have crept in alongside my constant searches for everything in the virtual airing cupboard. Unlike the laundry sitting dormant on the shelves in my cupboard in the hall, my laundry I air online is accessible to all. What if my airing cupboard in the hall now decides to join in too? Could I stop it from making connections with the virtual airing cupboard? Fortunately, yes, I do have that choice right now (I think).

I also have a choice though to actively connect my airing cupboard water tank to my wifi network via a new app that will give me visibility on every aspect of my hot water activity. To put it another way, I can join the 'Internet of Tanks' and learn what I wish about my hot water cylinder's story, as shown in Figure 31.

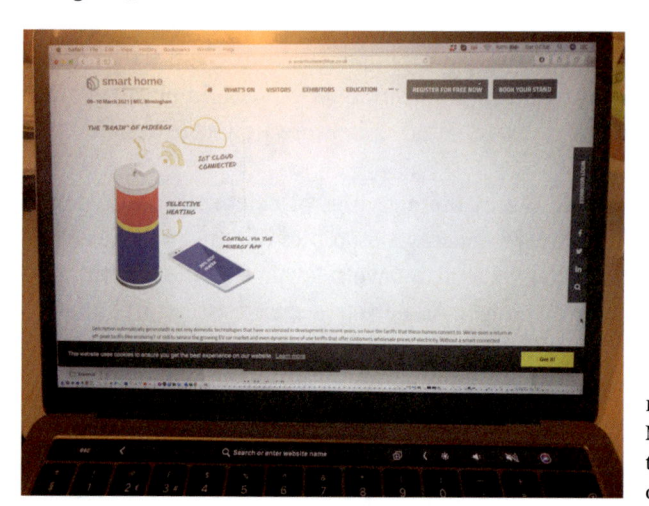

FIGURE 31
My laptop showing
the Internet of Tanks
opportunity

This includes the exact percentage of hot water available in the cylinder, how much energy has been used, the status of pasteurisation cycles, switching of energy sources and even, information about the energy mix and carbon

152 CHAPTER 2

intensity of the national grid's energy (Mixergy, 2020). In this sense, as I leave home to go for a drink in a nearby pub (before the next lockdown forbids it) I am taking my airing cupboard cylinder along with me, to be sociable too. Given that we can connect home devices in this way and carry any number of apps with us on our mobile phones, in a sense they have already made it into the small room on campus or online where people are busy discussing and writing the next university inclusivity policy. Digital solutions bring additional complications and unpredictability to a world that is already rapidly changing in response to a global pandemic. Data-driven systems are involved across all of our postdigital society. They have earned their place at the policy table (which may well be a virtual table currently). We need to accommodate their actions alongside our own, in ethical debates on social justice, human rights and capabilities in all HE policy discourse that seeks to effect change.

2.4 *Virtual Airing Cupboards Ventilate and Constitute Viewpoints*

Our large societal, postdigital 'airing cupboard' allows ventilation of many mutually constitutive viewpoints across both physical and online spaces. These are not set apart from universities as further examples will show. University policies cannot socially isolate either from the broader cultural/technical communication taking place on the communicable Covid-19 virus. Conditions in the virtual airing cupboard are not unlike the acts of droplets we fear coming into contact with from the virus, if we have too close an encounter with someone who might spread the disease. Our shared digital online communications systems have made it easy for any dialogue to pick up traces from other different institutional or personal positionalities, with implications for how inclusive practices in HE, and related policy, are now constructed and perceived.

In recent examples, ranging from the activities of celebrities to academics, the complexities of actions and reactions on topics relating to race can be noticed. The stances individuals take also have relevance to the institutions in which they work. When the singer Adele was accused of cultural appropriation, others argued that this is cultural celebration, in the context of the Notting Hill Carnival. The arguments posted online after she was pictured on Instagram wearing bantu knots, a traditional African hairstyle and a bikini in the design of the Jamaican flag, ranged from intense criticism to compliments and support for the musician (PA Media, 2020). One person concluded that 'this officially marks all of the top white women in pop as problematic', another suggested 'she should go to jail no parole for this'. Different viewpoints (including Labour members of parliament and other celebrities) tweeted in

RATIONALISATION OF HIGHER EDUCATION   153

her defence: 'Poppycock! This humbug totally misses the spirit of Notting Hill Carnival and the tradition of "dress up" or "masquerade" Adele was born and raised in Tottenham she gets it more than most. Thank you, Adele. Forget the Haters' (Lammy, 2020).

However, new dimensions of personal positionality (and potential cultural implications) were revealed when Jessica Krug, the 'prominent activist and professor of African American history at George Washington University', when writing on a blog called Medium, 'admitted that she has been pretending to be a black woman'. She 'revealed that she had assumed many false identities including "North African Blackness, US rooted Blackness (and) Caribbean rooted Bronx Blackness"' (Sibthorpe, 2020). Her blog claimed too that her own trauma and mental health in her teens may have contributed to her claiming identities that were not her own:

> I have eschewed my lived experience as a white Jewish child in suburban Kansas City under various assumed identities within a Blackness that I had no right to claim... I am not a culture vulture. I am a culture leech. (Krug, 2020)

These revelations raise some different questions on cancel culture. What happens when a person cancels themselves to the extent that they feel they no longer have a positionality? Then there are the intersections between inclusivity and mental health that are also presented by this case.

The global 'war' against Covid-19 has a dual effect, as the communicable, biological aspects of the contagion are fought by science and technology. At the same time technology, culture and language are 'transmitting' the informational aspects of the biological threat (Peters, Jandrić & McLaren, 2020). Examining how dimensions of 'cancel culture' flow through HE via digital technologies and human beings (together) demonstrates why such dynamic forces cannot simply be 'owned' by a set of inclusion guidelines. This is partly for cultural reasons, because any guidelines and related data have been shaped by the values, deadlines and critical levels of understanding or bias of the individual or committee who have written them, or adapted them from another university policy document (Hayes, 2019a). Then there are issues of inherent bias already discussed which may be programmed into technologies themselves that can also be responsible for 'cancelling' humans in all sorts of ways. Such bias is continually in interaction with data of many kinds which is also potentially biased. Datasets reflect the values and ideologies of their collectors, whether the topics concern ability, disability, ethnicity or gender, or indeed other terms we have come to use. As such they perform such concepts 'into being' (O'Keeffe, 2017: 133).

2.5 *The Contagion of Cancel Culture and the Educationalisation of Inclusivity*

Elsewhere I have written with co-authors about the problems arising from *educationalisation* of many different societal issues into agendas for schools and universities to be responsible for (Peters, Jandrić & Hayes, 2018, Jandrić & Hayes, 2020d). Larry Cuban, in discussion with Petar Jandrić (2020) described the process of 'educationalising' as:

> Transferring societal structural problems to the institution of schooling so individual students and teachers then become first, an easy target to blame, and second, responsible for solving the problem. For example, national health problems of smoking tobacco and drinking alcohol in the prior century got translated into school courses for youth about the physical and cognitive damages done by both drugs. Too many road accidents? Driver training and completing a safe driver's course for high school graduation became a school-based solution to a national problem. And as you pointed out in your question, the harnessing of schools to an increasingly high-tech economy means that children and youth are engaged early and persistently in using electronic devices so that they can easily fit into a high-tech workplace. (Cuban, in Jandrić, 2017: 13)

It is therefore not that unexpected to see the notion of 'cancel culture' being shipped into schools for teachers to tackle. Reserving any personal judgement on the pros and cons of linking cancel culture with teaching about bullying in schools, the initiative is being aimed at secondary schools:

> As part of the Government's drive to protect freedom of speech, secondary school students will learn that people with controversial opinions should be respected. (White, 2020)

MP Andrea Jenkyns tweeted (with an integral pun on the Commons):

> Great, commons sense prevails! Woke 'cancel culture' is a form of bullying, pupils will be taught, as part of the Governments drive to protect free speech. (Jenkyns, 2020b)

RATIONALISATION OF HIGHER EDUCATION   155

Taking steps to address cancel culture has importance though across all parts
of society. It requires ongoing critical debate that universities could potentially
lead on, but are not in a position to control any more than schools are:

> In Department for Education training manuals, teachers are instructed to
> tell pupils that the 'cancel culture' which has taken root at many universi-
> ties – where individuals call for a boycott of a person or company whose
> views they don't agree with, in the hope they lose their job or clients – is
> not part of a 'tolerant and free society'. (White, 2020)

Stating: 'the 'cancel culture' which has taken root at many universities' as a
justification for educationalising a deeply ingrained socio-technical practice
raises a number of issues. Firstly, it gives an impression that university is simply
a continuation of school. The bias here is against lifelong learners, those made
redundant through the pandemic seeking to retrain, apprentices and indeed
university staff. Secondly, there is a more fundamental problem of persistently
separating the teaching of cultural values from critical digital skills that would
raise awareness of how these intertwine and constitute each other. Thirdly, a
rather more 'sinister' link can be made. One that reveals another irrationality
in how one set of rational agendas to promote inclusivity can effectively 'cancel' another.

Whilst only flagged as guidance or principles, schools have been asked not
to use resources from organisations that take extreme political stances, including those who express a desire to 'end capitalism' (gov.uk, 2020b). In guidance
on how schools might set up the relationship between sex and health in the
curriculum, the DfE categorised anti-capitalism as an 'extreme political stance',
equating it with opposition to freedom of speech, anti-Semitism and endorse-
ment of illegal activity (Speare-Cole, 2020). A further issue concerns why, if we
do seek to educationalise ways to address cancel culture, would we only begin
programmes at the secondary school level, when infants now operate iPads,
phones and laptops as soon as they are able to hold these. The State of Data
(2020) report recently suggested too that:

> Children have lost control of their digital footprint by their fifth birthday
> from being in state education. (The State of Data, 2020)

This raises two interconnected issues in relation to the dialectics between technology and culture. If, as part of a tolerant and free society, children are to be
taught not to 'cancel each other' as part of their cultural education, why does it

seem that, from the earliest age possible, technological systems are effectively 'cancelling' the positionalities of children, through the school system, as they become 'datafied' as individuals? (Lupton & Williamson, 2017).

2.6   *Stalked by Data in an Ongoing Identity Theft?*

The State of Data report (2020) charts an alarming 'datafication of children' in the UK and points to how England's education system has also managed the 'exclusion and "managed moves" of outliers – the disabled, the lower achieving and those who won't get good grades' (The State of Data, 2020: 74). Particularly alarming is the forcing of schools:

> to turn the complexity of children's lives into simplified progress scores or attendance ratings without context, to be ranked and spanked in league tables by the national Regulator. (The State of Data, 2020: 75)

The authors argue that a form of identity theft is taking place from an early age through which children are no longer afforded space to make mistakes. This would seem to be upheld too by concerns over a use of AI to read young children's emotions whilst they learn. Yet a software called 4 Little Trees that measures muscle points on children's faces via a camera on their computer or tablet, and identifies emotions such as happiness, sadness, anger, surprise and fear, is argued to 'make the virtual classroom as good as – or better than – the real thing' (Chan, 2021). Claims that the software facilitates better interaction need to be balanced though with other elements of positionality, such as privacy and potential bias. Given that research has shown that some emotional analysis technology has difficulties 'in identifying the emotions of darker skinned faces, in part because the algorithm is shaped by human bias and learns how to identify emotions from mostly white faces' (Chan, 2021) the goal 'to train machines to be better than the average human' at reading facial expressions in relation to learning still sparks controversy (Chan, 2021).

Whilst the conditions of the pandemic lockdowns may seem like a separate set of challenges for schools, children and their families, through a postdigital perspective these are likely to compound each other in relation to both technology and culture. The physical restrictions placed on children, such as new sets of rules and regulations to observe, even in local play areas (Figures 32 and 33), do not sit apart from those they are required to follow in school or online. It is worth reflecting more broadly therefore on the different forms of identity theft that might impact young people, through physical Covid-19 restrictions and virtual encounters.

RATIONALISATION OF HIGHER EDUCATION 157

FIGURE 32
Covid-19 government guidance to 'stop the spread' whilst in a children's play area

FIGURE 33
Covid-19 list of rules displayed in a children's play area

158   CHAPTER 2

Indeed, just because data systems make an activity possible does not mean that it is beneficial and in fact 'historic data can cause harm' (The State of Data, 2020: 75). To address this situation there are calls for a greater prioritising of access, inclusion, safety, privacy and a platform for young people's views on their digital rights (Coleman, Pothong, Vallejos & Koene, 2017).

The process of airing the dirty laundry was once by word of mouth. Perhaps nods and whispers would have indicated that some people knew something about us we would have preferred them not to know. These days we really do not know what any person or agency could have access to, or whether it will work for or against us, as individuals. The data streams feeding the decisions that other humans or algorithms make about us are not at our disposal to learn why an application for a job, finance, a public service or a place at university is rejected. Such a situation impacts on the positionality of each of us in different ways in a postdigital society. Out there in the virtual airing cupboard are trails of my dirty laundry, but unlike the cupboard in my hallway I don't have a hope of clearing it out.

2.7   *Implications for HE Policy*

The university is no longer a discrete separate project detached from any of the examples raised so far. The virtual airing cupboard has seen to that. This leaves universities with the post-pandemic option of attempting to return to a 'normal' where a generation of discrete policies, one-by-one ticks a box for each issue as it arises, so that it can be educationalised into the curriculum or absorbed into staff training. However, issues of mental health and welfare do not reside in universities any more than disability or racism. Even if they did it seems unhelpful for the mental health concerns in relation to students and staff in HE to occupy a different set of policies to those concerning Technology Enhanced Learning (TEL), when the lockdown has clearly revealed just how interconnected these experiences can be.

An alternative to the singular, 'topic-based' manner in which HE strategies are frequently constructed could take a more person-focused, rather than topic-focused understanding. This approach could help to reveal the need to surface positionality instead of generality.

2.8   *Airing Cupboards and HE Policies Re-imagined as Living Literacies*

If humans are now data (Cheney-Lippold, 2018) then the question on my mind is: how much of this data is our own human narrative that is being rendered into something different? What routes might be open to us to preserve our own literacies? Recalling that a key 'challenge facing the university today is to link cultural reproduction and technological reproduction' (Delanty, 2001: 157) then perhaps there is a need to accept that our postdigital positionalities are made up of both. We are cultural and we are technological then, but we are also living conscious beings who bring our own literacies that are shaped by our identities and positioning. We breathe (when the virus lets us) and it is this living quality that could be helpful to remember in the process of collectively re-imagining our post-pandemic policymaking in universities.

In 'Living Literacies: Literacy for Social Change', Pahl, Rowsell, Collier, Pool, Rasool and Trzecak (2020) describe a living literacies approach as inclusive of official, schooled activities, such as reading, writing, speaking, and listening but also of tacit activities like scrolling through Instagram, watching the news footage and listening to music. This is a re-framing that goes beyond literacy as an object of study, to reimagine literacy as constantly in motion, vital, and dynamic and filled with personal affective intensities. They suggest that such a 'lived literacies' approach implies a turn to activism and to hopeful practice and creativity (Pahl, Rowsell, Collier, Pool, Rasool & Trzecak, 2020).

Important to my earlier critique of McPolicy, is the way that these authors examine literacies through a series of active verbs, like seeing, disrupting, hoping, knowing, creating, and making. Where in McPolicy these verbs were so often ascribed to strategies and technologies, taking instead the notion of living literacies into policy would be to position policy itself differently. Rather than topic, or institution focused, policymaking would be positionality focused. Rather than talk of 'equality', 'diversity' or 'inclusivity' as detached 'objects' of study, these would be explored in the contexts of the individual 'subjects' they relate to. Such an approach has more chance of supporting inclusivity because it also raises awareness that all interactions surrounding inclusive practices are dynamic, not static. They are both human and nonhuman, digital and nondigital. They can exert agency in unseen ways, as can policy.

In *The Good, the Bot, and the Ugly: Problematic Information and Critical Media Literacy in the Postdigital Era*, Jiang and Vetter (2020) argue for a pedagogy of postdigital critical media literacy. Their postdigital examination of bots points out the ideological nature of the Wikipedia community and:

> recognises bots as 'agents' that co-produce meanings with other social actors and human editors. Even though bots have contributed to the epistemic process of information validation on Wikipedia, the process has inevitably been made messy by the infiltration of misogyny, systemic bias, and conflict of interest on the online platform. A postdigital critical media literacy would encourage students to become more reflexive

of online information validation through identifying and analyzing bot-human interaction. (Jiang & Vetter, 2020)

In a similar fashion it is timely now to look at the manner in which HE inclusivity policy is formed and to become more reflexive about the possibility that, in its current shape, it simply confirms, rather than disrupts, existing systemic bias and entrenched inequalities.

CHAPTER 3

Postdigital Positionality as a Learner

1 Learning, Experience and Inclusion as Personal and Embodied, Not Rationally Audited

We will each have personal ideas on what it means to learn anything. In a broad sense, every person is a learner of some sort, whether they are assessed for formal qualifications or not. However, not all learning comes for free and routes into accessing education can vary greatly depending on each person's situation and context. Despite its potential worth to human beings, an education can be very expensive, and not only in economic terms. Education often involves making sacrifices, some that I can personally identify with, and others that people have shared with me. I have been moved by hearing individual experiences, challenges, discomfort, accounts of 'imposter syndrome', progression, setbacks and successes. People have discussed their living narratives with me as students in classrooms in which I have taught, in tutorials and supervisions, as staff on professional development programmes, in mentoring meetings, over Internet-based communication systems, in different geographical parts of the world (Lamb, Bartholomew & Hayes, 2017: 214, Traxler, Smith, Scott & Hayes, 2020) and across time zones and different locations during the 2020 Covid-19 crisis (Peters & Wang et al., 2020, Jandrić & Hayes, 2020a, Jandrić & Hayes, 2020b).

Learning through personal experience is different though to simply being told something. I can listen to (and be moved by) these powerful accounts, but I cannot personally embody them. Neither can I label them in any rational terminology that would retain the individuality and authenticity of each person's version of what they learned, how they learned something and the emotions that were involved. Learning through first-hand experiences can effect change in the way that a person perceives the world, and it may alter how they act in it, if they are able to examine their experiences reflexively. The idea of 'lived experience' is also a reminder that this is an active process taking place within a human being's body, even if they are in close interaction with technology too. Their body may, or may not, have a disability, be of a particular gender, ethnicity, or social class, but experiences of feeling included will then be felt across these intersecting factors (Hector, 2020: 66). Thus, it is hard to imagine these intimate authentic accounts from human beings about their experiences of learning, inclusion or discrimination, rendered into something simply called 'data' or 'the student experience'.

© KONINKLIJKE BRILL NV, LEIDEN, 2021 | DOI: 10.1163/9789004466029_005

162   CHAPTER 3

Yet data can be rich and qualitative, as well as descriptive and summative, or it can be both, depending on how it is collected and with what purposes, in a cultural political economy. The line of argument in this book so far has been that we now occupy a postdigital context where past and present cultural and technological concerns cannot sit apart from each other, or from biological challenges such as Covid-19. Concerns over student wellbeing cannot be isolated in policy from the use of AI to power learning or the IoT to modernise the campus. However, rather than institutions trying to educationalise and regulate all aspects of student experiences within walls that have ceased to exist, there is a role for universities as sites of knowledge at the intersection of key societal debates (Delanty, 2001: 158). Inclusivity is just one of these debates, but it concerns citizenship as a whole, not the student population alone. This shift requires a change of focus away from rational McPolicy towards postdigital positionality.

Universities over recent decades have gathered a lot of data about their own activities as institutions have become increasingly subordinate to what has been described as an 'audit culture'. This has come to embody 'a new rationality of governance' (Shore & Wright, 1999) where data is collected, and efficiency measured, on many activities surrounding student learning and support (Office for Students, 2019). Not only has this approach involved 'the re-invention of professionals themselves as units of resource whose performance and productivity must constantly be audited so that it can be enhanced' (Shore & Wright, 1999: 559), this has also reconstructed students as 'vulnerable' beings and even as 'thwarted consumers' (Brooks, 2018: 745). There has been a subtle but ongoing shift where an acknowledgement of the challenges and emotional aspects of learning, such as those I referred to at the start of this chapter, have come to be considered as if these were 'treatable' (Ecclestone & Hayes, 2019: 155) aspects of the package of 'experience' that students now pay for and universities 'deliver'. A key problem we have faced for some time is that:

> The language of markets, targets and tests is not only increasingly regulating education, but is driving out the possibility of other languages and closing the educational field to other possibilities. (Stevenson, 2010: 342)

This 'consumption of any space for alternative discourse' (Hayes, 2015: 27) has led to new identities being ascribed to students where they routinely require therapeutic interventions to counter the emotionally difficult aspects of learning. Unfortunately, this then leads to a preoccupation with feelings over the challenges of 'mastering a difficult subject' (Ecclestone & Hayes, 2019: 156) or the assessment that accompanies it. These changes have introduced new

POSTDIGITAL POSITIONALITY AS A LEARNER · 163

terminology too, which when placed within rational policy imperatives, takes on an independence from the individual human positionalities I described above. This is because any generalised description of the 'shared trauma' of being a student along with a set of prescribed antidotes is not the same thing as an individual narrative from a person who has overcome challenges to learning. The first is a rationality that treats students as deficient. The second is a positionality from which a student shares details of their personal journey and their identification with eventually becoming proficient.

It is important to stress that these arguments are not against the provision of support for students: far from it. They are though, a critique of a rationale where students are treated as 'lacking' rather than 'operating from a place of plenty' where they might experience and contribute to a 'genuine curiosity and joy in learning' (Kahane, 2009). Kahane argues that: 'students are reminded repeatedly of what they lack and come to treat education as a treadmill to gain praise and avoid humiliation' (Kahane, 2009: 57). Yet even a treadmill requires input from a human to keep it moving and often the hope of improved self-esteem is behind the choice that people make to exercise on a treadmill. Ecclestone and McGiverny (2005: 8) suggest that if educators focus on self-esteem this need not imply 'a view of learners as emotionally frail, weak or vulnerable', instead it implies:

> a recognition that, in order to progress, some individuals need to change their self-image and raise their estimation of their talents and potential. (Ecclestone & McGiverny, 2005: 8)

This however does not seem to be an analysis that sits well with a university culture of writing McPolicy. As previously argued, the linguistic structure of HE McPolicy is distinctive in that it appears to require hardly any input from humans at all (Hayes, 2019a). There is little space for living narratives and literacies because the focus is mostly on describing what detached objects (such as strategies, buzz phrases or technologies) have achieved, rather than accrediting diverse human subjects with the labour of their own learning. McPolicy mostly comments on student experience (not experiences), on digital literacy (not literacies) and therefore what is plural, diverse and ongoing, is simply omitted from these texts. What is static seems to get counted, whilst what is dynamic is frequently discounted. McPolicy does have its advantages though if you wish to discuss humans only in rational terms, *as* data. Under these circumstances, data may also be assumed to be 'facts', and facts (along with their associated metrics) can form a basis for all kinds of calculations and reasoning that can easily bypass the complications of human positionality.

Yet McPolicy could have begun to encounter a problem. Whilst this reductive form of discourse may have reinforced the rational governance of some forms of objective quality assurance, accreditation, accountability and so called 'best practices', when it comes to inclusivity policy, it continually falls short. This is because the writing of rational policy for the purposes of diversity and inclusion moves quickly into irrationality, if the activities of people are not mentioned in it. Furthermore, it hits another hurdle when it fails to engage explicitly with new digital developments that now have huge implications for how learning takes place. This includes the potential promise of AI powered education to improve access and approaches to education. It also encompasses the potential technological or commercial bias and ethical concerns surrounding many data-driven systems already actively used for student learning and related analytics. In seeking to measure inclusivity within narrow categories, the diverse fluid encounters of staff and students become reified into static data. This has implications for what then gets excluded. The aspects of identity that are argued to be valued, become absorbed into generalities. This ultimately makes it harder to effect meaningful change in any institution.

Even as I write, a phenomenal amount of data is being processed as the US election vote of 2020 draws to a close amid some dispute over the outcomes by the current president. Earlier in the year, as Covid-19 took hold in many parts of the world, different populations around the globe experienced first-hand the responses of their national leaders and their country's policies towards a pandemic. In the US, it was argued in March 2020: 'America has learned a lot about Trump during the coronavirus crisis' (D'Antonio, 2020). This report called for Donald Trump to step aside and to 'even go into self-quarantine for a while'. Only a few months later, Trump himself released a video on Twitter explaining that he is now the person learning. Having tested positive for the virus and received treatment, he discussed how he 'learned a lot about Covid. I learned it by going to school, the real school. This isn't the read the book school. I get it. I understand it' (Trump, 2020). Despite this personal declaration, it seems that what was learned through experience was not applied as others might have hoped. Trump staged 'an "insane" surprise drive-by visit to supporters outside the Walter Reed military medical center', where the president had been treated, placing others in the car with him at unnecessary risk of infection and obliged them to also quarantine for 14 days (Luscombe and Sullivan, 2020). Learning from experience then is intensely personal. Positionality concerns the values and prejudices we each hold and how we construct meaning to alter, or be altered by, such power relations. A positional perspective on learning is drawn from personal and historical experiences and changing contexts. As illustrated here then, one person's positionality on a topic such as Covid-19 will differ considerably from others.

Also, at the time of writing, students in the UK (and in many other cities around the globe) are persistently hitting the news headlines as potential spreaders of the Covid-19 virus. As cities seek to keep their cases low, the language of signage, such as 'shield our city' (Figure 34) makes the bold claim too that 'distance makes us stronger'.

FIGURE 34   A 'shield our city' sign proclaiming that: 'distance makes us stronger'

We are not told on what basis this is believed to be true. Students are in a rather different set of circumstances to those of a US president, but they are still experiencing various forms of public criticism across the virtual airing cupboard too:

> Whoever thought it a good idea to disperse 2 million Covid super-spreaders across British cities this month? (Jenkins, 2020)

Aside from the realities that some university courses cannot be conducted entirely online (for example those that require work in laboratories, hospitals, industry, stadiums and even at sea) the return of students to campus during Autumn 2020 raised a complex situation. Not only were university campuses reported as key sites of localised Covid-19 outbreaks, students were instructed to self-isolate in their halls of residence and reacted in different ways to being 'caged' (Arundel, 2020). Given that McDonaldised university campuses have in recent years come to resemble leisure and hotel complexes, as they have mimicked other forms of consumer services, students are hardly now experiencing the 'educational consumption' (Ritzer, 2005) that they were promised. Yet in late October 2020, universities had little time to edit their messages of welcome to students on institutional websites:

> World-class facilities. Beautiful campuses. A city that is full of life and buzzing with culture, sport and nightlife. All this makes for a student experience you won't find anywhere else. (University of Nottingham, 2020)

Below this warm greeting is a Coronovirus update, as simultaneously, Nottingham was moving into the 'very high' Covid-19 restrictions (Nottinghamshire County Council, 2020). With warnings too that they may not get to return to their family homes during the Christmas break, students across the UK were understandably questioning why they were encouraged to attend campus at all. These events gave rise to a new set of HE iconography in the UK, as students decorated their windows with appeals to the general public about their plight. Where once there may have been an expensive etching of disembodied words like: 'ambition', 'impact' or 'excellence', such objective icons were covered by rather more subjective appeals revealing personal positionalities. Appearing in the windows of university halls of residences were home-made signs referring to the sizable fees paid by students as they asked: '9k 4 what?'. Others pointed to their concerns of claustrophobia and mental health deterioration, alongside SOS messages and more whimsical images of beer and requests for food supplies (Rao, 2020). This was not quite 'the student experience' that has been so heavily marketed by universities on their websites during much of the last two decades and written into so many HE policy documents. These are though striking visual reminders that students never were a single, generalised body to whom universities delivered 'the student experience' to (Hayes, 2019a), despite claims like these repeated across many policy statements:

> It is the responsibility of every member of the College to help develop and deliver an exemplary Student Experience. (St Patricks, 2015–2017)

In contrast, the current circumstances of many students are anything but exemplary:

> From overcrowded lecture halls in France to a ban on sleepovers in Ireland, special coronavirus apps in the UK, snitching on dorm parties in the US and shuttered campus gates in India, students face a range of experiences when – or if – universities reopen. (Carroll, 2020)

In this chapter I will firstly, provide a little further background on the increasingly irrelevant discourse of 'the student experience' that has developed as a generalised buzz phrase in HE policy and intensified following the introduction of tuition fees in the UK (Dearing, 1997; Browne, 2010). Though marketised discourse can be noticed globally in university policies, in the UK context, a strong emphasis on a particular form of 'measurement' of HE activity reveals many misconceptions of what can be actually be quantified in a postdigital society. An educationalisation of many social issues into universities has now reached a crisis point. This is demonstrated by recent attempts to house all aspects of inclusive practices in institutional policies and then to attempt to deliver aspects of these back to students, as part of 'the student experience' package deal. In a year when pre-university students have seen their exam results placed at the mercy of algorithms, students arrived at university to find themselves confined to rooms on campus and were then told there is no guarantee they can return home during holidays, a review of 'the student experience' discourse and its isolation from realities is needed. It was already overdue. Alongside an urgency to review HE policy rhetoric to be a more inclusive discourse in itself, there is a pressing need to also recognise:

> the profound and dynamic impact of artificial intelligence (AI) on societies, ecosystems, and human lives, including the human mind, in part because of the new ways in which it influences human thinking, interaction and decision-making, and affects education, human, social and natural sciences, culture, and communication and information. (UNESCO, 2020c)

How we come to recognise these changes, in relation to human empowerment in learning, or simply as displacement of people whilst technology 'enhances' is part of this ongoing debate. What Covid-19 has also revealed is that in the communities surrounding universities there is still considerable digital exclusion. As educational institutions, agencies and charities have responded to the crisis they have discovered a lack of devices, connectivity, spaces in which people might work and learn, a lack of skills and confidence and other barriers to inclusion. Nor is this a static situation as people lose work, cannot feed children and cannot access online services to seek support, let alone learning.

Rather than take a reactive approach, with universities continuing to write a separate policy for each individual 'issue' that arises in these times of profound change, more critical and ecological approaches are required. These concern both the promises and ethical challenges of AI, as it comes to take up its place across the whole range of lifelong learning, human wellbeing and education

(Eynon, Davies, Salveson, 2018). Suddenly 'the student experience' (whatever this may be) is orderable as a takeaway from many more places than universities. Learning requirements can be personalised for each individual. Therefore, to be distinctive as institutions, universities will need to offer something less instrumental, narrow and process-driven (Eynon, Davies & Salveson, 2018). This moves the focus away from a collection of student data by each institution, focused on 'measuring', towards a more individual focus, where a learner's data will follow them on their life wide journey of learning what is needed, at the time it is needed. Positionality steps forward, and the instrumental marketing of 'the student experience' as a generalised product, moves off the menu.

Universities in collaboration with cross-sector agencies can though, take the initiative on this. Not as another player in the hospitality sector which has struggled so badly through the pandemic, but as a leading authority in the production and communication of knowledge. The debate on postdigital positionality needs a chair. As Delanty argued in 2001, the university needs a new unifying purpose which is not 'dominated by either the institutional context or by a reductive understanding of knowledge as information' (Delanty, 2001: 154). Policies can no longer sit apart from each other or the wider postdigital context surrounding universities. However, 'neither 'cultural politics nor the market offer a principle of unity' (Delanty, 2001: 151). The new global emphasis on sustainability and education just might do (UNESCO, 2020d). Delanty argued that as the university has lost its status as the sole site of knowledge it has become 'more and more drawn into the communicative structure of society' (Delanty, 2001: 152). Universities are therefore able to explore a new positionality of their own in postdigital society as biodigital philosophy, technological convergence, and new knowledge ecologies begin to emerge (Peters, Jandrić & Hayes, 2021a). I will return to these possibilities in later chapters. The implication for those learning though, is that, as diverse individual citizens, they will have greater choice of routes to learn and to further personal and collective goals. As students who learn in universities and take up roles in society relating to their discipline, they are entering diverse, fluid and changing work contexts. The critical reflexivity to appreciate their positionality in this postdigital landscape is key to their empowerment, rather than their displacement.

In the second half of the chapter I will examine this alternative to the current approach, where an overly inflated and generalised experience is discussed as the main attraction on the campus 'menu'. By applying the tenets of positionality, as put forward by Torres, Olave and Lee (2019), it becomes possible to notice just how different each student's individual experience is likely to be in a postdigital society. At a time when many larger areas of life (cultural, historical, technological, biological, political and economic, for example) can be observed to be merging, converging and overlapping in our postdigital global context, what individuals encounter through their own positionality, seems to be more diverse than ever.

It is therefore necessary to counter a strong suffocating marketing rhetoric of a generic 'student experience' with a more autonomous approach where each citizen recognises the possibilities before them. There are a number of authors who have begun to refer to personal 'learning ecologies' (González-Sanmamed, Sangrà, Souto-Seijo & Estévez, 2020, Fawns, Aitken & Jones, 2020) because these offer 'self-directed' ways to update personal knowledge and capabilities at the point that this is needed. This alters more traditional models of the labours of learning and teaching. However, digital advances that have brought AI into education, with chatbots and automated functions replacing teacher activities might also be discussed as developmental of both student and teaching roles. Very often rational McPolicy sets up an oppositional relationship between those learning and those teaching when they may in fact become more closely constitutive of each other, in some cases. Considering how student identities are complex, fluid, enmeshed in power relations and contextually bound offers new possibilities for inclusivity agendas that actually connect students and teachers as individuals. This requires a shift from delivering an assumed 'mass experience' that teachers are audited on, in terms of their efficiency, towards new appreciation of diverse postdigital positionality. Though students may feel somewhat 'caged' right now, there are possibilities ahead where we no longer need to detach the cultural, technological and biological wellbeing of students or teachers from all aspects of their lives or from the wider community. What is missing currently is a convergence of HE policies to recognise these interconnections.

2   Resisting the Iron Cage of 'the Student Experience'

Over recent decades in universities, as audit culture has taken hold, students have become rational objects *of study* in university policy, rather than individual human subjects, *who study* their chosen subject disciplines from their own diverse positionalities. In UK policy and more globally, students have become defined for some time now as 'customers', particularly since an introduction of tuition fees (Dearing, 1997; Browne, 2010). Customer 'experience' gets routinely evaluated, but this reduces knowledge to information that is easily processed as data. Universities are using the processing power of computing to construct the identity of the students that they admit, in a reductive 'measurement' of access, participation and success, via audits such as the Teaching Excellence

170   CHAPTER 3

and Student Outcomes Framework (TEF) (Office for Students, 2019).Yet the implications of this datafication cannot be separated from the related onto-logical and epistemological dilemmas that accompany it (Van Dijck, 2014).

Presently, universities have restricted their enormous capacity for critically reflexive dialogue about knowledge to one limited by, and obsessed with, insti-tutional information. Furthermore, at the same time as attempting to address every imaginable issue any student might encounter by generating endless policy information, universities are adding to potential issues of bias, as they trust student data to corporate platforms. University policy cannot be said to uphold social justice if the commercial values surrounding data collection, use and any hidden design and programming processes that reinforce existing inequalities are not transparently examined. This requires a critical appraisal of the ideology behind the 'whole ecosystem of connective media' (Van Dijck, 2014) that universities have bought into.

University policy focusing on inclusive practices for students does sit apart from social media, the corporate platforms that universities have adopted, or any flawed approaches towards collecting and measuring student data. In post-digital society, interpersonal communications are mediated by platform capi-talism and big data. As part of these networks universities have expanded their data infrastructure and performance metrics and are becoming experimental sites for commercial AI systems (Williamson, 2017, 2019b, 2020b, 2020c). Dur-ing the Covid-19 pandemic new commercial edtech partnerships have acceler-ated these developments but with little time to critically examine where this shifts the power.

2.1   *Inclusivity Is More Than an Item on 'the Student Experience' Menu*

There is now a pressing need for critical dialogue that takes a different starting point on university equality, diversity and inclusion policy from the assump-tion that such principles have already been 'embedded'. It is not enough for universities to simply act like another branch of the hospitality sector and add these into 'the student experience' menu. As part of the ecosystem of communicative media (Van Dijck, 2014) in postdigital society, the university now needs a strong sense of its own positionality. This requires fundamental changes to the routine generation of isolated McPolicy.

In *The Labour of Words in Higher Education* (Hayes, 2019a), I argued that through related HE policy discourse (McPolicy), we appear to have constructed an iron cage of 'the student experience' (Hayes & Jandrić, 2018). I demonstrated through a corpus-based Critical Discourse Analysis (CDA) of policy docu-ments how this package of 'the student experience' can also appear to 'act' to achieve things, concealing also the labour of the diverse humans who work

POSTDIGITAL POSITIONALITY AS A LEARNER 171

with students in universities. My analysis showed how this linguistic positioning of students has contributed to both detaching humans from their own labour and 'a separation of the labour of teaching from the labour of learning' (Hayes, 2019a: 20). For a more detailed explanation of corpus-based CDA, see Hayes and Bartholomew (2015) and Hayes (2019a).

In placing huge emphasis on learning experiences in isolation from teaching and research activities this reconceptualising of students has not only culturally divided the university, it has led to a 'therapeutic' turn (Ecclestone & Hayes, 2019) also dubbed a 'snowflake' culture. So whilst on the one hand, many authors have critiqued the 'student-as-consumer' approach in HE policy (Molesworth, Nixon & Scullion, 2009, Bunce, Baird & Jones, 2017, Peters, Jandrić & Hayes, 2018) for treating education as a customer transaction, other authors have discussed how this has led also to a rhetoric of students as weak or defenceless (Furedi, 2016). However, if a rationalised experience is constructed on behalf of students, then universities align themselves with any other provider of consumer experiences, where the thinking has all been taken care of for students. In such a discourse, students are not necessarily conceptualised as empowered consumers either (Brooks, 2017) but are trapped instead within an 'iron cage', even before they set foot in the workplace. Students' 'vulnerability is emphasised by both government and unions' (Brooks, 2018: 745). This has its uses too because it can deflect past failures by governing agencies to address inequalities, if the spotlight remains on students as deficient. This now sits uncomfortably though, alongside scenes where (if students are thought to be vulnerable) they were encouraged onto campus, detained in their rooms, had limited social contact due to Covid-19 restrictions and were prevented from visiting parents, if homesick or in need of support. Rather than viewing Covid-19 as a hiatus, it may be useful to view it as exposing institutional policy weakness.

2.2   *Student-Centred Culture*

A rational 'student-centred' culture (Hayes & Wynyard, 2002, 2016) can sound like a positive development that is difficult for staff or students to question. Statements like 'placing students at the centre of all that we do' is a common line that is found in university policies following an increased marketisation of the sector. This has though also proved to be a far from empowering rhetoric in practice (Jarvie, 2014, Furedi, 2016, Ecclestone & Hayes, 2019) as an emphasis on pedagogies for student-centred learning (O'Neill & McMahon, 2005) has become conflated in HE policy with the problematic notion of 'the student experience' (Hayes & Jandrić, 2018). There has been a tendency in policy discourse to discuss access to HE for particular groups of people in ways that can overlook complex social phenomena and further only narrow, therapeutic agendas (Ecclestone & Hayes, 2019). For example, much has been written concerning the important aspects 'of belonging' or 'wellbeing' as a student in HE. However, these campaigns can sound as if issues are being addressed by institutions alone, rather than in a two-way flow, where students themselves are active in shaping institutional understanding too. The levels of belonging that individuals choose to opt into are also relevant when such choices may be based on many different facets of a person's identity. HE policy has a tendency to focus only on a single aspect of a person's identity, such as their gender or their race, which limits understanding concerning the fluid 'intersections of race, class, nationality, gender and sexual orientation' (Wheaton & Kezar, 2019: 65). Such fluidity suggests that aspects of our identity are processes, rather than conditions (Dixson, Trent, Ladson-Billings, Anderson & Suarez, 2020), and so subject to new dynamic understandings related to social and historical contexts and change.

Terminology in social theories about learning can come to mean different things to different people, but this can also be the basis for interesting critical pedagogical debate which reveals complexities regarding the positionality of individuals. This could concern for example the differences that teachers perceive between experiential learning, self-directed learning or other flexible forms of pedagogy (O'Neill & McMahon, 2005). Whilst the experiences of students could be very different in each of these scenarios, the use of the term 'the student experience' has taken on a much larger overall presence, beyond debates about learning in university policies. It has come to act as an expanding container for many social issues to be placed under, but rather like my airing cupboard in the hall, it has become overly full and it now needs a clear out.

2.3 The Student Experience McPolicy Discourse

A key critique levelled at this phrase is that it has come to embody the notion that students paying for their education are purchasing a package they can consume, just like any other McDonaldised service. What this McPolicy discourse closes down, due to a singular objective construction in: 'the student experience', is the opportunity in policy for students to be discussed as diverse individuals and for them to input that diversity back into policy. The student experience is a linguistic construction that firstly, has emphasised the role of a degree as a consumer 'product' purchased to secure future employment (Peters, Jandrić & Hayes, 2018), rather than an experiential learning 'process' with transformative potential that continues well beyond student life (Hayes, 2015: 130). Secondly, a narrow understanding through a student-as-consumer approach in HE policy has developed into a strong rhetoric emphasising 'the student experience' as a package deal (Hayes & Jandrić, 2018). The impression generated is that universities are delivering a broad packaged experience of consumption itself, to students (Argenton, 2015: 921). This assumption has recently swelled further still to incorporate a range of egalitarian ideas, such as fairness, justice, equality of opportunity, diversity and well-being, but it is a fallacy that these can be packaged up for delivery in this way. Exactly what experience is being delivered and based on whose values?

In a document published by The Higher Education Academy (HEA) entitled: *Managing the student experience in a shifting higher education landscape* (Temple, Callender, Grove & Kersh, 2014), it stated:

> We describe the student experience as the totality of a student's interaction with the institution.

What though, if the 'totality' of each individual student's experience is constructed through multiple, mutually constitutive factors that do not cluster within the gates (or control) of an academic institution? What if the decision to accept considerably more students into university (based on predicted grades following the backlash from algorithmic predictions) has left many new students ill-prepared for what degree studies will require from them? Add to this situation unequal access to digital equipment (when trapped in student accommodation with no chance to physically visit the computer rooms, library or laboratories on campus) and it is not hard to see how these circumstances, due to a biological threat, can mingle with other existing disadvantages.

Universities responded to support students with food parcels and financial compensation, but it is challenging to also attend to their anxieties, diverse needs and the expectations of each student. The demands already placed on personal tutors will have increased in complexity. Even without the Covid-19 pandemic complicating the social, economic, educational and technological circumstances of each student's interaction with the institution, there is still huge variation in positionality amongst students. What defines each student's interaction with the institution in postdigital society does not remain static either. The pandemic has laid bare the problems with an approach to HE policy that seeks to 'embed' everything from digital platforms to wellbeing, inclusivity and even student ambitions, within institutions:

> The purpose of this Student Experience Strategy is to deliver the student experience ambitions of Edinburgh Napier University as set out in Strategy 2020. (Napier University, 2020: 3)

174   CHAPTER 3

Statements like this help to draw attention to the issues of seeking to control everything that students now experience under university 'ambitions', as if these were internally consistent for the place of study and for each student. The diverse experiences and ambitions of students from all walks of life do not exist only within a walled university garden controlled by the staff therein:

> It is vital that every member of staff fully understands their contribution and that of their colleagues in delivering the Student Experience. (Hayes & Jandrić, 134 :2018)

Placing aside for the moment the problem that individual staff contributions to a generic idea of 'the student experience' cannot easily be separated out to be quantified and measured, the emphasis on 'delivery' by an institution has long been a problematic concept too. The diverse experiences of each student cannot be ordered from the university, delivered and rated, as if sent out by any other commercial provider, such as Amazon or Argos, with the follow-up question: *what did you think of your purchase?* (Hayes & Jandrić, 2018). As students currently confined to their rooms in lockdown have discovered though, right now it seems easier to get a free Deliveroo order through, than to access the 'package' of higher education they have paid such high fees for:

> Students can also use the Morrisons on Amazon service which includes free same-day delivery and Morrisons service on Deliveroo. (Morris, 2020b)

In these unusual times, examples of this kind help to illustrate why a rational university policy discourse of delivering 'the student experience' remains an irrational claim for institutions to make. It is a problematic buzz phrase, but one which has also had its uses: 'as a construct to which all manner of expectations can be attached (Hayes, 2019a). Indeed, the educationalisation of social issues as problems for universities to solve, seems to be a defining feature of our times (Peters, Jandrić & Hayes, 2018). The concerns themselves may be ill-defined, ranging from mental health and wellbeing to transport and support from animals on campus, but still they have powerfully re-shaped popular understandings of 'the student' and their role in HE (Hayes, 2019a). A reconceptualisation of students has been achieved in part through this therapeutic turn, which according to Apperley (2014), includes:

> Increased emphasis on the student experience, signalled in part by the rhetoric of student-centred education, but also by the forced emphasis

POSTDIGITAL POSITIONALITY AS A LEARNER

on universities as 'learning institutions' as opposed to teaching institutions. The idea that universities might be *educational* institutions involving *both* learning and teaching has increasingly been suppressed by these rhetorical strategies. (Apperley, 2014: 732)

I will return to this separation of the labour of teaching from the labour of learning in the next chapter, but as one of the casualties of marketisation, it has brought both increased academic workloads and what Furedi argues is a 'deficit' model of students, within an infantilised university (Furedi, 2016).

2.4 *A Victimisation of Students*

From a 'Disneyfication' of academic courses, and ultimately to the preservation of the elusive and burgeoning notion of 'the student experience' (Hayes, 2017: 106), it has been suggested then that such factors have actually turned students into 'victims' (Furedi, 2016: 9). This is because the 'experience' generated is based on 'a diminished view of human subjectivity, which regards individuals not as agents of change, but as potential victims of the circumstances they face' (Furedi, 2016: 9). Furedi pinpoints the issue with this discourse where 'rhetorically, it preaches the value of diversity; in practice, it refuses to tolerate a diversity of opinions' (Furedi, 2016: 9): hence the concern that as cancel culture has grown in society it seems naïve to imagine that (like any other concern) it can simply be added to the list of social issues we 'educationalise' into school and university inclusivity policy.

Furedi points to a paternalistic form of governance (Furedi, 2016) which is behind the victimisation of students. This is echoed by Bartram, who suggests that the UK Teaching Excellence Framework (TEF) has also cemented a 'consumerist machismo' via a 'fetishisation of satisfaction' (Bartram, 2020: 6). Furedi contends that therapeutic culture requires continuous intervention, whilst Apperley suggests that against this background, 'public policy – including that of education – must be redirected towards shoring up the emotional deficit of the individual' (Apperley, 2014: 734). Analysis by Brooks (2017) of how students are now constructed in contemporary English HE policy supports these concerns. Whilst students may be assumed to be 'empowered consumers' in today's commercially driven universities, their vulnerability is emphasised in policy by both government and student unions (Brooks, 2017: 1). This then feeds into broader government narratives, legitimising contemporary reforms and excusing apparent failures of previous policies (Brooks, 2017: 1, Hayes, 2019a: 35). There is considerable difference though between knowing cohorts of students well and building important connections with them as a teacher, and the victimisation culture that has trapped students in a 'cage' of

176   CHAPTER 3

weakness, vulnerability and dependence. The Covid-19 crisis has brought such
dynamics into the spotlight as well as demonstrating striking knock-on effects
across different levels of the educational sector.

2.5   *Training Key Workers of the Future*
As universities have donated equipment and laboratories to support the pandemic effort, as well as sent many of their trainee health professionals into
frontline work, there are calls to protect and sustain university programmes
which meet the need for key workers of the future. There are though many
aspects of the broad landscape being referred to as 'key work' that the pandemic has also brought to public attention.

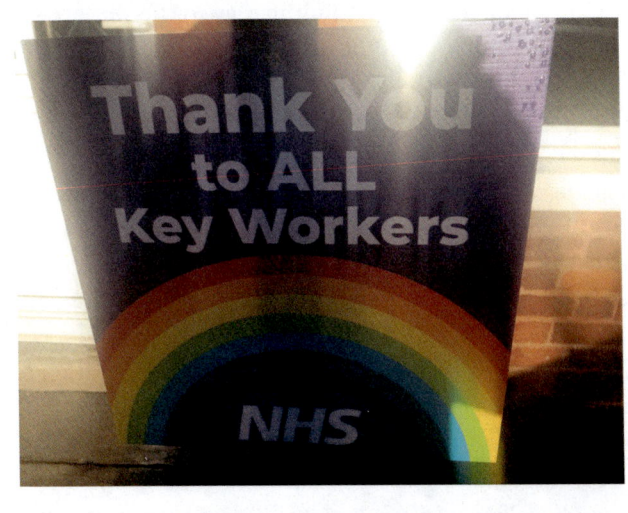

FIGURE 35
A sign with a rainbow
thanking all key workers

Whilst health and care workers immediately come to mind (Figure 35),
there is a broader spectrum of essential workers whose labour might be considered 'foundational' given that it can't be shut down (Foundational Economy
Collective, 2020). Many people working in cleaning, delivery and supermarket roles, as well as those in education, care and health services may also be
a part of the 'gig economy', on precarious or zero hour contracts, facing economic risks and potentially high levels of stress, whilst working through the
pandemic. As many graduating students enter the harsh conditions of the
gig economy and take up key roles, even temporarily, there are risks if their
treatment in university has emphasised only their weakness, vulnerability and
dependence.

Even for highly trained medical professionals, new challenges have emerged
as frontline, lifesaving healthcare environments have intermingled with
aggressive forms of cancel culture in the virtual airing cupboard. As Rachel

Clarke's 2021 book: *Breathtaking: Inside the NHS in a Time of Pandemic* attests, nurses and doctors are now facing physical and virtual forms of abuse from Covid deniers and sceptics denigrating their work and even trying to physically remove sick and dying patients from wards (Clarke, 2021). A generic policy discourse of 'the student experience' is inadequate and inaccurate as universities plan to train key workers for the future. New policies will be required that reflect the multiple changes to workplaces where students undertake placements and seek to develop their careers.

2.6   'Learning Never Stops' But My Future May Be Decided by an Algorithm

The #Learning never stops campaign (UNESCO, 2020a) provides further individual insights from around the world through the UNESCO Associated Schools Network. The quotations and comments from school students, teachers and parents describe the pressing need for personal contact between staff and students, when teachers know their student's backgrounds, strengths and weaknesses. They discuss the use of every possible form of communication when many students are without computers or laptops. Teachers say that they feel they are now working all of the time and they describe concern too for their own students' mental health. Parents add their concerns about whether their children are learning sufficiently at home and there is of course considerable anxiety over exams (UNESCO, 2020a). These audible and readable accounts from different locations mean that many aspects of what it means to learn and teach through the crisis and from home can be noticed.

Even as lockdowns are eased, accounts of what it means to run a school and seek to control social distancing take their toll on staff and students, as in this anonymous headteacher diary of the shape just one week took at the beginning of term (Guardian, 2020c). This is indicative of so many accounts and testimonies that have been shared by individuals online. The physical symbols of lockdown discussed earlier have made certain things visible, such as the chalk drawings on homes that reminded us that children were not at school and the many lists of rules that have appeared detailing various 'steps to safer working together' (Figure 36) or 'stay safe' rainbow trails (Figure 37).

Yet there are other less visible new partnerships in the lives of students seeking to complete their studies, move on to university and plan their futures in these challenging circumstances. The complex interplay between viral biology on the one hand and information science on the other, can be clearly observed in the A level algorithm example as this played out in the UK during Summer 2020. Many computer algorithms use statistical models, to good effect. For example, they are used in pharmaceutical trials, in order to test the

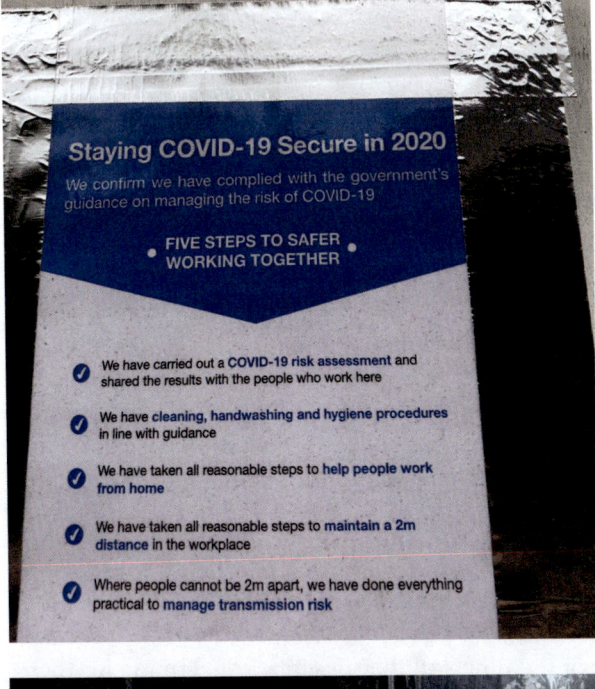

FIGURE 36
A staying Covid-19 secure sign detailing five steps to safer working together

FIGURE 37
A 'stay safe' sign as part of a Rainbow Trail

effectiveness of a new drug. Typically, the drug is tested against a control, since it is the systematic difference between the performances of the drug and the control group that must be evaluated. The statistical models, inherent in the algorithm, enable this systematic difference to be separated from the natural variation that is always present. In a very real way therefore, statistical models can save lives.

The use of such statistical algorithms can, though, be more controversial as observed in the recent move to deflate A'level, GCSE and other predicted student grades. The moderation of grades from public exams has always been part of the quality assurance process. The aim has been to ensure parity between different educational institutions and uniformity, and where possible, between year groups. The requirement for such a process became critical though when, due to a government decision, no final exams were taken in the Summer of 2020. Predicted grades, supplied by teachers, have always been a requirement, prior to exams in general. They have tended to be the basis of appeals too, for example when a student has been absent, through illness. The predicted grades for the summer of 2020 were though significantly higher than the corresponding examination grades had been in previous years. This was not unexpected and historic data was used to redress this perceived imbalance.

It is understandable though that individual students would feel aggrieved that their predicted grades had been reduced when they had not had an opportunity to sit any exam. The situation was made somewhat worse however when reductions in grade appeared to lack uniformity between various institutions. Students from lower performing institutions appeared to have been affected worse; presumably historic data suggested that the disparity between predicted grades and actual grades was more marked in some institutions than in others. There also appeared to be bias built into the algorithm and the situation soon became untenable. To put these events into another context, it could be asked: what boxer, athlete or sportsperson would accept an adverse outcome from a virtual, computer-modelled contest, when deprived of the opportunity for a real competition? How much more aggrieved would they feel if the algorithm had used their postcode to predict the outcome? Of course, such a sporting analogy is not quite the same as using historic data for deflating overly high grades in education. No one places all sportspeople under one blanket discussion of 'the sporting experience' either.

So whilst using historic data was seen by some to be an objective part of a valid quality process, once the data was in the public domain, the use of such an algorithm for assessing grades was open to ridicule, mass dispute and protests from students and teachers:

> We don't sentence people for crimes committed by someone else, so why sentence students to grades someone else got in the past? That's exactly what the Government has done with its disgraceful approach to A levels. (Payne, 2020)

Whilst the mantra of *Trust the Teachers* was adopted as an appealing slogan, it is not quite obvious as to what they should be trusted with. The inflated aggregate grades remain for this year at least, with all of the consequences this may have, both for those who have since left for university and for those who did not take that route. There are those who argue that the 'exams fiasco is just the beginning' and that it was both absurd to attempt to 'determine individual attainment by computer model' or to think that 'teacher-predicted grades are any substitute for proper examinations'. Either way, each of these 'panicked responses to the coronavirus' is likely to 'cause one injustice after another' (Slater, 2020). What can be learned though, is that 'people want individual results' and the anger of both physical and online protests attests to this. Positionality comes into play as people are mostly concerned with their own individual results and fairness of them. They do not want to be the 'result of an aggregate' (Burgess, 2020).

2.7 The Student Experience Policy Discourse Lacks Inclusivity

Whilst no educational system can claim to be entirely fair for everyone across the board, the treatment of diverse students in this rationalised manner resulted in uproar. Sabri (2011) has argued that not only does 'the student experience' rhetoric homogenise students, depriving them of agency at the same time as purporting to give them a 'voice', it is potentially also 'a means of discriminating between the value of different experiences of education' (Sabri, 2011: 657). Regulators of HE (such as the Quality Assurance Agency and Higher Education Academy, but more recently, Advance HE and the Office for Students in the UK) have helped to established this discourse, but it could also be said to be performing a line of 'work' itself: 'in sustaining and developing the market-oriented disciplining of higher education' (Sabri, 2011: 657). Sabri adds that this has come at a price, because:

> the sacralisation of 'the student experience' has in fact obscured the educational form and function of experience for an ethnically and socio-economically highly diverse body of students. (Sabri, 2011: 657)

It is in this situation that the rational and seemingly empowering mantra of 'the student experience' has become increasingly irrational. Inventing, labelling and packaging this as a 'product' and delivering it to universities for a response may have given it the appearance of a concrete existence. It has though, served to mask the individual experiences of students of the equality, diversity and inclusivity agendas, that institutions are now scrambling to deliver.

The policy statements in which 'the student experience' is frequently embedded, sound as if everyone should believe that this is how the world of universities works. Instead of treating human identity and senses as personal and diverse, the policy discourse discusses what each student encounters in terms of generic ideas on 'belonging' or 'involvement', as if these were collective, not individual, and thus experienced uniformly by all. Such problematic assumptions even suggest that 'a sense of wellbeing' is included in 'the student experience' deal that gets delivered to students. As such, academic experience has become interconnected with all other experiences, but treated as if it were any other generic adventure or leisure deal on offer at a local hotel (Hayes & Jandrić, 139:2018). It is therefore not difficult to see why the students caged in their rooms currently are calling for their money back!

2.8 *Some Students Feel Like They've Been Scammed*

The is how one student described how they felt in relation to the promises of 'the student experience' in a year when this package is proving even harder for HE to 'deliver':

> The experience we're getting simply doesn't match up to what we were promised before arriving at Uni this year. Within the months prior to term starting, we received an array of polite emails from the Uni expressing their acknowledgment of the "current situation" and how they were doing "everything in their power" to make sure we have an "amazing experience". What a load of rubbish that was. (Arundel, 2020)

Other students added that they would have deferred if they had known the realities, mentioning that they 'felt robbed' and had 'been forced into something without our consent'.

> It seems many students, like me, feel scammed by false promises of a "close to normal" experience. We've walked right into what feels like a trap: get students to Uni, tell them it's all going to be sunshine and rainbows, then tell them they can't leave their bedrooms. (Arundel, 2020)

It is clear from student accounts like this that even one face to face class a week would be welcomed under the current circumstances and that human contact is needed:

> Now, more than ever, we need to be able to contact our professors when we need them. I appreciate that online learning is stressful for staff too, but the most depressing part about it is that, although the Unis are trying to "deliver a high quality of online learning", many students are reporting their emails aren't being replied to by lecturers, leaving them left without access to the tuition they are paying for. (Arundel, 2020)

Though the pandemic could not have been predicted by universities, perhaps it will yet provide a portal through which institutions might distance themselves from the policy fallacy of 'the student experience'. When each of us is instructed: 'keep your social distance' (Figure 38) this is not one collective 'experience', but rather it plays out as an understanding that each of us has to individually navigate. For some this is likely to yield trauma, panic, emotion and fear. For others it may be more of a relief, or something to endure

Finding 'space' for debate on more ecological approaches (Bronfenbrenner, 1994, Fawns, Aitken & Jones, 2020) than 'the student experience' rhetoric is necessary, where positionality not assumed generic knowledge, is central to addressing inequities in postdigital society.

2.9 *Debating Ways to Address Inequities through Postdigital Positionality*

As an intensely 'studied' group of people, students in universities have been categorised in all sorts of ways in recent decades. Jones (2010) has questioned, 'so just what is the student experience?'. In a literature review examining various conceptual frameworks, he states:

> Paradoxically while there are many studies that consider aspects of the student experience, there are very few which attempt to define it. (Jones, 2010)

FIGURE 38
A 'keep your social distance' sign

POSTDIGITAL POSITIONALITY AS A LEARNER

Examining the literature, Jones found that seven main themes could be identified: students' expectations about university and student life, transition, peers, others: parents, culture and the media, the degree programme, extra-curricular activity, what happens post graduation: employability (Jones, 2010). Jones then examined these within Bronfenbrenner's ecological model (1994) as a potential framework in which to evaluate the student experience and understand a student journey. This approach towards understanding human development is one way to begin considering ecological approaches to understanding human development. The idea of 'micro-systems' is used to examine the relationship between the individual and their immediate environments. Micro-systems may operate in the 'meso-system', which is the location of closest proximity to the individual and the area having greatest influence on their development, or they may operate in the 'exosystem', which is where further individual micro-systems operate, but have less influence on the individual because of their lack of close proximity. Bronfenbrenner also refers to 'macrosystems' which are about the overarching pattern of systems and chronosystems which allow for the impact of time (Bronfenbrenner, 1994). Whilst this conception begins to map out some broader contexts interacting with individual learners, it is necessary to bring to such a framework the dynamic ways in which computing systems and data now alter human experience in new unpredictable ways.

Therefore, as well as examining student positionality in such a model, interactions with and between non-human actors in the messy and unpredictable postdigital context surrounding learners, needs to be considered. For example, our learning and inclusivity experiences are now 'flesh-electric' (Lewis, 2020) as discussed earlier. Torres, Olave and Lee (2019) argue that despite a robust literature on positionality, HE research often neglects engagement with people's varied, fluid, and complex positionalities. They suggest that personal positionality is constructed around three main tenets: (1) identities are complex and fluid, (2) they are enmeshed in power relations and (3) they are contextually bound. It is therefore worth considering how such an understanding could bring new alternative ways to understand inclusivity and to appreciate the diversity of students. This offers one way to move away from the restricted and swollen rhetoric of the student experience.

2.10   *Student Identities as Complex and Fluid*

Students are also citizens, members of communities online and offline. They may work or have family or caring commitments, a personal disability, may be studying in a different country to their own and writing in a language that is not their native tongue. Their perceived identities also intersect across fluid and changing contexts (Collins & Bilge, 2016). As such, students have 'multidimensional subjectivities' and complex relationships with the spaces and places they inhabit (Torres, Olave & Lee, 2019: 6). By subjectivity, it is understood that this refers to the condition of being a person. This includes the processes through which each of us become a person. Therefore, *subjectivity* is about 'how we are constituted as cultural subjects and how we experience ourselves' (Barker & Jane, 2016: 260). These subjectivities are inextricably linked with our personal values and *self-identity*, which are understood to concern 'the conceptions we hold about ourselves and our emotional identification with those self-descriptions' (Barker & Jane, 2016: 260). Closely linked to both subjectivity and self-identity is our *social identity*, which refers to 'the expectations and opinions that others have of us' (Barker & Jane, 2016: 260).

Despite the complexities described above, there has been a tendency in HE policy over recent decades to persistently objectivise student identity. Other examples beyond 'the student experience', include for example referring to an 'international student' which is another socially constructed label that may aid institutional categorisation, but also projects a monolithic and static view of the individuals concerned (Torres, Olave & Lee, 2019: 7). Taking an approach that focuses on student positionality instead enables students themselves to identify their multiple subjectivities as a dynamic negotiation. Recognising the 'nonunitary subjectivity' (Hollway, 1989) of students is not only a more accurate, context-responsive and inclusive approach it is also one that AI in education is increasingly able to appeal to, in terms of providing personalised forms of learning.

Torres, Olave and Lee (2019: 8) discuss how the positionality of a student can additionally vary through space and time, as they adopt different roles, such as that of an expert to present something at a conference, or as a doctoral candidate to receive supervisory advice. Some students are also supervisors of others in workplaces and/or parents of children. Taking a perspective of lifelong learning, positionality shifts over time, location and changes of role alongside the countless subjective variables at play in individual identities. All of this takes place in relationships with others that are powerful and not symmetrical (Sheppard, 2002). Additionally, in postdigital society positionality is altered through a messy, complex interplay of both people and things. This brings new implications for positionality, such as examples described in the previous chapter where forms of discrimination do not only take place between humans. These can travel from human design processes into systems and data and back into further social interactions between people. These are influences that need to be acknowledged in university policymaking for inclusivity, because equality, diversity and all manner of inequalities are now intimately constructed, and reconstructed, via digital interactions with computers that can keep people on the margins (Jandrić & Hayes, 2019).

2.11   Student Identities Enmeshed in Power Relations

The power relations surrounding student identities are therefore mutually constitutive, as students either accept or resist conditions that they find themselves in. A student 'simultaneously negotiates the multiple dimensions of language, various forms of capital, as well as evolving social identities' in different contexts (Torres, Olave & Lee, 2019: 2). However, when it comes to digital contexts where oppression is less obvious there are new power relations that affect inclusivity. Costanza-Chock (2018: 7) points out that closely linked to intersectionality is the concept of the 'matrix of domination' which refers to 'race, class, and gender as interlocking systems of oppression'. Describing factors such as power, oppression, resistance, privilege, penalties, benefits, and harms as 'systematically distributed' these will structure different people's lives in different ways (Costanza-Chock, 2018: 7).

Placing these observations in the context of data-driven AI systems it is argued that at the personal level, a student could experience an interface that either 'affirms or denies' their identity, through features such as 'a binary gender dropdown during account profile creation'. At the community level, AI systems design may foster 'certain kinds of communities while suppressing others, through the automated enforcement of community guidelines, rules, and speech norms, instantiated through content moderation algorithms and decision support systems'. Such rules may decide who is included in a protected category in relation to hate speech or certain content moderation guidelines. Then, at an institutional level there are further considerations as universities both adopt data driven AI systems for teaching but also train computer scientists, developers, and designers on courses in the institution (Costanza-Chock, 2018: 8). There are therefore important considerations for universities to examine drawing on intersectional theory to reflexively look at how their own stance on inclusivity might now be undermined at different levels. This could include isolated decisions being taken concerning technologies for use in learning and research and related commercial partnerships that bring a different set of marketised values to education (Williamson, 2017, 2019b, 2020a, 2020b, 2020c). Or it may concern the design and deployment of 'AI systems that shape the distribution of benefits and harms across society' (Costanza-Chock, 2018: 8).

As discussed earlier, there are many powerful influences surrounding what is being put forward by universities as an 'inclusivity' policy agenda or framework. Covid-19 highlighted the problem that large numbers of students had no laptop of their own, triggering schemes by universities to rapidly respond. However, there are the additional related challenges of wifi bandwidth in shared housing and a lack of space to work. These and other inequalities demonstrate why inclusivity agendas do not sit apart either from a political digital economy where opportunities sit alongside dangers of exclusion (Bukht & Heeks, 2017). Having access to a computer and the skills to use it imaginatively can bring about support from the wider community, even from celebrity benefactors. In one example, Russell Crowe donated nearly £3,000 to a student who could not afford to take up the place they were offered on a prestigious drama course. The student created a GoFundMe page in an effort to raise the necessary cash and caught the attention of the film star (Zahid, 2020). Not an isolated incident, when only the previous week, Taylor Swift had donated £23,000 to a different student so that she could afford to attend a UK university (Sky News, 2020). These instances are part of wider ecological streams of communication and activity in the virtual airing cupboard, but they are not accessible by all.

Assumptions made in policy are problematic when they are not cognisant of these intimate flows of knowledge passing between humans and computers in the form of bioinformational capitalism (Peters, Jandrić & McLaren, 2020) and feeding into the positionality of each student in different ways. These are not scenarios that can be educationalised, but this is a dynamic context that requires honest and inclusive critical representation in university policy, to acknowledge that student experiences are plural, unequal, and contextually bound.

2.12   *Student Identities as Contextually Bound*

Torres, Olave and Lee (2019: 22) point out that any student or scholar's 'self-understanding is mutable and context-responsive'. This means that the self-conceptions students hold and their emotional identification with these are subject to multiple influences, including those they encounter in the virtual airing cupboard. As such, students face a challenge in 'managing the presentation of who they are and who they are perceived to be' (Hult, 2013). Postdigital positionality is a powerful way to point to the problems associated with any decontextualised understanding of student subjectivities and to provide more plural accounts which fill in the gaps that are omitted in McPolicy for the student experience.

A recent BBC news story covering the decision made by student Zoe Petre from Wales to post her revision notes on Instagram provides one example of postdigital positionality, as enacted by a biomedical science student (BBC, 2020g). Zoe's choice to do this when her exams were not going well was based on her feeling that she needed new techniques to motivate herself. Zoe photographed her handwritten revision notes, uploaded these to her @ZoeStudies account on Instagram and added her own comments on her motivation to do this and what she has learnt on how best to study. The process that Zoe chose to follow illustrates her personal postdigital context, through the combination of transferring what she worked on with pen and paper, onto a digital system, adding her thoughts and emotions. Initially followed just by her own friends, her postings have now gained a worldwide audience of followers who were encouraging her to succeed at her course. Zoe describes how she wanted her notes 'to look nice so I want to look at them and learn'. Her notes have become something she wants to revisit. She adds that: 'I also really try and understand them, then condense them so it's easier for revision' and she comments that 'I find Instagramming pushes me and helps me to track my progress, as I always record my highs and lows' (BBC, 2020g). Numerous embodied and external aspects are therefore at play, as each of us live learning experiences and perceive meaning via personal positionality. Our perceptions of identity may be altered too at any number of complex intersections.

2.13   *The Changing Labours of Learning and Teaching*

Earlier in this chapter the issue of a separation between the interconnected labours of learning and teaching was raised in relation to placing students in a 'deficit' model and 'victim culture' (Furedi, 2016). During the pandemic there have been questions of 'scapegoating' too where a blame culture has attributed students as a group who haven't followed the rules or have indulged in 'wilful misbehaviour' (Reicher, 2020). The problem once more of treating students as if they were a homogenous category arises when viewpoints like this flood the virtual airing cupboard. There is scope for such ideas to be conflated too, with standardised views of generations, such as 'Millenials' or 'Generation Z' meeting with backlash from young people who simply prefer not to be called anything (Bromwich, 2018). The issue of cohesive generations, and seeking scapegoats amongst them, has also been addressed by Caitlin Fisher (2019) who argues that a form of gaslighting (or psychological manipulation) takes place around young people now on 'a societal level'. She raises the issue that terms like 'Millenials' seem to be used in relation to how university faculties should 'handle' this generation of students. She cites divisive forms of knowledge that seem to accompany this perspective, including notions that 'Millenials need participation trophies' or Millenials are 'hard to work with' or 'special snowflakes' (Fisher, 2019).

There are other authors who maintain though, that students attending university now are very different from those entering universities a few decades ago. They suggest 'attention should be paid to the characteristics of students, their expectations and needs, as an important criterion for determining the university's role and its contributions at this time' (González-Sanmamed, Sangrà, Souto-Seijo & Estévez, 2020: 86). Characteristics are though, rather different to a mass categorisation or the assumption of a mass shared 'experience'. They argue that at the same time, the role of university teachers also merits reflection across the range of demands that they are now required to meet and the implications this has for their training and professionalisation. In the light of earlier discussion about the educationalisation of so many social issues into universities as well as the overcrowding aspects, it is hard to see how expectations of high levels of quality and personalised attention can be achieved (González-Sanmamed, Sangrà, Souto-Seijo & Estévez, 2020: 86). These authors also argue that young people have grown up in a very different cultural environment to previous generations, which is reflected in their behaviours, relationships and expectations as well as their way of attending, participating and learning at university (González-Sanmamed, Sangrà, Souto-Seijo & Estévez, 2020: 86). Whilst these are factors that might be attributed to a good number of undergraduates, avoiding generalisations is important. There are also many other diverse learners of different ages and circumstances whose positions will vary too.

2.14   *Inclusivity as Personalised AI or Access and Participation*

In a postdigital landscape there are new configurations also of what a human is, or might be, that will alter our former perceptions of equality, diversity and inclusivity. This is because there are new intersections to consider between AI and perceptions of what is meant by a discourse of 'inclusive education', related teacher functions and pedagogical approaches. Breines and Gallagher (2020) undertook research to identified use cases for bots. They asked, in what educational spaces bots might be situated, and how these would supplement the teacher function, rather than replace it. They advocate a continuous engagement with the community of educators and students in order to shift away from marketised discourses and students as passive recipients of information towards more collaborative development of educational technologies. (Breines & Gallagher, 2020: 1). Given that universities 'generally rely heavily on third party commercial services for their educational technologies' there has been a problem where 'narratives of solutionism' (Morozov, 2013) have been the dominant discourse. Instead, AI could be a means to support teachers, and augment teaching roles and human intelligence (Cukurova, Kent & Luckin, 2019: 3033). This then reinforces the types of entanglements that this book is concerned with, where policies for inclusive teaching practices now need to address not only the relations between humans, but also 'the networks of humans and things through which teaching and learning are translated and enacted' (Fenwick, Edwards & Sawchuk, 2015: 6).

Knox, Wang and Gallagher (2019) examine and compare the discourses that can typically accompany AI technology which is expected: 'to disrupt and enhance educational practice' and, on the other hand, the policy discourse

POSTDIGITAL POSITIONALITY AS A LEARNER   189

that 'appeals for greater inclusion in teaching and learning'. They suggest that
in both discourses a future of 'education for all' is envisaged. However, in AI
in education (AIEd) 'the idea of an automated, and personalised, one-to-one
tutor for every learner' is put forward, whilst the broad mantra of 'inclusive
education often appears more concerned with methods of involving marginalised and excluded individuals and organising the communal dimensions of
education' (Knox, Wang & Gallagher, 2019). The distinctions between 'attempts
at collective educational work through inclusive pedagogies and the drive for
personalised learning through AIEd' are critically discussed:

> A quest for personalisation through AIEd is concluded to have 'a prob-
> lematic grounding in the myth of the one-to-one tutor and questionable
> associations with simplistic views of 'learner-centred' education. In con-
> trast, inclusive pedagogy is suggested to be more concerned with devel-
> oping a 'common ground' for educational activity, rather than developing
> a one-on-one relationship between the teacher and the student. Inclu-
> sive education is therefore portrayed as political, involving the promo-
> tion of active, collective, and democratic forms of citizen participation.
> (Knox, Wang & Gallagher, 2019)

Examining diversity via a postdigital lens holds relevance for all citizens, who
now share the commonality of being digitised and datafied, whether they
actually opt to go online or not.

2.15   *The Lives of Both Learners and Teachers Are Digitised and Datafied*
In the light of rapid digital and biodigital changes discussed so far, different
configurations to the taught disciplines are likely to follow. Furthermore,
shared global aspirations around sustainability and the bioeconomy give
promise of much interdisciplinary and cross-sector collaboration (Peters,
Jandrić & Hayes, 2021b). Changes to how teachers and students interact would
seem to be inevitable too. These developments seem likely to begin to override
the increasingly tired McPolicy argument that teachers are simply delivering
'the student experience' and need to be measured to become more efficient in
doing so. When both learners and teachers are digitised and datafied across
corporate platforms there are related ontological and epistemological considerations (Van Dijck, 2014). Critical debate is needed to redraw educational
roles and critical pedagogies when critical reason itself now requires a biodigital interpretation (Peters, Jandrić & Hayes, 2021a).

There is much scope for research to be undertaken jointly by students and
teachers to learn more about their mutually constitutive relationships with

non-humans and with each other, as blurred, but not separate narratives. At the institutional level too, new values will need to be explored with regard to decisions to supplement teacher functions and to understand the implications relating to visibility and invisibility online, transparency and aspects of hidden curricula of both HE and educational technology itself (Gallagher & Breines, 2020, Gallagher, Breines & Blaney, 2020). Teachers and learners alike are now caught up in the 'entire ecosystem of connective media' (Van Dijck, 2014) where the cultural, technological and biological wellbeing of students or teachers cannot be separated from all aspects of their lives, or from the wider community across the virtual airing cupboard. The discourse of McPolicy, that seeks to measure the perceived excellence of teaching practices as somehow separate from other parts of this ecosystem can only produce flawed results. Instead the diverse positionalities of all of those in the ecosystem need to be considered if inequalities that occur at numerous intersections are to be addressed (Equality and Human Rights Commission, 2017: 50). What is missing currently is a consensus, in this context of broader postdigital convergence, of how HE policies now need to converge too.

CHAPTER 4

Postdigital Positionality as a Teacher

1   Measuring What Exactly, and Why?

At the beginning of *The Labour of Words in Higher Education,* I asked the question, *when did the academic labour of teaching become 'best practice'?* The use of this phrase seemed to appear in policy discourse about education during the 1990s as something teachers should aspire to providing, alongside mantras where academics needed to respond to the demands of a 'knowledge-based economy' (KBE), to be ready for an 'information age' and to ensure 'competitive advantage' in the 'global marketplace' (Hayes, 2019a). The opaque notion of best practice is not confined to education and has been picked up across many professions and workplaces, but others too, have called for a different discourse, one more 'relevant' to individuals, communities and universities (Hambleton, 2020). Not unlike some biological viruses, policy discourse of this kind seems to take on a form of contagion in our language, as described by Mann (2018) and linger in the atmosphere of HE. Through complex integrations of human and digital systems, such discourse seems to be 'self-renewing' (Peters, 2012). When I critiqued the linguistic structuring of HE McPolicy I argued that multiple repetitions of statements like these are problematic when phrases (not people) enact academic activities:

> World class research and engaging teaching approaches provide an excellent learning experience.
>   Support and celebrate innovations and best practice in enhancing the student experience. (Hayes, 2019a: 85)

Not only do these statements omit any direct reference to the academic labour involved in teaching students and in student learning, they are also hard to contest. The concepts expressed sound as if they are positive ones, yet they arouse disquiet when considered next to what we each personally experience in diverse contexts as teachers. Like many educational buzz phrases, the notion of 'measuring excellence' is an approach that has taken on a viral nature in recent years in HE policy discourse. Biesta (2009) argues that:

> the rise of the measurement culture in education has had a profound impact on educational practice, from the highest levels of educational

192   CHAPTER 4

policy at national and supra-national level down to the practices of local schools and teachers. (Biesta, 2009)

There are though, irrationalities that emerge from rational forms of 'measuring excellence' when an expression of implied values in McPolicy tends to close down any further need to 'engage explicitly with values in our decisions about the direction of education' (Biesta, 2009). Teacher positionalities are altered in this situation too because the impression that we are all proceeding 'towards a pre-specified end' requires no further debate. Biesta provides an example in the emphasis placed on the idea of 'educational effectiveness':

> Effectiveness is an *instrumental* value, a value which says something about the quality of *processes* and, more specifically, about their ability to bring about certain outcomes in a secure way. But whether the outcomes themselves are desirable is an entirely different matter – a matter for which we need value-based judgements that are not informed by instrumental values but by what we might best call *ultimate* values: values about the aims and purposes of education. (Biesta, 2009)

Due to recent technological and cultural shifts, education may now have an *ultimate* value in supporting human endeavours for survival in the context of biodigital convergence and our societal response (UNESCO, 2020d). How an emphasis on sustainability (UNESCO, 2020: 65) might help to disrupt a 'means-end' consumer based approach that has persisted over decades (Hlynka & Belland, 1991: v) remains part of this debate. Through a postdigital perspective we might ask too which former educational models might be revisited, discarded or redesigned, as 'advances in the biological sciences, including psychophysiology and biometrics, neuroscience and genomics' bring 'fresh questions about the intersections of biology with society, politics and governance' (Williamson, 2019).

Then there are the value-based judgements that relate to the positionality of each individual teacher, which are complex and fluid, enmeshed in power relations and contextually bound (Torres, Olave & Lee, 2019). As such, teachers are ideally placed to raise critical questions concerning the purpose and direction of educational processes and practices amid postdigital change. However, in Pauline Palmer's exploration of the positionality and agency of teacher educators working in HE, she found that powerful neoliberal discourses required teachers to 're-position themselves'. This has had varying degrees of success and has come at a high price in terms of a 'deep sense of loss of professional agency and identity' (Palmer, 2017).

In *Pursuing Teaching Excellence in Higher Education: Towards an Inclusive Perspective*, Wood and Su (2020) argue that despite the international significance placed on the idea of 'teaching excellence' for HE worldwide, the notion is opaque and poorly defined. The importance of engaging multiple voices in discussions of what teaching excellence might entail is emphasised. There is a need to adopt different lenses and a take a plurality of stakeholder perspectives into account. Given that HE is a vital element of the public sphere, they claim that vitality is diminished when an ideologically informed discourse prevails in the absence of informed public debate and more democratic and inclusive perspectives (Wood & Su, 2020). Whilst these arguments support positionality from a human vitality perspective, there are others who would broaden these arguments further, to include more relational elements that are not all human.

For Gravett and Kinchin (2020), it is necessary to rethink the contested concept of 'teaching excellence' in HE via posthumanist theory, because this helps to shift the gaze beyond the measured individual to explore a wider context of relationality and fluidity of practice. There is a need to avoid what has become a 'sedative discourse' (Guattari, 2014: 27) that closes down debate rather than inviting criticality. Thus, extending debate to include ecological crises resulting from the expansion of capitalism brings in arguments that link education with recent global challenges and all living and technological systems. This perspective is consistent with a growing emphasis across the globe on sustainability as a much broader shared goal internationally, that is closely linked to education. At the same time as legislation and agreements amongst international partners to improve global environmental standards and to develop a circular bioeconomy based on biodigital progress (Peters, Jandrić & Hayes, 2021b), the role of education is being recast in more ecological models (Bronfenbrenner, 1994, Fawns, Aitken & Jones, 2020) and exploratory postdigital ecopedagogies (Jandrić & Ford, 2020).

Saachi, Lotti & Branduardi place education at the centre of a model for a bio-based economy, arguing that more flexible educational frameworks are needed to facilitate the new interdisciplinary combinations we will require to meet sustainability goals. They suggest that education will need to cross the boundaries of a single sector and begin to integrate tools, language and knowledge drawn from across different disciplines and sub-disciplines. The design of 'high-level education programmes' that cut across subjects such as science, innovation, economics and education are more likely 'to promote and guide society towards bio-based innovation' (Saachi, Lotti & Branduardi, 2020). In the United Nations Educational, Scientific and Cultural Organization (UNESCO) report on Education for Sustainable Development (ESD) (2020d) a roadmap is provided to support such change where the primary emphasis is placed on learning to live sustainably on the planet. The UNESCO 2030 agenda also recognises that alongside addressing the 17 Sustainable Development Goals (SDGs) intended to eradicate poverty, education can no longer afford not to engage with the implications of a new biodigital context, where: 'the tipping points will eventually change not only our lives and environments, but also our discourse on sustainability. Some 'old' problems will be resolved, but new challenges and risks will arise. ESD for the future cannot afford not to address the implications of the technological era (UNESCO, 2020d).

In this chapter, the positionality of teachers is examined firstly, in relation to the culture of measuring excellence and performativity that has been adopted and absorbed across HE in recent decades. Biesta (2009) argues that this has marginalised the question of 'purpose' in educational discussions. The question of what gets included and audited, and what becomes excluded in this discourse, is significant in relation to inclusivity policies and frameworks. This is because a narrow framing of McDonaldisation of HE (Hayes, D., 2017) has yielded a 'macho consumerist identity' (Bartram, 2020) that teaching, and teachers, are constrained by. This has redefined teacher identities within one narrow, rational purpose but has irrationally closed down other more inclusive areas of exploration that acknowledge the positionality of teachers and students in postdigital society. Whilst new lecturers spend considerable time learning and discussing powerful educational theories and models, as well as exploring their own identities as educators, much of this positionality gets erased in a model of competition and compliance. A separation of learners from the broader context and relationships that exist and develop through education are discussed. We seem to have been laying a rather narrow path for AI to be applied in education to follow a diminished 'learner centred' model of teaching in which the key dimensions of McDonaldisation appear to be alive and well. This marketised, metrics-based approach makes assumptions about what should be measured, but it also excludes many key aspects of our postdigital lives, in its own form of 'cancel culture'.

In the second half of the chapter new personal and plural starting points are explored. The pandemic has taken the majority of teaching abruptly into online contexts and also into the homes of students and teachers. With little time to prepare or reflect on this 'pivot', the question of positionality has come to the forefront as students and teachers have shared their individual narratives. Individuals relate many knock-on or compounded effects that are relevant to equality, diversity and inclusivity policy. Some have gained new skills, others merely new anxieties. The challenge of sharing inadequate workspaces and equipment has been voiced, setbacks to gender equalities as childcare, home schooling and caring responsibilities have added pressures to already busy academic lives, less travel has been welcomed by some (Figure 39), but for others less accessibility to support for disability has been raised (Jandrić & Hayes, 2020a, Jandrić & Hayes, 2020b).

FIGURE 39
An 'only travel if you need to' sign

Looking towards a post-pandemic university, more ecological approaches are being explored which could help shift rational policy discourse to something more positional. Alternatives to the current model may help to restore subjectivity, agency and identity for individuals and within teaching contexts, to look beyond the cancel culture of excellence. We need to be cognisant though that a commodification of subjectivity could also take place, via widespread digitalisation (De Vos, 2020). This could reconfigure the conditions for knowledge production and alter beyond recognition what we currently believe to be human. Whether these new scientific paths lead to emancipation or alienation could therefore depend heavily on perceptions of educational purpose and on universities continuing to 'engage explicitly with values in our decisions about the direction of education' (Biesta, 2009).

1.1 *What Gets Included and What Becomes Excluded*

Referring to recent decades, Biesta (2009) highlights a 'remarkable rise in interest in the measurement of education' and educational 'outcomes' to support the banner of 'raising standards' in teaching. Many competitive league tables and comparative studies have also accompanied this culture of measurement. These provide information on how national institutions and international education systems perform alongside each other. Biesta points out the irony in adopting this form of accountability that (in a McDonaldised fashion) 'is often limited to choice from a set menu and thus lacks a real democratic dimension' (Biesta, 2009). This leads into questions therefore on what exactly gets included and what else gets missed out in such a culture of measurement? When new teachers in universities undertake an academic practice certificate (such as a Postgraduate Certificate for HE) they become aquainted with a wealth of educational theory that crosses disciplinary boundaries. They are required to reflexively explore their identity as a teacher, to learn how to design taught courses that may help students to learn, to undertake a research project to explore their own teaching practice and to participate in reciprocal peer review processes. A new lecturer will therefore need to make value-based judgements on methods to adopt across diverse contexts and cohorts of students. Teacher positionality is therefore complex and fluid and enmeshed in the power relations and contexts encountered (Torres, Olave & Lee, 2019).

This pathway of teaching development as critical practice based on personal, value-based judgements seems to sit uncomfortably with any generalised notion of excellence or best practice. Yet policies adopted for measuring excellence, outcomes and employability prospects for students have pre-defined variables, categories and attributes that surveys seek to quantify. The accompanying policy discourse has emphasised rational, systematic forms of improvements as goals, which seems to irrationally exclude the diversity of critical methods and reflexivity that a new lecturer is required to assimilate during their academic practice certificate. This contradiction leads into the issue of whether we are simply adopting generic categories that appear easy to measure, or whether we are actually measuring what we really value (Biesta, 2009). Closely related to this dilemma is an emphasis on performativity that 'requires individual practitioners to organize themselves as a response to targets, indicators and evaluations'. This means that teachers must 'set aside personal beliefs and commitments and live an existence of calculation' (Ball, 2003: 215). Such a regulation of performance can leave teachers with little human agency to perform. It also produces opacity in organisations rather than transparency. As professionals compete to 'realise their potential', this can also marginalise less instrumental routes to knowledge in HE (Hayes, 2019a: 24). Biesta points to a further problem where performativity can build a 'culture in which means become ends in themselves so that targets and indicators of quality become mistaken for quality itself'. Furthermore, this can lead to only certain topics that seem to fit this judgement of quality being funded for research, based on 'this particular methodology in order to generate scientific knowledge' to add to the list of 'what works' (Biesta, 2009).

1.2 Adding Items to the McPolicy Menu in Order to Measure Them

As well as omitting important aspects of authenticity, positionality and reflexivity that new teachers engage with, there are other problematic assumptions linked to inclusivity when only some pre-selected items join the McPolicy menu to be measured. Whilst a startling number of general policy topics are now addressed in university strategy documents, these themes tend to sit apart from each other as if such matters affect students or staff, in isolation from each other. Repeated attempts to 'fix' societal issues (such as student engagement, employability, sustainability, digital capability, wellbeing, inclusivity and mental health) by educationalising these into university strategies, seems to result in documents that fail to address combinations of these themes. Students are likely to be experiencing further challenges that do not get a mention but that intersect across several of these areas, as any lecturer who is also a personal tutor will testify. As an example, a policy aiming to address discrimination may not necessarily refer to forms of algorithmic exclusion or cancel culture in the same policy that addresses digital capability. As more ecological approaches towards education to support sustainability emerge, the interdisciplinary collaborations anticipated need to be reflected in converged policies. Just as measuring excellence has focused on a menu of isolated variables to aid audit, ecological approaches towards teaching quality recognise the messy postdigital contexts that teachers now occupy and their unique, fluid, positionalities within these.

1.3 Educational Purpose Will Differ across Contexts

Biesta (2009) suggests though that there is a 'remarkable absence in many contemporary discussions about education of explicit attention for what is educationally desirable'. Instead the focus remains on 'educational processes and their improvement but very little about what such processes are supposed to bring about'. This may perhaps be because 'the question of educational purpose might be seen as too difficult to resolve' and also because 'ideas about the purpose(s) of education are seen as being entirely dependent upon personal – which often means: subjective – values and beliefs about which no rational discussion is possible' (Biesta, 2009). It would seem therefore that the more democratic discussions concerning educational purpose largely get left within the sessions on the Postgraduate Certificate for HE and may get little airing in the wider institutional context outside. Biesta suggests that HE has come to rely on 'a particular commonsense view of what education is for'. It is a view though, that 'often serves the interests of some groups (much) better than those of others' (Biesta, 2009). This view could take the form that 'what matters most is academic achievement in a small number of curricular domains, particularly language, science and mathematics', a view that is constructed mainly with a focus on the 'qualification function of education'. However, for some students, vocational skills may be more important than academic knowledge depending on 'the access such knowledge gives to particular positions in society' (Biesta, 2009). It is therefore not hard to see how social inequalities via education can become reproduced.

1.4   *The Rise of Learning and the Decline of Education*

The issue discussed in the previous chapter, where an increased emphasis on 'learning' has led to a decline in the concept of 'education' has impacted on how teachers are now positioned as 'facilitators' of learning and learners, rather than teachers of students (Biesta, 2009). Education in turn becomes a much larger container into which 'the provision of learning opportunities or learning experiences' has attracted an array of additional elements that now cluster under 'the student experience' which McPolicy seeks to measure in terms of 'enhancement' and 'value for money' (McRae, 2018). Teachers are then required to 'encourage, support and celebrate' fabricated concepts like 'best practice' that might be measured in terms of how much this can enhance other fabricated concepts like 'the student experience':

> Encourage, support, and celebrate innovations and best practice to enhance the student experience. (Hayes, 2019a: 19)

Such statements leave out an abundance of what might have been said concerning education, which becomes recast with a sole focus 'in terms of learning and learners' (Biesta, 2009). Biesta attributes a combination of factors to this situation, including new theories of learning, process driven roles, a huge rise in informal learning throughout people's lives, the erosion of the welfare state, and the rise of neoliberal policies in which the individual is prioritised as a learner consumer. Whilst a number of these could be empowering, the accumulative effect can be to structure some 'ways of thinking, doing and reasoning to the detriment of other ways of thinking, doing and reasoning' (Biesta, 2009).

Biesta raises the issue that firstly, a learner focus is basically an *individualistic* concept. Thus it 'stands in stark contrast to the concept of education

POSTDIGITAL POSITIONALITY AS A TEACHER   199

which always implies a relationship: someone educating someone else and the person educating thus having a certain sense of what the purpose of his or her activities is'. Secondly, 'learning is basically a *process* term. It denotes processes and activities but is open – if not empty – with regard to content and direction' (Biesta, 2009).

1.5 *Measuring Human Intelligence Based on Which Educational Theories and Values?*

The detachment of learning from education (and in turn from the associated relationships that education involves with people and pedagogy) and the treatment of learning as process-oriented makes learning ripe for an application of AI in this vein. Luckin (2020) argues that AI enables smarter ways to 'understand ourselves, the world and how we teach and learn':

> For the first time we will be able to extend, develop and measure the complexity of human intelligence – an intellect that is more sophisticated than any AI. This will revolutionise the way we think about human intelligence. (Luckin, 2020)

But, 'revolutionise the way we think about human intelligence' *from which point of view*? There are indeed many as any trainee lecturer will attest. If there were not abundant approaches for thinking about human intelligence, then an enormous wealth of educational and interdisciplinary literature and staff development roles might as well be dispensed with. Perhaps this is a consideration. As mentioned earlier, new teachers are trained to be educators through perspectives that cross disciplinary boundaries. They are required to reflexively explore their unique identities as educators as they develop techniques and design activities for diverse contexts and cohorts of students. Students come in every variety, background, age group, culture and bring their own visions and needs. If AI is to be applied in ways that might be empowering, then it is necessary to question the route through which such systems have been developed and designed and are likely to then be deployed. It is not enough to bring in AI techniques without both interrogating the commercial background and educational theory behind them, any more than we would recruit a new teacher to take responsibility for a taught programme, without checking their qualifications, inclusive practice and experience to teach.

1.6 A *'Track and Trace'* on the Background to AI in Education

Williamson and Eynon (2020) have examined some of the historical threads connected with AI in education as well as future directions. In an editorial to a recent special issue that they convened, they discuss a range of interests, ethical and social implications that can get overlooked in the 'current hyperbole' surrounding AI in education (AIEd). They include the background and links to sets of 'associated ideas about adaptive systems, pedagogic agents, personalized learning, intelligent tutors, and automated governance' (Williamson & Eynon, 2020: 224) and suggest that rather than a linear history, a convergence is taking place of many 'genealogical threads'. These include:

1. several decades of AIEd research and development in academic centres and labs
2. the growth of the commercial education technology (edtech) industry
3. the influence of global technology corporations on education
4. the emergence of data-driven policy and governance.

Their genealogical analysis approach therefore 'tracks and traces', so to speak, 'how contemporary practices and institutions emerged out of specific struggles, conflicts, alliances, and exercises of power'. This includes contingent processes, disciplinary conflicts and encounters, funding schemes, 'methodological advances and sectoral encounters between academic research and commercial imperatives' (Williamson & Eynon, 2020: 224). Tracing such links, as well as the effects of Covid-19 in accelerating these interests, is a reminder of the powerful dialectics between universities and the flow of commercial edtech interests and alliances connected through the virtual airing cupboard. If these dominant and controlling trajectories are not highlighted, then a digitalisation of human intelligence can happen very quickly, without much examination of the blueprints that lie behind it.

1.7 McAI Values Support Efficiency, Calculability, Predictability and Control in Education

In Ritzer's McDonaldisation thesis (2018) the key techniques of rationalisation described are: *efficiency, calculability, predictability and control.*

These dimensions are supported across many contemporary institutions through the ability to train computers to perform tasks without human intervention. This detachment from people has proved to be rather useful during the pandemic with renewed interest in deploying robots to undertake basic cleaning and administrative tasks and reduce risk of person to person contact with the virus, along with the incessant need for sanitiser (Figure 40). Given that 'McDonaldisation is a force for increasing global homogeneity' (Ritzer & Dean, 2019: 188) though, it is worth bearing in mind the fifth dimension of McDonaldisation: *irrationality of rationality.* In universities, when does increased homogenisation (evidenced for example through emphasis on 'best practice' and 'the student experience') move the rationality behind AIEd concerning *predictability,* as just one example, into a problematic *irrationality*?

FIGURE 40
A sign reminding people to use sanitiser

Perotta and Selwyn (2020) have examined scholarly work carried out by data scientists around the use of 'deep learning' to predict aspects of educational performance. They take into account a wealth of theory from Science and Technology Studies (STS) and report issues with 'units of analysis: flawed data, partially incomprehensible computational methods, narrow forms of educational knowledge baked into the online environments, and a reductionist discourse of data science with evident economic ramifications' (Perrotta & Selwyn, 2020: 251). They argue that, particularly when framed ethnographically, doubt is cast on AI as an objective scientific endeavour. Given the converged routes that AI has developed along, where emphasis has been placed on 'epistemic expertise in the learning sciences and educational data science that is related to, but not reducible to, commercial and economic interests' (Williamson & Eynon, 2020: 226) there are a particular set of values travelling comfortably and silently with AI into universities, and into the lives of teachers and students.

This has far reaching implications in a discussion of postdigital positionality where emphasis is placed on empowerment through deeply individual educational encounters. These cross multiple intersections that relate to the positionality of each individual teacher, which is complex and fluid, enmeshed in power relations and contextually bound (Torres, Olave & Lee, 2019). Instead

'AI techniques of 'automated knowledge discovery' such as pattern recognition and correlational analysis are based on a mechanical, inductivist epistemology that assumes all patterns are interpretable in the same standardized ways across all cultures and contexts' (Williamson & Eynon, 2020: 226).

1.8   *Automating Empowerment or Inequality*

Standardised interpretation across cultures and contexts bypasses a wealth of interdisciplinary knowledge. This includes educational techniques with disadvantaged individuals and groups across global and local contexts. For example, a raft of work by universities on education for sustainable development seems to be treated as something of a trajectory that does not feed back into core institutional education policy. In our research on *Learning through the Crisis* for the DFID EdTech Hub (Traxler, Smith, Scott & Hayes, 2020) our Delphi technique revealed repeated agreement from experts in development education and policy from across the globe that 'context is king'. The Covid-19 pandemic has provided many insights to local and global contexts of disadvantage where the challenges facing teachers and students are not so different, but what is being learned reflects the positionality of those involved (Jandrić & Hayes, 2020a, 2020b). Others emphasise a deeply relational nature of teaching and learning, where no 'complex problems can be effectively solved by one autonomous component' (Czerniewicz et al., 2020). There are therefore many potential learning practices, processes and theories within our so-called knowledge economy that fail to connect and inform our approaches towards inequalities. There are powerful postdigital dialogues though at our fingertips, but these need to also cross disciplines, sectors and locations to inform new personal and plural understandings.

This is a perspective that is also echoed through the intersectional HCI studies discussed in Chapter 2. It is important to learn how AI has been applied in a wider community context to inform how it might empower rather than exacerbate inequalities. In Virginia Eubanks' (2018) *Automating inequality: how high-tech tools profile, police, and punish the poor,* locational studies and observations provide rich insights into the flaws of algorithmic predictions. These are flaws though, that intersect with societal arrangements regarding gender, class and race, policies for welfare reform and digital deprivation. Eubanks refers to these constitutive elements creating a 'digital poorhouse' of the twenty-first century, but the effects are rapid and at a larger scale. There are much greater complexities than in the case of the physical poorhouses that existed in previous centuries, yet many struggles involve the same racial and class-based fights for social justice.

These observations make it necessary to reintroduce the very broad nature of education, from the most basic concerns about child or adult literacy right through to the most advanced scientific and philosophical reasoning and research. From literacy in language, digital skills, data, or all of these and other literacies, may now require a new hybrid concept to refer to where these integrate. The connections for example, with how 'citizen literacy' (Casey, 2020) might develop at the intersections where biology, technology, economy and politics meet are not separate from university recruitment, participation and retention or from equality, diversity and inclusion agendas. At the same time as discussing the very latest biodigital advances, there are questions to consider relating as to how literacy is now enacted by citizens. Universities now need to address these complexities in a more organic approach towards policy, if they hope to widen participation. They need to engage with deeply interconnected questions if institutions hope to broaden opportunities for diverse learners. Such concerns cannot be separated from new techniques that fall under 'precision education' (Williamson, 2019), where interdisciplinary educational science is focused on 'the quantification of students' affects, bodies and brains'. Wealthy investors and philanthropic donors are involved alongside commercial entities, university researchers and scientists:

> Set in the context of intensive scientific advances in the biological sciences, including psychophysiology and biometrics, neuroscience and genomics, precision education raises fresh questions about the intersections of biology with society, politics and governance. (Williamson, 2019)

Education has always needed a spread of provision and techniques to reach society's most disadvantaged. It is currently hard to visualise whether all citizens can, will or even should be, absorbed into such advances (Peters, Jandrić & Hayes, 2021c). In *Brain Culture: Shaping Policy through Neuroscience*, Jessica Pykett (2015) argues:

> Learning can never be understood simply as a brain process. Rather, there are high political stakes in neuroscientific explanations of the learning process in terms of delimiting learning norms and dealing with learning differences in real places. Education is more than the aggregate sum of people learning. The shaping of conduct, behaviour and educational outcomes is a social and cultural endeavour essential to the governing of citizens in specific contexts. The brain of the learning person is not just an algorithm to be optimised.

Therefore, a focus on 'learners' alone cuts off the flow of contextual knowledge that teachers and students from all manner of locations bring to this debate. Projects like *Republic of Learning* (Garnett, 2019) encourage self-determined places of learning. A strong emphasis is on positionality means that individuals represent their learning however they wish. This is different though to a trend towards 'personalised learning' that only sounds empowering in its application of AI to connect with the individual positionality of students. This is critiqued for encouraging rational, simplistic views of 'learner-centred' education (Knox, Wang & Gallagher, 2019) and individualistic discourse that overemphasises market-inspired logics and the interests of technology companies through metrics, automation and the pervasive collection of data (Perrotta & Selwyn, 2020). In contesting these issues, there is also the need to put forward alternative, more empowering discourses for AIEd:

> In this sense, AI in education needs to be talked about more often in controversial and circumspect terms, rather than accepted as a computational fait accompli. (Perrotta & Selwyn, 2020: 267)

It is therefore necessary to continue a debate about teaching with technology that has been ongoing and reshaping for decades concerning the 'technological means-end model' (Hlynka & Belland, 1991: v) that McPolicy endorses, and what alternatives might now be open to us.

2   Finding New, Personal and Plural Starting Points from Which to Teach

The starting point that McPolicy has bestowed on each of us thus needs to be re-evaluated. This is because it is 'a politically imposed discourse, which is to say that it constitutes the hegemonic discourse of western nation states' (Olssen & Peters, 2005: 314) thus diverting us from other potentially richer dialogues emerging from different nations and in a postdigital context. In seeking to measure excellence and improve outcomes in HE, a set of rational starting points have been introduced. These share similarities with dimensions of McDonaldisation, where humans have been 'valued' in a particular (rather functional, but also increasingly disposable) manner as observed in the running of fast food outlets (Ritzer, 1993). They have also been positioned in a particularly disempowering manner, in relation to the emphasis on technology for enhancing learning in McPolicy that omits human labour and values (Hayes, 2019a).

Penny Welch (2020) argues that:

> The subordination of human values to market values within the higher education system today detracts enormously from its success in extending opportunities to students, providing jobs for staff and contributing to local economies. Any claims made for excellence are hollow when the achievements of institutions come at the expense of the wellbeing of students and staff. Academic analysis, collective campaigns and individual actions that promote human values have never been more necessary.

Taking a pause to consider how we might voice alternative, exciting and empowering perspectives that are drawn from different, more personal and plural starting points, is the essence of what this book is about.

2.1   *Postdigital Perspectives on the McPolicy of Measuring Excellence*

In a recent special issue in *Postdigital Science and Education* journal a range of different views are taken to critique the 'measuring of excellence' in HE, taking a postdigital perspective (Hayes, 2020).

FIGURE 41
University iconography where a window is inscribed with the word 'EXCELLENCE'

The measuring of excellence has become a familiar but disputed notion in universities, despite the etching of such words into windows (Figure 41).

Dennis Hayes argues that unquestioning compliance with this concept ignores a responsibility that academics have 'to refuse to be told what to think', as such, we each have a duty towards academic freedom that overrides any 'rationality of governance' (Hayes, D., 2019). Over decades of measuring efficiency via an 'audit culture' (Shore & Wright, 1999) this has emphasised certain teaching outcomes at the expense of others. Teaching staff have been required to acquire higher levels of recognition for their 'excellence' by mapping themselves to national frameworks of recognition. However, research undertaken by Warnes (2020) found that there was little impact on teaching quality itself from the award of higher fellowships. Instead recipients did not change practice, perceiving that they were 'already excellent', their managers showed little interest and their students were mainly unaware of their receipt of excellent teaching awards (Warnes, 2020). As well as the problems of measuring teaching excellence, applying measurement to research has brought one 'particular concept of research excellence into being' (Jandrić, 2020) at the expense of others. As a result, universities have tended to segregate their policies related to innovative digital and scientific research from their policies aimed at inclusive practices in teaching. Not only are important dialectical relationships between the practices of research and teaching at risk in this rational approach, irrationalities are surfacing in this separation across policy too.

As Covid-19 has illuminated human dependencies on digital platforms for teaching and research it has also revealed the problems of trying to control diversity and inclusion within the boundaries of a university that no longer exists. Universities have been forming public/private partnerships across recent decades that have taken advantage of the 'pervasive and ubiquitous connectivity and mobility' afforded by the virtual airing cupboard. This has, at the same time, been 'profoundly transforming the production, ownership, distribution and nature of learning and knowing and problematising the role and status of universities and lecturers' (Traxler, 2020). There are new data flows between the digital infrastructure of universities and the commercial platforms and companies they have built alliances with. Extracted data is used for aggregation, analysis, and monetisation (Komljenovic, 2018, 2020). Therefore, universities are no longer environments set apart from the outside world selecting who or what they will or will not engage with. The focus has shifted towards the importance now of 'the inclusion of the higher education system into the world outside' (Traxler, 2020). Traxler discusses factors that are 'threatening to overturn a world of steady change and stable argument' (Traxler, 2020) that our HE policies have for so long been based on. As such, 'our capacity to understand, let alone measure, these and their relationship to equity and education will be poorly understood for years to come' (Traxler, 2020).

2.2 Regional Positionalities and Place-Based Debate
Whilst universities are often discussed as an HE sector, this can detract from the considerable diversity that exists between institutions, their activities, priorities, focus and surroundings. These institutional positionalities are important

POSTDIGITAL POSITIONALITY AS A TEACHER 207

to remember in a context where homogeneity can silence regional voices and diverse contributions to this debate. As such:

> territorially agnostic discourse about universities, downplays institutional history and purpose, risks concealing innovative practices, and fails to tackle entrenched inequalities. (Hayes, Jopling, Hayes, D, Westwood, Tuckett & Barnett, 2020)

In raising this challenge, there is a value and role for live, place-based debate in HE institutions to highlight distributional inequities concerning funding, raise local voices from the community and connect these with national policy. Even though such debate has had to take place virtually during the Covid-19 pandemic, such events provide opportunities to voice 'the essential part that regional universities play in connecting global technological and biological change, with local social projects, citizens and industry' (Hayes et al., 2020). They open space too, for recognition through postdigital perspectives that Covid-19 does not sit apart from other political economic challenges for teachers, students, researchers and policy makers in HE and beyond. Whilst HE policies may address many topics separately in live debate they are discussed simultaneously. These take on a more organic and transparent nature during live debate, raising the regional academic voices that are all too often silenced by the data-driven measures of excellence that currently dominate policy.

2.3   *A More Ecological Model*

The measurement of excellence model of the university will always encounter issues where activities (such as valuable live debate) are not easily quantified. The emphasis placed on evaluating simplistic notions of processes and isolated variables simply leaves universities constrained in their operations, and also vulnerable. Barnett (2017) argues that in universities we are currently failing to see the ecological nature of our activities, that the ecological university is upon us, ahead of us, and here even now:

> But we do not see it, being blind to its presence. Its manifestations are unrecognised, so blinkered are we by the dominant ideologies of our age, in much of what matters in higher education is that which generates income and secures markets, positioning in world rankings and student satisfaction. (Barnett, 2017)

Barnett proceeds to point out that 'ecology' hints at the character of the situation and an interconnectedness, where the university is 'increasingly interconnected with so many facets of the world, human and non-human'. He argues that the university is neither in crisis nor in ruins but it is instead 'falling woefully short of its responsibilities *and* its possibilities in the world' (Barnett, 2017). There is a longer history to such calls for ecological approaches in academia, including the 'three spheres of ecology' (environmental, social and mental) discussed by Guattari (2000) and prior to that the 'ecology of mind' proposed by Gregory Bateson (Bateson, 1972, Stratford, 2015).

In *The Eco-university in the Green Age,* Michael Peters (2016) traces a 'conceptual ancestry' for the term 'eco' pointing to its root in both ecology and economics (Peters, 2016: 60). He describes the eco in ecology in terms of its 'relationship of living organisms to their environment' and the eco in economics as the management or stewardship of this. There are relations across these ideas that deeply connect with how the contemporary university might shift in focus. Our currently largely managerial focus is on the eco in economy, where our political economy of neoliberalism, processes of McDonaldisation and discourse of McPolicy dictate the path of education. If a more balanced approach where the environment, place and context surrounding each of us (in terms of positionality) becomes a reality, then there is a possibility for radically altering the discourse. Peters argues that the debate on whether the household, estate or environment around us is a discipline or a branch of knowledge has a long history but by the end of the eighteenth century what we refer to as 'political economy had severed its ancient links' (Peters, 2016: 62). Peters describes a 'conceptual and epistemological tug-of-war' between 'science on one side, with a mainstream, "no-limits-to-growth" economics of development' or modernisation and 'a Romanticist anti-modernism' which 'by contrast, attempts to hold onto organicist metaphors, resists the instrumental rationality that characterises the perceived positivism of the sciences, and courts "deep ecology" principles, "local knowledge" and the naturalism of other cultures' (Peters, 2016: 66).

2.4 Changing Curriculum and Policy to Reflect a Sustainable Global Digital University Ecosystem

So here we have it, in terms of a much longer background to the 'measuring' that we seem to have become obsessed with right now in universities and the marginalisation of context and positionality. There is, as Peters puts it, a longstanding opposition:

> the whole intersecting matrix of grand narratives of modernism and its oppositional anti-modernist counter-narratives – which, incidentally is still very much part of the on-going "culture wars" of the early twenty-first

POSTDIGITAL POSITIONALITY AS A TEACHER 209

century, is fundamental to understanding how we might break free of this controlling dualism, and thus move beyond modernity. (Peters, 2016: 67)

It is necessary to understand a new interdisciplinary and integrative science in order to address sustainability. This new integration requires changes to the curriculum, to education of students and new postdigital ecopedagogies that help us navigate 'genealogies, contradictions and possible futures' (Jandrić & Ford, 2020). It brings new points to consider in the design of postdigital learning and teaching (Matthews, 2019) and in the evaluation of teaching quality in more ecological and less rational, datafied ways (Fawns, Aitken & Jones, 2020). Peters argues that a fundamental starting point:

> is signified in the "eco" root meaning shared by ecology and economy. It provides the basis for various conceptions of the university and higher education in general in its contribution to knowledge economies and ecologies within the concept of the emerging global digital university ecosystem. It includes not only the advent of social media, knowledge sharing and collaboration, but also the development of "big" publishing systems, the emergence of "big data", open access and other innovations in the field of academic publishing. The dual cross-over purpose is the question of a going beyond a productionist metaphysics that dominates the industrial age, to a new ethos and new possibilities for exploring the post-industrial green or sustainable economy. (Peters, 2012)

These are questions that we have turned to in a collection of articles (Peters, Jandrić & Hayes, 2021a, 2021b, 2021c) that also inform a larger forthcoming project in the edited book: *Bioinformational Philosophy and Postdigital Knowledge Ecologies*. Singapore: Springer. This compilation will explore how the new ecological possibilities of the bioeconomy offer alternative postdigital knowledge ecologies to the rational means-end, consumer dominated capitalism that has underpinned education for too long. There is now an urgency for the university to respond and to take up a key role in advancing understanding on these matters in the public realm. If HE fails to do this it will otherwise remain negatively positioned (Barnett, 2017). Reflecting on the arguments put forward by Delanty (2001: 158) earlier in this book, the university has a societal responsibility for connecting technology to citizenship, 'the solution resides in linking the challenge of technology with cultural discourses'. If the positionality of the university shifts in this way, then the McPolicy discourse may become less of a focus than these key intersubjective exchanges concerning the widespread digitalisation of humanity.

2.5 Developing an Inclusive, Shared Language about Education, Teachers and Students

In their model to support a sustainable, bio-based economy (and its different focus to a KBE), Saachi, Lotti and Branduardi (2020) refer to 'education', not 'learning'. It is education that will help to facilitate important interdisciplinary combinations, to cross boundaries and integrate tools, language and knowledge from many different disciplines and sub-disciplines (Saachi, Lotti & Branduardi, 2020). In their vision, innovation requires a move beyond single sector competences, where a novel and flexible educational framework can help create a shared language. They recognise that to transition to a bio-based economy entails the support of the social sciences and also a personal consciousness that can guide desirable technological transitions (Saachi, Lotti & Branduardi, 2020). There appears to be a much stronger focus on teachers in this educational approach, but with space for broad and inclusive collaboration across teachers, other teachers and students. Given the emphasis on developing a shared language, it is hard to imagine the McPolicy rhetoric in use here. McPolicy is based on a flawed model that cannot support the above sustainable, ecological model now required.

CHAPTER 5

Postdigital Positionality as a Researcher

1 The McPolicy of Research Excellence

When I chose to place the concept of positionality next to the word postdigital for the title of this book, I smiled at the possibility that I could simply be creating a form of buzz phrase myself, not unlike those that sit within the McPolicy discourse that I have critiqued over a number of years now. I thought that I will need to be reflexive about that possibility, to explain myself and my reasoning in placing these two words together. Policy aimed at research in HE is not without its buzz phrases, such as 'world class research', or the huge emphasis placed on 'research excellence' and the elusive, related concept of 'impact'. Both research and teaching policies and practices sit within what has broadly been discussed as a marketisation of HE or the neoliberal university with features that support 'corporate competitiveness' in the 'global knowledge-based economy' (Slaughter & Rhoades, 2000). Authors putting forward alternatives to neoliberalism, such as a 'democratic educator' model as opposed to an 'industrial trainer' or 'old humanism' one, tend to focus on what people might do, in terms of reorganisation of values that would further education as an entitlement (Rustin, 2016). Less emphasis has been placed though on how research and scientific progress might contribute to such a restructuring, because many of the popular arguments retain a focus at the level of a critique of neoliberal HE policy. We may soon be entering rather new territory though, as this chapter will discuss.

In *The Labour of Words in Higher Education,* I examined how particular linguistic patterns could be noticed around certain buzz phrases in HE policy discourse. I undertook a corpus-based Critical Discourse Analysis (CDA) of many strategy texts written about isolated ideas such as 'employability' and 'student engagement' and I explained the research design, methods, terminology, data collected, ethical implications, findings and conclusions drawn from my analysis. These are all recognised stages in any research project that is expected to meet a certain standard of quality and coherence. I also provided a reflexive account of my positionality, which is generally expected of researchers in social scientific, humanities and interdisciplinary research in particular. Positionality is closely related to power and values and to how a researcher might reflexively account for their own personal role and positioning as they conduct a research study. It occurred to me that positionality has a potentially wider role to play

© KONINKLIJKE BRILL NV, LEIDEN, 2021 | DOI: 10.1163/9789004466029_007

though, than simply its adoption as a process through which I explain how my values (e.g. as a female of a certain age from a particular background) may have influenced a research study I undertook, or restricted what participants might be prepared to tell me.

This broader vision of positionality is closely related to the notions of both intersectionality and reflexivity and where these concepts may meet in any aspect of our lives in postdigital society. It is intended to contribute to the broad debate on inclusivity and related rational policies in universities, which I argue to be inadequate, due to what these (rather irrationally) exclude. Inclusivity policies in HE generally adopt the rational McPolicy approach where perceived student success might be measured in terms of access, participation and retention and associations between characteristics of students in relation to certain outcomes (Office for Students, 2018, 2019, 2018–2022). An increased focus on equality, diversity and inclusivity in universities has become closely interrelated with the dominant policy discourse of 'the student experience' and 'learner centred' approaches. This has led to universal claims about categories where outcomes might be easily measured, but less attention has been given to more situated, individual accounts of positionality. Furthermore, very little attention has been paid within HE inclusivity policies to the inequities that might be addressed or exacerbated by a broad digitalisation of life and scientific research, including the role of algorithmic activities across opaque, data-driven systems.

As such, I propose that further debate on how we might understand and apply positionality theory in this new postdigital context is now needed. This is firstly, because whatever stance we adopt towards our own research, learning and knowledge, it is now mediated through complex sociotechnical as well as sociocultural interactions. This makes problematising positionality more challenging and this needs to be stated explicitly by those undertaking research. As Cousin has observed, a form of 'positional piety' can sometimes be adopted by researchers who claim moral authority through their affinity with what is being researched (Cousin, 2010: 9). However, there are now new digital filters of many kinds through which what, or whom, we are researching is now mediated. Just as new understandings have emerged about language as 'value laden' (Cousin, 2010: 9), the postdigital context surrounding researchers and those who are being researched cannot be ignored.

Positionality, along with reflexivity became part of methodological conversations in research because these concepts and practices bring insights to situated knowledges. Situating personal experiences within the perspectives of those that they concern, stems from feminist theory (Harding, 1993). Situated knowledges 'disrupt the authority of research and any claims of universal knowledge' helping to legitimate the perspectives of diverse individuals (Ulmer, 2017). Such accounts provide powerful alternatives to universal rhetoric like 'the student experience' or 'the international student' because the rich narratives of individuals attest to a fluidity of identity and personal experiences 'among very different and power-differentiated communities' (Haraway, 1988: 580). There is though, something of a dilemma in following through my argument, that if positionality is to help inform inclusivity policy it needs to take into account the activities of non-human as well as human beings. Taking such a 'posthuman' approach towards positionality 'decentres' the role of humans, when the situated knowledges argument stemming from feminist theory was intended to 'centre' those whose perspectives risked being marginalised (Ulmer, 2017: 836). Yet in our postdigital society, we cannot be inclusive in inclusivity policy, unless we ensure that all material activities of human and nonhuman bodies are retained in any frameworks that we generate.

Ulmer (2017: 832) argues that 'the posthuman turn has radically shifted what is possible in research methodology' via a 'renewed attention to materiality, vitalism, ecologies, flora, fauna, climate, elements, things, and interconnections'. This has implications across all current and newly emerging academic fields in relation to 'who and what has the capacity to know' and it alters perspectives on what positionality includes:

> If humans are not the only possible subjects or objects of study in research, then a wealth of different possibilities emerge. This is why fields such as education, cultural geography, ecofeminism, and philosophy are contending with what it means to do research in an epoch in which humans are a geological force with planetary impact. Critical approaches to inquiry are no exception. (Ulmer, 2017: 832)

My reasoning in writing a book entitled postdigital positionality was not only to capture this wider context of research, but also to demonstrate why positionality has relevance in all of our lives in postdigital society. I could have discussed 'posthuman positionality' alone, but it is the broader postdigital and messy nature of everyone's lives that I have sought to apply positionality to, as it provides a wider overview through which to invite all into this debate.

In this chapter I will firstly, examine some background to how the McPolicy discourse has contributed to bringing about a strong divide between different (but connected) academic activities conducted in universities. A neoliberal form of discourse, as opposed to a classical liberal discourse has altered the positionality of academics as a new liberalism based on the logic and rules of market competition has been applied to the public sector. This has led to a 'displacement of public good models of governance, and their replacement with individualised incentives and performance targets, heralding new and more stringent conceptions of accountability and monitoring across the higher education sector' (Olssen, 2016: 129). Olssen argues that 'impact assessment' in particular, 'represents a new, more sinister phase of neoliberal control'. This is a model of accountability that sits at odds with the 'idea of the public good' and also with new cutting-edge scientific research in support of sustainable futures (Peters, Jandrić & Hayes, 2021a, 2021b, 2021c). Therefore I raise a question that is central to the focus of this book: *if we are intent on working towards a set of established inclusive practices in universities, where inequities are addressed, why is it that our HE policies seem intent on excluding so many important aspects of society that now impact on inclusivity for individuals?*

In the second half of the chapter, the 'industrialised' nature of science and a global division of labour with its accompanying inequalities (Jandrić & Hayes, 2019) is initially considered. There is the problem of just what vast quantities of scientific data and writing have been now been generated at speed with implications for quality, that have emerged as a by product from the intense focus on impact. There has also been a blurring of lines across what might be thought of as information or knowledge. This has been particularly apparent between politics, journalism and science during the Covid-19 crisis (Rose, 2020). The intense pressure to draw on results from science (which take time to generate in terms of reliability) for policymaking has contributed too. A convergence of relationships across scientific disciplines arise now from mutual interactions between information, biology, politics and the economy. These changes are unfolding before the eyes of a global audience in the virtual airing cupboard and could be profoundly disruptive to who we actually are as humans. Inviting in non-humans as participants is no longer an option, they are a constitutive part of what will become of us.

It is therefore necessary to debate how such scientific convergence might now be reflected in more holistic and organic approaches to critical inquiry and HE policy. In a postdigital society all manner of reconfigurations between technologies and humans are imaginable and indeed probable. In this broad postdigital world view, new possibilities from digitalisation, bioinformation and biodigitalism go way beyond the 'means-end' McPolicy discourse that has developed over decades (Peters, Jandrić & Hayes, 2021c). Sustainability has taken centre stage supported by cutting edge research, leaving the university with a new, broad educational purpose to step up to. HE now needs new merged and inclusive policies that reflect the postdigital positionality of the university itself, which is the focus of Chapter 6.

POSTDIGITAL POSITIONALITY AS A RESEARCHER   215

1.1   *Positionality as Neoliberal or Classical Liberal Discourse*

Neoliberalism has been discussed by Olssen (2016) as 'an application of the logic and rules of market competition to the public sector'. It is helpful though to consider the differences between neoliberal and classical liberal discourse, because it provides broader insight into the structuring of HE policy during the last three decades:

> Classical liberalism represents a negative conception of state power in that the individual was taken as an object to be freed from the interventions of the state, neoliberalism has come to represent a positive conception of the state's role in creating the appropriate market by providing the conditions, laws and institutions necessary for its operation. Whereas in classical liberalism the individual is characterised as having an autonomous human nature and can practice freedom, in neoliberalism the state seeks to create an individual that is an enterprising and competitive entrepreneur. (Olssen, 2016: 130)

Therefore, with regard to the positionality of an individual subject, a shift can be noticed where self-reliance and autonomy in classical liberalism are altered in neoliberal forms of welfare. Instead a perception of self-interested individuals who might slack in their duties in some way results in reliance by the state on monitoring, surveillance, performance appraisal and accountability. With regard to accountability, Olssen points out some of the neoliberal strategies that include:

- contracting out services to the private sector
- increasing competition between units within the public sector
- placing all potentially conflicting responsibilities into separate institutions
- separating the commercial and non-commercial functions of the state
- separating advisory, regulatory and delivery functions into different agencies
- introducing an assortment of accountability and monitoring techniques
- strategies to overcome sources of inequity, inefficiency, corruption
- ensuring international competitiveness, efficiency and excellence

On this basis, 'public-sector reforms relating to health, security or education have sought to restructure the basis of accountability through notions tied to individually attached incentives and targets, and through monitoring and assessment through audits' (Olssen, 2016: 133). Soon after the election of the Margaret Thatcher led Conservative government in the UK in 1979, the first

216　　　　　　　　　　　　　　　　　　　　　　　　　　　　　　　　　　CHAPTER 5

major external measurement mechanism introduced in universities was to assess accountability in research.

1.2　　*The Research Assessment Exercise and Research Excellence Framework*

In the UK, the Thatcher years (1979–1990) sought to restore wealth through a conviction that a free enterprise economy is the only secure basis for individual freedom. Of course, the question could be raised once more: *individual freedom from exactly whose positionality?* Along with many changes in the mode of regulation of public and private sectors there were changes to the structure of policy discourse (Fairclough, 1989: 177, Hayes, 2019a: 66). A shaping of new professional subjectivities led to 'self-appraising individuals' who were urged to continually notice where they might improve their performativity (Ball, 1997: 263). Such ideas were later developed further under Tony Blair, as the New Labour government took up office in the late 1990s.

The Research Assessment Exercise (RAE) was first implemented in 1986, but then again in 1989, 1992, 1996, 2001 and 2008. The RAE was intended to 'survey the quantity and scope of research in order to provide data for the distribution of funding through the Funding Councils' (Olssen, 2016: 134). Disciplinary research structured under certain Units of Assessment (UoAs) was peer-reviewed by panels comprised of experts from across the disciplinary areas. The RAE has since been replaced with a Research Excellence Framework (REF, 2014, 2021) which is similar, but the change in language to stress 'excellence' has been accompanied by a move beyond demonstrating productivity and quality of research alone. Olssen refers to a 'new concern to assess and authorise the relevance of research being undertaken in terms of the contribution and significance for the wider society' (Olssen, 2016: 137). The set of criteria used by the assessment panels includes the categories of originality, significance and rigour. In later RAEs work was also codified in terms of 'quality', 'excellence', 'international status' and 'robustness' (Olssen, 2016: 134).

However, the pattern set by RAE and REF for certain academics to be 'returnable' based on items of research published over the period preceding each assessment exercise has also led to a divide between and amongst academic roles in universities. RAE and later REF gave rise to criticism given that 'subjectivity can change depending on who is making the judgement' and 'who gets to read the actual individual pieces and make recommendations' can 'heavily influence the outcome' (Finsden, 2008, 65). Over the years, dissatisfaction amongst academics with these research excellence audits has been apparent in the comments on issues like internal departmental politics that favour some paradigms or forms of research over others. There have been protests at the

POSTDIGITAL POSITIONALITY AS A RESEARCHER   217

narrowly defined norms for constructing models of academic research success
and the lack of support for more varied research approaches and undertakings.
Issues regarding routes for maximising publications citations and metrics,
stress, anxiety and emotional costs have also been well documented, along
with concerns about the competitive nature and complexity in this form of
compliance (Olssen, 2016: 135, Barnett, 2000).

1.3 Separation and Distortion If Positionality Is Not Reflected in Research

It could be argued too that these frameworks for the measuring of either
research or teaching excellence not only separate and segregate university staff
from each other, they can also have distorting effects on what is 'reported'. In
the case of REF, Olssen (2016: 137) discusses 'deep structural fissures at the core
of the impact system – concerning what is impact, as well as how to assess it'.
Each item of research has its own positionality and context as well as the positionality of the researchers and participants, but an 'epistemic difficulty' arises
in assessing impact (Collini, 2009). Collini provides examples concerning the
work of historians and how long term the effects might be in terms of any long-
term changes in social practices. Olssen adds to this the concerns that:

> The assessments of impact are, we could say, inextricably 'entangled'
> with the privileged positions of the REF panel who establish them. (Ols-
> sen, 2016: 138)

Olssen argues further that the impact agenda constitutes a new 'structural
selectivity', or 'lever', contributing to the major transformation of academia,
extending the neoliberal project from accountability for how academics have
met their responsibilities to control over the content of research itself (Olssen,
2016: 139). It is the basis on which research impact is considered in terms of
'uptake' by external parties in industry or policy that Olssen suggests

> Constitutes a new definition of research and of what is allowed, and per-
> haps more importantly not allowed, which is dangerously open to inter-
> pretation by the hegemony of dominant and powerful groups. (Olssen,
> 2016: 139)

These arguments need to be connected with others where an erosion of individual autonomy is taking place across many areas of the university and is as
a result altering the positionality of universities themselves as independent
agencies within wider political economy.

218   CHAPTER 5

1.4   *The Challenges That Have Arisen Surrounding Education Research*
Hammersley (2002) has addressed some of the complexities that have also
arisen in relation to the measurement, and practical application of, educational research. In a neoliberal model of monitoring, surveillance, appraisal
and accountability, there are conflicting expectations where research into education is concerned. Arguments that education research has failed to prop-
erly serve policymaking and practice, tend to lay blame at the door of either
researchers themselves, or with policymakers and practitioners (Hammersley,
2002: 59). It is important to look also though, at expectations that have arisen
for educational research to serve a form of managerialism, rather than to be
channelled into the development of teaching. As such there has been an expec-
tancy that education research will support the project of transforming the education system into a more 'transparent' public management organisation.

The discourse that arises in policy from a conceptualising of a direct relationship between education research and an application to practice resembles
an 'engineering model and the metaphors of application, implementation, and
dissemination associated with it' (Hammersley, 2002: 77). Such structures can
be noticed in McPolicy, particularly in relation to the assumption that educational technology research will feed directly into an enhancement of learning
(Hayes, 2019a) but then:

> Any failure in this respect is taken to indicate a defect in the way in which
> one or other activity is being performed. (Hammersley, 2002: 77)

This is a very different model from the role that education research might
potentially play if placed at the centre of global plans for sustainable development, as put forward in *Education for Sustainable Development: a roadmap*
(UNESCO, 2020). A new interdisciplinary and integrative science that is able to
address sustainability though needs a more flexible dialogue between research,
education and society 'within the concept of the emerging global digital university ecosystem' (Peters, 2012).

Scientific progress has presented us with new opportunities and challenges
in the digitalisation of biology and the biologisation of digital processes, reflecting the need for a different kind of political economy. The emphasis on production that has dominated the industrial age has seen capitalism 'surpass both its
material boundaries and the need for concrete people' (De Vos, 2020). In *The
digitalisation of (inter) subjectivity: a psy-critique of the digital death drive,* De
Vos suggests that when faced with events that have potential to change both
the world and ourselves, we are forced to pose the *what will become of us?* question. Pointing out that humans always have the capacity to imagine themselves

as something different, De Vos asks: 'does this not signal that one never simply coincides with oneself, that one is always already other to oneself? (De Vos, 2020). Such then is our potentially reflexive postdigital positionality as we begin to explore the post-industrial green or sustainable economy (Peters, 2012) through bioeconomy. It is now necessary to imagine more empowering and inclusive routes than measuring excellence for research and education policy. Reflexive questions need to be raised too about the nature of reality and who we believe we are as humans. This dialogue needs to 'engage explicitly with values in our decisions about the direction of education' (Biesta, 2009), but also to address some of the recent crises that have befallen research itself in the old industrial model.

2 Scientific Research, Crises and Convergences

Ravetz (2016) has raised ongoing concern that despite all of our research measurement and evaluation processes, 'quality control has failed to keep pace with the growth of science' (Ravetz, 2016). Amid the new the biodigital convergence (Policy Horizons Canada, 2020) and resulting reconfigurations to traditional scientific disciplines, there are existing issues of scientific credibility that are now 'older than most junior faculty members' (Bishop, 2019: 435). From concerns over reproducibility (Open Science Collaboration, 2015), abuse of metrics (Wilsdon, 2016), problems of peer review in publishing (Jandrić, 2020) and other areas of integrity, there is a crisis that has effects on what we believe we can actually 'know'. This situation has become more complex as humans have ceased to be able to process big data and algorithms now have considerable agency in all stages of research. This means that questions of reproducibility need to be levelled at both human and non-human researchers together, given their close collaboration, with related challenges for ethics and inclusivity.

In our recent article "Biodigital Philosophy, Technological Convergence, and New Knowledge Ecologies" (Peters, Jandrić & Hayes, 2021a) we reflected that this crisis in integrity in science has spanned both predigital and postdigital times. Biodigital convergence needs to be explored across all of the emerging ecologies of knowledge with questions and implications of scientific credibility considered alongside other characteristics of biodigital systems, such as: democratisation, decentralisation, geographic diffusion, scalability, customisation and reliance on data (Policy Horizons Canada, 2020). There are other combined factors to discuss too, such as how our political economy has put in place systems of control and rewards that have produced positivist incentives for researchers (Jandrić, 2020b). This has mixed with the 'industrialised' nature of science and the global division of labour with its accompanying inequalities (Jandrić & Hayes, 2019). Short-term contracts afforded to researchers and teachers, where renewal rests in the hands of individuals or lead investigators, has meant that maintaining 'ideals of independence and integrity becomes increasingly difficult' (Ravetz, 2016). We are faced too with an enormous proliferation of scientific writing which remains unread in its original form (Jandrić & Hayes, 2019).

2.1 The Pace and Utility of Scientific Research

Among other factors that can alter credibility, Sutton (2020) argues that, as we have seen during the pandemic, a 'frantic pace of the 24-hour news cycle and competition from social media mean the bandwidth through which complex ideas must be relayed to the public is very narrow'. Added to this are incentives for broadcasters to gain 'a catastrophising 10-second soundbite' rather than 'a level-headed exposition' concerning the 'challenges of various competing strategies' (Sutton, 2020). Then there are government scientific advisers who when 'funded by the public purse and bearing considerable social responsibility' should not be excused 'from providing cynical interpretations of data, of questionable validity, and drawn from a weak evidence base, all in order to justify further restrictions' (Sutton, 2020). Given the speed at which innovative ideas quickly become old news, a prioritisation of novelty over replication has developed.

There is a problem that, as research excellence frameworks demonstrate, quality becomes instrumentalised because impact is the name of the game. Even more concerning is the issue that perhaps those who engage in 'shoddy' or 'sleazy' science don't know what is in fact, sub-standard (Ravetz, 2016). Whilst sociological critics have attacked the epistemological foundations of science, less attention has been given to imperfections in its practice (Ravetz, 2016). Picking up on these issues, Bishop (2019: 435) reflects that over the last four decades threats to reproducibility have been recognised but have remained unaddressed. Furthermore, 'many researchers persist in working in a way that is guaranteed not to deliver meaningful results'. Bishop (2019: 435) argues though that 'new forces' such as the field of metascience, documentation, and awareness of the issues, may finally help to address irreproducibility, as 'we can no longer dismiss concerns as purely theoretical'. Then there is the fact that 'social media enables criticisms to be raised and explored soon after publication'. In scientific publishing, 'more journals are adopting the registered report format, in which editors evaluate the experimental question and study design before results are collected'. Finally, those who fund research have introduced requirements 'that data and scripts be made open and methods be described fully' (Bishop, 2019: 435). Given that biodigital convergence is surfacing new

POSTDIGITAL POSITIONALITY AS A RESEARCHER   221

knowledge ecologies, this brings to the forefront questions concerning what our image of science is, or should be, as we face changes that could be profoundly disruptive to our assumptions about society, the economy, and our human bodies (Policy Horizons Canada, 2020, Peters, Jandrić & Hayes, 2021a). In terms of inclusivity, we might ask though, *who in fact should we invite along to such a debate?*

2.2   *Including All of Our Environmental Research Partners*

James Ball (2020: 219) makes the point that many of the scientists, technologists and entrepreneurs behind the Internet and major systems and scientific advances under discussion, are actually still alive. If they are willing to participate, such pioneers might be invited to join postdigital debates to discuss new knowledge ecologies, biodigital technologies and the role of the new bioeconomy (Peters, Jandrić & Hayes, 2021a). There are others though, that now need to be included in these debates and when policy is written, or when ethics is discussed. This is because they already act as partners with us in our research, in new and varied ways, regardless of whether or not, they actually have a voice.

Jasmine Ulmer (2016) raises the question, *what if critical inquiries encompassed more than humanity?* The stance taken in this book is that they do, but with the acknowledgement that such are the implications from biodigital convergence that critical inquiry itself may experience a shift (Peters, Jandrić & Hayes, 2021a). Ulmer puts forward the case that critical inquiries take a 'more-than-human turn' via posthumanism, which raises issues for research methodology. Furthermore, taking a position as I have in this book, she argues that:

> Knowledge frameworks that privilege the human at the expense of the more-than-human could therefore be viewed as incomplete, as well as a potential injustice to non-human entities. (Ulmer, 2016: 834)

Not only do we now need to attend to and include human entanglements with data and digital technologies, there are other material and non-human environmental actors to account for, as well as connections and relationships described already, where the IoT and AIoT welcome objects like my airing cupboard hot water tank to participate.

2.3   *Human-Centred Approaches to Critical Research Inquiries Are Not Enough*

In critical research studies there is an emphasis on inclusion. Qualitative or mixed methods are applied to support inquiry into questions concerning race, ethnicity, gender, sexuality, class, culture, spirituality, ability, language, and other aspects of identity and anyone can offer insights based on their own sociocultural experiences. (Ulmer, 2016: 833). There is a wealth of literature that covers matters of inequity or injustice and fields of study such as Critical Race Theory, disability and gender studies have sought to interpret and better understand the experiences of those who may be marginalised in some form. To this background, arguments from posthuman theory suggest that 'given the state of the planet, human-centred approaches to research may not be enough' and justice involves more than what can be found solely within the realm of human relations (Haraway, 1988, Alaimo, 2016, Braidotti, 2019a, 2019b. Justice then is argued to be also:

> material ecological, geographical, geological, geopolitical, and geophilosophical. Justice is a more-than-human endeavour. (Ulmer, 2016: 833)

This stance does not involve removing humans from research but deemphasising the focus on them. Humans being treated for Covid-19 may have symptoms and be required to isolate (Figure 42) but they do not sit in isolation from the contact tracing apps, equipment helping them to breathe, or the locations in which different variants of the virus may have taken hold.

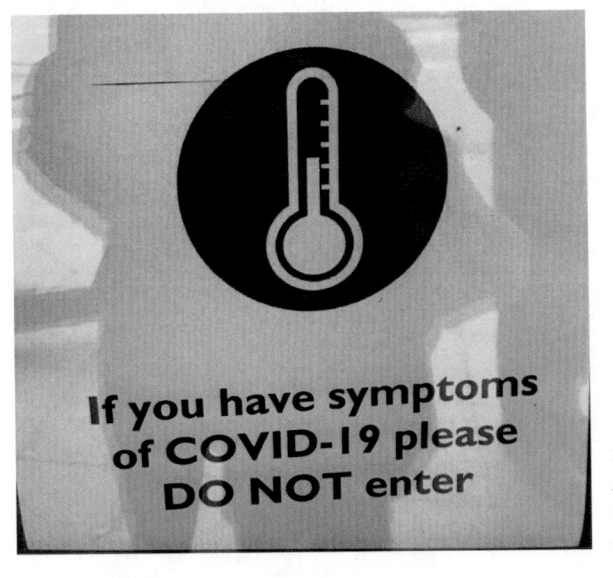

FIGURE 42
A sign asking those with Covid-19 symptoms not to enter a building

This involves recognising that:

> non-human elements are always already present. How we live, eat, drink, breathe, commute, hear, see, smell, touch, sense, and experience life are inextricable from our local ecologies. Humans are characters in a cast of many. (Ulmer, 2016: 833)

POSTDIGITAL POSITIONALITY AS A RESEARCHER   223

Thus, in a posthuman approach any frameworks that privilege the human at the expense of the 'more-than-humans' might be viewed as incomplete which has implications for research methodology and positionality.

2.4   *Implications for Research Methodologies*

Related methodological questions concern who then is producing or contributing to what we understand knowledge to be and from what positionality? Delanty (2011) argues that 'the idea of a critical theory of society' is in itself in 'urgent need of clarification both theoretically and methodologically. At least five major uses of the term can be found within sociological theory Delanty, 2011: 68). There is also a need to interrogate questions that ask how, where, when, with what, and why certain knowledge is being produced (Ulmer, 2016: 834). This raises considerations for researchers in how they locate their own positionality and also render visible other subjective influences within critically reflective frameworks. There are discussions to reflexively include on who or what influenced their research and also how.

Whilst Ulmer is not particularly keen on the term posthuman (rather like postdigtial) she recognises it as useful in the ways that it is invoked by an array of authors whose focus is on matter and the meaning of material things in peoples' lives. She raises the significant point that 'when humans are decentred as the only possible knowers, a wealth of research possibilities emerge' and 'it is no longer enough to produce piecemeal knowledge through interviews, observations, and texts', indeed:

> Language – whether it be in the forms of texts, sounds, or images – insufficiently represents the interactions among society, culture, geology, and ecology. (Ulmer, 2016: 834)

By problematising distinctions between and among species and other forms, things, objects or beings the recognition that humans are not the only ones with capacity to 'know' can lead to 'profoundly different ways of thinking about research design' (Ulmer, 2016: 834). There are many different disciplinary traditions (e.g. geology, geography, feminism, cultural studies, science studies, political science, economics, and philosophy, among others) feeding in also to the posthuman debate about how environmental aspects of our existence are to be included.

What can be observed is that during the Covid-19 crisis there are now so many personal narratives attesting to the effects that material elements have in individual lives that such accounts (and their implications for HE research, teaching and policy) cannot be ignored (Jandrić & Hayes, 2020a, 2020b, Teräs, Suoranta, Teräs & Curcher, 2020, Sapon-Shevin, SooHoo, 2020). Humans have

FIGURE 43
A sign listing a set of rules for
visitors to an office to observe
if their visit is essential

been required to adapt to new sets of rules in language that has separated them from each other, as in Figure 43.

At the same time many of us have spent even more time using devices and material objects to avoid encountering other people, as we follow scientific advice. Therefore, as these human and beyond-human narratives encounter the effects emerging from radical technological changes, there are questions to be raised about scientific research that feed into points concerning HE policy in Chapter 6.

2.5 Changing Ecologies of Knowledge about Science, Technology and Policy

In a paper entitled *Changing Ecologies of Knowledge and Action (CEKA)*, Peter Healey points to the radical changes to the 'familiar landscapes in which science and technology are produced, distributed and used and are accountable to wider society' (Healey, n.d.). In this working paper, Healey raises a set of questions concerning:

1. *What kind of science is done?* – given accelerating development of new sciences, technologies and fields of radical application, e.g. biosciences; additive manufacturing and advanced IT

2. *How is science done?* – given radical improvements in the cost-effectiveness of computing, improved analysis across all fields of science, control of increasingly complex processes in additive manufacturing, increasing reliance on modelling, simulation and 'big data'.

3. *Where is science done?* – science is increasingly being done beyond the conventional settings of the university and industrial labs e.g. in garage labs, public labs, collaborative facilities of various kinds, some local, some international, sharing opportunities and risks of new technologies, bringing together combinations of industrial, academic and state partners.

4. *Who does science?* – science is increasingly performed not only by career scientists in university, government and industry labs but also performed directly, or commissioned on behalf of, patient groups, environmental campaigners, entrepreneurs, and hobbyists, with individuals sometimes occupying more than one role in parallel.

5. *How is science owned and communicated?* – changing approaches to, and uses of, intellectual property regimes and publishing models are developing in the light of open access especially to publicly funded science, and the growth of crowd-funded science.

6. *How is science governed, regulated and socially mediated?* – despite a growing disconnect between hierarchical institutions and distributed practice, closer inspection reveals a rich variety of linkages, ranging from complete autonomy to full capture by commercial science outlets. Intermediary organisations and networks are playing a developing role in shaping distributed practice through supplying equipment and experimental materials and brokering deals for new scientific outputs or capacities. In macro-issues of governance and regulation many jurisdictions are still evolving (potentially divergent) approaches.

7. *What do different sectors of society expect science to do?* – states and cities increasingly build political imaginaries around sociotechnical narratives. In parallel to these symbolic uses of science in political attempts to build high-level consensus around broad visions of the future, the pragmatic decisions about particular technologies are often highly contested between different interests and values.

Peter Healey argues that the background to the above developments 'is a set of broader longer term, specific and more immediate changes affecting how science and technology are produced, consumed and perceived (Healey, n.d.: 7).

Such changes have implications for our knowledge of physical and organic things when these are conceived of as code, or as informational building blocks. There are questions concerning manipulation and redesign of life in potentially reductionist ways. In relation to policy benefits, Healey concludes that research conducted under CEKA helps with understanding the development of new decentralised and citizen-centred knowledge production across the whole system by which knowledge is produced, validated and utilised. In particular to help us assess:

- whether and in what respects this new production is disruptive, and what new patterns of innovation may be emerging.
- whether and how new modes of doing science affects the balance between the traditional prime governmental target of knowledge in support of economic development, on the one hand, and broad social equity in enjoying the fruits of new knowledge (United Nations, 2012), and democratic accountability/approval for the uses of science, on the other
- policy mechanisms currently being used in the governance and regulation of these new sites and processes for performing science and technology at various scales, with particular attention to issues of safety and quality control
- future science and technology policy pathways, including possible new priorities for the university by which the new knowledge production might be supported and encouraged (Healey, n.d.: 6).

Healey's paper has laid out the broad and dynamic postdigital landscape in which science and technology have converged, with many far-reaching consequences for positionality and university policy that Chapter 6 will now pick up.

CHAPTER 6

Postdigital Positionality as a Leader and Policy Maker

1 **What Is Shaping the University and What Might the University Now Shape?**

Policy reviews will address the effects of the pandemic from numerous angles going forward to point to both existing and new inequities that Covid-19 has brought to light. Whilst this book has shared some of these examples, as contexts have unfolded, the main focus has been to encourage broad open debate on new policy discourse that will recognise the postdigital environment that universities now occupy and the diversity of human positionality within it. These theories together create a productive dialogue that might inform 'more inclusive' and critically sustainable inclusivity policy. As discussed already, universities are not contained institutions. Their activities are local, national, international, institutional and individual. All of these are aspects that are now also interconnected with what takes place in the virtual airing cupboard of the Internet. However, not all people in the communities surrounding universities have access to the Internet, to devices that might help them connect or to the skills that might enable participation.

An amusing, but also revealing illustration of the kinds of hybrid postdigital connections emerging across local government and the Internet, can be watched in a clip of a UK parish council meeting that went viral in early 2021 (YouTube, 2021). Posted online by people present, it was viewed on Twitter and YouTube by hundreds of thousands and also reported in national media, due to the altercations between those present. The video clip demonstrates the challenges of establishing points of order and regulations in an online meeting, as well as the different positionalities of those present attempting to also navigate the technology they are using. At one point a phone rings in the background and is answered during the meeting, whilst a form of cancel culture is enacted as the council chair is removed from the Zoom meeting by another councillor. Fierce objections from the vice chair ensue as he argues for the standing orders to be read. Requests to be respectful follow, with other members laughing in disbelief at how the meeting has unfolded.

This scenario is an anecdote worth reflecting on in relation to the local contexts and communities in which universities are located and the identities that

© KONINKLIJKE BRILL NV, LEIDEN, 2021 | DOI: 10.1163/9789004466029_008

HE institutions assume. Parish councils do not often hit the headlines, yet as the lowest tier of local government in different cities they play a valuable role in providing representation and consultation with district and county councils in matters such as planning, environment and recreation (Farrer & Pidd, 2021). The sudden trending on Twitter of such a meeting is a powerful illustration of the reach of the virtual airing cupboard of the Internet, triggered through the necessity of meeting online during lockdown. In a further example of the challenges that can arise for community groups navigating online meetings in unfamiliar technology, an entire school board in California had to resign when a Webex meeting they believed to be private was publicly streamed. Members of the board made disparaging remarks about parents who were upset at school closures and quickly realised they had been heard and tweeted. A petition calling for their resignation followed (BBC Technology, 2021).

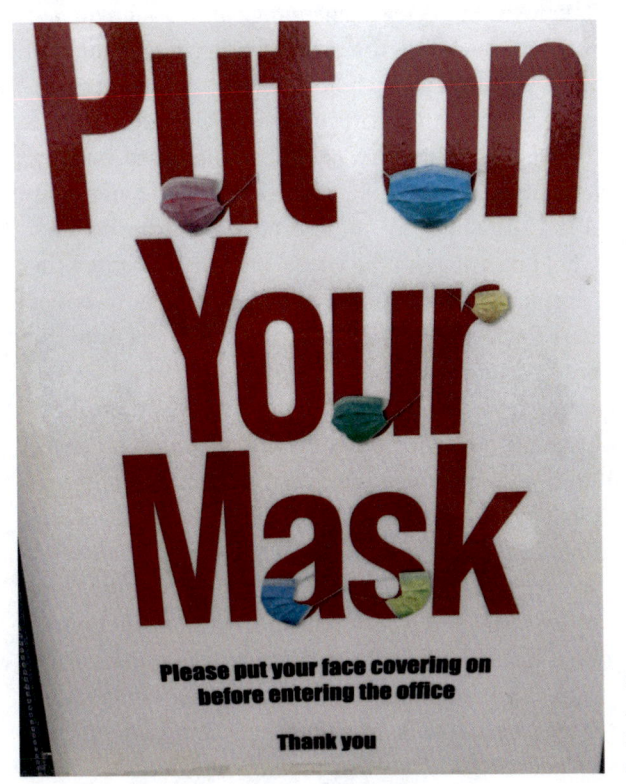

FIGURE 44
A reminder to 'put on your mask' before entering the office

In earlier chapters, this book pointed to some of these complex, postdigital interactions relating to the positionalities of students, teachers and researchers in this context, all of whom are also members of local communities and regions. The positionality of the postdigital university as an institution and

POSTDIGITAL POSITIONALITY AS A LEADER AND POLICY MAKER   229

that of its leaders located in hybrid learning spaces (Cohen, Nørgård & Mor, 2020) is now the focus for this chapter.

In this introductory section to the chapter, I will set the context a little to discuss how the pandemic has revealed many underlying inequalities in the areas surrounding universities before outlining what the other sections will cover.

In a recently published Health Foundation report (2020), *Build back fairer: the Covid-19 Marmot review, the pandemic, socioeconomic and health inequalities*, a stagnation in health improvement in the UK is identified as a status quo that existed prior to the pandemic, that the country should not return to:

> The levels of social, environmental and economic inequality in society are damaging health and well-being. As the UK emerges from the pandemic it would be a tragic mistake to attempt to re-establish the status quo that existed before the pandemic. (Health Foundation, 2020)

The report argues that 'this pandemic exposes the underlying inequalities in society and amplifies them' (Health Foundation, 2020: 5). On this basis this inquiry seeks to demonstrate effects from the pandemic and societal response on social and economic inequities, mental and physical health and their likely effects on health inequalities in the future. Yet in taking a socioeconomic focus, there are still only eight references to 'digital' in the main body of the report. All of these concern 'digital access' to services or 'digital exclusion' due to a lack of devices or infrastructure. Whilst digital access is a hugely important issue (not everyone can SmartShop as in Figure 45, or make online bookings as in Figure 46, or click and collect as in Figure 47) there are countless complex and deeply intertwined challenges that accompany digital access and the contexts of those who are disadvantaged (Traxler, Smith, Scott & Hayes, 2020).

Understanding who will address these (frequently opaque) aspects of digital inequality is an ongoing issue for governments, universities, regional agencies, charities and all who seek to improve digital skills in communities.

The Not-Equal project (2020) discovered numerous challenges that digital ways of working throw up for already vulnerable groups. These include: safeguarding young people, a lack of moderation of their activities, patchy wifi connections, screen fatigue, online isolation, exhaustion from learning new platforms, physical issues, lack of skills and digital literacy, fear of technology, lack of trust, no consistent device if phones or laptops are swapped, shared, sold or stolen, exacerbation of existing mental health problems, a loss of intimacy, wariness of how to interact, privacy concerns, fears concerning protection and aversion to seeing one's own face on screen, or to being seen (Not-Equal project, 2020).

FIGURE 45
A reminder to download the SmartShop app to help avoid checkout queues

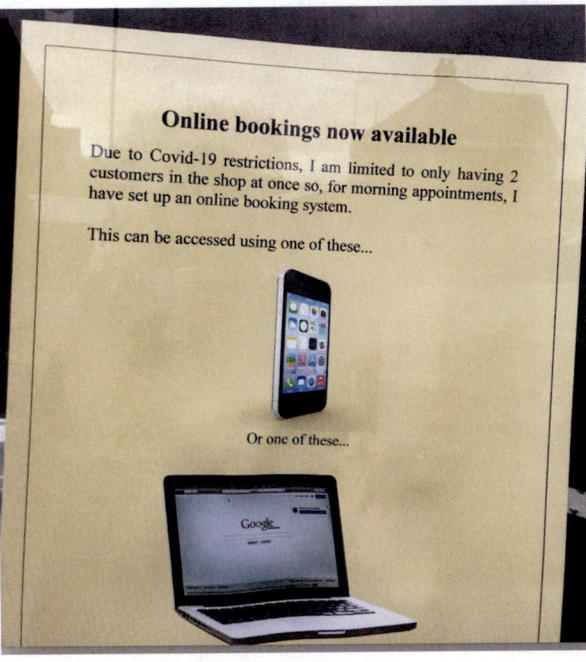

FIGURE 46
A sign indicating that due to Covid-19 an online booking system has been set up for appointments

FIGURE 47   A sign reminding people that 'only orders placed online are available at this store'

All of these point to the individual and positional nature of the messy post-digital facets of our lives. Yet when digital devices or systems are mentioned in relation to inequality, diversity and inclusivity, university or government policy reports frequently omit these dimensions in an analysis that barely skims the surface.

In referencing issues of access to digital and online facilities in isolation, countless forms of bias, exploitation and discrimination are overlooked, alongside human agency, system legibility and negotiability (Mortier et al., 2020). Digital opportunities are understandably emphasised, along with skills and employability too, but it remains unclear as to who actually takes responsibility to attend to the many real but less visible aspects of digital life, that will still continue to hamper 'building back fairer'.

At the close of *The Labour of Words in Higher Education, is it time to reoccupy policy?* I explained why the current McPolicy discourse institutions still work to, is inadequate:

> Attention needs to be paid to these documents. Not least because contradictory statements around social justice risk cancelling each other out, if widening participation and student retention are enacted by generic statements, projects and technology, rather than diverse staff and students themselves. (Hayes, 2019a: 150)

A persistent rational McPolicy discourse has been conducting its own form of cancel culture, by writing out the staff and students whose diverse labour constitutes the university, but also in omitting complex and far reaching digital interconnections with inequality and inclusion. Drawing on Ritzer's McDonaldisation thesis, McPolicy reached its point of irrationality then in a year when a pandemic revealed the 'contents' of the university for all to see. By contents, I refer to the humans and the 'more-than-humans' (Ulmer, 2017, Braidotti, 2019a, 2019b) in HE whose postdigital activities do not sit neatly within the walls of an institution. The virtual airing cupboard of the Internet connects and disconnects what people are and who they might become, in an epoch of broad and potentially irreversible digitalisation of life (OECD, 2020).

McPolicy closes down debate (Hayes et al., 2020). Or it did, until Covid-19 brought into the public domain the diverse and unique postdigital position-alities of students and academics across the globe (Jandrić & Hayes, 2020a, 2020b, Watermeyer et al., 2020, UNESCO, 2020a). These testimonies that have flooded the virtual airing cupboard with a very different discourse to the sani-tised impression of what happens in university activities that is generated in McPolicy. So, in a sense, my call below has already received a unanimous response:

> It therefore is time for staff and students, as a collective community, to protest this language and change the way in which divisive forms of HE policy are written. (Hayes, 2019a: 150)

Rational approaches in McPolicy omit these distinctive and varied aspects of who each of us are, as individual people. They omit the communicative pow-ers concerning knowledge that are now afforded to the wider population in the virtual airing cupboard. Thus, they omit the global citizenship we each hold alongside any institutional membership. A generic, repetitive McPolicy reflects the consumer culture of our current political economic structuring of society. It is unsustainable though to represent a new political bioeconomic discourse that our global society now seeks (OECD, 2009, The Bioeconomy Council, 2019, UNESCO, 2020d).

Linking positionality with postdigital theory yields a broader understand-ing too of why these concepts need to remain in continual dialogue to inform inclusivity policy in this context. University policy documents and frameworks for inclusivity currently fail to acknowledge the dialectical nature of human activity, computer systems, learning, research, data, material and biological change. The technological and cultural split already discussed can be noticed clearly as some policies home in on matters of social justice and human rights but omit any reference to the ethical issues that are ingrained in our data gathering and data-driven technological platforms across the Internet. Mean-while, policies that urge a use of technology tend to frame this in the weary arguments of best practice, an unquestionable enhancement of the student experience and a measurement of excellence. In a wider global context this separation of policy interests that concern cultural issues, from those that concern technological ones, tends to serve a variety of commercial interests. It does not though adequately serve an emancipatory inclusivity agenda in universities. Reflecting on educational reform from a global perspective, Saltman and Means (2019) highlight trends that are converging to fundamentally alter education from a democratic to a commercial endeavour across the world:

> Transnational institutions, such as the Organisation for Economic Cooperation and development (OECD), the World Bank, the World Trade Organisation, and powerful transnational corporations, such as Pearson, are promoting an interconnected set of global educational reforms that seek to align national systems of education with the demands of transnational capitalism and elite economic and political interests. (Saltman & Means, 2019: 1)

Given this situation, where many universities have now invested in corporate partnerships on the grounds of improved efficiencies and rational ideas of progress, there are some key choices looming for leaders and policy makers in relation to AI, algorithmic activity, data, cloud ethics (Amoore, 2020) and equality, diversity and inclusivity agendas. As discussed earlier, we cannot inhabit only the parts of 'the cloud' we choose to, as individuals or as institutions. Nor can we easily track down accountable humans outside of algorithms to hold them to account when 'algorithms are implicated in new regimes of verification, new forms of identifying a wrong or of truth telling in the world' (Amoore, 2020). Such a situation now requires university leaders to revisit their whole mission as sites and producers of knowledge, when they are no longer the main users of knowledge (Delanty, 2001: 152). Furthermore, that knowledge is inextricably intermingled with information and data that has huge commercial value. The increased instances of cyberattacks, ransomeware and phishing emails targeting universities further attest to this (Afifi-Sabet, 2020, Hellard, 2020).

Rather than write an inclusivity framework and trust that 'the principles of inclusive practice are well established' (Department for Education, 2017), there is a need to confront what is constantly being re-worked in the cloud to understand how this alters how inclusivity is actually experienced by individuals. Huge corporations now control human online identities. Such control does not cease when students or staff log off from a computer or a phone. Our datafied selves continue to be shaped, altered, celebrated, exploited or cancelled, but nor do they disappear. Deeply personal facets of our identities, including race, gender, disability and religion are 'described by 'ones and zeros' and 'defined by templates of data' (Cheney-Lippold, 2018). Furthermore, 'algorithmically produced categories replace the politicised language of race, gender and class with a proprietary vocabulary that speaks *for* us' (Cheney-Lippold, 2018) and this is speaking to commercial monopolies, that have different values to universities. This then severely hampers the ambitions of any university committee to 'embed' or 'mainstream' practices for inclusivity which do not remain static. A new approach is needed that plays to the strengths of universities, rather than one that simply exposes their weaknesses in the corporate playing field. Here universities are faced with decisions on claiming their own postdigital positionalities and shaping their own response as leaders in this field, before becoming simply additional resources for the big commercial monopolies.

Peter Scott (2018) has argued that 'the contemporary university is subject to two (apparently contradictory), forces'. He describes firstly:

> the drive towards the modernisation of its governance and management, often in ways that reflect corporate structures more familiar in the private sector (and other parts of the reformed public sector). This drive has been accompanied by the growth of performance management, both of institutions and individual teachers and researchers; the more prescriptive identification of goals and targets (at the expense, perhaps, of traditional notions of autonomy and academic freedom); and more explicit – and intrusive? – forms of audit, accountability and evaluation. (Scott, 2018: 35)

I demonstrated in my analysis of McPolicy how such rational forms of governance have come to be represented in strategic discourse. Common sense statements suggest that technologies, policies and institutions, not people, have the autonomy to 'act' to accomplish all aspects of academic work. If people are left feeling 'insignificant' (Leone, 2020) then perhaps this is happening to institutions too. Scott then describes the second force as:

> new modes of learning, a more open curriculum and more distributed patterns of research. Examples include the popularity of (technology-enhanced) self-directed learning, the growth of massive open online courses (MOOCs), the spread of open-source publication and greater emphasis on the impact and application of research. (Scott, 2018: 35)

As a former Vice Chancellor, Scott's argument is that whilst both of these forces reflect deep-rooted changes in the nature of modern higher education:

> it would be misleading to see them as always or inevitably in conflict. However, they do pose new dilemmas about how to maintain an appropriate

POSTDIGITAL POSITIONALITY AS A LEADER AND POLICY MAKER   235

balance between the necessary management of the large, complex and heterogeneous organisations that modern universities have become and their capacity for innovation and creativity. (Scott, 2018: 35)

Thinking about this analysis in relation to the broad observations on a need to re-link cultural reproduction and technological reproduction in HE, Delanty discussed a market-driven capitalism 'shaping the university in the image of technoscience', as disengaged from 'battles of cultural identity' (Delanty, 2001: 157). Nearly twenty years later we are in the grip of a pandemic that has revealed just how closely interconnected these economic, technological, cultural and biological battles really are. The underpinning economic focus on productivity has in recent decades replaced an 'open intellectual enquiry' (Olssen & Peters, 2005) through which we might debate postdigital connectivities. Complex intersections across the virtual airing cupboard now necessitate this open dialogue when inclusivity is the focus. Davies (2016) discussed different phases and policy dynamics of neoliberalism over recent decades that have sought to 'prop up' the broken model of capitalist accumulation (Davies, 2016: 133). In a sense these mutate in a fashion analogous to different strains of the Covid-19 virus, which also disadvantages the vulnerable. What remains a problem is that persistent rational approaches omit the distinctive and varied aspects of who each of us are and the variable positions we find ourselves in. They also omit the communicative powers concerning knowledge that are now afforded to much of the wider population.

However different authors choose to frame these arguments, there seems to be some broad agreement that tensions between corporate structures, compliance and prescriptive targets for excellence have driven divisions that could hamper creative approaches deeply connected with our human cultural identities. Our current HE policy discourse structures set out the boundaries of what staff and students come to believe is possible, even if as individuals they do not closely engage with the processes of policymaking themselves. The related narratives and arguments of McPolicy make their way into all of the realms of activity in universities and resisting such dominant rhetoric becomes challenging.

As discussed in Chapter 2, postdigital positionality and the twofold debate this book is concerned with for inclusivity policy, centres around the interactions, back and forth across humans and machines in personal, individual contexts, and across interpersonal relations. AI has enabled machines to mimic the cognitive functions that humans use, whilst interacting with humans. How this is experienced is unique for each person and thus also significant to how leaders respond towards inclusivity in postdigital HE. This is because multiple

and diverse 'actors' (that are not all human, and not all machine) are now altering much of what is still being described as 'established' or 'inclusive' practices
in universities.

Scott (2018) points out that tensions and even contradictions between
compliance and creativity are not though inevitable. He argues for systems
of coordination and balanced solutions where creativity can be nurtured and
strengthened, pointing out that this is:

> essential to the healthy functioning of universities in the twenty-first
> century because of the complexity and heterogeneity of their missions.
> (Scott, 2018: 46)

Work undertaken by Adrianna Kezar and Jaime Lester (2010) suggests that
positionality theory expands knowledge concerning leadership. This is because
too simplistic an approach can often be taken towards the role played by the
social identities of leaders. Policy rhetoric that imposes broad categorisations
on human beings tends to uphold the image of leaders in static positions from
which they take rational decisions based on common sense. The placing of
people into any kind of grouping objectifies the human qualities of this group.
This can translate into linguistic constructions in policy that also attribute
actions and feelings to this socially constructed category of people. Positionality theory points instead to multiple overlapping identities (Kezar, 2002: 96).
Kezar & Lester argue that our understanding of leadership in an HE context
remains partial without taking into account features of identity such as race,
disability or gender.

Postdigital positionality theory can expand this approach further, to recon-
ceptualise leadership and policymaking by including people's 'postdigital
identities'. These have a 'dialectic relationship' (Freire, 2000: 50) with the other
key elements of our existence and how we each perceive ourselves as individuals. This takes into account the complexities of postdigital experiences as
part of the multiple identities that affect leaders and the processes of leadership. There are now intricacies arising to show that statements like 'the principles of inclusive practice are well established' (Department for Education,
2017) are misconceptions. The principles of inclusive practice instead require
a dynamic ongoing dialogue. Prior (2020) points however to the problem that
'there is still sector-wide ignorance surrounding how to deal with knowledge
that is subjective and embodied' (Prior, 2020: 188). Yet this is also knowledge
that is a crucial aspect of any inclusivity programme, if equality and diversity
are to be celebrated and if marginalised groups are to be supported to recognise opportunities.

In the remainder of this chapter, rational conceptions of leadership in HE will be examined firstly, in terms of the current positionality of universities in postdigital society. As complex marketised and multi-layered institutions where McPolicy is generated, this form of discourse is culturally distant from individuals and their academic identities. An examination of cultural forces at play within universities cannot sit apart from individuals, or from the global and transnational technological advances already discussed. The work of multinational corporations and alliances now shape our lives based on the data we have become in the cloud (Ball, 2020, Cheney-Lippold, 2018, Amoore, 2020, Selwyn, Macgilchrist & Williamson, 2020). This data is deeply personal, it relates to our identities and perceived possibilities of who each of us might become as diverse citizens and human beings. Komljenovic (2020) argues that universities have tended to focus on data privacy issues which are important, but from a political economic perspective, the data value models of commercial ed tech companies need our attention too. These are quietly restructuring cultural and technological values in HE.

The implications for inclusivity policy in institutions are too huge to ignore, or to allow cultural concerns to be raised independently of the technological ones. Then there is the question of control. Whilst universities attempt to control and embed inclusivity agendas, as if these existed apart from digital advances and new educational technologies, their partnerships with major commercial players are also bringing new consequences for inclusive practices in relation to data driven systems. The ongoing privatisation and commercialisation of education has rapidly advanced across the globe during the 2020 pandemic. Leaders in governments and universities alike were ill-equipped to catch up with the rapid technological changes in postdigital society and so they relied heavily on the advice of corporate business partners. These companies are not disinterested advisers though when it comes to data. They take rational, solution-based and profitable decisions. Therefore, in a sense this is not unlike trusting foxes to take care of the hens. The values and intentions of the parties involved are somewhat different. It is also a blurred area too where wealthy philanthropists have funded private technology companies to become embedded in public education systems bringing long-term reforms (Hogan & Williamson, 2020). This provides new powers for technology consortiums to influence educational policies but based on values of investment and profit. It places considerably less emphasis though on the interests of emancipatory education that seeks to bring opportunities for knowledge to those on the margins, in terms of levelling up.

The second half of this chapter is concerned with the responses that are open to university leaders and policymakers. These require a reflexivity that is a key strength of universities to be applied in re-shaping how institutions are positioned in postdigital society. Rather than seek to control aspects of the virtual airing cupboard by embedding them inside the structure of the institution, universities are re-visualised as centres of critical, cross-sector postdigital dialogue. In this vision the university, as a key producer of critical forms of knowledge, becomes more of an arbiter of postdigital communication, not another bystander looking on. In this role there can be an acceptance that inclusivity agendas are not simply regulated as if they lived inside the university, when so many powerful societal forces now act upon these. Therefore, the future of the university lies in preserving 'relatively non-institutional space' and 'seeing the university as the site of reflexively constituted knowledge' in order to 'appreciate its role in contemporary society' (Delanty, 2001: 155). This a perspective that treats digital skills and online activities as every bit as 'real' as place-based opportunities for those in disadvantaged situations. It is a positionality that can engage with the notion of 'critical sustainability as part of a post-corporate cultural model and as an alternative to the neoliberal conception of sustainability (Delanty, 2020: 1). Therefore, rather than acting as a resource for corporate business to simply mould, the university becomes instead, a critically reflexive authority at the intersection of powerful cross-sector, postdigital debates.

1.1   *What Is an Institution?*

Much research has been undertaken on ways of understanding institutions and organisational structures. There have been recent attempts to consolidate these ideas too in the light of social change and to examine institutional structures, processes and interplays at the world system, transnational, societal and industry levels alongside micro forces (Scott, 2010). In terms of the concept of postdigital positionality, this is an emerging debate that can also be examined at micro, personal and interpersonal levels right through to macro transocietal levels.

Reeves (2019) argues that:

> Framing an organisation as a complex adaptive system shifts focus away from the individual and towards the organisation as the unit of analysis, and such a shift is consistent with the anti-reductionist rhetoric of postdigital to move beyond a conception of an organisation as something that can be reduced to individual people, resources, and data. (Reeves, 2019: 156)

Increasing human agency to shape organisational evolution is argued to be dependent on a reconceptualisation of value. This requires a more conscious approach to determining what is important in the activity of organisations

POSTDIGITAL POSITIONALITY AS A LEADER AND POLICY MAKER   239

(Reeves, 2019: 156). As institutions, universities tend to describe their top-level mission statements and strategic plans and ambitions. The policies that sit beneath this overview may or may not articulate well with it. As I have shared my findings on McPolicy from *The Labour of Words in HE* at different institutions I have consistently been told by staff and students that they do not recognise themselves in the policy discourse of their university. They view it as disconnected from them personally and from their academic activities. This is not therefore a good starting point for inclusivity policy to be cast in the same vein. Scott (2010: 6) defines institutions as:

> Social structures that have attained a high degree of resilience [and are] composed of cultural-cognitive, normative, and regulative elements that, together with associated activities and resources, provide stability and meaning to social life. (Scott, 2010: 6)

This suggests that individuals are deriving meaning at different levels that do not sit neatly in one element of organisational management. Rather there is an interdependence across the diverse elements, making it important to look at these holistically and reflexively, in terms of positionality, rather than rationally and objectively. Scott describes three interdependent elements of organisational management as:

- *Regulative*: these elements are formalised and rational, easily planned and strategically manipulated, with a need for clear directives, alignment of incentives, and surveillance. Regulative elements, if not supported by cultural beliefs, are more likely to be evaded and behaviour of staff becomes decoupled from the rules and formal structures.
- *Normative:* actors are seen more as social persons who care deeply about their relations to others and adherence to the guidelines is motivated by their own identity, personal ties and informal relations with co-workers.
- *Cultural-cognitive*: elements are socially constructed symbolic representations that frame individual perceptions and decisions. Deeply entrenched assumptions and conceptions of the 'way the world is' are likened to culture as 'the software of the mind' (Hofstede, 1991). Cultural-cognitive elements provide the bedrock for normative prescriptions and regulative controls, because norms and rules must refer to institutionally constituted entities (Scott, 2010: 6).

Scott argues that this 'three pillars' framework (that many HE institutions often structure a strategic plan around) becomes emasculated if not closely connected to human and physical resources. As such it is necessary to be aware of: institutional variety, the interdependence of and interactions between organised units at multiple levels, the effects of non-local, as well as local factors, appreciation of the temporal nature of social life, the ongoing effects of the past on the present and future, to emphasise the importance of ideas that mediate between environmental conditions and actions to promote diversity, and new types of social behaviour and novel systems (Scott, 2010: 18).

This understanding sits well with the ideas from Reeves on the 'anti-reductionist rhetoric' of the postdigital (Reeves, 2019: 156). However, there seem to be few forums where the identity of the university might be critically examined and reimaged outside of the constraints of institutional McPolicy.

1.2 Bureaucratisation, Rationality and Positionality

Ginsberg (2011: 25) points to the challenges that have emerged from a rational bureaucratisation of HE but one that has irrationally failed to free up time for academic staff 'to dedicate themselves to their main tasks, teaching and research' (Jandrić & Hayes, 2020d). Universities are filled with:

> armies of functionaries – the vice presidents, associate vice presidents, assistant vice presidents, provosts, associate provosts, vice provosts, assistant provosts, deans, deanlets, deanlings, each commanding staffers and assistants – who, more and more, direct the operations of every school. Backed by their administrative legions, university presidents and other senior administrators have been able, at most schools, to dispense with faculty involvement in campus management and, thereby to reduce the faculty's influence in university affairs. (Ginsberg, 2011: 25)

Further irrationalities have emerged as the layers within universities have become more complicated to meet the demands from regulatory bodies, such as audits of data on student access, participation, retention and progression (Office for Students, 2018, 2019). Whilst all of these topics are important, a narrow focus has been adopted for inclusivity in this context. It has largely engaged with the humans concerned, and rather ironically has done so, through engagement with data, not people. Furthermore, in removing faculty from central institutional administration including policymaking, it becomes hard to argue that faculty do not engage with policy. Meanwhile members of faculty can find that they still spend many hours on the layers of local administration that still exist in their department (Jandrić & Hayes, 2020d).

1.3 How Might HE Policy Pivot to Postdigital Policy?

Teachers are urged to continually improve on what they teach in HE, researchers are urged to improve the impact from what they publish, but this is not

POSTDIGITAL POSITIONALITY AS A LEADER AND POLICY MAKER   241

a discourse heard very often in relation to policymaking processes and the related discourse that is written up. Scrutiny in this area seems to have been missed off the quality assurance and enhancement grid, as I don't remember noticing The Policy Excellence Framework (the PEL perhaps?) being devised to join the other REF, TEF and KEF frameworks that UK universities are required to work to. In *The Labour of Words in HE* I observed that:

> These are the decades in which academic labour has been increasingly, rationally audited for quality and performance (Shore & Wright, 1999; Ball, 2003). Yet somehow, rather irrationally, we have failed to quality assure or enhance, the very language of McPolicy in which we write our strategies for enhancement. (Hayes, 2019a: 6)

Policy writing committees could be more inclusive (and creative) given the shift during the pandemic to write university policy via online systems, rather than gathered around a table on campus. A focus is heavily placed on how teachers might flip a classroom and pivot to online education, but where are

FIGURE 48
A sign instructing people to please stay apart from each other

the discussions for opening up creativity in policy making, now that there are captive experts and audiences, just as there are for online conferences?

In recent decades universities have omitted a crucial part to policy making and policy writing. Indicative of a productivity-driven, neoliberal approach across all of academia perhaps (particularly since student fees were introduced), the broader dialogue that would reflect the 'sociocultural dynamism of policy processes' (Nudzor, 2009: 503) has been bypassed. Instead, the rational problem-solving approach has dominated and the documents we have to show for it (closely examined in *The Labour of Words*) have been in social isolation from each other since long before Covid-19.

Yet, even lonely HE strategies aimed at solitary topics were constituted within a context (despite a use of language that frequently omits this background). They demonstrate (if we really take time to look) what HE policymaking had become prior to the pandemic, a set of socially distanced topics that persist in addressing cultural issues in isolation from technological ones (Delanty, 2001).

Opening a dialogue now concerning the new possibilities before universities, where they might take into account the dynamic personal postdigital context around individuals and reflect this in policy, would offer a liberating and potentially more effective route forwards. If any further evidence were needed as to why such dialogue is necessary, then much can be sourced from the post-pandemic debates already taking place at this time of writing (Carrigan, 2020a). Given that policy is neither a problem-solving tool, nor a process, but both (Nudzor, 2009), there is time yet to shape a dynamic 'new normal' for HE policy discourse. One that draws more closely on a global focus on sustainability. This could soon show us what a more ecological, political bioeconomic discourse looks like, rather than a political economic one which emphasises only productivity and consumption.

1.4 Digitalisation, Convergence and the Need for a Shift in University Policy

The technological and scientific convergences that are described in recent reports on digitalisation have far reaching consequences for what we do in HE both globally and locally that 'cannot be overstated' (OECD, 2020: 20). Digitalisation runs deep and it is happening quickly therefore university leaders have a challenge before them as to how exactly to engage with this in policy. There are European plans to 'overhaul' the digital market too, including how tech giants operate' (BBC Technology, 2020). This is aimed at addressing a dominance that big players like Google and Facebook have assumed. In particular their use of the data they have gathered from one service that is used to

POSTDIGITAL POSITIONALITY AS A LEADER AND POLICY MAKER 243

'improve or develop' a new one in a different area, making it difficult to compete with them. They have become 'gatekeepers' who have set the rules of the game for their users and their competitors (BBC Technology, 2020). Ball (2020: 232) argues that we 'need to work out how to treat personal data now it is so valuable'. He suggests though that this may require many smaller fixes rather than one big one if we are hoping for sustainable change.

Universities could also adopt this smaller fix approach and feed into different policies, each of the various related compliances that legislation requires, but there are broader responsibilities for university leaders to consider. These go beyond the *regulative* elements identified earlier by Scott (2010). There are also *normative* and *cultural-cognitive* elements to deliberate, if the university is to consolidate its positionality in postdigital society. University leaders will need to take debate well beyond what Williamson refers to as 'political computational thinking' where assumptions are made that 'policy problems can be addressed using the right code'. In this model students are inculcated into 'the material practices and systems of thought associated with computer coding' and encouraged to become contributors to new forms of digital governance (Williamson, 2016: 39). However, all this does is shift responsibility elsewhere rather than confronting more fundamental inequalities that exist in the digital realm. Instead universities need to be ready to link probing concerns about digitalisation and sustainability, with inclusivity policy, which requires a fundamentally different discourse.

1.5   *Convergence of Global and Local Policy Dialogues*

It is also a discourse where there is much to be learned at both global and local levels from interventions during the pandemic. This is demonstrated in a recent research project that was conducted by a team in the Education Observatory, at University of Wolverhampton (Traxler, Smith, Scott & Hayes, 2020). The research, which was commissioned by the Department for International Development (DFID) EdTech Hub was intended to (1) identify digital ideas, in whatever form that might maintain the continuity of education systems and (2) that might stop existing or potential disadvantages being amplified or exacerbated by Covid-19 or by the responses to it. The report which emerged from this project is based on a large-scale review of literature, from both academic sources and non-academic sources, on consultations with specific groups of experts and policy makers and on material and ideas from a wide network of contacts and collaborators (Traxler, Smith, Scott & Hayes, 2020). The relevance this research has for new approaches towards HE policy discourse arises from its deeply dialogic and dynamic approach towards understanding the positionality of those in crisis and their postdigital contexts across the globe.

As mentioned earlier, HE policies that self-isolate from each other *within* institutions are a problem because they fail to connect all of the factors affecting inclusive practices, particularly in overlooking postdigital factors and individual positionality. However, the practice of universities simply reproducing similar policies on different topics is also a trend that risks these documents being meaningless to those they are aimed at. Now that the Covid-19 crisis has revealed how so many problems arising in the Global North have already been experienced and addressed in creative ways across the Global South, there is much to be learned from how other nations are developing inclusive practices. Research publications from the Global North have dominated knowledge about HE, due to the underpinning global economy on which universities have largely based their research and policy making. These papers and indeed the related policies should not be read in isolation from those bearing insights on crises from the Global South because Covid-19 has presented many similar challenges to those already being tackled in the developing world. Steps to improve access and continuity of education for marginalised groups through technologies in Low to Middle Income Countries (LMIC) hold relevance for disadvantaged groups living in local regions of developed countries. The Learning through the Crisis report (Traxler, Smith, Scott & Hayes, 2020) explains how amongst the research methods undertaken, a Delphi process and ideas from a wide network of contacts and collaborators informed policy recommendations. The Delphi method is a systematic means for a panel of experts to respond to questions and share views (Brady, 2015, Okoli & Pawlowski, 2004) which was adapted in this research to gather opinion via Google Forms. This enabled rapid insights to be shared amongst policy makers from different countries alongside those teaching, researching and supporting the use of digital technologies and analogue interventions, to address disadvantage. In this way, the individual lived experience on what has worked and what hasn't in contexts of crisis was brought into dialogue. There are many ways that Delphi can be adapted as a process to support more dynamic and inclusive forms of policymaking using online systems across different cultures and communities.

Our own adaptation of Delphi demonstrated that dialogue is crucial in the policy making decisions to address crises. Digital technologies make these exchanges possible now in much broader contexts to develop new approaches towards inclusivity. Those who participated in the Delphi exchange with us were working with different minority groups or were specialists in different regions of Africa. Others had considerable experience in distance learning or expertise in policy making in different regions or with marginalised groups. More detailed explanations of the Delphi process (which was really a digitally-enabled simulation of a face to face discussion) can be read in the report. At a time when many university staff are already communicating across online forums to conduct their daily activities, the chance to involve local regional agencies or international ones to inform policy on inclusivity has never been more relevant. This allows an honest approach to towards including human (and technological) experience in policy making rather than simply writing about a package that universities are claiming to 'enhance' called 'the student experience'.

The simplistic McDelivery approach to policy not only treats students as if they are on a production line, the policy texts themselves then suggest that 'the student experience' has power to act on behalf of both students and academics alike (Hayes, 2019a: 6).

2 Ecological Approaches towards Policy That Begin from Positionality Not Rationality

Beginning to address matters of inclusivity from any point of rationality needs to be questioned as it is only one possible starting point. In a recent publication entitled *Incalculable experience* (Bertelsen, 2019) the importance of positionality with regard to experience is expressed. The starting point here is that rather than a rational measuring of student experience, such 'pre-determining pretences of the neoliberal education system' should be resisted in favour of exceeding 'the count':

> Thought and research, reading and writing are activities whose value should never be determined in advance. Neither should their value be reduced to the post-determinations of metrics. (Bertelsen, 2019)

Currently universities seek to control each of the various challenges that present themselves from 'outside' by placing them within rational frameworks that measure pre-determined ideas about inclusive practices or employability and what counts as 'success'. To move beyond a simple calulative model that sat within the current neoliberal political economy model and took a mostly *regulative* approach, a more critical dialogue is needed for the *normative* and *cultural-cognitive* levels to strengthen the postdigital university. Neither inclusivity nor sustainability agendas can be simply regulated, as if these lived inside universities when so many powerful global forces now act upon these areas of life. There is though, a choice for university leaders to take between either attempting to treat the sustainability agenda as if it were just another in the line-up of corporate policies or adopting a more critically reflexive stance in a 'post-corporate cultural model' (Delanty, 2020: 1).

2.1 Critical Sustainability

If the university adopts a more ecological approach then 'critical sustainability as part of a post-corporate cultural model' provides one 'alternative to the neoliberal conception of sustainability' (Delanty, 2020: 1). This would provide a different route for universities from their current purpose which has tended to see them reduced to something of a resource for corporate businesses to mould and a supply system providing work-ready graduates for companies to employ. Given that digitisation is promising to fundamentally disrupt current understandings of humanity itself, the university has responsibilities as a critically reflexive facilitator located at the very intersection of these powerful cross-sector, postdigital debates.

At a time when education is being placed as central to the United Nations Educational, Scientific and Cultural Organization roadmap for sustainable development (UNESCO, 2020d) and global activities towards sustainable futures (The Bioeconomy Council, 2019), Delanty argues that 'a clear relation to critique' has not yet been established. He points out that there are good reasons to be critical when sustainability derives from a 'global policy and corporate discourse' that is 'replete with contradictions and ambivalence'. Citing a fundamental problem (that I would argue sits well alongside the sorts of irrationality of rationality described by Ritzer), he suggests that:

> the notion of sustainability seeks to sustain that which has now become unsustainable and is therefore incompatible with radical political ecology and a concept of nature in keeping with the age of the Anthropocene. (Delanty, 2020: 2)

Delanty contests that it is only when the idea of 'unsustainability' is brought into the picture that the notion of 'sustainability' takes on a wider significance, in responding to calls for alternatives to endless growth and the widely felt need for a more collective responsibility. Whilst there is consensus on the need in general for sustainable environmental policies, in terms of 'what needs to be done', there is little consensus on 'how it should be done'. In proposing a post-corporate cultural model as an alternative to a neoliberal conception of sustainability, this also offers something of a corrective to ideas of 'post-sustainability' (Foster, 2017), 'namely the argument that sustainability has become devoid of relevance and has become an empty term' (Delanty, 2020: 3).

Whilst sustainability, like so many other buzz terms has been made 'banal' in corporate discourse, with multiple meanings concerning what is to be sustained and by whom, 'the term has now become integral to the very nature of

POSTDIGITAL POSITIONALITY AS A LEADER AND POLICY MAKER 247

democracy, such that it no longer resides in a domain separate to social and political institutions and practices. To this end Delanty argues that 'sustainability is an inherently cultural category and needs to be understood as such' (Delanty, 2020: 4).

2.2 Cross-Sector Postdigital Dialogue Led by Humanities and Computing

The arguments above, coupled with Delanty's (2001) call for a reconnection in universities of the discourse between technology and culture, offer productive routes to think through future possibilities for ecological pathways for university policies. However, these then require a dual resistance from both humanities and computing, to totalising McPolicy agendas. They need to be widely inclusive too, of cross-sector postdigital dialogue.

So how might humanities and computing together lead such a debate? Michael Peters argues that currently we find ourselves in a 'bad ecology', a storm that 'links data, life and the planet', it:

> Integrates human beings into systems as part of the hive intelligence that harnesses big data and puts its analysis to new commercial uses. (Peters, 2020: 593)

Computing therefore has a place and a ready supply of data, but as discussed in Chapter 2, there are probing HCI questions and complex intersectional debates already taking place. In the humanities on the other hand there is also broad debate across different branches, from digital humanities to philosophy, but perhaps it is important to re-examine what remains in the former categories of thought:

> Meanwhile, philosophy is still busy debating its age-old questions: freedom, agency, happiness, the good life. (Peters, 2020: 593)

At this point of crisis where the information age is meeting new bioinformational and bioeconomic challenges and possibilities, Peters points out that:

> Philosophy in the age of information has gone off-shore to the AI engineer. The old categories are empty containers formulated in the Enlightenment and form an ideal board game with no winners. They are not able to describe or analyse the current fifth generation cybernetic system rationality that engulfs us all changing the very conditions of existence. (Peters, 2020: 593)

248   CHAPTER 6

Therefore, the question of positionality is key here, if the fields of humanities and computing are to jointly lead a cross-sector postdigital debate, particularly one in which our human biological status itself is in the process of being digitised.

2.3   *Academic Freedom of Speech in the Postdigital Debate*

Meanwhile, on the topic of postdigital debate there are also issues for universities who don't rise to the challenges of taking such a dialogue into the wider community. Dorrell (2020) picks up on the risks that arise for academia in failing to engage with the broader politics and agencies outside of institutions.

FIGURE 49
A local business details its policy for operating as 'normal' during the Covid-19 pandemic

On the issue of 'academic freedom of speech' he perceives there are 'escalating culture wars'. Referring to a report by a particular think tank and adviser to government he suggests that:

> If universities can make themselves central to this conversation, then they might no longer be seen as an enemy to defeat. (Dorrell, 2020)

All the more so, 'if universities place themselves at 'the centre of the conversation about improving the lives of those who live in the satellite towns beyond their immediate horizons' (Dorrell, 2020). This includes building strong connections with local government and the many businesses that have struggled through the pandemic lockdowns (Figure 49).

Thus, universities who engage with the place-based agendas of 'levelling up' (University Partnerships Programme Foundation, 2018) will be in a better position to lead cross-sector debate. However, this also requires a stronger focus on

POSTDIGITAL POSITIONALITY AS A LEADER AND POLICY MAKER 249

local priorities and not just on institutional ones. It is only through a stronger connection with citizens themselves that universities will be able to develop their postdigital inclusivity agendas to become active and meaningful.

2.4 University Strategy and Postdigtial Organisational Change

University strategy therefore cannot be based only on lessons learned from the past or on solutionist views of digital technologies to simply 'enhance' what HE already does. The shift taking place as life itself becomes digitised and a convergence of disciplines follows could provide us yet with new critical and sustainable routes out of the crisis. Reeves suggests that it is not enough to 'place a passive trust in technologies that we barely understand', but in taking a postdigital perspective on organisations, we might 'prioritise the experiences that we want organisations to provide'. This concerns what is valued 'for society and the environment' but we need to adapt our behaviour accordingly' (Reeves, 2019: 197).

Meanwhile, Scott (2010: 17) points to a need to:

> consider the full range of mechanisms that allow institutional forms to emerge, the struggles over their shape and meaning, and the efforts to create institutional settlements as well as to destabilize, dismantle, and reconfigure them. All are important moments in the ways of the social world. (Scott, 2010: 17)

Of the many approaches that have been devised to construct frameworks for understanding social change, Scott draws together some key features that are distinctive to an institutional perspective:

- A detailed attention to existing institutional variety at the organisation, sector field, or societal level;
- A focus on the interdependence of and interactions between organised units at multiple levels;
- An awareness of the effects of non-local, as well as local factors;
- An appreciation of the temporal nature of social life, the ongoing effects of the past on the present and future;
- emphasis on the importance of ideas (symbolic systems) that mediate between environmental conditions and actions;
- an awareness that processes may produce convergence of procedures and forms but also promote diversity and the emergence of new types of social behaviour and novel systems.

Scott concludes that:

250   CHAPTER 6

> Important changes are proceeding apace throughout the developed and
> developing world, and while there are signs of increasing homogeniza-
> tion and convergence, equally strong indicators attest to the preservation
> and development of diversity. (2010: 18)

It is therefore a diverse and inclusive postdigital debate that universities are in
a unique position to lead on and institutional theory has its place in helping to
'tease out and untangle the complex structures involved and the diverse processes and mechanisms at work' (Scott, 2020: 18). This could include taking forward cross-sector debate on possible postdigital scenarios, and their strengths
in this context for new approaches towards inclusivity.

2.5   *Postdigital Scenario Planning and Inclusivity*

Matt Finch describes future scenario planning as 'instructional fables for
organisations' (Finch, 2020). With the pace of digitalisation and scientific
change that is before us, fables could soon become realities. Therefore, some
postdigital scenario planning could help us examine different possible futures
that would offer alternative to a neoliberal conception of sustainability and
take us in the direction of a post-corporate cultural model of critical sustainability (Delanty, 2020: 4). For example, Michael Peters raises the question:

> Are we destined to evolve into bioinformational beings that become more
> and more integrated into a single evolving data processing system? Once
> the link between bioinformational technologies and cognitive sciences is
> made at the nano-level... then, surely, corporations and governments will
> be able to hack human beings. Goodbye humanism as an educational
> and pedagogical philosophy. (2020: 600)

Here then is a question that has to involve both the disciplines of Humanities
and Computing. Finch suggests there are a very broad range of questions that
are yet to become clear:

> The pandemic has accelerated or triggered numerous transformations
> whose full consequences are yet to become clear, while other, previously
> existing trends may now bend or break as a result of 2020's crises. The
> pandemic response may, in turn, cause new uncertainties – from the
> long-term health of the economy to the immediate question of university
> admissions. (Finch, 2020)

However, what remains important is that universities develop new strategic
capabilities. This includes:

rigorous and disciplined approaches to uncertainty which allow us to make leadership decisions on bases other than the evidence and experience of a past which may never repeat. (Finch, 2020)

The use of scenario planning therefore offers:

one method to convene a community of forward-thinking practitioners and engage them in the serious discussion of our strategic blindspots, informing and enriching future decision-making for the post-pandemic university. (Finch, 2020)

University leaders are no exception to the intersecting aspects of positionality discussed earlier by Torres-Olave and Lee (2019). Therefore, in postdigital debate across a range of scenarios there is power to bring together the communities Finch describes to influence our collective futures. It is necessary though for this debate to combine both academic and cross-sector civic leadership if the broad and contentious concerns that fall under inclusivity are to be addressed. The scenarios may sound futuristic but they may also be potentially current circumstances, bringing both complexities but also unintended consequences to plan for.

CHAPTER 7

Conclusions on Postdigital Futures

1   When Biological Environments Change, Social Arrangements Need
     to Alter Too

Seven years before Covid-19 became a reality across the globe, Dingwall, Hoffman and Staniland (2013) called for a *Sociology of Pandemics*. They argued:

> Infectious disease has re-emerged as a public health threat in an increasingly globalised era, adding transnational actors to traditional national and local government actors. (Dingwall, Hoffman & Staniland, 2013)

With a background in Sociology, I am not likely to disagree with applying critical theory to theorise pandemics (particularly when the year in which this book has been written has revealed just what global, local and individual reach a virus like Covid-19 has). Sociology can enable deep insights into social behaviour and society. It supports debate on complex relationships, power structures, social interaction and the language and culture that surrounds our everyday lives. Via empirical investigation and critical analysis, Sociology is a discipline that contributes to a body of knowledge about social order and social change, such as effects from the mandatory wearing of face masks, or shopping alone (Figure 50). Yet Sociology cannot tackle an analysis of the new postdigital positionalities we now find ourselves in on its own. In our rapidly changing postdigital context, interdisciplinary consortiums, cross-sector cooperation, analysis and interpretations are needed in order to capture powerful narratives across traditional, emerging and converging disciplinary shifts, amid rapid digital change.

In universities we have at our fingertips a wealth of academic disciplines, with new ones arriving regularly, alongside the social, scientific and technological changes that bring them into being. The pandemic has made our society 'anthropologically strange' to us (Dingwall, Hoffman, & Staniland, 2013) and it has accelerated many technological and scientific changes that were already bringing fundamental shifts to how we might perceive ourselves as humans (Hall, 2013, Fuller & Jandrić, 2018, Braidotti, 2019a, 2019b, De Vos, 2020, Savin-Baden, 2021). From simply spending much more time conducting activities online, right through to far reaching bioinformational and biodigital changes that are yielding new postdigital knowledge ecologies (Peters, Jandrić

© KONINKLIJKE BRILL NV, LEIDEN, 2021 | DOI: 10.1163/9789004466029_009

CONCLUSIONS ON POSTDIGITAL FUTURES

FIGURE 50
A reminder of government
regulations during the
pandemic

& Hayes, 2021a), what we currently perceive as 'inclusivity' policy necessitates ongoing, interdisciplinary debate. In turn, universities and the regions around them, require new pathways for more dynamic postdigital policies, that are informed and updated organically through cross-sector dialogue and diverse positionalities.

Positionality has traditionally involved a reflexive dialogue between self, and the social and political context that creates individual identity, in terms of e.g. race, class, gender, sexuality, ability, status (England, 1994, Bourke, 2014, Luttrell, 2019). Positionality now needs to reflexively encompass too, the multiple reconfigurations between technologies and humans that alter who, and what, humans are. In their reconfigured status, human identities converge with effects from widespread digitalisation (OECD, 2020) raising new challenges in terms of equality, diversity and inclusivity agendas. Who, or what, contributes to discrimination, and who, or what, becomes a victim of bias, are new ethical questions to anticipate and debate. Then there are questions of whose logic influences related strategies and regulations and how this shift may now begin to alter the structure and values underpinning McPolicy discourse.

In HE we have been required to distance ourselves from many structures we had come to accept due to Covid-19 and these measures have intermingled with the wider restrictions placed on our lives. Such fundamental alterations indicate that our 'social arrangements can, and must, change when biological environments change' (Dingwall et al., 2013). There is a recognition then in this acknowledgement of much wider infrastructures where dialogue between different forms of governance (technological, material, scientific, public health, economic, security, surveillance, media and communications, to name just a few) needs to aid a more critically sustainable response (Delanty, 2020). Berlant argues that 'infrastructure is not identical to system or structure' (Berlant, 2016: 393). Indeed, narrow calculative structures restrict what is knowable and thinkable in complex patterns of human interaction (Hayes, 2020). A 'glitch' like Covid-19 renders these structures visible for what they always were: not a reflection of infrastructure, just one form of structural organisation (Hayes, 2020). As such, HE requires new 'thinking infrastructures' that reflect the living mediation of what now organises life and learning, to help us to redo and rework previously restrictive policy models (Kornberger et al., 2019).

I argued in *The Labour of Words in HE* that it was time for humans to reoccupy the restricting McPolicy discourse we have worked within, but which has failed to linguistically acknowledge our academic labour (Hayes, 2019a). With no room for debate, McPolicy has provided a powerful structure to legitimate a series of measuring exercises of what activities might be enhanced across HE. Yet still inequities persist, as intersections where policies need to meet are overlooked (Czerniewicz & Rother, 2018, Hayes, 2019: 135, Equality Act Review, 2020b). This is but one structuring of policy that emerged as an exercise of control to support the neoliberal, McDonaldised organisation of our universities. Based on a notion of a student as a passive consumer with a generalised experience that might be 'measured', this is a structure that now sits uncomfortably with new collaborative global sustainability goals and the ecological and positional approaches needed to support these. Furthermore, as universities prepare to admit a new generation of young people, already being referred to as 'generation Covid' (Wonkhe, 2021) who have lived with the disadvantages and mental health challenges of a pandemic (ImpactEd, 2021), it is necessary to review the issues that taking a simple therapeutic approach exacerbates (Apperley, 2014, Furedi, 2016, Ecclestone & Hayes, 2019) and to respond to feedback from students on their online learning experiences (Jackson, 2021) to learn from this, beyond the pandemic. New values require new policies, and it is time to consider what policy shaped by postdigital dialogue (Jandrić et al., 2018) might offer us in terms of inclusion of diverse positionalities to address inequalities.

CONCLUSIONS ON POSTDIGITAL FUTURES   255

I opened this book then with an intention to explore positionality in these postdigital times by raising a twofold debate. This has explored firstly, the new postdigital context that HE now occupies in society. This was examined in a year where a global pandemic has illuminated human digital dependencies and digital exclusion alike, out in the virtual airing cupboard of the Internet. Multiple and diverse 'actors' that are not all human, not all computer, are now shifting what, just a few years ago, were upheld as 'established' inclusive practices in universities (Department for Education, 2017). Therefore, I suggested secondly, that we might both recognise and explore what these rapid postdigital changes alter in our interpersonal relations and take a broader more inclusive view through positionality theory, on what strategies need to change in postdigital universities.

In our current approach towards equality, diversity and inclusivity agendas the focus has remained heavily tipped towards human interaction alone, with other non-human or beyond-human factors barely discussed, despite the powerful ways in which these now intersect across peoples' lives. Some have suggested that the pandemic has opened a portal through which humans might pivot from unsustainable levels of consumption. Others are arguing that we must 'build back fairer' (Health Foundation, 2020). As we look towards bio-economic solutions and possibilities, complex questions of 'digital health' (Petersen, 2018) and 'human dignity' (Zwijnenberg, 2014) join a fundamental challenge raised at the start. This concerns how universities might link the disengaged forces of cultural reproduction and technological production (Delanty, 2001: 157). A convergence is happening now though that needs to be recognised in HE policy. Even the application of critical theory by humans to analyse the world around them looks set to shift, as critical theory itself may find it occupies a new or different positionality, as a result of a widespread digitalisation of biology (OECD, 2020).

1.1   *What Are We Airing and What Remains in the Cupboard?*

When I introduced my airing cupboard as a participant it was a tongue-in-cheek, playful analogy intended to draw attention to the intermingled 'airing' of so much information and human emotion across the Internet. Amid the broad dimensions of cancel culture there are complex rationalities at play, where even an author of a book on cancel culture itself, Julie Burchill, found herself cancelled by her publisher due to remarks she made over Twitter (BBC Entertainment & Arts, 2020). Regardless even of the politics of this particular debate, it is perhaps interesting to note how this gets categorised under the 'entertainment' section of the BBC News website. Mark Carrigan has drawn attention to both the promise of social media in academia and also some deeply problematic strands we need to notice and be personally aware of. Drawing on the way in which platforms are designed to subtly encourage our compulsive use of them, this brings a theoretical background of behaviourism into people's everyday lives, homes and families. Therefore, whilst the '*mass* character of commercial social media platforms breaks down the stable boundaries between the university and wider society, opening up a liminal space in which new ways of working can thrive', unfortunately there is a new 'professionalisation of Twitter within UK universities' which 'progressively undercuts this':

> Its use becomes something which intersects with the institutional context in deeply obscure and rapidly evolving ways. I worry it has come to be something which hybridises the personal and the professional in the most subtly violent manner, leading work to become life and life to become work. (Carrigan, 2020b)

This is a topic picked up by Aral (2020) in a book: *The hype machine: How social media disrupts our elections, our economy, and our health – and how we must adapt,* who claims the pandemic ignited the online world like 'a digital forest fire' (Aral, 2020). Providing both 'human connectivity, social support and lifesaving information' but also acting as 'a cauldron of misinformation about impending national lockdowns and false cures', Aral argues that 'the threat of surveillance capitalism morphed into lifesaving disease surveillance' (Aral, 2020: xiv). Then there are the problems of a lack of legislation that will help to capture activities of hateful extremism across social media platforms, including hate crime, terrorism and incitement of violence. In a report: *Operating with impunity: legal review* (Commission for Countering Extremism, 2021) the balance between dangerous extremist activity and freedom of expression is confronted, with a call for a new legal framework to protect democracy.

1.2   *How Will HE Inclusivity Policy Include the Internet of Things?*
As discussed already, we are living currently with the irrationalities of our McDonaldised rational society and maybe a sense of the ridiculous can also help, as we seek to imagine possible alternative, postdigital futures. Static though it may appear then, there seem to be few barriers to me now inviting my hot water tank (just like other material or organic items) to become digitally intelligent and add its input to this debate. As part of the algorithmic internet of things (AIoT), the contents of my airing cupboard might join 'a paradigm shift where anything and everything can become interconnected', adding new security and privacy issues to existing ethical challenges (Pal, Hitchens, Rabehaja & Mukhopadhyay, 2020). It then becomes necessary to question

CONCLUSIONS ON POSTDIGITAL FUTURES

what reforms are needed to inclusivity policies (that still centre mostly around human-to-human discriminatory practices). Inclusivity policies themselves need to be inclusive of the hybrid assemblage of devices and potential data bias that humans now intimately interconnect with.

The connectivity that has made it possible to link up all manner of appliances, devices and objects through the Internet of Things (IoT) permits the territories of cultural reproduction and technological reproduction to become deeply interconnected across the virtual airing cupboard of the Internet. We are using the same complex virtual space to rant our hearts out across social media in one form of dialogue, and simultaneously we are conducting dialogue with doorbells, heating, appliances and the water tank in the hallway airing cupboard. All of this capability for gathering big data has arrived with us so recently that we are unable to conclude its fuller meaning. It is important that we try though, or as Thomas Ramge (2020) puts it, 'how can human beings use artificial intelligence, intelligently?'

1.3   *Internet or Splinternet?*

Yet, even whilst contemplating such challenges, there are suggestions that cracks are appearing in the virtual airing cupboard of the Internet:

> Over the last year, the worldwide web has started to look less worldwide. (Iyengar, 2021)

This claim is partly based on a series of potential bans of tech companies such as TikTok, WeChat and Twitter by various countries. It is also linked to a Facebook clash with the Australian government 'over a proposed law that would require it to pay publishers. Facebook 'briefly decided to prevent users from sharing news links in the country in response to the law, with the potential to drastically change how its platform functions from one country to the next' (Iyengar, 2021). Whilst a deal was reached to resolve this particular example, Facebook has suggested similar clashes are on the cards for the future. There is the concern that if:

> territorial agreements become more common, the globally connected internet we know will become more like what some have dubbed the 'splinternet' or a collection of different internets whose limits are determined by national or regional borders. (Iyengar, 2021)

Such potential regulatory crackdowns around the world are attributed to a combination of rising nationalism, trade disputes and concerns about the market dominance of certain global tech companies. The major problem that arises however is that this is not just a process of 'upending the tech companies that built massive businesses on the promise of a global internet' as discussed by James Ball (2020). This is a situation that now threatens 'the very idea of building platforms that can be accessed and used the same way by anyone anywhere in the world' (Iyengar, 2021).

1.4 Fragmentation or Sustainability and Inclusion?

This potential fragmentation of the Internet adds a further layer of complexity to the arguments I have put forward for university policies for inclusivity to also be inclusive of all aspects of the postdigital contexts we occupy. If the Internet is now meeting persistent barriers from different laws in different nations, then this presents a major global challenge to both inclusivity and sustainability. Yet on the other hand, reining in the big tech companies is something that many countries around the world are now gaining confidence to do. As Iyengar (2021) points out, these 'companies are ultimately dependent on continued access to billions of users around the world, and governments have shown they are willing to cut off that access in the name of protecting their citizens and sovereignty online' (Iyengar, 2021).

As possibilities for developing new synthetic forms of life, organic memory and algorithmic medicines become realities in this context, we might question also the implications for how we understand 'digital health' (Petersen, 2018). As we contemplate these challenges to traditional understandings of the human body, there are legal, practical, methodological and ethical questions that cluster, not to mention those concerning research funding bodies and policy. Further convergence between digital and biological science is rapidly following and we are still grappling with how best to regulate algorithmic capabilities. This has left little time to discuss how to reconnect the 'old pipes' of HE (such as our theories, practices, processes and policies) with these new digital and biological wires, amid rapid, cross-sector societal change. These examples are reminders of the 'plumbing' we now need to undertake, if we are to address societal inequalities via new technological possibilities.

Reforms to inclusivity policies focused on human-to-human discriminatory practices alone, need to now be more inclusive of all kinds of hybrid reshaped humans and computers. The Humanities and Computing disciplines need to step up their dialogue too, but as an inclusive cross-sector, cross-disciplinary, exchange. Our HE policy making processes and discourse now require a more ecological basis of critical sustainability (Delanty, 2020) through which we might organically anticipate new forms of bias, accountabilities and possibilities, that these intimate encounters will bring.

CONCLUSIONS ON POSTDIGITAL FUTURES

1.5   *Reviewing What Is Meant by Equality*

The Covid-19 pandemic has thus brought to light complex intersections where human biology and digital technologies intersect with human rights, data, environment and fluid aspects of personal identity and positionality. The post-digital nature of these interactions is revealed in the dialectics between human behaviour, such as social distancing, isolation, use of hand sanitiser and wearing of face coverings, alongside other technological and scientific innovations aimed at conquering the virus, as well as the use of data to inform decisions on when to lift lockdown restrictions. These aspects have interspersed with language too, as the mantras of 'hands, face, space' (Figure 51) and 'stay alert, control the virus, save lives' (Figure 52) have become adopted in physical places as well as online.

Ramge argues that 'artificial intelligence will not be able to relieve us of the burden of thinking, nor will it be able to tell us the right way to act socially' (Ramge, 2020). This means that we need approaches towards policy that can speak to both the diversity of people's positionalities and the rapidly changing postdigital contexts they find themselves in.

Objective forms of rationality, as revealed in McPolicy, are not likely to be able to address the linkages we require in universities between the disengaged

FIGURE 51
Reminders of the 'hands, face, space' hygiene routine

FIGURE 52
Reminders of the requirement to
wear face coverings in all shops

forces of cultural reproduction and technological production (Delanty, 2001: 157). Many examples of why this is the case have already been cited throughout the book but are also apparent in a recent review of the Equality Act 2010. In a campaign to review the Equality Act (Equality Act Review, 2020b) the convergence of multiple issues begins to be addressed in a suggested move away from a discrete list of protected characteristics alone.

An urgency to address poverty, unemployment, and inaccessibility to social and cultural capital exacerbated by the pandemic is being voiced in many related studies and reports.

1.6   What Disadvantages Didn't Covid-19 Intersect With?

On this basis we might wonder at whether there are any disadvantages that Covid-19 has not intersected with. Amid the conclusions in the *Predicting Futures* 2.0 report (Equality Act Review, 2020b) that the handling of predicted grades algorithmically amidst the Covid-19 pandemic has widened the inequality gap and will continue to do so, there is a reference to a 'toxic intersection'. This is an adaptable notion concerning the point at which numerous disadvantages cluster together to compound existing inequalities for individual citizens. As many research studies follow the effects from the pandemic it is not difficult to demonstrate why 'the role of education as a vehicle for social

CONCLUSIONS ON POSTDIGITAL FUTURES

mobility' is currently not working. In examples where there are low household incomes, there may also be challenges arising for different racial and ethnic identities. There may be additional influences too concerning the socioeconomic background people come from, or in relation to their gender. Then there is the 'largely unresolved gender pay gap that is widespread across all industries' along with the 'unconventional marker within intersectionality theory' of religion (Equality Act Review, 2020b). To add to these and many more characteristics that can merge in an individual's life to affect their positionality, education and employment opportunities, are the complex technological examples this book has discussed.

Yet technology alone cannot fix the challenges of equality and inclusivity in education either. As Reich puts it, technology is only as strong as the community of educators around it (Reich, 2020). Technology is frequently omitted in any depth from policies or reports on inclusivity, but Covid-19 has clearly shown us why the 'dialectics of digitalisation' (Ramge, 2020) with biological and cultural change can no longer be sat on the sidelines of this debate. Indeed, this is an inclusive topic in itself that each of us has a stake in.

1.7   *Digitalisation, Positionality and (Inter) Subjectivity*
De Vos (2020) argues that our very (inter) subjectivity is at stake now. Pointing to the way in which psychological interpretations about a problematic use of our data are often made at the point when there is some kind of breach, or bias, De Vos reminds us that it is psychology that actually underpins the platforms we use across the Internet. Digital platforms like Google, Facebook, Twitter and others 'function fundamentally via heuristics that are informed by psychology' (De Vos, 2020). Silicon Vally companies have a principal interest in knowing our searches, clicks and likes and so in other words, our desires. Given how much we share, they know the dirty laundry we each air too. Or as DeVos puts it 'our thoughts, images, emotions, memories' present themselves in this 'amphitheatre for our psychological life'. As such, De Vos recommends that psychologists need to proceed critically with regard to digitalisation and to disentangle their (neuro) psy-theories from their implications given that these actually structure the digital technologies themselves that are under scrutiny.

Here then we have a matter of positionality for the researchers in psychology to reflexively address. Still though it is one that involves us all when DeVos poses the question that: 'if psychoanalysis constitutes the most expedient critique of how the psychoanalytic infrastructure of digitality is compliant with, and even fundamental to, what one might designate as digital capitalism, then could psychoanalysis also offer an alternative for a different mode of

262   CHAPTER 7

digitality?' It is an important question to pose, and also to raise it from many different disciplinary angles, when we contemplate the place that data intensive biology appears to be taking up now in education.

1.8   *Data intensive Biology in Education*

Whilst the digital may have become 'the master narrative of our world' (Fuller & Jandrić, 2019: 215), the biological is more important than ever (Mañero, 2020). Ben Williamson has drawn attention to how advanced technologies that can process complex biological data have now transformed the human sciences and are now being used to conduct studies and generate new knowledge in the field of education (Williamson, 2019a). Pickerskill (2020) has demonstrated how epigenetic processes are of increasing interest to a range of professionals beyond biomedicine. This he says is piqued by the notion of 'the plastic body' and 'the belief that bioscientific research is demonstrating new molecular mechanisms through which the social and physical environment impact upon the bodies of humans and other animals' (Pickerskill, 2020: 72). These are far reaching interventions that extend the idea of what education is and what it can do. The problem lies in what rationality sits behind the interpretations that are being made, such as visions of biology that ahere to certain ideas of a 'good society' and the policies and practices need to reach this (Pickerskill, 2020: 79). Citing some 'problematic ontological moves from specific behaviours in rats to assemblages of actions and ideas in humans when theorising about the import of epigenetics for education', Pickerskill uncovers some worrying pathways. He suggests therefore that:

> If biological and education researchers are going to be increasingly wading into each other's waters, substantive, thoughtful, and self-critical dialogue between them is surely warranted. (Pickerskill, 2020: 72)

Williamson has adopted a categorisation of 'precision education' for these and other developments such as brain-based teaching (Pykett, 2015), neurotechnologies and polygenic scoring (Williamson, 2019a) and argues for the necessity of interdisciplinary collaborative research across areas such as education technology and governance, social and political geography and sociology of science and medicine.

1.9   *What Visions May Lie Ahead in a Bioeconomic Political Economy?*

Taking into account these, and indeed all of the digital challenges and possibilities that have been 'aired' in this book to aid the debate on postdigital positionality and inclusivity in HE, I will turn finally to reflect on what a

CONCLUSIONS ON POSTDIGITAL FUTURES

bioeconomic political economy might offer not only as an alternative to our current neoliberal political economy, but in changing the McPolicy discourse. Delanty (2020) discussed the notion of critical sustainability and a post-corporate HE. In a series of recent papers Michael Petars, Petar Jandrić and I have recently explored ideas on what biodigital philosophy and technological convergence might yield in terms of new and powerful knowledge ecologies (2021a). In a follow up paper, we then discussed biodigital technologies and the bioeconomy in relation to the global new green deal (2021b) and in a third paper, we embarked on a postdigital-biodigital debate to raise varied questions that had been occurring to each of us in writing the previous two papers (2021c). In a fourth paper (2021d), we revisited the concept of the 'edited collection' itself, to explore new values and approaches that might emerge in collaboration with other authors on the *Bioinformation Philosophy and Postdigital Knowledge Ecologies* book (forthcoming). Our work on these papers has helped to consolidate our positionalities on many interesting questions and ideas, but there are many more questions ahead for us all.

Currently there are far reaching consequences for our environment and ourselves if a change of direction from our current political economy is not realised. Now that technological and scientific progress towards a circular bioeconomy presents possible solutions, there are questions that the social sciences and humanities need to raise, alongside new educational programmes to help effect far reaching and critically sustainable change (Saachi, Lotti and Branduardi, 2020). Therefore, for me and my interest in altering the tired McPolicy discourse in HE, I have wondered whether 'political bioeconomy' represents a new, extended field of thought, or an alternative way that society is organised. What new discourses and related behaviours might emerge then through political bioeconomy? Might we witness a change of direction from the dominant, growth focused, market-led discourse about how technology will automatically enhance experience (as if experience were something universal that we all share)? If new forms of 'political bioeconomic discourse' are on the horizon for us, then such a discourse would contribute to new directions for the postdigital debate that I have proposed on inclusivity. It leaves me wondering too, what kinds of reasoning powers will we be likely to require for our debate in a political bioeconomy? (Peters, Jandrić & Hayes, 2021c).

1.10 What Might a Political Bioeconomic Discourse Look Like in HE Policy?

Thirty years ago Hlynka and Belland (1991: v) argued that whilst the paradigm shift identified by Thomas Kuhn (1962/2012) drew attention to alternative methods of research, it is 'ironic that educational technology, a field which prides itself on being within the vanguard of change, suddenly appears instead to be lagging behind other fields and disciplines'. They added that 'educational technology appears to have become stuck fast in a technological means-end model' (Hlynka & Belland, 1991: v). In the disappointing decades that have followed, this quick-fix identity for technology within education has been overlaid and repeated in the policy discourse that has accompanied many years of digital development. Furthermore, it left us ill-prepared to meet individual learners at their point of need during successive lockdowns, as widespread digital poverty and exclusion has been revealed (Holmes & Burgess, 2020, Westwater, 2021). The 'coronavirus pandemic has injected fresh urgency into the education technology conversation' and 'it is important to note that there is no "one size fits all" solution to modernising education; it will very much depend on individual courses or student needs' (Li, 2021).

If a political bioeconomic discourse is to offer a more ecological and inclusive alternative to McPolicy in HE, then it will require critical understandings to develop across education, government agencies and commercial providers to finally shift from a widely critiqued 'student-as-consumer' approach (Driscoll & Wicks, 1998, Molesworth, Nixon & Scullion, 2009, Bunce, Baird & Jones, 2017, Brooks, 2018, Peters, Jandrić & Hayes, 2018, Hayes and Jandrić, 2018: 128, Hayes, 2019a). A consumer model of student learning derived from our neoliberal political economy (Olssen & Peters, 2005) and a McDonaldisation of HE (Hayes, D, 2017) reflected in a discourse of McPolicy (Hayes, 2019a) will no longer align with the aspirations of a resilient, sustainable bioeconomy (Peters, Jandrić & Hayes, 2021b). Therefore, HE policy needs a new relationship with the postdigital environment that universities now occupy. This includes an analysis of evolving new working patterns during lockdown that can be observed to some extent even via examining electricity usage (National Grid, 2020). Then there are the benefits and risks involved in home working, including additional 'vulnerability to cyber crime' through the Internet that has arisen for many during the pandemic. In a report entitled: *The UK's Response to Cyber Fraud A Strategic Vision* 'a response that goes beyond the incremental change that has occurred over the past few years' is called for. This is because 'cyber fraud now accounts for most of the fraud committed in the UK' (Dawda, Janjeva & Moiseienko, 2021). The authors argue too that it poses distinct challenges compared to 'traditional', offline types of fraud, such as:

> A need for high-quality digital forensic skills in the investigation of cyber fraud; the virtually unlimited pool of possible offenders from around the world; and the likelihood that – in contrast to the investigation of other

CONCLUSIONS ON POSTDIGITAL FUTURES   265

types of crime – state-of-the-art expertise and resources may reside in
the private sector rather than law enforcement agencies. (Dawda, Janjeva
& Moiseienko, 2021)

Whilst Gary Hall (2013) argued that the digital humanities does not bring
computing and humanities together as 'equivalent', digitisation has extended
such a reach across disciplines, life and work that Braidotti (2019a) has called
for a theoretical framework for the critical posthumanities to incorporate new
fields of transdisciplinary knowledge. Her work also brings new insights for how
a so-called non-human might be suitably acknowledged alongside a human.
As I have argued throughout this book, all humans and non-humans need to
be given their place as participants in inclusivity strategies. This emphasises
also that rather than reduce the role of the humanities, arts and literature in
universities, as recent developments have indicated, a new emphasis might be
drawn on why literary communities actually 'matter to human rights' (Stonebridge, 2020). This links well with postdigital understandings and Delanty's
arguments for a critical sustainability discourse that might move us forward in
a post-corporate model for HE.

To appreciate how a widespread digitalisation across all aspects of life in the
virtual airing cupboard has shifted positionality, we might reflect once more on
Braidotti's argument that in our online activities we are increasingly required
to verify that we are in fact a human, and not a robot of some sort (Braidotti,
2019a). To this example we might add many other instances where a constant
and fatiguing verification of our human identity and permissions is required in
the virtual airing cupboard. We make repeated 'sign ins' that require complex
passwords to be updated, an acceptance of cookies is expected from us at every
turn. Autocorrect does its utmost to cause embarrassment whenever we send
a text hastily and don't look to see what has been altered. Then there are the
unexpected reminders we may never recall requesting, such as details of our
daily or weekly screen time flashing up before us, or the latest news stream pop-
ping up alongside many inconvenient system updates which provoke automatic
computer shutdowns. This situation 'assumes as the central point of reference
the algorithmic culture of computational networks – not the human' (Braidotti, 2019a), but we are rapidly moving towards a more ambiguous situation still,
where digital processing of complex biological data has now started to alter disciplinary focus in the sciences (OECD, 2020) and to bring 'precision education'
into universities (Williamson, 2019a). Such advances are yielding new postdigital knowledge ecologies (Peters, Jandrić & Hayes, 2021a) and an urgent need for
these developments to be reflected in new forms of HE policy for inclusivity.

1.11 Giving the Final Word to the Airing Cupboards, Silos, Apps and Climate Change

Whilst people can take to the streets (when not in a pandemic lockdown) and protest for greater equality and acceptance of diversity, when they take to the 'sheets' within the virtual airing cupboard, they may find that their human liberty and positionality is continually overridden. Not only is it pretty 'heated' out there in the virtual airing cupboard of the Internet, through cancel culture between people, our data and verbal exchanges travel through many more 'collaborators' than we can see or possibly know.

It is a state that has become normalised, but it alters how human rights, diversity and inclusivity are enacted. Amoore (2020) raised the problem that 'machine learning algorithms that anticipate our future propensities are seriously threatening the chances that we have to make possible alternative political futures' (Amoore, 2020: 1). Braidotti (2019b: 31) therefore questions: 'what are the parameters that define a posthuman knowing subject, her scientific credibility and ethical accountability?' She refers to 'posthuman times', which is a matter for critical debate in itself, when there are others who would argue that 'we have always been posthuman' (Matthewman, 2011: 172). Setting this debate in a postdigital context is just one way to acknowledge a landscape of global, cross-sector, biodigital and disciplinary change, along with the complexities that this brings to individual positionalities.

Price (2020) has put forward the case for examining 'human-virus-data relations' and issues of social justice that arise as governments have come to rely on contact tracing apps to help address the global public health emergency (Price, 2020: 772). This provides another route into looking at forms of postdigital hybrid assemblages that Covid-19 is illuminating and the impact these have on people's individual postdigital positionalities. The apps collect data via people's smart phones for analysis by a risk-scoring algorithm to determine if public health authorities should be alerted if a user has come into contact with a person with Covid-19. The apps may be a tool, but they are more than this, they are 'biological-more-than-human-entities'. Given that use of contact-tracing apps is mandatory in certain countries and some groups in society may be stigmatised or disenfranchised by contact-tracing apps. Contact-tracing apps 'may increase the vulnerability of those who are already vulnerable, reduce and weaken data security and privacy, and undermine trust in healthcare provision' (Price, 2020: 787). Placing these arguments within our broader, global environmental challenges, and the multispecies entanglements that are needed to sustain life on Earth, Price argues that humans are just as likely to exploit them and that:

CONCLUSIONS ON POSTDIGITAL FUTURES   267

Covid-19 most likely arose because of the human exploitation of another species. Only when we acknowledge these contradictions, can we move forward in addressing the problems we are collectively facing. Whilst it may not be immediately obvious what the relationship is between the Anthropocene and Covid-19, the two are inextricably linked. (Price, 2020: 776)

Gergen (2009) puts forward the idea that we live in a world of 'co-constitution'. Suggesting that we are always already emerging from relationship, that we cannot step out of relationship and that even in our most private moments we are never alone. Gergen argues that for the wellbeing of the planet we must protect the 'generative processes of relating' (Gergen, 2009). With this idea in mind, postdigital positionality provides one way to examine how we might inclusively relate all aspects of our postdigital society to each of our diverse positionalities. Our environment has changed and, as we alter and adapt to new convergences and possibilities, the challenge is for HE policy to recognise the impact of these co-constituted matters in the lives of students and staff.

Our current political economy is predicated on consumer consumption rather than environmental renewal, but even the discourse of activism now needs to change. Indeed, as observed by the Venerable Dr Rosemarie Mallett, Archdeacon of Croydon, there is a distinct lack of diversity amongst climate activists. This is particularly apparent in this big year for environmental activism as preparations take place for the landmark COP26 conference to be held in Glasgow, UK in November 2021.

Mallett suggests that it is time to move beyond the merely disruptive 'shocking' protests, as this kind of action could be deemed to be a 'white middle-class activity', with black people more aware of the impact on their lives if they get arrested (Holland, 2021). Questioning whether the climate movement is now 'at a crossroads' she points out that 'change often doesn't come via revolution but via evolution' (Holland, 2021). It is therefore time for HE to take a leading role in such cross-sector and cross-societal evolutionary change. To begin to relate university policies for inclusivity to the wider environment of critical sustainability that has already accepted our more-than-human collaborators, is a good place to start. Thus, to conclude on a final point of wackiness, Scott (2010: 18) suggests that 'we need to better exploit and learn from the multiple natural experiments in institution building, maintenance, and demolition now underway in our rapidly changing world'. Having drawn on a few metaphors during the course of this book, as well as people's concerns over the 'behaviourist' stance that our digital technologies have emerged from, I may as well

FIGURE 53
A snowman sports a face
mask alongside the more
traditional carrot during
Winter 2020

return to these considerations. Given that a silo (we understand) is already engaged in 'constructive thinking', the question to bring to our next postdigital debate is, are we?

Even as I conclude this book, a university consortium is bringing together several ground-breaking threads of biodigital research to create the Active Living Infrastructure: Controlled Environment (ALICE). A prototype that could revolutionise housing and replace fossil fuels through 'living bricks', ALICE:

> creates a living, breathing, energy-generating microbial system that can simultaneously supply power to your home and talk to you through augmented reality to tell you how productive and 'happy' it is. (UKRI, 2021)

Price points out that we need to find ways to live alongside our apps and other 'more-than-human counterparts'. As such, we 'need to learn to stay with the trouble and not to be afraid to stand up to what we are unsure of' (Price, 2020: 789).

Perhaps if we manage to bring the bricks, silos, contact tracing apps and airing cupboards on board with inclusive forms of 'critical thinking', as part of the intimate flow of knowledge passing between the humanities and computing, and critically and honestly represent these relationships in university policy discourse, then we may really begin to know where we stand.

Glossary

Airing cupboard   a cupboard where a hot water tank is kept. It stores water that has been heated either by a boiler or within the tank itself. Such cupboards are usually near a stairway, bedroom or bathroom. Due to the warmth, people air clothes and towels on shelves in them.

Artificial Intelligence (AI)   a broad branch of computer science concerned with building smart machines capable of performing tasks that typically would require human intelligence. AI is an interdisciplinary science with multiple approaches, but advancements in machine learning and deep learning are creating a paradigm shift across the technology industry.

Biodigital convergence   the interactive combination, sometimes to the point of merging, of digital and biological technologies and systems.

Biodigitalism   the mutual interaction and integration of information and biology, where the manipulation of biological systems in computational biology is beginning to fundamentally reconfigure all levels of theory and practice.

Bioeconomy   a knowledge-based production and use of natural or biological resources, together with biological processes and laws, that allow the provision of goods and services in an environmentally friendly way.

Bioinformationalism   new organic forms of computing that apply computer science and information technology to the field of biology to better understand biological processes. The creation of databases, algorithms, computational and statistical techniques and theory to solve formal and practical problems arising from the management and analysis of biological data.

Cancel culture   an Internet-based practice of ostracising someone for something they have said. Sometimes referred to as call-out culture, the objection can sometimes be aggressive, or involve a painful, widely broadcast form of shaming of individuals or public figures.

Circular bioeconomy   an economic model where biological resources are renewable, sustainably managed, recovered and reused as much as possible. A way to deliver society's needs while responding to sustainability issues.

Digitalisation   refers in general to any aspect of society that is being digitally transformed and to related evolving discussions of such processes, strategies and business models in society, academia and industry.

Flesh electric   a term that Tyson Lewis adopts in reference to the postdigital 'instead of assuming as a starting point a dichotomy between analog and digital educational forms of life, it assumes that they are always already plugged into one another: a flesh electric' (Lewis, 2020: 265).

Genomics   the study of all of a person's genes (the genome), including interactions of those genes with each other and with the person's environment.

Inclusivity   the quality, practice or policy of trying to include all different types of people and treat them fairly and equally, such as providing equal access to opportunities and resources for those who might otherwise be excluded, marginalised in some form.

McDonaldisation   a term developed by the American sociologist, George Ritzer. He defines McDonaldisation as the process by which the principles of the fast-food restaurant are coming to dominate more and more sectors of society.

McPolicy   a term I developed, drawing on Ritzer's work, to refer to a McDonaldisation of HE Policy. McPolicy discourse is characterised by strong patterns of repetition in HE policy statements, where technologies, strategies and other objects are attributed with human labour.

Political economy   the interdisciplinary study of the way in which governments influence or organise their nation's economic resources under e.g. socialism, communism, capitalism or neoliberalism and interrelationships between the resulting public policy and individuals.

Positionality   the social and political context that creates a person's identity, e.g. race, class, gender, sexuality, ability status. Positionality also describes how each person's identity influences, or potentially biases, their understanding of and outlook on the world.

Postdigital   refers to the idea that people are increasingly no longer in a world where digital technology and media are separate, virtual, or 'other' to a 'natural' human and social life. Both a rupture in our existing theories and their continuation, postdigital life is unpredictable, digital and analog, technological and non-technological, biological and informational.

Postdigital positionality   is a concept I develop in this book by placing the terms of postdigital and positionality side by side, to demonstrate how individuals will experience postdigital contexts in unique and diverse ways, depending on their positionality.

Posthumanism   a critical, theoretical and eco-conscious paradigm that looks beyond humanism and 'opens up the world to its contents. It recognises that our technologies are always in attendance, and that they are far from the only party to our human being' (Matthewman, 2011: 164).

Rationality   interpreted as a narrow form of reasoning that seeks the optimum means to any given end and is shaped by regulations, institutions and social structures.

Rationalisation   a development of Weber's theory of bureaucracy by Ritzer, to show how rationalisation extends into global cultural homogenisation via McDonaldisation. Efficiency, predictability, calculability and control are key concepts in this discussion of rationalisation.

Reflexivity the process of becoming self-aware to critically consider one's own thoughts and actions, in the light of different contexts, and to interrogate how these may influence or impact on others, in terms of experience, understanding or generation of knowledge.

Technoscience refers to technology and science viewed as mutually interacting disciplines, or as two components of a single discipline, where there is a reliance on science for solving technical problems and technological knowledge is applied to solve scientific problems.

References

7News. (2020, February 3). *Coronavirus rumour that pets can carry virus results in animals thrown to their deaths*. https://7news.com.au/news/animals/coronavirus-rumour-that-pets-can-carry-virus-results-in-animals-thrown-to-their-deaths-c-678046

Abblitt, S. (2019). A postdigital paradigm in literary studies. *Higher Education Research & Development, 38*(1), 97–109. https://doi.org/10.1080/07294360.2018.1541313

Adamu, M. S. (2020, April). Adopting an African standpoint in HCI4D: A provocation. In *Extended abstracts of the 2020 CHI Conference on human factors in computing systems* (pp. 1–8). https://doi.org/10.1145/3334480.3382833

Afifi-Sabet, K. (2020, July 23). *Six universities among those hit by Blackbaud ransomware attack*. ITPro. https://www.itpro.co.uk/security/ransomware/356553/reading-and-leeds-universities-swept-up-in-blackbaud-ransomware-attack

Aguilar, A., Twardowski, T., & Wohlgemuth, R. (Eds.). (2020). Trends in bioeconomy. *New Biotechnology*. https://www.sciencedirect.com/journal/new-biotechnology/special-issue/10JHZ84SNZ2

Ahmed, M. (2020, October 8). UK passport photo checker shows bias against dark-skinned women. *BBC*. https://www.bbc.co.uk/news/technology-54349538

Alaimo, S. (2016). *Exposed: Environmental politics and pleasures in posthuman times*. University of Minnesota Press.

Alcoff, L. (1988). Cultural feminism versus post-structuralism: The identity crisis in feminist theory. *Signs: Journal of Women in Culture and Society, 13*(3), 405–436. https://doi.org/10.1086/494426

Alpaydin, E. (2020). *Introduction to machine learning*. MIT Press.

Althusser, L. (1971). Ideology and ideological state apparatuses (Notes towards an investigation). In *Lenin and philosophy and other essays* (B. Brewster, Trans.). Monthly Review Press.

Amnesty International. (2020). *Bahrain, Kuwait and Norway contact tracing apps among most dangerous for privacy*. https://www.amnesty.org/en/latest/news/2020/06/bahrain-kuwait-norway-contact-tracing-apps-danger-for-privacy/

Amoore, L. (2020). *Cloud ethics: Algorithms and the attributes of ourselves and others*. Duke University Press.

APM Research Lab. (2020). *The color of coronavirus*. https://www.apmresearchlab.org/covid/deaths-by-race#age

Apperley, A. (2014). Revisiting dearing: Higher education and the construction of the 'belabored' self. *Culture Unbound: Journal of Current Cultural Research, 6*(4), 731–753.

Aral, S. (2020). *The hype machine: How social media disrupts our elections, our economy, and our health – and how we must adapt*. Currency.

REFERENCES   275

Argenton, G. (2015). Time for experience: Growing up under the experience economy. *Educational Philosophy and Theory, 47*(9), 918–934. https://doi.org/10.1080/00131857.2015.1035158

Arts and Humanities Research Council (AHRC). (2020, August 21). *AHRC supports British Library and University of Manchester project to help record the NHS voices of COVID-19.* https://ahrc.ukri.org/newsevents/news/nhs-voices-of-covid-19/

Arundel, S. (2020, November 13). My last bit of in person teaching was cancelled and now I've had enough. Quite frankly, I feel like I've been scammed. *The Leeds Tab.* https://thetab.com/uk/leeds/2020/11/13/my-last-bit-of-in-person-teaching-was-cancelled-and-now-ive-had-enough-52931

Ball, S. J. (1997). Policy sociology and critical social research: A personal review of recent education policy and policy research. *British Educational Research Journal, 23*(3), 257–74.

Ball, S. J. (2003). The teacher's soul and the terrors of performativity. *Journal of Education Policy, 18*(2), 215–228. https://doi.org/10.1080/0268093022000043065

Ball, S. J. (2020). *The system: Who owns the Internet, and how it owns us.* Bloomsbury.

Balloo, S. (2020, April 2). Graffiti mural to thank NHS appears amid coronavirus lockdown – but not everyone is happy. *Birmingham Live.* https://www.birminghammail.co.uk/news/midlands-news/graffiti-mural-thank-nhs-appears-18031390

Barker, C., & Jane, E. (2016). *Cultural studies: theory and practice.* Sage.

Barnett, R. (2017). *The ecological university: A feasible utopia.* Routledge.

Barnett, R. (2000). *Realising the university in an age of supercomplexity.* Open University Press.

Barnett, R., & Di Napoli, R. (Eds.). (2008). *Changing identities in higher education: Voicing perspectives.* Routledge.

Barrett, G. (2018, May 23). Why it's time to ditch the term 'BAME'. *Refinery29.* https://www.refinery29.com/en-gb/2018/05/199526/what-does-bame-stand-for

Bartram, B. (2020). Queering the TEF. In *Challenging the teaching excellence framework.* Emerald Publishing Limited.

Bateson, G. (1972). *Steps to an ecology of mind: Collected essays in anthropology, psychiatry, evolution, and epistemology.* Chandler Pub. Co.

BBC. (2020a, June 18). Black lives matter: Where does 'taking a knee' come from? *BBC.* https://www.bbc.co.uk/news/explainers-53098516

BBC. (2020b, August 18). A-level and GCSE results: Call for urgent review into grading 'fiasco'. *BBC.* https://www.bbc.co.uk/news/uk-53826305

BBC. (2020c, September 20). Coronavirus: Students' return could spark lockdown, say locals. *BBC.* https://www.bbc.co.uk/news/education-54205401

BBC. (2020d, September 26). Coronavirus: Students trapped by 'shambolic' return to university, says union. *BBC.* https://www.bbc.co.uk/news/uk-54308329

BBC. (2020e, May 19). Coronavirus: Home-schooling six children with just one phone. *BBC*. https://www.bbc.com/news/av/education-52717519/coronavirus-homeschooling-six-children-with-just-one-phone

BBC. (2020f, October 10). Covid in Scotland: Bar workers dump leftover ice in closure protest. *BBC*. https://www.bbc.co.uk/news/uk-scotland-54491598

BBC. (2020g, January 1). Instagram hit for Cardiff student who posts revision notes. *BBC*. https://www.bbc.co.uk/news/uk-wales-50630400

BBC Technology. (2020, December 15). EU digital services act set to bring in new rules for tech giants. https://www.bbc.co.uk/news/technology-55307115

BBC Technology. (2021, February 22). Entire school board resigns after accidental public livestream. https://www.bbc.co.uk/news/technology-56156795

BBC Entertainment & Arts. (2020, December 16). Julie Burchill's book about cancel culture cancelled over Twitter row. *BBC*. https://www.bbc.co.uk/news/entertainment-arts-55331063

Beardmore, R. (2020, September 17). Webcams and speakers set for installation in Wyre town centres 'will not be used for monitoring'. *Fleetwood Weekly News*. https://www.fleetwoodtoday.co.uk/news/politics/webcams-and-speakers-set-installation-wyre-town-centres-will-not-be-used-monitoring-2975347

Beattie, A. R., & Hayes, S. (2020). Whose domain and whose ontology? Preserving human radical reflexivity over the efficiency of automatically generated feedback alone. In *Mobility, data and learner agency in networked learning* (pp. 83–99). Springer.

Beer, D. (2020). *The writing moment: Three difficulties with writing in this time of upheaval*. https://davidbeer.substack.com/p/the-writing-moment

Bell, D. (1976). *The cultural contradictions of capitalism*. Basic Books.

Berg, L. D., Huijbens, E. H., & Larsen, H. G. (2016). Producing anxiety in the neoliberal university. *The Canadian Geographer, 60*(2), 168–180. https://doi.org/10.1111/cag.12261

Berlant, L. (2016). The commons: Infrastructures for troubling times. *Environment and Planning D: Society and Space, 34*(3), 393–419. https://doi.org/10.1177%2F0263775816645989

Berners Lee, T. [@timberners_lee]. (2012, July 27). *This is for everyone #london 2012 #one web #opening ceremony @webfoundation @w3c* [Tweet]. Twitter. https://twitter.com/timberners_lee/status/228960085672599552

Bertelsen, L. (2019). Incalculable experience. *The Fibreculture Journal, 30*. http://thirty.fibreculturejournal.org/wp-content/pdfs/FC30_FullIssue.pdf

Biesta, G. (2009). Good education in an age of measurement: On the need to reconnect with the question of purpose in education. *Educational Assessment, Evaluation and Accountability (Formerly: Journal of Personnel Evaluation in Education), 21*(1), 33–46. https://doi.org/10.1007/s11092-008-9064-9

Bishop, D. (2019). Rein in the four horsemen of irreproducibility. *Springer Nature, 568*, 435. https://doi.org/10.1038/d41586-019-01307-2

REFERENCES

Bloomberg News. (2020, March 8). Driverless delivery van startup sees demand surge amid outbreak. *Hyperdrive.* https://www.bloomberg.com/news/articles/2020-03-08/they-won-t-catch-the-virus-so-chinese-robovan-maker-s-sales-jump?sref=QYc4Et5D

Bodenheimer, G., & Shuster, S. M. (2020). Emotional labour, teaching and burnout: Investigating complex relationships. *Educational Research, 62*(1), 63–76.

Boellstorff, T. (2016). For whom the ontology turns: Theorizing the digital real. *Current Anthropology, 57*(4).

Bourke, B. (2014). Positionality: Reflecting on the research process. *The Qualitative Report, 19*(33), 1–9.

Bowcott, O. (2020, November 30). International lawyers draft plan to criminalise ecosystem destruction. *The Guardian.* https://www.theguardian.com/law/2020/nov/30/international-lawyers-draft-plan-to-criminalise-ecosystem-destruction

Brady, S. R. (2015). Utilizing and adapting the Delphi method for use in qualitative research. *International Journal of Qualitative Methods, 14*(5). https://doi.org/10.1177/1609406915621381

Braidotti, R. (2019a). *Posthuman knowledge.* Wiley.

Braidotti, R. (2019b). A theoretical framework for the critical posthumanities. *Theory, Culture and Society, 36*(6), 31–61. https://doi.org/10.1177%2F0263276418771486

Breines, M. R., & Gallagher, M. (2020). A return to teacherbot: Rethinking the development of educational technology at the University of Edinburgh. *Teaching in Higher Education,* 1–15. https://doi.org/10.1080/13562517.2020.1825373

Brewis, H. (2020, August 11). Ben & Jerry's hits out at Priti Patel over 'inhuman' treatment of migrants. *Evening Standard.* https://www.standard.co.uk/news/uk/ben-jerrys-ice-cream-migrants-priti-patel-a4522351.html

Bromwich, J. E. (2018, January 31). We asked generation Z to pick a name. It wasn't Generation Z. *The New York Times.* https://www.nytimes.com/2018/01/31/style/generation-z-name.html

Bronfenbrenner, U. (1994). Ecological models of human development. In *International encyclopedia of education* (Vol. 3, 2nd ed.). Elsevier.

Brooks, L. (2020, June 12). J K Rowling row hints at generational rift on transgender rights. *The Guardian.* https://www.theguardian.com/society/2020/jun/12/jk-rowling-row-hints-at-generational-rift-on-transgender-rights

Brooks, R. (2017). The construction of higher education students in English policy documents. *British Journal of Sociology of Education, 39*(6), 745–761. https://doi.org/10.1080/01425692.2017.1406339

Brunel University London Equality and Diversity Strategy. (2015–2020). Webpage. https://www.brunel.ac.uk/about/documents/pdf/equality-and-diversity-strategy-2015-to-2020.pdf

Bukht, R., & Heeks, R. (2017). Defining, conceptualising and measuring the digital economy. *Development Informatics Working Paper, 68.* https://www.researchgate.net/profile/Rumana_Bukht/publication/327356904_Defining_Conceptualising_and_Measuring_the_Digital_Economy/links/5c69cb07299bf1e3a5af02d0/Defining-Conceptualising-and-Measuring-the-Digital-Economy.pdf

Bunce, L., Baird, A., & Jones, S. E. (2017). The student-as-consumer approach in higher education and its effects on academic performance. *Studies in Higher Education, 42*(11), 1958–1978. https://doi.org/10.1080/03075079.2015.1127908

Burgess, M. (2020, August 20). The lessons we all must learn from the A-levels algorithm debacle. *Wired.* https://www.wired.co.uk/article/gcse-results-alevels-algorithm-explained

Cantrell, K., & Palmer, K. (2019, May). The casualties of academia: A response to the conversation. *Overland,* 1–6.

Carrigan, M. (2020a). *The Post-Pandemic University.* https://postpandemicuniversity.net/about/

Carrigan, M. (2020b, December 4). Twitter hybridises the personal and the professional in the most subtly violent manner. *The Post-Pandemic University.* https://postpandemicuniversity.net/2020/12/04/twitter-hybridises-the-personal-and-the-professional-in-the-most-subtly-violent-manner-leading-work-to-become-life-and-life-to-become-work/

Carroll, R. (2020, September 25). Dorm snitches and party bans: How universities around the world are tackling Covid. *The Guardian.* https://www.theguardian.com/world/2020/sep/25/universities-respond-to-covid-surge

Casey, J. (2020, February 2). Citizen literacy: A white paper. *Citizen Literacy Community Interest.* https://citizenliteracy.com/wp-content/uploads/2020/09/Citizen_Literacy_White-Paper_02_Sep_2020.pdf

Centers for Disease Control and Prevention (CDC). (2020). *Covid-19 cases, hospitalisation and death by race/ethnicity.* https://www.cdc.gov/coronavirus/2019-ncov/downloads/covid-data/hospitalization-death-by-race-ethnicity.pdf

Chan, M. (2021, February 17). This AI reads children's emotions as they learn. *CNN Business.* https://edition.cnn.com/2021/02/16/tech/emotion-recognition-ai-education-spc-intl-hnk/index.html

Chang, B. (2020). From 'Illmatic' to 'Kung Flu': Black and Asian solidarity, activism, and pedagogies in the Covid-19 era. *Postdigital Science and Education, 2,* 741–756. https://doi.org/10.1007/s42438-020-00183-8

Charles, A. (2020, October 6). Too much social media is bad for your health... and I should know. *Grazia.* https://graziadaily.co.uk/life/real-life/social-media-addiction-social-dilemma/

Cheney-Lippold, J. (2018). *We are data: Algorithms and the making of our digital selves.* NYU Press.

REFERENCES

Clancy, S. (2019). A new vision for adult education. *Soundings, 72*(72), 105–116.

Clarke, R. (2021). *Breathtaking: Inside the NHS in a time of pandemic*. Little, Brown.

Clarke, R. (2021). 'I've been called Satan': Dr Rachel Clarke on facing abuse in the Covid crisis. https://www.theguardian.com/books/2021/feb/06/ive-been-called-satan-dr-rachel-clarke-on-facing-abuse-in-the-covid-crisis

Clarke, R. I., & Schoonmaker, S. (2020). The critical catalog: Library information systems, tricksterism, and social justice. In *Proceedings of the 2020 CHI Conference on human factors in computing systems* (pp. 1–13). https://doi.org/10.1145/3313831.3376307

Codding, D., Mouza, C., Rolón-Dow, R., & Pollock, L. (2019). Positionality and belonging: Analyzing an informally situated and culturally responsive computer science program. In *Proceedings of FabLearn 2019* (pp. 132–135). https://doi.org/10.1145/3311890.3311909

Coeckelbergh, M. (2020). The postdigital in pandemic times: A postment on the Covid-19 crisis and its political epistemologies. *Postdigital Science and Education.* https://doi.org/10.1007/s42438-020-00119-2

Cohen, A., Nørgård, R. T., & Mor, Y. (2020). Hybrid learning spaces – Design, data, didactics. *British Journal of Educational Technology, 51*(4), 1039–1044. https://doi.org/10.1111/bjet.12964

Coleman, S., Pothong, K., Vallejos, E. P., & Koene, A. (2017). *The internet on our own terms: How children and young people deliberated about their digital rights*. University of Nottingham, Horizon Digital Economy Research, 5Rights.

Collini, S. (2018). *Speaking of universities*. Verso Books.

Collini, S. (2020, April 28). Covid-19 shows up UK universities' shameful employment practices. *The Guardian.* https://www.theguardian.com/education/2020/apr/28/covid-19-shows-up-uk-universities-shameful-employment-practices

Collins, P. H., & Bilge, S. (2016). *Intersectionality*. John Wiley & Sons.

Commission for Countering Extremism. (2021). Webpage. https://assets.publishing.service.gov.uk/government/uploads/system/uploads/attachment_data/file/963156/CCE_Operating_with_Impunity_Accessible.pdf

Connor, S., Mahoney, M., & Lewis, N. (2019). *Anticipating a 4th industrial revolution and the futures of learning: A discussion paper for Wolverhampton Learning City Region.*

Corona24 News. (2020, October 17). Coronavirus: 'Fat finger error' gives contact tracking app users wrong alert levels. *Science and Tech News.* https://www.corona24news.com/2020/10/coronavirus-fat-finger-error-gives-contact-tracking-app-users-wrong-alert-levels-science-tech-news.html

Costanza-Chock, S. (2018). Design justice, A.I., and escape from the matrix of domination. *Journal of Design and Science (JoDS).* https://doi.org/10.21428/96c8d426

Cousin, G. (2010). Positioning positionality: The reflexive turn. In *New approaches to qualitative research* (pp. 25–34). Routledge.

Cramer, F. (2015). What is 'post-digital'? In *Postdigital aesthetics* (pp. 12–26). Palgrave Macmillan.

Crenshaw, K. (1989). Intersectionality, identity politics and violence against women of color. *Kvinder, Køn & Forskning, 2–3.* https://doi.org/10.7146/kkf.v0i2-3.28090

Cukurova, M., Carmel, K., & Luckin, R. (2019). Artificial Intelligence and multimodal data in the service of human decision-making: A case study in debate tutoring. *British Journal of Educational Technology, 50*(6), 3032–3046. https://doi.org/10.1111/bjet.12829

Czerniewicz, L., Agherdien, N., Badenhorst, J., Belluigi, D., Chambers, T., Chili, M., ... Ivala, E. (2020). A wake-up call: Equity, inequality and Covid-19 emergency remote teaching and learning. *Postdigital Science and Education, 2*(3), 946–967. https://doi.org/10.1007/s42438-020-00187-4

D'Antonio, M. (2020, March 14). America has learned a lot about Trump during coronavirus crisis. *CNN.* https://edition.cnn.com/2020/03/14/opinions/in-coronavirus-crisis-america-has-learned-a-lot-about-triump-dantonio/index.html

Davies, W. (2016). The new neoliberalism. *New Left Review, 101.*

Dawda, S., Janjeva, A., & Moiseienko, A. (2021). *The UK's response to cyber fraud a strategic vision.* https://rusi.org/sites/default/files/cyber_fraud_final_web_version.pdf

Dawson, G., & Thompson, O. (2019, July 11). Should the term 'BAME' be ditched when referring to people of African descent, Asian and minority ethnic people? *KLTV.* http://kirkleeslocaltv.com/news/should-the-term-bame-be-ditched-when-referring-to-people-of-african-descent-asian-and-minority-ethnic-people/

Dawson, M. (2019). Algorithmic culture, networked learning and the technological horizon of theory. *Technology, Pedagogy and Education, 28*(4), 463–472. https://doi.org/10.1080/1475939X.2019.1643780

Day, A. (2020, August 17). 'Don't Kill Granny' – Why these grandmothers love the new Coronavirus slogan. *HuffPost.* https://www.newsbreak.com/news/2042364560049/dont-kill-granny-why-these-grandmothers-love-the-new-coronavirus-slogan

Deepwell, K. (2020). Postdigital education, feminism, women. *Postdigital Science and Education, 2,* 248–253. https://doi.org/10.1007/s42438-019-00096-1

Delanty, G. (2001). *Challenging knowledge: The university in the knowledge society.* Open University Press.

Delanty, G. (2008). Academic identities and institutional change. In R. Barnett & R. Di Napoli (Eds.), *Changing identities in higher education: Voicing perspectives.* Routledge.

Delanty, G. (2011). Varieties of critique in sociological theory and their methodological implications for social research. *Irish Journal of Sociology, 19*(1), 68–92. https://doi.org/10.7227%2FIJS.19.1.4

Delanty, G. (2020). Critical theory as a critique of UnSustainability: 'Damaged life' in the anthropocene. *Estudios Públicos, 159,* 7–37.

REFERENCES

Deloitte. (2019). *Smart campus: The next-generation connected campus.* https://www2.deloitte.com/content/dam/Deloitte/us/Documents/strategy/the-next-generation-connected-campus-deloitte.pdf

Department for Education. (2017). *Inclusive teaching and learning in higher education.* https://www.gov.uk/government/publications/inclusive-teaching-and-learning-in-higher-education

DeVito, M. A., Walker, A. M., Lustig, C., Ko, A. J., Spiel, K., Ahmed, A. A., ... Gray, M. L. (2020). Queer in HCI: Supporting LGBTQIA+ researchers and research across domains. In *Extended abstracts of the 2020 CHI Conference on human factors in computing systems* (pp. 1–4). https://doi.org/10.1145/3334480.3381058

Dickey, M. R. (2020, September 9). Instagram is building a product equity team and hiring a director of diversity and inclusion. *TechCrunch.* https://techcrunch.com/2020/09/09/instagram-is-building-a-product-equity-team-and-hiring-a-director-of-diversity-and-inclusion/

Dingwall, R., Hoffman, L. M., & Staniland, K. (2013). Introduction: Why a sociology of pandemics? *Sociology of Health & Illness, 35*(2), 167–173. https://doi.org/10.1111/1467-9566.12019

Dixson, A. D., Trent, W. T., Ladson-Billings, G. J., Anderson, J. D., & Suarez, C. E. (Eds.). (2020). *Condition or process? Researching race in education.* American Educational Research Association.

Dorrell, E. (2020, October 12). The government is serious about winning the culture wars – universities need to be ready. *Wonkhe.* https://wonkhe.com/blogs/government-culture-wars-universities-ready/

Driscoll, C., & Wicks, D. (1998). The customer-driven approach in business education: A possible danger? *Journal of Education for Business, 74*(1), 58–61. https://doi.org/10.1080/08832329809601663

Ecclestone, K., & Hayes, D. (2019). *The dangerous rise of therapeutic education.* Routledge.

Ecclestone, K., & McGiveney, V. (2005). Are adult educators obsessed with developing self-esteem? *Adults Learning, 16*(5), 8–13.

Electronic Frontier Foundation (EFF). (2020). *Covid-19 and digital rights.* https://www.eff.org/issues/covid-19

Ellis, M. (Ed.). (2019). *Critical global semiotics: Understanding sustainable transformational citizenship.* Routledge.

Elliss, H. (2014). The dirty secrets of clickbait. This post will blow your mind! *Econsultancy.* https://econsultancy.com/dirty-secrets-clickbait/

England, K. V. L. (1994). Getting personal: Reflexivity, positionality, and feminist research. *The Professional Geographer, 46*(1), 80–89. https://doi.org/10.1111/j.0033-0124.1994.00080.x

Equality Act. (2010). https://www.equalityhumanrights.com/en/equality-act/equality-act-2010

Equality Act Review. (2020a). https://www.equalityactreview.co.uk

Equality Act Review. (2020b, December 4). *Predicting futures 2.0. Examining student concerns amidst Coronavirus exam cancellations.*

Equality and Human Rights Commission. (2017). *Measurement framework for Equality and Human Rights.* https://www.equalityhumanrights.com/sites/default/files/measurement-framework-interactive.pdf

Equality and Human Rights Commission. (2019). *Protected characteristics.* https://www.equalityhumanrights.com/en/equality-act/protected-characteristics

Equality and Human Rights Commission. (2020). *Public sector equality duty.* https://www.equalityhumanrights.com/en/advice-and-guidance/public-sector-equality-duty

Eubanks, V. (2018). *Automating inequality. How high-tech tools profile, police, and punish the poor.* St. Martin's Press.

Eynon, R., Davies, H., & Salveson, C. (2018, June 13). *Understanding the potential of AI for lifelong learning: The need for a critical perspective.* https://www.oii.ox.ac.uk/blog/understanding-the-potential-of-ai-for-lifelong-learning-the-need-for-a-critical-perspective/

Fabiani, A. (2020, June 29). Why the Chinese app TikTok is a data privacy problem. *Screen Shot.* https://screenshot-media.com/technology/social-media/tiktok-data-privacy/

Farrer, M., & Pidd, H. (2021, February 5). Insults and expletives turn parish council Zoom meeting into internet sensation. *The Guardian.* https://www.theguardian.com/uk-news/2021/feb/05/handforth-insults-and-expletives-turn-parish-council-meeting-into-internet-sensation

Fawns, T., Aitken, G., & Jones, D. (2020). Ecological teaching evaluation vs the datafication of quality: Understanding education with, and around, data. *Postdigital Science and Education.* https://doi.org/10.1007/s42438-020-00109-4

Fazackerley, A. (2020a, May 12). Women's research plummets during lockdown – but articles from men increase. *The Guardian.* https://www.theguardian.com/education/2020/may/12/womens-research-plummets-during-lockdown-but-articles-from-men-increase

Fazackerley, A. (2020b, August 21). We were already full: Universities face nightmare of exams chaos and Covid-19. *The Guardian.* https://www.theguardian.com/education/2020/aug/21/universities-warn-of-pandemic-risk-if-upgraded-a-level-students-admitted

Fazackerley, A. (2020c, September 19). UK universities predict record student dropout rate. *The Guardian.* https://www.theguardian.com/education/2020/sep/19/uk-universities-predict-record-student-dropout-rate

REFERENCES

Feenberg, A. (2019). Postdigital or predigital? *Postdigital Science and Education, 1*, 8–9. https://doi.org/10.1007/s42438-018-0027-2

Fenwick, T., Edwards, R., & Sawchuk, P. (2015). *Emerging approaches to educational research: Tracing the socio-material.* Routledge.

Finch, M. (2020, September 28). Scenario planning for digitalised education: Managing uncertainties through the pandemic and beyond. *The Post-Pandemic University.* https://postpandemicuniversity.net/2020/09/28/scenario-planning-for-digitalised-education-managing-uncertainties-through-the-pandemic-and-beyond/

Finsden, B. (2008). The RAE in Scotland: A Kiwi participant-observer in an ancient university. *Critical Perspectives on Communication, Cultural & Policy Studies, 27*(1–2), 61–72.

Fisher, C. (2019). *The gaslighting of the millennial generation: How to succeed in a society that blames you for everything gone wrong.* Mango Publishing.

Fisher, E. (2020). Can algorithmic knowledge about the self be critical? In M. Stocchetti (Ed.), *The digital age and its discontents: Critical reflections in education* (pp. 111–122). Helsinki University Press. https://doi.org/10.33134/HUP-4-6

Flood, A. (2016, November 15). 'Post-truth' named word of the year by Oxford dictionaries. *The Guardian.* https://www.theguardian.com/books/2016/nov/15/post-truth-named-word-of-the-year-by-oxford-dictionaries

Foundational Economy Collective. (2020). *What comes after the pandemic? A ten-point platform for foundational renewal.* https://foundationaleconomycom.files.wordpress.com/2020/03/what-comes-after-the-pandemic-fe-manifesto-005.pdf

Freire, P. (2000). *Pedagogy of the oppressed* (30th anniversary ed.). Continuum.

Fuchs, C. (2011). Web 2.0, prosumption, and surveillance. *Surveillance and Society, 8*(3), 288–309. https://doi.org/10.24908/ss.v8i3.4165

Fullan, M. (2020). Learning and the pandemic: What's next? *Prospects, 49*, 25–28. https://doi.org/10.1007/s11125-020-09502-0

Fuller, S., & Jandrić, P. (2019). The postdigital human: Making the history of the future. *Postdigital Science and Education, 1*(1), 190–217. https://doi.org/10.1007/s42438-018-0003-x

Furedi, F. (2016). *What's happened to the university? A sociological exploration of its infantilisation.* Routledge.

Gabrielle, M. (2020, June 1). The Coronovirus has hastened the post-human era. *TechCrunch.* https://techcrunch.com/2020/06/01/the-coronavirus-has-hastened-the-post-human-era/

Gallagher, J. (2020, October 14). Covid: Two-week circuit breaker 'may halve deaths', report says. *BBC.* https://www.bbc.co.uk/news/health-54538278

Gallagher, M., & Breines, M. (2020). Surfacing knowledge mobilities in higher education: Reconfiguring the teacher function through automation. *Learning, Media and Technology*, 1–13.

Gallagher, M., Breines, M., & Blaney, M. (2020). Transparency, (in)visibility, and hidden curricula: Surfacing critical pedagogy through contentious edtech. *Postdigital Science and Education*.

Gamsu, S., & Hall, R. (2019). *A new vision for further and higher education, essay collection* [Project report]. Centre for Labour and Social Studies. http://dro.dur.ac.uk/29119/1/29119.pdf?DDD34+drmg83

Gant, J. (2021, February 13). Government set to fine universities who 'cancel' people due to their views as ministers 'defend British history and culture'. *MailOnline*. https://www.dailymail.co.uk/news/article-9258031/Government-appoint-woke-warden-powers-fine-universities-cancel-people.html

Garnett, F. (2019). *Republic of learning: Our common wealth of learning*. https://therepublicoflearning.wordpress.com/2019/09/17/21st-century-republic-of-learning/

Gergen, K. J. (2009). *Relational being: Beyond self and community*. Oxford University Press.

Gill, R. (2010). Breaking the silence: The hidden injuries of the neoliberal university. In R. Ryan-Flood & R. Gill (Eds.), *Secrecy and silence in the research process: Feminist reflections*. Routledge.

Gillespie, T. (2020, August 2). Jonathan Isaac: Orlando Magic star explains why he didn't kneel in honour of Black Lives Matter. *Sky News*. https://news.sky.com/story/jonathan-isaac-orlando-magic-star-explains-why-he-didnt-kneel-in-honour-of-black-lives-matter-12040372

Ginsberg, B. (2011). *The fall of the faculty*. Oxford University Press.

Gittos, L. (2020a, August 7). Racialising the crisis in policing. *Spiked*. https://www.spiked-online.com/2020/08/07/racialising-the-crisis-in-policing/

Gittos, L. (2020b, August 31). The black lives we don't talk about. *Spiked*. https://www.spiked-online.com/2020/08/31/the-black-lives-we-dont-talk-about/

González-Sanmamed, M., Sangrà, A., Souto-Seijo, A., & Estévez, I. (2020). Learning ecologies in the digital era: Challenges for higher education. *Publicaciones, 50*(1), 83–102. https://doi.org/10.30827/publicaciones.v50i1.15671

Gramsci, A. (1971). Americanism and Fordism. In Q. Hoare & G. F. Smith (Eds.), *Selections from the prison notebooks* (pp. 277–318). International Publishers.

Gravett, K., & Kinchin, I. (2020). Revisiting 'A "teaching excellence" for the times we live in': Posthuman possibilities. *Teaching in Higher Education*, 1–7.

Gregory, J. (2020, February 28). The coronavirus 'infodemic' is real. We rated the websites responsible for it. *Stat*. https://www.statnews.com/2020/02/28/websites-spreading-coronavirus-misinformation-infodemic/

REFERENCES   285

GOV.UK. (2020a). *UK national data strategy consultation.* https://www.gov.uk/
government/consultations/uk-national-data-strategy-nds-consultation/uk-
national-data-strategy-consultation

GOV.UK. (2020b, September 24). *Guidance: Plan your relationships, sex and health
curriculum.* https://www.gov.uk/guidance/plan-your-relationships-sex-and-health-
curriculum

Guardian. (2020a, July 3). Harry Potter fan sites distance themselves from JK Rowling
over transgender rights. *Gender.* https://www.theguardian.com/world/2020/jul/03/
harry-potter-fan-sites-distance-themselves-from-jk-rowling-over-transgender-
rights

Guardian. (2020b, September 11). BLM dance routine on Britain's Got Talent triggers
15,500 complaints: Performance by Diversity was inspired by the killing of George
Floyd in the US. *PA Media.* https://www.theguardian.com/tv-and-radio/2020/
sep/11/blm-dance-routine-britains-got-talent-triggers-complaints

Guardian. (2020c). 'Our first case of Covid. Parents are hounding me, staff are afraid':
Diary of a headteacher's week. *Schools.* https://www.theguardian.com/education/
2020/sep/26/our-first-case-of-covid-parents-are-hounding-me-staff-are-afraid-
diary-of-a-headteachers-week

Guattari, F. (2000). *The three ecologies.* Athlone Press.

Habermas, J. (1972). *Knowledge and human interests.* Beacon Press.

Hall, R. (2018). *The alienated academic: The struggle for autonomy inside the university.*
Palgrave Macmillan.

Hall, R., & Bowles, K. (2016). Re-engineering higher education: The subsumption of
academic labour and the exploitation of anxiety. *Workplace, 28,* 30–47.
https://doi.org/10.14288/workplace.v0i28.186211

Hall, S. (1990). Cultural identity and diaspora. In J. Rutherford (Ed.), *Identity: Community, culture, difference* (pp. 2–27). Lawrence & Wishart.

Hall, S., Critcher, C., Jefferson, T., Clarke, J., & Roberts, B. (2013). *Policing the crisis: Mug-
ging, the state and law and order* (rev. ed.). Macmillan. (Original work published
1978)

Hambleton, R. (2020). From 'best practice' to 'relevant practice' in international city-
to-city learning. In *Strategies for urban network learning* (pp. 31–56). Palgrave Macmillan.

Hammerley, M. (Ed.). (2002). *Educational research, policymaking and practice.* Sage.

Haraway, D. (1988). Situated knowledges: The science question in feminism and the
privilege of partial perspective. *Feminist Studies, 14,* 575–599. https://doi.org/
10.2307/3178066

Harding, S. (1993). Rethinking standpoint epistemology: What is 'strong objectivity?'. In
L. Alcoff & E. Potter (Eds.), *Feminist epistemologies* (pp. 49–82). Routledge.

Harman, G. (1984). Conceptual and theoretical issues. In J. R. Hough (Ed.), *Educational
policy: An international survey.* Croom Helm Australia, Pty Limited.

Hatmaker, T. (2020a, August 14). Clearview AI landed a new facial recognition contract with ICE. *TechCrunch*. https://techcrunch.com/2020/08/14/clearview-ai-ice-hsi-contract-2020/

Hatmaker, T. (2020b, September 10). Portland passes expansive city ban on facial recognition tech. *TechCrunch*. https://techcrunch.com/2020/09/09/facial-recognition-ban-portland-oregon/

Hayes, D. (2017). *Beyond McDonaldization: Visions of higher education*. Taylor and Francis.

Hayes, D. (2019). How the university lost its way: Sixteen threats to academic freedom. *Postdigital Science and Education*. https://doi.org/10.1007/s42438-019-00079-2

Hayes, D., & Wynyard, R. (2002). *The McDonaldization of higher education*. Praeger.

Hayes, J. (2019, August 23). When the public feared that library books could spread deadly diseases. *Smithsonian Magazine*. https://www.smithsonianmag.com/history/during-great-book-scare-people-worried-contaminated-books-could-spread-disease-180972967/

Hayes, S. (2015). Counting on the use of technology to enhance learning. In P. Jandrić & D. Boras (Eds.), *Critical learning in digital networks*. Springer.

Hayes, S. (2019a). *The labour of words in higher education: Is it time to reoccupy policy?* Brill.

Hayes, S. (2019b). Regional voices in national policymaking. *Wonkhe*. https://wonkhe.com/blogs/regional-voices-in-national-policymaking/

Hayes, S. (2019c). Employable posthumans: Developing HE policies that strengthen human technological collaboration not separation. In M. A. Peters, P. Jandrić, & A. J. Means (Eds.), *Education and technological unemployment*. Springer.

Hayes, S. (2020). Postdigital perspectives on the McPolicy of measuring excellence. *Postdigital Science and Education*. https://doi.org/10.1007/s42438-020-00208-2

Hayes, S., & Bartholomew, P. (2015). Where's the humanity? Challenging the policy discourse of technology enhanced learning. In J. Branch, P. Bartholomew, & C. Nygaard (Eds.), *Technology enhanced learning in higher education*. Libri.

Hayes, S., & Jandrić, P. (2014). Who is really in charge of contemporary education? People and technologies in, against and beyond the neoliberal university. *Open Review of Educational Research, 1*(1), 193–210. https://doi.org/10.1080/23265507.2014.989899

Hayes, S., & Jandrić, P. (2017). Resisting the final word: Challenging stale media and policy representations of students' performative technological encounters in university education. In S. Cranmer, N. B. Dohn, M. de Laat, T. Ryberg, & J. A. Sime (Eds.), *Research in networked learning*. Springer.

Hayes, S., & Jandrić, P. (2018). Resisting the iron cage of 'the student experience'. In M. Sardoč (Ed.), *The language of neoliberal education*. Šolsko polje. https://www.pei.si/ISSN/1581_6044/1-2-2018/1581_6044_1-2-2018.pdf

REFERENCES 287

Hayes, S., Jopling, M., Hayes, D., Westwood, A., Tuckett, A., & Barnett, R. (2020). Raising regional academic voices (alongside data) in Higher Education (HE) debate. *Postdigital Science and Education*. https://doi.org/10.1007/s42438-020-00131-6

Hayes, S., Hayes, D., Jandrić, P., Traxler, J., Jandrić, P., Welch, P., ... Barnett, R. (2021). 'Measuring excellence' in higher education. *Postdigital Science and Education, 3*(1) (Special issue). https://link.springer.com/journal/42438/volumes-and-issues/3-1

Healey, P. (n.d.). *Changing Ecologies of Knowledge and Action (CEKA)*. Working paper. InSIS, University of Oxford. https://www.insis.ox.ac.uk/files/cekasummaryproposalpdf

Health Foundation. (2020). *Build back fairer: The Covid-19 Marmot review, the pandemic, socioeconomic and health inequalities.* http://www.instituteofhealthequity.org/resources-reports/build-back-fairer-the-covid-19-marmot-review/build-back-fairer-the-covid-19-marmot-review-full-report.pdf

Hector, M. (2020). Arriving at thriving: Learning from disabled students to ensure access for all. *Policy Connect.* https://www.policyconnect.org.uk/research/arriving-thriving-learning-disabled-students-ensure-access-all

Hellard, B. (2020, September 2). Exams cancelled after Northumbria University cyber attack: 'IT difficulties' force clearing hotline and student portal offline. *ITPro.* https://www.itpro.co.uk/security/cyber-attacks/356965/northumbria-university-shutdown-after-cyber-attack

Hemment, D., Belle, V., Aylett, R., Murray-Rust, D., Pschetz, L., & Broz, F. (2019). Toward fairness, morality and transparency in Artificial Intelligence through experiential AI. *Leonardo, 52*(5). https://doi.org/10.1162/leon_a_01795

Hern, A. (2020, October 6). Covid: How Excel may have caused the loss of 16,000 test results in England. *The Guardian.* https://www.theguardian.com/politics/2020/oct/05/how-excel-may-have-caused-loss-of-16000-covid-tests-in-england

Hirsch, A. (2020, August 27). We should be free to talk about racism without being penalized. *The Guardian.* https://www.theguardian.com/commentisfree/2020/aug/27/racism-david-olusoga-tv-industry

Hlynka, D., & Belland, J. C. (Eds.). (1991). *Paradigms regained: The uses of illuminative, semiotic, and post-modern criticism as modes of inquiry in educational technology: A book of readings.* Educational Technology.

Hofstede, G. (1991). *Organizations and cultures: Software of the mind.* McGrawHill.

Hogan, B., & Williamson, A. (2020). Commercialisation and privatisation in/of education in the context of Covid-19. *Education International.* https://www.researchgate.net/profile/Ben-Williamson-2/publication/343510376_Commercialisation_and_privatisation_inof_education_in_the_context_of_Covid-19/links/5f2d6f05a6fdcccc43b2cf99/Commercialisation-and-privatisation-in-of-education-in-the-context-of-Covid-19.pdf

Holland, L. (2021, February 4). Climate activists say 'shock' protests need to evolve to get people of colour involved. *Sky News*. https://news.sky.com/story/climate-activists-say-shock-protests-need-to-evolve-to-get-people-of-colour-involved-12207783

Holliday, A. (2007). *Doing & writing qualitative research*. Sage.

Hollister, S. (2019, October 2). Google contractors reportedly targeted homeless people for Pixel 4 facial recognition. *The Verge*. https://www.theverge.com/2019/10/2/20896181/google-contractor-reportedly-targeted-homeless-people-for-pixel-4-facial-recognition

Holloway, W. (1989). *Subjectivity and method in psychology: Gender, meaning and science*. Sage.

Holmes, H., & Burgess, G. (2020). *Coronavirus has highlighted the UK's digital divide*. University of Cambridge Centre for Housing and Planning Research (CCHPR). https://www.cchpr.landecon.cam.ac.uk/Research/Start-Year/2017/building_better_opportunities_new_horizons/digital_divide/presentation_slides/at_download/file

Holon IQ. (2020). Webpage. https://www.digitalcapability.org

hooks, B., & McKinnon, T. (1996). Sisterhood: Beyond public and private. *Signs: Journal of Women in Culture and Society, 21*(4), 814–829.

Hope, C. (2021, February 13). Exclusive: Universities face fines as part of 'twin assault' on cancel culture. *The Telegraph*. https://www.telegraph.co.uk/politics/2021/02/13/exclusive-universities-face-fines-part-twin-assault-cancel-culture/

HRH the saboteur [@DoomlordVek]. (2020, August 12). *I'm happy to delete, after an explanation supporting Ben and Jerry's in their fight with the Home Office* [Tweet]. Twitter. https://twitter.com/DoomlordVek/status/1293597294449893377

Hult, F. M. (2013). Covert bilingualism and symbolic competence: Analytical reflections on negotiating insider/outsider positionality in Swedish speech situations. *Applied Linguistics, 35*(1), 63–81. https://doi.org/10.1093/applin/amt003

Hunsinger, J. (2020). On the current situation: Normal violences, pandemics, emergencies, necropolitics, zombies, and creepy treehouses. *Fast Capitalism, 17*(2).

Huxstable, S. A., Fowler, C., Kefalas, C., & Slocombe, E. (2020). *Interim report on the connections between colonialism and properties now in the care of the National Trust, including links with historic slavery*. National Trust. https://nt.global.ssl.fastly.net/documents/colionialism-and-historic-slavery-report.pdf

Hyacinth, B. T. (2017). *The future of leadership: Rise of automation, robotics and artificial intelligence*. Lightening Source UK.

Ienca, M., & Andorno, R. (2017). Towards new human rights in the age of neuroscience and neurotechnology. *Life Sciences, Society and Policy, 13*, 5. https://lsspjournal.biomedcentral.com/articles/10.1186/s40504-017-0050-1

ImpactEd. (2021). *Pupil learning and wellbeing during the Covid-19 pandemic*. https://drive.google.com/file/d/19tcaSSfyxzTXWjBlj8LsgtJM-frrfbXu/view

REFERENCES

Interguard. (2020). *Employee monitoring made simple.*
https://www.interguardsoftware.com/?utm_campaign=brandINT&utm_source=
google&utm_medium=GSN&utm_term=interguard&gclid=
EAIaIQobChMI5N7q98Xl6wIVSLLVCh36HQ5NEAAYASAAEgL_9vD_BwE

International Commission on the Futures of Education. (2020). *Education in a post-COVID world: Nine ideas for public action.* UNESCO. https://unesdoc.unesco.org/ark:/
48223/pf0000373717/PDF/373717eng.pdf.multi

Ivancheva, M. (2020, March 20). The casualization, digitalization, and outsourcing of academic labour: A wake-up call for trade unions. *FocaalBlog.*
http://www.focaalblog.com/2020/03/20/mariya-ivancheva-the-casualization-digitalization-and-outsourcing-of-academic-labour-a-wake-up-call-for-trade-unions/

Iyengar, R. (2021, February 23). The worldwide web as we know it may be ending, *CNN Business.* https://edition.cnn.com/2021/02/23/tech/splinternet-tech-regulation-facebook/index.html

Jackson, A. (2021, February 3). The expectation gap II – students' hopes for learning and teaching in the next normal. *Wonkhe.* https://wonkhe.com/blogs/the-expectation-gap-ii-students-hopes-for-learning-and-teaching-in-the-next-normal/

Jackson, L. M. (2017, August 22). We need to talk about digital blackface in reaction GIFs. *Teen Vogue.* https://www.teenvogue.com/story/digital-blackface-reaction gifs

Jandrić, P. (2017). *Learning in the age of digital reason.* Sense.

Jandrić, P. (2019). We-think, we-learn, we-act: The trialectic of postdigital collective intelligence. *Postdigital Science and Education, 1,* 275–279. https://doi.org/10.1007/
s42438-019-00055-w

Jandrić, P. (2020). Postdigital research measurement. *Postdigital Science and Education.*
https://doi.org/10.1007/s42438-020-00105-8

Jandrić, P., & Hayes, S. (2019). The postdigital challenge of redefining education from the margins. *Learning, Media and Technology,* 381–393. https://doi.org/10.1080/
17439884.2019.1585874

Jandrić, P., & Hayes, S. (2020a). Writing the history of the present. *Postdigital Science and Education.* https://doi.org/10.1007/s42438-020-00168-7

Jandrić, P., & Hayes, S. (Eds.). (2020b). Teaching in the age of Covid-19. *Postdigital Science and Education.* https://doi.org/10.1007/s42438-020-00169-6

Jandrić, P., & Hayes, S. (2020c). Postdigital we-learn. *Studies in Philosophy and Education.* https://doi.org/10.1007/s11217-020-09711-2

Jandrić, P., & Hayes, S. (2020d). Technological unemployment and its educational discontents. In M. Stocchetti (Ed.), *The digital age and its discontents.* Helsinki University Press.

Jandrić, P., & Ford, D. (2020). Postdigital ecopedagogies: Genealogies, contradictions, and possible futures. *Postdigital Science and Education.* https://doi.org/10.1007/
s42438-020-00207-3

Jandrić, P., Jaldemark, J., Hurley, Z., Bartram, B., Matthews, A., Jopling, M., Manero, J., MacKenzie, A., Irwin, J., Rothmuller, N., Green, B., Ralston, S. J., Pyyhtinen, O., Hayes, S., Wright, J., Peters, M. A., & Tesar, M. (2020). Philosophy of education in a new key: Who remembers Greta Thunberg? Education and environment after the Coronavirus. *Educational Philosophy and Theory.* https://doi.org/10.1080/00131857.2020.1811678

Jandrić, P., Knox, J., Besley, T., Ryberg, T., Suoranta, J., & Hayes, S. (2018). Postdigital science and education. *Educational Philosophy and Theory, 50*(10), 893–899. https://doi.org/10.1080/00131857.2018.1454000

Jandrić, P., Knox, J., Macleod, H., & Sinclair, C. (2017). Learning in the age of algorithmic cultures. *E-learning and Digital Media.* https://journals.sagepub.com/doi/pdf/10.1177/2042753017731237

Jandrić, P., Ryberg, T., Knox, J., Lacković, N., Hayes, S., Suoranta, J., Smith, M., Steketee, A., Peters, M., McLaren, P., Ford, D. R., Asher, G., McGregor, C., Stewart, G., Williamson, B., & Gibbons, A. (2018). Postdigital dialogue. *Postdigital Science and Education,* 1–27. https://doi.org/10.1007/s42438-018-0011-x

Jenkins, S. (2020a, September 25). Why do students travel to university? Covid has proved they don't need to. *The Guardian.* https://www.theguardian.com/commentisfree/2020/sep/25/covid-students-travel-university-freshers-glasgow

Jenkyns, A. [@andreajenkyns]. (2020b, September 26). *Great, commons sense prevails! Woke 'cancel culture' is a form of bullying, pupils will be taught* [Tweet]. Twitter. https://twitter.com/andreajenkyns/status/1309955203328815110

Jiang, J., & Vetter, M. A. (2020). The good, the bot, and the ugly: Problematic information and critical media literacy in the postdigital era. *Postdigital Science and Education, 2*(1), 78–94. https://doi.org/10.1007/s42438-019-00069-4

Johnson, M., Maitland, E., & Torday, J. (2020). Covid-19 and the epigenetics of learning. *Postdigital Science and Education.* https://doi.org/10.1007/s42438-020-00190-9

Jones, J. R. (2010). So just what is the student experience? The development of a conceptual framework for the student experience of undergraduate business students based on the themes emerging in the academic literature. In *SRHE Annual Research Conference.* Newcastle University. https://www.srhe.ac.uk/conference2010/abstracts/0146.pdf

Kaeser-Chen, C., Dubois, E., Schüür, F., & Moss, E. (2020). Positionality-aware machine learning: Translation tutorial. In *Proceedings of the 2020 Conference on fairness, accountability, and transparency* (pp. 704–704).

Kahane, D. (2009). Learning about obligation, compassion, and global justice: The place of contemplative pedagogy. *New Directions for Teaching and Learning, 118,* 49–60. https://doi.org/10.1002/tl.352

REFERENCES

Katwala, A. (2020, August 15). An algorithm determined UK students' grades. Chaos ensued: This year's A-levels, the high-stakes exams taken in high school, were cancelled due to the pandemic. The alternative only exacerbated existing inequities. *Wired*. https://www.wired.com/story/an-algorithm-determined-uk-students-grades-chaos-ensued/#google_ads_iframe_3379/conde.wired.native/in-content/business/article/1_0:~:text=Forgetthetriplelockethnicminority,schoolcareersthatthey'reassessedanonymously

Keele University. (2018–2022). *Equality, diversity and inclusion strategy.* https://www.keele.ac.uk/media/keeleuniversity/policyzone20/humanresources/EDI%20STRATEGY%202018-22.pdf

Kezar, A. (2002). Reconstructing static images of leadership: An application of positionality theory. *Journal of Leadership Studies*, *8*(3), 94–109. https://doi.org/10.1177%2F107179190200800308

Kezar, A., & Lester, J. (2010). Breaking the barriers of essentialism in leadership research: Positionality as a promising approach. *Feminist Formations*, 163–185. https://doi.org/10.1353/nwsa.0.0121

Kliff, S., Satariano, A., Silver-Greenberg, J., & Kulish, N. (2020, March 26). There aren't enough ventilators to cope with the Coronavirus. *NYTimes*. https://www.nytimes.com/2020/03/18/business/coronavirus-ventilator-shortage.html

Knox, J. (2019). What does the 'postdigital' mean for education? Three critical perspectives on the digital, with implications for educational research and practice. *Postdigital Science and Education, 1*(2), 357–370. https://doi.org/10.1007/s42438-019-00045-y

Knox, J., Wang, Y., & Gallagher, M. (2019). Introduction: AI, inclusion, and 'everyone learning everything'. In *Artificial Intelligence and inclusive education* (pp. 1–13). Springer.

Komljenovic, J. (2018). Making higher education markets: Trust-building strategies of private companies to enter the public sector. *Higher Education*, *78*(1), 51–66. https://doi.org/10.1007/s10734-018-0330-6

Komljenovic, J. (2020). The future of value in digitalised higher education: Why data privacy should not be our biggest concern. *Higher Education*. https://doi.org/10.1007/s10734-020-00639-7

Kornberger, M., Bowker, G. C., Elyachar, J., Mennicken, A., Miller, P., Nucho, J. R., & Pollock, N. (Eds.). (2019). *Thinking infrastructures*. Emerald Group Publishing.

Köver, C., & Reuter, M. (2019, December 2). TikTok curbed reach for people with disabilities. *Netzpolitik*. https://netzpolitik.org/2019/discrimination-tiktok-curbed-reach-for-people-with-disabilities/

Krug, J. A. (2020, September 3). The truth, and the anti-black violence of my lies. *Medium*. https://medium.com/@jessakrug/the-truth-and-the-anti-black-violence-of-my-lies-9a9621401f85

Kucharski, A. (2020, February 8). Misinformation on the coronavirus might be the most contagious thing about it. *The Guardian*. https://www.who.int/dg/speeches/detail/director-general-s-remarks-at-the-media-briefing-on-2019-novel-coronavirus---8-february-2020

Kuhl, P. K., Lim, S. S., Guerriero, S., & Van Damme, D. (2019). *Developing minds in the digital age*. OECD Publishing.

Kuhn, T. S. (2012). *The structure of scientific revolutions* (50th ann. ed.). University of Chicago Press. (Original work published 1962)

Kumar, N., & Karusala, N. (2019). Intersectional computing. *Interactions, 26*(2), 50–54. https://doi.org/10.1145/3305360

Lacković, N. (2020a). Thinking with digital images in the post-truth era: A method in critical media literacy. *Postdigital Science and Education*, 1–21. https://doi.org/10.1007/s42438-019-00099-y

Lacković, N., & Olteanu, A. (2020b). Rethinking educational theory and practice in times of visual media: Learning as image-concept integration. *Educational Philosophy and Theory*, 1–16. https://doi.org/10.1080/00131857.2020.1799783

Lamb, J., Bartholomew, P., & Hayes, S. (2017). Transnational academic staff development: Cultural, practical and policy challenges. In J. Branch, A. Hørsted, & C. Nygaard (Eds.), *Globalisation in higher education*. Libri Publishing.

Lammy, D. [@David Lammy]. (2020, August 31). *Poppycock! This humbug totally misses the spirit of Notting Hill Carnival and the tradition of "dress up" or "masquerade" Adele* [Tweet]. Twitter. https://twitter.com/DavidLammy/status/1300413774126551040

Lea, J. (2010). *Political correctness and higher education: British and American perspectives*. Routledge.

Lem, P. (2020, September 17). Covid-19 could worsen the digital divide. *Research Professional*. https://researchprofessionalnews.com/rr-news-europe-universities-2020-9-covid-19-could-worsen-digital-divide/

Leone, M. (2018). Semiotics of the selfie: The glorification of the present. *Punctum, 4*(2), 33–48.

Leone, M. (2020). *On insignificance: The loss of meaning in the post-material age*. Routledge.

Leslie, D. (2020). *Understanding bias in facial recognition technologies: An explainer*. The Alan Turing Institute. https://www.turing.ac.uk/sites/default/files/2020-10/understanding_bias_in_facial_recognition_technology.pdf

Lewis, T. E. (2020). Everything you always wanted to know about being postdigital but were afraid to ask a vampire squid. *Postdigital Science and Education, 2*(2), 265–266. https://doi.org/10.1007/s42438-019-00082-7

Li, J. (2021, February 3). Putting an end to digital poverty. *New Statesman*.

Liesch, K. (2020). Don't do unconscious bias training. *Tidal Equality*. https://www.tidalequality.com/blog/dont-do-unconscious-bias-training

REFERENCES 293

Lister, T. (2021, February 5). Why COVAX could become the most important acronym of 2021. *CNN Health.* https://edition.cnn.com/2021/02/05/world/covax-explainer-intl/index.html

Luckin, R. (2020, March 10). AI in education will help us understand how we think. *The Financial Times.* https://www.ft.com/content/4f24adca-5186-11ea-8841-482eed0038b1

Lukács, G. (1971). *History and class consciousness.* Merlin.

Lupton, D., & Williamson, B. (2017). The datafied child: The dataveillance of children and implications for their rights. *New Media & Society.* https://doi.org/10.1177%2F1461444816686328

Luscombe, R., & Sullivan, H. (2020, October 5). 'This is insanity': Walter Reed physician among critics of Donald Trump drive-by visit. *The Guardian.* https://www.theguardian.com/us-news/2020/oct/04/trump-walter-reed-drive-by-visit-criticism

Luttrell, W. (2019). Reflexive qualitative research. In *Oxford research encyclopaedia of education.*

MacKenzie, A., & Bhatt, I. (2020). Opposing the power of lies, bullshit and fake news: The value of truth. *Postdigital Science and Education,* 2(1), 217–232. https://doi.org/10.1007/s42438-019-00087-2

MacKenzie, D., & Wajcman, J. (1999). Introductory essay: The social shaping of technology. *The Social Shaping of Technology,* 2, 3–27.

Macpherson Report. (1999). *The Stephen Lawrence inquiry.* UK Government, Cm 4262-I. https://assets.publishing.service.gov.uk/government/uploads/system/uploads/attachment_data/file/277111/4262.pdf

Maher, F. A., & Tetreault, M. K. (1993). Frames of positionality: Constructing meaningful dialogues about gender and race. *Anthropological Quarterly,* 118–126.

Mañero, J. (2020). Postdigital brave new world and its educational implications. *Postdigital Science and Education,* 2(3), 670–674. https://doi.org/10.1007/s42438-020-00129-0

Mann, A. (2018). *Reading contagion: The hazards of reading in the age of print.* University of Virginia Press.

Manthorpe, R. (2020, August 28). Exams algorithm not 'mutant' and contained 'predictable' errors, says top statistician. *Sky News.* https://news.sky.com/story/exams-algorithm-not-mutant-and-contained-predictable-errors-says-top-statistician-12058124

Marr, B. (2019, December 20). What is the Artificial Intelligence of things? When AI meets IoT. *Forbes.* https://www.forbes.com/sites/bernardmarr/2019/12/20/what-is-the-artificial-intelligence-of-things-when-ai-meets-iot/

Matias, C. E. (2020). Do you SEE the words coming out of that text? Seeing whiteness in digital text. *International Journal of Multicultural Education,* 22(2). http://dx.doi.org/10.18251/ijme.v22i2.2411

Matthewman, S. (2011). *Technology and social theory.* Palgrave Macmilan.

Matthews, A. (2019). Design as a discipline for postdigital learning and teaching: Bricolage and actor-network theory. *Postdigital Science and Education.* https://doi.org/10.1007/s42438-020-00170-z

Mautner, G. (2005). The entrepreneurial university: A discursive profile of a higher education buzzword. *Critical Discourse Studies, 2*(2), 95–120. https://doi.org/10.1080/17405900500283540

Mayer-Schönberger, V., & Cukier, K. (2014a). *Big data: A revolution that will transform how we live, work, and think.* Eamon Dolan/Mariner Books.

Mayer-Schönberger, V., & Cukier, K. (2014b). *Learning with big data: The future of education.* Eamon Dolan Book.

McCall, L. (2005). The complexity of intersectionality. *SIGNS: Journal of Women in Culture and Society, 30*(31), 1771–802. https://doi.org/10.1086/426800

McDonald, H. (2019, December 12). AI expert calls for end to UK use of 'racially biased' algorithms. *The Guardian.* https://www.theguardian.com/technology/2019/dec/12/ai-end-uk-use-racially-biased-algorithms-noel-sharkey

McRae, A. (2018, February 22). What does 'value for money' mean for English higher education? *Times Higher Education.* https://www.timeshighereducation.com/features/what-does-value-money-mean-english-higher-education

McVeigh, T. (2013, March 2). Amazon acts to halt sales of 'Keep Calm and Rape' T-shirts. *The Guardian.* https://www.theguardian.com/technology/2013/mar/02/amazon-withdraws-rape-slogan-shirt

Means, A. J. (2018). Platform learning and on-demand labor: Sociotechnical projections on the future of education and work. *Learning Media and Technology.*

Metro News Reporter. (2021, February 12). Librarians troll book lover who built 'swap box' outside home in lockdown. *Metro.* https://metro.co.uk/2021/02/12/librarians-troll-book-lover-who-build-swap-box-outside-home-in-lockdown-14066956/

Micrashell. (2020). *A suit that allows you to safely socialise in times of a pandemic.* https://production.club/micrashell/

Miltner, K. M., & Highfield, T. (2017). Never gonna GIF you up: Analyzing the cultural significance of the animated GIF. *Social Media + Society, 3*(3), 1–11. https://doi.org/10.1177%2F2056305117725223

Mirzaei, A. (2019, September 8). Where 'woke' came from and why marketers should think twice before jumping on the social activism bandwagon. *The Conversation.* https://theconversation.com/where-woke-came-from-and-why-marketers-should-think-twice-before-jumping-on-the-social-activism-bandwagon-122713

Mixergy Ltd. (2020, September 30). The 'internet of tanks' – a hot water cylinder story. *Smart Home.* https://www.smarthometechlive.co.uk/news/the-internet-of-tanks-a-hot-water-cylinder-story

Molesworth, M., Nixon, E., & Scullion, R. (2009). Having, being and higher education: The marketisation of the university and the transformation of the student into consumer. *Teaching in Higher Education, 14*(3), 277–287. https://doi.org/10.1080/13562510902898841

Morozov, E. (2013). *To save everything, click here: the folly of technological solutionism.* Public Affairs.

Morris, N. (2020a, April 1). The race problem with artificial intelligence: 'Machines are learning to be racist'. *Metro.* https://metro.co.uk/2020/04/01/race-problem-artificial-intelligence-machines-learning-racist-12478025/

Morris, N. (2020b, September 28). Morrisons launches SOS food delivery service for students. *Metro.* https://metro.co.uk/2020/09/28/morrisons-launches-sos-food-delivery-service-for-students-13337540/

Mortier, R., Haddadi, H., Henderson, T., McAuley, D., & Crowcroft, J. (2014). *Human-data interaction: The human face of the data-driven society.* https://arxiv.org/pdf/1412.6159.pdf

Mortier, R., Haddadi, H., Henderson, T., McAuley, D., Crowcroft, J., & Crabtree, A. (2020). Human-data interaction. In *The encyclopedia of human-computer interaction* (2nd ed.). Interaction Design Foundation. https://nottingham-repository.worktribe.com/preview/819355/Human-Data%20Interaction.pdf

MOTH. (2020). *Moving to online teaching and homeworking, UCL.* https://www.ucl.ac.uk/ioe/departments-and-centres/centres/ucl-knowledge-lab/research/ucl-moving-online-teaching-and-homeworking-moth

Mozilla Manifesto. (2003). *Let's unfck the Internet.* https://foundation.mozilla.org/en/

Murphy, S., & Walker, A. (2020, September 21). MPs urged to do unconscious bias training as dozens of Tories set to reject it. *The Guardian.* https://www.theguardian.com/world/2020/sep/21/mps-urged-to-do-unconscious-bias-training-as-dozens-of-tories-set-to-reject-it

Napier University. (2020). *Student experience strategy 2020.* https://www.napier.ac.uk/~/media/documents/corporate-documents/student-experience-strategy.pdf

National Grid. (2020, July 21). *4 ways lockdown life affected UK electricity use.* National Grid. https://www.nationalgrid.com/uk/stories/grid-at-work-stories/4-ways-lockdown-life-affected-uk-electricity-use

Negroponte, N. (1998). Beyond digital. *Wired, 6*(12), 288.

NIHR. (2020). *Living with Covid-19.* https://evidence.nihr.ac.uk/themedreview/living-with-covid19/

Noodle Partners. (2020). Webpage. https://partners.noodle.com

Nottinghamshire County Council. (2020, October 28). *Nottingham and Nottinghamshire move to tier 3 Very high restrictions for Covid-19.* https://www.nottinghamshire.gov.uk/newsroom/news/nottingham-and-nottinghamshire-move-to-tier-3-very

Nudzor, H. (2009). Re-conceptualising the paradox in policy implementation: A postmodernist conceptual approach. *Discourse: Studies in the Cultural Politics of Education, 30*(4), 501–513. https://doi.org/10.1080/01596300903237255

OECD. (2020). The digitalisation of science (2020). In *The digitalisation of science, technology and innovation: Key developments and policies.* OECD Publishing. https://read.oecd-ilibrary.org/science-and-technology/the-digitalisation-of-science-technology-and-innovation_b9e4a2c0-en#page5

Office for Students. (2019, September 26). *Associations Between Characteristics of Students (ABCS). How do outcomes differ when accounting for multiple student characteristics?* OfS 2019.34. https://www.officeforstudents.org.uk/publications/associations-between-characteristics-of-students/

Office for Students. (2018–2022). *Equality and diversity objectives for the Office for Students.* https://www.officeforstudents.org.uk/media/od3ocb3f-2e49-4541-ad57-f5823a4d3893/ofs-e-and-d-statement-and-objectives.pdf

Office for Students. (2019). *The Teaching Excellence and Student Outcomes Framework (TEF).* https://www.officeforstudents.org.uk/data-and-analysis/differences-in-student-outcomes/

O'Keeffe, C. (2017). Economizing education: Assessment algorithms and calculative agencies. *E-Learning and Digital Media, 14*(3), 123–137. https://doi.org/10.1177/2042753017732503

Okoli, C., & Pawlowski, S. D. (2004). The Delphi method as a research tool: An example, design considerations and applications. *Information & Management, 42*(1), 15–29. https://doi.org/10.1016/j.im.2003.11.002

Olson, P. (2020, April 10). My girlfriend is a chatbot. *The Wall Street Journal.* https://www.wsj.com/articles/my-girlfriend-is-a-chatbot-11586523208

Olssen, M. (2016). Neoliberal competition in higher education today: Research, accountability and impact. *British Journal of Sociology of Education, 37*(1), 129–148. https://doi.org/10.1080/01425692.2015.1100530

Olssen, M., & Peters, M. A. (2005). Neoliberalism, higher education and the knowledge economy: From the free market to knowledge capitalism. *Journal of Education Policy, 20*(3), 313–345. https://doi.org/10.1080/02680930500108718

O'Neill, G., & McMahon, T. (2005). Student-centred learning: What does it mean for students and lecturers. In *Emerging issues in the practice of university learning and teaching I.* AISHE.

Open Covid Pledge. (2020). *Make the pledge to share your intellectual property in the fight against Covid-19.* https://opencovidpledge.org/2020/08/27/creative-commons-to-steward-the-open-covid-pledge/

Open Covid Pledge for Research in Education. (2020). *Sign the open Covid pledge for research in education.* Association for Learning Technology. https://www.alt.ac.uk/open-covid-pledge

Open Science Collaboration. (2015). Estimating the reproducibility of psychological science. *Science, 349*(6251).

REFERENCES

Osamor, K. (2020, October 17). BAME is past its sell-by date. *Politics Home.*
https://www.politicshome.com/thehouse/article/bame-is-past-its-sellby-date

Ovetz, R. (2020). The Algorithmic University: On-line education, learning management systems, and the struggle over academic labor. *Critical Sociology.* https://doi.org/10.1177%2F0896920520948931

Pahl, K., & Rowsell, J., with Collier, D., Pool, S., Rasool, Z., & Trzecak, T. (2020) *Living literacies: Re-thinking literacy research and practice through the everyday.* MIT Press.

Palmer, P. M. (2017). *Changing times, changing values: An exploration of the positionality and agency of teacher educators working in higher education* (Doctoral dissertation). Manchester Metropolitan University. https://e-space.mmu.ac.uk/619874/1/Thesis%20final%20version%2018th%20December%202017.pdf

PA Media. (2020, September 1). Adele accused of cultural appropriation over Instagram picture. *The Guardian.* https://www.theguardian.com/music/2020/sep/01/adele-accused-of-cultural-appropriation-over-instagram-picture

Park, S., Freeman, J., & Middleton, C. (2019). Intersections between connectivity and digital inclusion in rural communities. *Communication Research and Practice, 5*(2), 139–155. https://doi.org/10.1080/22041451.2019.1601493

Partington, A. (2020). Developing inclusive pedagogies in HE through an understanding of the learner-consumer: Promiscuity, hybridisation, and innovation. *Postdigital Science and Education.* https://doi.org/10.1007/s42438-020-00110-x

Parveen, N. (2020, April 11). Milk floats ride to the rescue of locked-down British households. *The Guardian.* https://www.theguardian.com/world/2020/apr/11/milk-floats-ride-to-the-rescue-of-locked-down-british-households

Parveen, N. (2021, February 12). Priti Patel hits out at 'dreadful' Black lives matter protests. *The Guardian.* https://www.theguardian.com/politics/2021/feb/12/priti-patel-hits-out-at-dreadful-black-lives-matters-protests

Payne, B. (2020, August 17). Trusting a bizarre algorithm over teachers like me is a terrible mistake. The Government's computerised grading system is discriminatory and ridiculous. *The Telegraph.* https://www.telegraph.co.uk/news/2020/08/17/trusting-bizarre-algorithm-teachers-like-terrible-mistake/

Pedro, F., Subosa, M., Rivas, A., & Valverde, P. (2019). *Artificial Intelligence in education: Challenges and opportunities for sustainable development.* UNESCO. https://unesdoc.unesco.org/ark:/48223/pf0000366994

Pepperell, R., & Punt, M. (2000). *The postdigital membrane: Imagination, technology and desire.* Intellect Books.

Perrotta, C., & Selwyn, N. (2020). Deep learning goes to school: Toward a relational understanding of AI in education *Learning, Media and Technology, 45*(3), 251–269. https://doi.org/10.1080/17439884.2020.1686017

Peters, M. A. (2012). Bio-informational capitalism. *Thesis Eleven, 110*(1), 98–111. https://doi.org/10.1177%2F0725513612444562

Peters, M. A. (2016). The eco-university in the green age. *Review of Contemporary Philosophy*, *15*, 60–69.

Peters, M. A. (2019). Posthumanism, platform ontologies and the 'wounds of modern subjectivity'. *Educational Philosophy and Theory*. https://doi.org/10.1080/00131857.2019.1608690

Peters, M. A. (2020a). Critical philosophy of technological convergence: Education and the Nano-Bio-Info-Cogno paradigm. In M. Stocchetti (Ed.), *The digital age and its discontents* (pp. 235–252). Helsinki University Press. https://doi.org/10.33134/HUP-4-12

Peters, M. A. (2020b). Platform ontologies, the AI crisis and the ability to hack humans 'An algorithm knows me better than I know myself'. *Educational Philosophy and Theory*, *52*(6), 593–601. https://doi.org/10.1080/00131857.2019.1618227

Peters, M. A., & Besley, T. (2020). *Pandemic education and viral politics*. Routledge.

Peters, M. A., Besley, T., Jandrić, P., & Zhu, X. (Eds.). (2020). *Knowledge socialism. The rise of peer production: Collegiality, collaboration, and collective intelligence*. Springer.

Peters, M. A., & Jandrić, P. (2019). Posthumanism, open ontologies and bio-digital becoming: Response to Luciano Floridi's OnlifeManifesto. *Educational Philosophy and Theory*, *51*(10), 971–980. https://doi.org/10.1080/00131857.2018.1551835

Peters, M. A., Jandrić, P., & Hayes, S. (2018). The curious promise of educationalising technological unemployment: What can places of learning really do about the future of work? *Journal of Educational Philosophy and Theory*. https://doi.org/10.1080/00131857.2018.1439376

Peters, M. A., Jandrić, P., & Hayes, S. (2021a). Biodigital philosophy, technological convergence, and new knowledge ecologies. *Postdigital Science and Education*. https://doi.org/10.1007/s42438-020-00211-7

Peters, M. A., Jandrić, P., & Hayes, S. (2021b). Biodigital technologies and the bioeconomy: The global new green deal? *Educational Philosophy and Theory*. https://doi.org/10.1080/00131857.2020.1861938

Peters, M. A., Jandrić, P., & Hayes, S. (2021c). Postdigital-biodigital: An emerging configuration. *Educational Philosophy and Theory*. doi:10.1080/00131857.2020.1867108

Peters, M. A., Jandrić, P., & Hayes, S. (2021d). Revisiting the concept of the 'edited collection': Bioinformation philosophy and postdigital knowledge ecologies. *Postdigital Science and Education*. https://doi.org/10.1007/s42438-021-00216-w

Peters, M. A., Jandrić, P., & Hayes, S. (Eds.). (2022). *Bioinformational philosophy and postdigital knowledge ecologies*. Springer (forthcoming).

Peters, M. A., Jandrić, P., & McLaren, P. (2020). Viral modernity? Epidemics, infodemics, and the 'bioinformational' paradigm. *Educational Philosophy and Theory*. https://doi.org/10.1080/00131857.2020.1744226

Peters, M. A., Rider, S., Hyvonen, M., & Besley, T. (2018). Post-truth, fake news. *Viral Modernity and Higher Education, Singapore*. Springer.

Peters, M. A., Wang, H., Ogunniran, M. O., Huang, Y., Green, B., Chunga, J. O., Quainoo, E. A., Ren, Z., Hollings, S., Mou, C., Khomera, S. W., Zhang, M., Zhou, S., Laimeche, A., Zheng, W., Xu, R., Jackson L., & Hayes, S. (2020). China's internationalized higher education during Covid-19: Collective student autoethnography. *Postdigital Science and Education*. https://doi.org/10.1007/s42438-020-00128-1

Petersen, A. (2018). *Digital health and technological promise: A sociological inquiry*. Routledge.

Pickersgill, M. (2020). Epigenetics, education, and the plastic body: Changing concepts and new engagements. *Research in Education*, *107*(1), 72–83. https://doi.org/10.1177%2F0034523719867102

Pledge.com. https://www.pledge.com/en-us

Pluckrose, H., & Lindsay, J. (2020). *Cynical theories: How activist scholarship made everything about race, gender and identity – and why this harms everybody*. Pitchstone Publishing.

Policy Horizons Canada. (2020, February 11). *Exploring biodigital convergence: What happens when biology and digital technology merge?* Government of Canada. https://horizons.gc.ca/wp-content/uploads/2020/02/Biodigital-Convergence-with-Links-Final-02062020.pdf

Porter, J. (2020, August 17). UK ditches exam results generated by biased algorithm after student protests: Protesters chanted 'Fuck the algorithm' outside the country's Department for Education. *The Verge*. https://www.theverge.com/2020/8/17/21372045/uk-a-level-results-algorithm-biased-coronavirus-covid-19-pandemic-university-applications

Postan, E. (2016). Defining ourselves: Personal bioinformation as a tool of narrative self-conception. *Journal of bioethical inquiry*, *13*(1), 133–151. https://doi.org/10.1007/s11673-015-9690-0

Powell, R. (2020, August 17). Exams U-turn fixes a political problem for the government but creates many more practical ones. *Sky News*. https://news.sky.com/story/exams-u-turn-students-may-feel-happier-about-their-career-prospects-gavin-williamson-probably-doesnt-12051199

Price, C. (2020). Covid-19: When species and data meet. *Postdigital Science and Education, 2*(3), 772–790. https://doi.org/10.1007/s42438-020-00180-x.

Prior, R. (2020). Afterword. In R. Mateus-Berr & R. Jochum (Eds.), *Teaching artistic research conversations across cultures*. De Gruyter.

Pykett, J. (2015). *Brain culture: Shaping policy through neuroscience*. Policy Press.

Ramge, T. (2020). *Postdigital: Using AI to fight Coronavirus, foster wealth and fuel democracy*. Murmann Publishers GmbH.

Rao, S. (2020, September 30). '9k4 what? Here are all the signs put up by students under forced lockdown in halls. *The Tab*. https://thetab.com/uk/2020/09/29/9k-4-what-here-are-all-the-signs-put-up-by-students-under-forced-lockdown-in-halls-176848

Ravetz, J. (2016, June 8). How should we treat science's growing pains? *The Guardian.* https://www.theguardian.com/science/political-science/2016/jun/08/how-should-we-treat-sciences-growing-pains

Readings, B. (1996). *The university in ruins.* Harvard University Press.

Rees, J. (2020, August 11). Facial recognition use by South Wales Police ruled unlawful. *BBC News.* https://www.bbc.co.uk/news/uk-wales-53734716

Reich, J. (2020). *Failure to disrupt: Why technology alone can't transform education.* Harvard University Press.

Reicher, S. (2020, September 9). Scapegoating young people for Britain's rising coronavirus rates is a poor strategy. *The Guardian.* https://www.theguardian.com/commentisfree/2020/sep/09/scapegoating-young-people-britain-coronavirus-rates

Rein, L. (2020, July 10). Drive-in movie theaters have come to NYC for Summer 2020. *Mommy Poppins.* https://mommypoppins.com/new-york-city-kids/drive-in-movie-theaters-nyc

Reeves, T. (2019). A postdigital perspective on organisations. *Postdigital Science and Education, 1*(1), 146–162. https://doi.org/10.1007/s42438-018-0018-3

Research Excellence Framework. (2021). *What is the REF?* https://www.ref.ac.uk/about/what-is-the-ref/

Rikowski, G. (2003). Alien life: Marx and the future of the human. *Historical Materialism, 11*(2), 121–164. https://doi.org/10.1163/156920603768311255

Ritzer, G. (1993). *The McDonaldisation of society.* Pine Forge Press.

Ritzer, G. (2005). *Enchanting a disenchanted world: Revolutionizing the means of consumption.* Pine Forge Press.

Ritzer, G. (2018). *The McDonaldisation of society: Into the digital age* (9th ed.). Sage Publications.

Ritzer, G., & Dean, P. (2019). *Globalisation: The essentials* (2nd ed.). WileyBlackwell.

Ritzer, G., Jandrić, P., & Hayes, S. (2018). The velvet cage of educational con (pro) sumption. *Open Review of Educational Research.* https://doi.org/10.1080/23265507.2018.1546124

Robinson, S. K. (2020). A global reset of education. *Prospects, 49,* 7–9. https://doi.org/10.1007/s11125-020-09493-y

Roy, A. (2020, April 4). The pandemic is a portal. *Financial Times.*

Roy, L. A. (2018). *Teaching while white: Addressing the intersections of race and immigration in the classroom.* Rowman and Littlefield.

Rudd, T. (2017). TEF: Re-examining its logic and considering possible systemic and institutional outcomes. *Journal of Critical Education Policy Studies, 2*(15), 59–90.

Russell, S., & Norvig, P. (2016). *Artificial intelligence: A modern approach* (global 3rd ed.). Pearson.

REFERENCES

Rustin, M. (2016). The neoliberal university and its alternatives. *Soundings, 63*(63), 147–176. https://doi.org/10.3898/136266216819377057

Ryberg, T. [@tryberg]. (2020, March 18). *Call for testimonies "teaching in the age of COVID-19". Share how #Corona has impacted your life as teacher and/or researcher* [Tweet]. Twitter. https://twitter.com/tryberg/status/1240360139653353472

Saachi, S., Lotti, M., & Branduardi, P. (2020). Education for a biobased economy: Integrating life and social sciences in flexible short courses accessible from different backgrounds. *New Biotechnology, 60,* 72–75. https://doi.org/10.1016/j.nbt.2020.10.002.

Sabri, D. (2011). What's wrong with 'the student experience'? *Discourse: Studies in the Cultural Politics of Education, 32*(5), 657–667. https://doi.org/10.1080/01596306.2011.620750

Saltman, K. J., & Means, A. J. (Eds.). (2018). *The Wiley handbook of global educational reform.* John Wiley & Sons.

Sandel, M. J. (2020). *The tyranny of merit: What's become of the common good?* Allen Lane.

Sandhu, R. (2018, May 17). Should BAME be ditched as a term for Black, asian and minority ethnic people? *BBC Politics.* https://www.bbc.co.uk/news/uk-politics-43831279

Sapon-Shevin, M., SooHoo, S. (2020). Embodied social justice pedagogy in a time of 'no touch'. *Postdigital Science and Education, 2,* 675–680. https://doi.org/10.1007/s42438-020-00177-6

Saunders, D. (2015). Resisting excellence: Challenging neoliberal ideology in postsecondary education. *Journal for Critical Education Policy Studies, 12*(2), 391–411.

Savin-Baden, M. (Ed.). (2021). *Postdigital humans: Transitions, transformations and transcendence.* Springer.

Scheuerman, M. K., Wade, K., Lustig, C., & Brubaker, J. R. (2020). How we've taught algorithms to see identity: Constructing race and gender in image databases for facial analysis. *Proceedings of the ACM on Human-Computer Interaction, 4*(CSCW1), 1–35. https://doi.org/10.1145/3392866

Schraer, R., & Triggle, N. (2020, September 3). Coronavirus: People sent long distances for Covid tests. *BBC News.* https://www.bbc.co.uk/news/health-53990068

Schwab, K. (2017). *The fourth industrial revolution.* Random House.

S C Johnson. (2020). Webpage. https://www.scjohnson.com/en/our-purpose/social-responsibility-news/health-and-well-being/coronavirus/coronavirus

Scott, P. (2018). Compliance and creativity: Dilemmas for university governance. *European Review, 26*(S1), S35–S47. https://doi.org/10.1017/S1062798717000527

Scott, W. R. (2010). Reflections: The past and future of research on institutions and institutional change. *Journal of Change Management, 10*(1), 5–21. https://doi.org/10.1080/14697010903549408

Seldon, A. (2020). *The fourth education revolution reconsidered: Will Artificial Intelligence enrich or diminish humanity?* University of Buckingham Press.

Shattock, M. (2018). Better informing the market? The Teaching Excellence Framework (TEF) in British higher education. *International Higher Education, 92*, Winter, 21–22. https://doi.org/10.6017/ihe.2018.92.10283

Shearing, H. (2020, June 18). Black lives matter: Statues are falling but what should replace them? *BBC News*. https://www.bbc.co.uk/news/uk-52995404

Sheppard, E. (2002). The spaces and times of globalization: Place, scale, networks, and positionality. *Economic geography, 78*(3), 307–330.

Shore, C., & Wright, S. (1999). Audit culture and anthropology: Neo-liberalism in British higher education. *Journal of the Royal Anthropological Institute, 5*(4), 557–575.

Sibthorpe, C. (2020, September 4). Jessica Krug: George Washington University professor admits she has been pretending to be Black. *Sky News*. https://news.sky.com/story/jessica-krug-george-washington-university-professor-admits-she-has-been-pretending-to-be-black-12063202

Simmel, G. (1950). *The sociology of Georg Simmel*. The Free Press.

Simpson, P., & Mayr, A. (2010). *Language and power*. Routledge.

Sinclair, C., & Hayes, S. (2019). Between the post and the com-post: Examining the postdigital 'work' of a prefix. *Postdigital Science and Education, 1*(1), 119–131. https://doi.org/10.1007/s42438-018-0017-4

Sky News. (2020, August 21). *Taylor Swift donates £23,000 to London student so she can afford UK university*. https://news.sky.com/story/taylor-swift-donates-23-000-to-london-student-so-she-can-afford-uk-university-12053406

Slater, T. (2020, August 20). The exams fiasco is just the beginning: Our panicked response to coronavirus will cause one injustice after another. *Spiked*. https://www.spiked-online.com/2020/08/20/the-exams-fiasco-is-just-the-beginning/

Slaughter, S., & Leslie, L. (1997). *Academic capitalism*. John Hopkins University Press.

Slaughter, S., & Rhoades, G. (2000). The neo-liberal university. In *New labor forum* (pp. 73–79). Labor Resource Center, Queens College, City University of New York.

Smithers, R. (2020, September 23). Uncle Ben's rice to get revamp after criticism over racial stereotyping. *The Guardian*. https://www.theguardian.com/business/2020/sep/23/uncle-bens-to-get-revamp-after-criticism-over-racial-stereotyping

Sodha, S. (2020, August 18). The fake meritocracy of A-level grades is rotten anyway – universities don't need them. *The Guardian*. https://www.theguardian.com/commentisfree/2020/aug/18/a-level-grades-universities-exams

Speare-Cole, R. (2020, September 26). Government tells schools in England not to use anti-capitalist material in teaching. *Evening Standard*. https://www.standard.co.uk/news/uk/schools-england-anti-capitalist-materials-a4557461.html

Stanford Graduate School of Education. (2014). *Technology can close achievement gaps, improve learning*. https://ed.stanford.edu/news/technology-can-close-achievement-gaps-and-improve-learning-outcomes

REFERENCES

Stevenson, N. (2010). Education, neoliberalism and cultural citizenship: Living in 'X Factor' Britain. *European Journal of Cultural Studies, 13*(3), 341–358. https://doi.org/10.1177%2F1367549410363201

Stonebridge, L. (2020). *Writing and righting: Literature in the age of human rights.* Oxford University Press.

St Patricks. (2015–2017). *Student experience strategy.* https://www.st-patricks.ac.uk/media/1129/sp_student_bookletpdfpagespeedceprccoilzpb-1.pdf

Stratford, R. (2015). What is the ecological university and why is it a significant challenge for higher education policy and practice. *PESA-Philosophy of Education Society of Australasia, ANCU, Melbourne.*

Stubley, P. (2020, August 29). Coronavirus: Fury as new schools' guidance released on Friday afternoon before pupils return. *The Independent.* https://www.independent.co.uk/news/education/education-news/coronavirus-schools-england-guidance-face-masks-latest-a9695066.html

Sudjic, O. (2021, January 23). Page refresh: How the internet is transforming the novel. *The Guardian.* https://www.theguardian.com/books/2021/jan/23/page-refresh-how-the-internet-is-transforming-the-novel

Suoranta, J. (2020). The Covid-19 world: Learning or downfall. *Postdigital Science and Education.* https://doi.org/10.1007/s42438-020-00189-2

Sutton, R. (2020, October 8). Don't blur the line between science and politics: The more scientists breach into politics, the more they risk damaging their credibility. *Spiked.* https://www.spiked-online.com/2020/10/08/dont-blur-the-line-between-science-and-politics/

Swinford, S. (2020, August 13). Benn and Jerry's accused of virtue signalling in migrant row. *The Times.* https://www.thetimes.co.uk/article/ben-jerry-s-accused-of-virtue-signalling-in-migrant-row-m2bzjjhqq

Taylor, C. [@Callum Taylor]. (2020, August 8). *Many young people have lost elderly grandparents during this pandemic and are still grieving* [Tweet]. Twitter. https://twitter.com/CallumTaylor95/status/1292194693330198528

Taylor, L., Sharma, G., Martin, A., & Jameson, S. (2020). *Data justice and COVID-19: Global perspectives.* Meatspace Press.

Temple, P., Callender, C., Grove, L., & Kersh, N. (2014). Managing the student experience in a shifting higher education landscape. *The Higher Education Academy, 1*(1), 1–25. https://www.heacademy.ac.uk/sites/default/files/resources/managing_the_student_experience.pdf

Teräs, M., Suoranta, J., Teräs, H., & Curcher, M. (2020). Post-Covid-19 education and education technology 'solutionism': A Seller's market. *Postdigital Science and Education, 2*(3), 863–878. https://doi.org/10.1007/s42438-020-00164-x

The State of Data. (2020). *Report: Mapping children's data in state education in England (2020) defenddigitalme.* https://defenddigitalme.org/the-state-of-data-2020/

Thomas, Z. (2020, April 18). Coronavirus: Will Covid-19 speed up the use of robots to replace human workers? *BBC News.* https://www.bbc.co.uk/news/technology-52340651

Thorén, C., Edenius, M., Lundström, J. E., & Kitzmann, A. (2019). The hipster's dilemma: What is analogue or digital in the post-digital society? *Convergence, 25*(2), 324–339. https://doi.org/10.1177%2F1354856517713139

TikTok. (2019, October 24). Statement on TikTok's content moderation and data security practices. *TikTok.* https://newsroom.tiktok.com/en-us/statement-on-tiktoks-content-moderation-and-data-security-practices

Torres-Olave, B., & Lee, J. J. (2019). Shifting positionalities across international locations: Embodied knowledge, time-geography, and the polyvalence of privilege. *Higher Education Quarterly.* https://doi.org/10.1111/hequ.12216

Traxler, J. (2020). Inclusion, measurement and relevance and Covid-19. *Postdigital Science and Education,* 1–9. https://doi.org/10.1007/s42438-020-00182-9

Traxler, J., Smith, M., Scott, H., & Hayes, S. (2021). *Learning through the crisis: Helping decision-makers around the world use digital technology to combat the educational challenges produced by the current COVID-19 pandemic.* Department for International Development (DFID) EdTech Hub. https://docs.edtechhub.org/lib/?all=john+traxler&page=2&page-len=1&sort=score&id=CD9IAPFX

Treusch, P., Berger, A., & Rosner, D. K. (2020, July). Useful uselessness? Teaching robots to knit with humans. In *Proceedings of the 2020 ACM designing interactive systems conference* (pp. 193–203).

Trump, D. [@realDonaldTrump]. (2020, October 4). *This Tweet is from a suspended account* [Tweet]. Twitter. https://twitter.com/realDonaldTrump/status/1312864232711520257

UK Research and Innovation. (2021, February 9). Living bricks can generate energy in the home. *UKRI.* https://www.ukri.org/news/living-bricks-can-generate-energy-in-the-home/?utm_medium=email&utm_source=govdelivery

UK Research and Innovation (UKRI). (2020). *Knowledge Exchange Framework (KEF).* https://re.ukri.org/knowledge-exchange/knowledge-exchange-framework/

Ulmer, J. B. (2017). Posthumanism as research methodology: Inquiry in the Anthropocene. *International Journal of Qualitative Studies in Education, 30*(9), 832–848.

UNESCO. (2020a, March 31). *Learning never stops: Testimonies from students and educators.* https://en.unesco.org/covid19/educationresponse/learningneverstops/testimonies

UNESCO. (2020b). *Education in a post-covid world.* https://unesdoc.unesco.org/ark:/48223/pf0000373717/PDF/373717eng.pdf.multi

UNESCO. (2020c, September 7). *Ad Hoc Expert Group (AHEG) for the preparation of a draft text of a recommendation on the ethics of Artificial Intelligence.* SHS/BIO/AHEG-AI/2020/4 REV.2Pa. https://unesdoc.unesco.org/ark:/48223/pf0000373434

REFERENCES

305

United Nations. (2020, April). *COVID-19 and human rights: We are all in this together.* United Nations. https://www.un.org/sites/un2.un.org/files/un_policy_brief_on_human_rights_and_covid_23_april_2020.pdf

United Nations Educational, Scientific and Cultural Organization (UNESCO). (2020d). *Education for sustainable development: A roadmap.* https://unesdoc.unesco.org/ark:/48223/pf0000374802

University and College Union (UCU). (2020). *Universities must not become the care homes of a Covid second wave.* https://www.ucu.org.uk/article/10964/Universities-must-not-become-the-care-homes-of-a-Covid-second-wave?list=1676

University of Greenwich. (2019–2022). *Equality, diversity and inclusion strategy and action plan.* https://docs.gre.ac.uk/__data/assets/pdf_file/0004/1067539/EDI-Strategy-and-Action-Plan-2019-2022-5.19.pdf

University of Leeds Equality and Inclusion Framework. (2014–2019). https://equality.leeds.ac.uk/wp-content/uploads/sites/64/2014/03/9400_EI_Report_Final_160114.pdf

University of Leicester Equality, Diversity and Inclusion Strategy. (2017–2021). https://www2.le.ac.uk/offices/equalities-unit/about-us/a-culture-of-equality-strategy

University of Nottingham. (2020). *Student experience.* https://www.nottingham.ac.uk/studywithus/student-experience/index.aspx

University of York. (2020). *How to be a white ally.* https://www.york.ac.uk/about/equality/talk-about-race/white-ally/

University Partnerships Programme (UPP) Foundation. (2018). *Truly civic: Strengthening the connection between universities and their places.* https://upp-foundation.org/wp-content/uploads/2019/02/Civic-University-Commission-Final-Report.pdf

Universities UK (UUK). (2020). *Equality, diversity and inclusion.* https://www.universitiesuk.ac.uk/policy-and-analysis/Pages/equality-diversity-inclusion.aspx

Universities UK (UUK) and National Union of Students (NUS). (2019). *Black, Asian and minority ethnic student attainment at UK Universities: #ClosingTheGap.* https://www.universitiesuk.ac.uk/policy-and-analysis/reports/Documents/2019/bame-student-attainment-uk-universities-closing-the-gap.pdf

Valinsky, J. (2020, March 26). McDonald's and other brands are making 'social distancing' logos. *CNN.* https://edition.cnn.com/2020/03/26/business/social-distancing-brand-logos-coronavirus/index.html

van Dijck, J. (2014). Datafication, dataism and dataveillance: Big data between scientific paradigm and ideology. *Surveillance and Society, 12*(2), 197–208. https://doi.org/10.24908/ss.v12i2.4776

van Splunder, F. (2020). *Language is politics: Exploring an ecological approach to language.* Routledge.

Varma, A. (2020). Evoking empathy or enacting solidarity with marginalized communities? A case study of journalistic humanizing techniques in the San Francisco homeless project. *Journalism Studies*. https://doi.org/10.1080/1461670X.2020.1789495

Verger, A., Lubienski, C., & Steiner-Khamsi, G. (2016). *The rise of the global education industry: Some concepts, facts and figures*. https://www.ei-ie.org/en/woe_homepage/woe_detail/4850/the-rise-of-the-global-%20education-industry-some-concepts-facts-and-figures

Verger, A., Fontdevila, C., & Zancajo, A. (2016). *The privatization of education: A political economy of global education reform*. Teachers College Press.

Wallace, J. D., Burton, B. G., Chandler, R. C., & Darby, D. G. (2020). Special issue for suddenly online – Considerations of theory, research, and practice. *The Journal of Literacy and Technology, 21*(2), Special Edition. http://www.literacyandtechnology.org/uploads/1/3/6/8/136889/jlt_vol_21_2__v1.02brevised2_wallace_burton_chandler_darby.pdf

Watermeyer, R., Crick, T., Knight, C., & Goodall, J. (2020). COVID-19 and digital disruption in UK universities: Afflictions and affordances of emergency online migration. *Higher Education*, 1.

Weber, M. (1930). *The protestant ethic and the spirit of capitalism*. Allen and Unwin.

Welch, P. (2020). Mass higher education in England – a success story? *Postdigital Science and Education*.

Warnes, M. (2020). Questioning the impact of teaching fellowships on excellent teachers. *Postdigital Science and Education*. https://doi.org/10.1007/s42438-020-00107-6

West, M., Kraut, R., & Ei Chew, H. (2019). *I'd blush if I could: Closing gender divides in digital skills through education*. UNESCO.

Westwater, H. (2021, January 14). Lack of laptops for remote learning is pushing families to the brink. *The Big Issue*. https://www.bigissue.com/latest/lack-of-laptops-for-remote-learning-is-pushing-families-to-the-brink/

Wheaton, M. M., & Kezar, A. (2019). Interlocking systems of oppression: Women navigating higher education leadership. In *Challenges and opportunities for women in higher education leadership* (pp. 61–83). IGI Global.

Whitchurch, C. (2013). *Reconstructing identities in higher education. The rise of the third space professionals*. Routledge.

Whitaker, S. [@Sue Whitaker]. (2020, September 21). *Up to 40 Tory MPs to refuse to undertake unconscious bias training* [Tweet]. Twitter. https://twitter.com/SueWhitaker11/status/1307977408340013056

White, J. (2020, September 26). Woke 'cancel culture' is a form of bullying and 'no platforming': An attack on free speech, pupils will be taught. *Mail Online*. https://www.dailymail.co.uk/news/article-8774625/Woke-cancel-culture-form-bullying-pupils-taught.html

REFERENCES

Williams, R. (2020, April 24). Coronavirus: Woman 'named and shamed' by neighbours on Facebook for not joining clap for carers. *Sky News*. https://news.sky.com/story/coronavirus-woman-named-and-shamed-by-neighbours-on-facebook-for-not-joining-clap-for-carers-11978192

Williamson, B. (2017). *Big data in education: The digital future of learning, policy and practice*. Sage.

Williamson, B. (2019a). Digital policy sociology: Software and science in data-intensive precision education. *Critical Studies in Education*, 1–17.

Williamson, B. (2019b). Policy networks, performance metrics and platform markets: Charting the expanding data infrastructure of higher education. *British Journal of Educational Technology*, 50(6), 2794–2809.

Williamson, B. (2020a). *New pandemic edtech power networks*. https://codeactsineducation.wordpress.com/2020/04/01/new-pandemic-edtech-power-networks/

Williamson, B. (2020b). Making markets through digital platforms: Pearson, edu-business, and the (e)valuation of higher education. *Critical Studies in Education*, March, 1–17.

Williamson, B. J. (2020c). New digital laboratories of experimental knowledge production: Artificial Intelligence and education research. *London Review of Education*.

Williamson, B., & Eynon, R. (2020). Historical threads, missing links, and future directions in AI in education. *Learning, Media and Technology*, 45(3), 223–235.

Wilsdon, J. (2016). *The metric tide: Independent review of the role of metrics in research, assessment and management*. Sage.

Winner, L. (1980). Do artifacts have politics? *Daedalus*, 109(1), 121–136.

Wonkhe. (2021, March 2). *Wonkhe@home: The future shape of admissions: What next for students, schools and universities?* https://wonkhe.com/events/future-shape-of-admissions/?utm_medium=email&utm_campaign=WonkheMondays2022February&utm_content=WonkheMondays22February+CID_6a40a09e7014389ed41546934064e519&utm_source=Emailmarketingsoftware&utm_term=Grabyourtickethere

Wood, M., Garbett, A., Morrissey, K., Hopkins, P., & Balaam, M. (2018). 'Protection on that erection?' Discourses of accountability and compromising participation in digital sexual health. In *Proceedings of the 2018 CHI Conference on human factors in computing systems* (pp. 1–12).

Workers' Educational Association (WEA). (2019). *Adult education 100*. https://www.wea.org.uk/get-involved/our-campaigns/adult-education-100

World Economic Forum (WEF). (2019). *Civil society in the fourth industrial revolution: Preparation and response*. https://www.weforum.org/whitepapers/civil-society-in-the-fourth-industrial-revolution-preparation-and-response

World Health Organisation. (2020). *Director-general's remarks at the media briefing on 2019 novel coronavirus on 8 February 2020*. https://www.who.int/dg/speeches/detail/director-general-s-remarks-at-the-media-briefing-on-2019-novel-coronavirus---8-february-2020

YouTube. (2021, February 5). Parish council meeting with Jackie Weaver, the guide liverpool. *YouTube.* https://www.youtube.com/watch?v=jB3P_oGAioI

Zahid, A. (2020, August 26). Russell Crowe donates nearly £3,000 to student who could not afford drama course. *Sky News.* https://news.sky.com/story/russell-crowe-donates-nearly-3-000-to-student-who-could-not-afford-drama-course-12057216

Zwijnenberg, R. (2014). Biotechnology, human dignity and the importance of art. *Teoria: Revista di Filosofia, 34*, 131–148. https://www.researchgate.net/profile/Robert_Zwijnenberg/publication/289115312_Biotechnology_Human_Dignity_and_the_Importance_of_Art/links/5919832a0f7e9b1db6519799/Biotechnology-Human-Dignity-and-the-Importance-of-Art.pdf?origin=publication_detail

Index

academia   30, 34, 43, 44, 58, 62, 63, 66, 140, 208, 217, 242, 248, 255

academic   22, 23, 33, 35, 36, 38, 39, 47, 59, 62, 63, 70, 71, 87, 88, 97, 108, 119, 120, 123, 124, 127, 130, 133, 138–140, 173, 175, 181, 191, 195, 196, 198, 200, 205, 207, 209, 213, 216, 217, 225, 234, 237, 239–241, 243, 248, 251, 252, 254

academic freedom   205, 248

access   3, 9, 11–13, 15, 17, 20, 24, 31, 34, 35, 45, 54, 58, 65, 67, 69, 74, 90, 100, 102, 120, 122, 123, 133, 137, 144, 147, 149, 158, 164, 167, 169, 171, 173, 174, 181, 186, 188, 198, 209, 212, 225, 227, 229, 231, 240, 244, 258

accessible   115, 151, 186

action   6, 23, 25, 44, 56, 58, 59, 65, 73, 77, 79, 87, 100, 146, 152, 183, 205, 224, 236, 240, 249, 262, 267

activist   20, 78, 82, 144, 153, 267

administration   36, 240

agency   10, 11, 13, 37, 40, 44, 59, 62, 64, 71, 89, 100, 126, 158, 159, 180, 192, 195, 196, 219, 231, 238, 247

AI in education (AIEd)   189, 200, 204

airing cupboard   1–3, 5–7, 9–12, 15–17, 38, 39, 41, 44, 49, 55, 56, 63, 70, 73, 76, 79–82, 86, 102, 107, 108, 115, 116, 118, 123, 126, 135, 143, 145, 146, 149–152, 158, 165, 172, 176, 186, 187, 190, 200, 206, 214, 221, 227, 228, 232, 235, 238, 255–257, 265, 266

algorithm   3, 16, 18, 39–41, 43, 72, 57, 65, 75, 76, 89, 100, 110–112, 116, 126, 128, 133, 146, 156, 158, 167, 177–179, 185, 203, 219, 233, 266

analysis   10, 13, 40, 43, 51, 53, 70, 80, 109, 119, 141, 142, 146, 147, 156, 163, 171, 175, 200–202, 205, 206, 211, 255, 234, 235, 238, 247, 252, 264, 266

analytics   3, 16, 22, 114, 164

app   60, 88, 121, 151, 230

application   22, 51, 74, 117, 120, 142, 148, 158, 199, 204, 215, 218, 224, 234, 255

argument   1, 20, 23, 40, 48, 50, 52, 56, 59, 68, 74, 79, 80, 82, 85, 92, 106, 108, 109, 111, 114, 118, 123, 124, 144, 146, 149, 152, 162, 163, 189, 193, 206, 209, 211, 213, 217, 218, 222, 232, 234, 235, 246, 247, 258, 265, 266

artificial intelligence (AI)   5, 22, 46, 51, 63, 65, 111, 112, 133, 140, 167, 257, 259

attainment   22, 65, 74, 141, 180

augmented   20, 51, 63, 84, 100, 119, 268

automated   120, 121, 169, 185, 189, 200, 202

autonomous   18, 61, 63, 111, 114, 169, 202, 215

bias   10, 19, 20, 23, 25, 40, 51, 54–57, 60, 62, 67, 74, 77, 87, 99, 117, 120, 121, 133, 139–142, 146, 147, 153, 155, 156, 159, 160, 164, 170, 179, 231, 253, 257, 258, 261

biodigitalism   11, 52, 214, 271

biodigital convergence   48, 192, 219–221, 271

bioeconomy   4, 6, 45, 50, 189, 193, 209, 219, 221, 232, 246, 263, 264, 271

bioinformational capitalism   186

bioinformationalism   9, 11, 271

biological   2, 7, 10–12, 20, 22, 24, 25, 31, 34, 38, 43, 44, 46, 48, 49, 50, 53, 89, 119, 133, 153, 162, 168, 169, 173, 190–192, 203, 207, 232, 235, 248, 252, 254, 258, 261, 262, 265, 266, 271

Black, Asian and minority ethnic (BAME)   144, 145

Black Lives Matter   79–81, 93

bodies   22, 27, 46, 65, 68, 102, 105, 121, 125, 203, 213, 221, 240, 258, 262

boundaries   2, 5, 11, 44, 68, 124, 131, 134, 137, 193, 196, 199, 206, 210, 218, 235, 256

brain   46, 61, 203, 262

bureaucratisation   52, 53, 240

businesses   3, 16–18, 26, 27, 67, 82, 97, 105, 112, 117, 118, 123, 128, 130, 140, 142, 237, 238, 246, 248, 258

buzz phrases   14, 33, 34, 58, 70, 71, 98, 108, 163, 167, 174, 191, 211

calculability   14, 28, 37, 92, 137, 200

campus   3, 16, 32, 44, 64, 106, 128, 143, 149, 152, 162, 165–168, 171, 174, 240, 241

cancel culture   11, 14, 76, 78, 81, 86, 116, 133, 146, 153–155, 175, 176, 194, 195, 197, 227, 231, 255, 266, 271 capabilities 17, 33, 37, 51, 121, 127, 152, 169, 250, 258

capitalism 14, 24, 38, 59, 66, 72, 98, 104, 105, 155, 170, 186, 193, 209, 218, 233, 235, 256, 261

challenges 1, 10, 22, 25, 33–35, 38, 47, 48, 58, 88, 91, 114, 122, 124, 133, 136–138, 141, 148, 156, 161–163, 167, 176, 185, 193, 194, 197, 202, 207, 218–220, 228, 229, 240, 244, 245, 247, 248, 253, 254, 256–258, 261, 262, 264, 266

children 15, 34, 75, 93, 95, 154–157, 167, 177, 184

circular bioeconomy 4, 50, 193, 263, 271

circumstances 9, 12, 17, 26, 31–34, 43, 49, 59, 70, 89, 93, 95, 97, 110, 117, 133, 136, 143, 163, 165, 166, 173, 175, 177, 181, 188, 251

citizen 6, 10, 12, 15, 16, 19, 37, 41, 63, 64, 82, 124, 140, 168, 169, 183, 189, 203, 207, 209, 226, 237, 249, 258, 260

civic 38, 61, 63, 65, 143, 251

class 2, 10, 11, 13, 29, 41, 59, 67, 68, 73, 76, 80, 134, 161, 166, 172, 181, 185, 191, 202, 211, 221, 234, 253, 267

climate change 12, 99, 103, 266

coding 18, 70, 110, 147, 148, 243

cognitive 11, 56, 61, 120, 154, 235, 239, 243, 245, 250

colour 79

collective 12, 49, 52, 59, 63, 77, 78, 97, 99, 105, 110, 123, 136, 168, 181, 182, 189, 205, 232, 246, 251, 267

commodification 195

commercial 3, 5, 8, 17, 18, 22, 24, 32, 37, 43, 46, 48, 50, 56, 61, 64, 98–100, 110, 111, 114–116, 118, 119, 133, 135, 141, 146, 149, 164, 170, 174, 175, 185, 188, 199–201, 203, 206, 215, 225, 233, 234, 237, 247, 256, 264

communication 2, 7, 9, 11, 12, 16, 17, 20, 54, 72, 81, 102, 110, 121–123, 130, 131, 133, 135, 140, 152, 161, 167, 168, 170, 177, 186, 238, 254

community 15, 37, 96, 99, 136, 142, 143, 148, 149, 159, 169, 185, 186, 188, 190, 202, 207, 228, 232, 248, 251, 261

complex 3, 12, 19, 20, 23, 24, 44, 50, 59, 62, 66, 67, 70, 76, 79, 80, 88, 98, 100, 101, 106, 116, 117, 119, 122, 124, 126, 133, 135, 137, 138, 147, 165, 169, 171, 177, 183, 184,

191, 192, 196, 201, 202, 212, 219, 220, 225, 228, 229, 231, 235, 237, 238, 247, 250, 252, 254, 255, 257, 259, 261, 262, 265

computer 8, 10, 49–51, 53–55, 57, 62, 63, 71, 87, 91, 110, 111, 116, 119, 121, 134, 137, 138, 142, 147, 148, 156, 173, 177, 179, 180, 185, 186, 232, 233, 243, 255, 265

conflicting 215, 218

consumer 8, 14, 29, 47, 64, 72, 104, 105, 109, 115, 116, 123, 147, 165, 171, 172, 192, 198, 209, 232, 254, 264, 267

consumption 22, 28, 30, 51, 52, 72, 109, 119, 123, 130, 149, 162, 166, 173, 242, 255, 267

contagious 7, 102, 110

context 1, 4, 5, 9, 13, 18–20, 24, 25, 28, 30, 32, 35, 39, 43–46, 49, 52, 54, 56–59, 61, 63–69, 73, 80, 87–89, 104, 106–110, 119, 121, 123, 126, 127, 130, 136, 138, 143, 149, 152, 156, 162, 167–169, 179, 183, 186, 194, 198, 202, 213, 217, 232, 240, 252, 253, 255, 256, 258, 266

control 9, 14, 16, 17, 19, 21, 24, 28, 30, 32, 37, 41, 42, 48, 50, 61, 65, 66, 81, 92, 100, 113–116, 119, 123, 136, 137, 142, 146, 155, 173, 174, 177, 178, 200, 206, 214, 217, 219, 225, 226, 233, 237, 238, 245, 254, 259

convergence 8, 10, 47, 48, 168, 169, 190, 192, 200, 214, 219–221, 242, 243, 249, 250, 255, 258, 260, 263

coronavirus 101, 166

corporations 6, 41, 200, 233, 237, 250

corpus 170, 171, 211

Covid-19 7, 9, 13, 17–19, 25–35, 37, 42, 44, 46, 47, 53, 60, 63, 66, 82, 90, 91, 92, 95–99, 101, 102, 104–108, 116, 117, 123, 124, 126, 135, 139, 143, 152, 153, 156, 157, 161, 162, 164–167, 171, 173, 185, 200, 202, 206, 207, 214, 222, 223, 227, 229, 230, 232, 235, 242, 243, 248, 254, 259, 266, 267

crisis 18, 33, 35, 63, 64, 80, 96, 98, 99, 101, 103, 106, 144, 161, 164, 167, 176, 177, 202, 208, 214, 219, 223, 243, 244, 247, 249

critical 3, 10, 11, 13, 46, 47, 49, 51, 63, 72, 74–76, 82, 89, 104, 106, 110, 118, 124, 125, 132, 138, 140, 141, 147, 153, 155, 159, 167, 168, 170, 189, 192, 211, 221–233, 238, 246, 249–251, 255, 258, 263–267, 269

critical discourse analysis 170, 211

cross-sector 15, 37, 96, 148, 168, 189, 238, 246–248, 250, 251, 253, 258, 266, 267

INDEX   311

cultural   1, 6, 7, 9, 10, 12, 14, 16, 18, 24, 25, 30,
        34, 37, 48, 50, 51, 55, 65, 68–70, 79, 86,
        87, 109, 117, 123, 127, 131, 134, 136, 145,
        152, 153, 155, 159, 162, 192, 245, 246, 250,
        255, 257, 260, 261
culture   3, 6, 8, 9, 11, 14–16, 20, 28, 29, 42–44,
        46, 47, 51, 66, 70, 75–81, 84, 86, 87, 90,
        98, 99, 104, 107, 109, 114–117, 119, 121, 122,
        127, 130, 132, 133, 135, 138, 141, 143, 146,
        153, 167, 169, 171, 175, 194, 196, 197, 203,
        208, 223, 227, 231, 251, 253, 265, 266
curriculum   114, 118, 155, 158, 208, 209, 234

data   2, 3, 5, 9, 10, 12, 13, 15–22, 38–41, 43–48,
        53–55, 57, 58, 60–66, 70–74, 76, 77,
        86–89, 99, 100, 107, 110–114, 116–118, 121,
        126, 127, 133, 137, 140, 141, 145, 146, 149,
        152–158, 161–164, 168, 170, 185, 201, 206,
        207, 220, 232, 237, 247, 250, 257, 259,
        262, 265
database   60, 146
data-driven systems   2
debate   1, 3, 7, 10, 12, 15, 19, 22–25, 34, 43–46,
        50, 51, 56, 59, 66, 67, 71, 75, 79, 125,
        133, 143, 167, 168, 182, 189, 192, 193,
        204, 206–208, 212, 213, 248, 250–256,
        261–263, 266, 268
debating   182, 247
democratic   6, 32, 63, 114, 189, 193, 196, 198,
        211, 226, 233
design   18, 38, 51, 52, 56, 70, 117, 118, 135,
        136–141, 152, 170, 184, 185, 193, 196, 199,
        209, 211, 220, 223
devices   3, 9, 10, 12, 13, 20, 22, 35, 43, 49, 55,
        57, 58, 60, 87, 90, 111, 112, 119, 126, 133,
        145, 147–148, 152, 154, 167, 224, 227–229,
        231, 257
dialectics   155, 200, 259, 261
dialogue   4, 11, 13, 15, 23, 43, 49, 65, 67, 68, 86,
        87, 97, 111, 118, 125, 128, 136, 139, 143, 152,
        170, 218, 219, 227, 232, 235, 236, 238, 242,
        244, 245, 247, 248, 253, 254, 257, 258, 262
digitalisation   3–5, 12, 24, 46, 48, 53, 195, 200,
        209, 212, 214, 218, 232, 242, 243, 250,
        253, 255, 261, 265
digital   10, 15, 23, 24, 36, 43, 44, 48, 49, 52, 53,
        56, 57, 59, 60, 63, 65–67, 70, 74, 76, 77,
        86, 89–91, 100, 107, 117, 120, 122, 143, 145,
        161, 162, 168, 169, 182, 186, 201, 213, 214,
        219, 235, 238, 262, 267

dignity   255
dimensions   4, 20, 37, 49, 56, 63, 70, 74, 76,
        78, 84, 97, 98, 107, 117, 144, 153, 185, 189,
        194, 196, 200, 204, 231, 255
diminished   49, 51, 66, 175, 193, 194
dirty   2, 7, 10, 82, 126, 151, 158, 261
disability   19, 22, 34, 60, 88, 127, 153, 158, 161,
        183, 195, 222, 233, 236
disadvantage   6, 13, 20, 23, 26, 35, 44, 45, 91,
        117, 144, 173, 202, 235, 243, 244, 254, 260
discipline   50, 75, 124, 135, 138, 168, 208, 252
discourse   5–9, 12–14, 16, 19, 25, 26, 28, 33,
        37, 39, 42–49, 51, 57, 58, 70, 82, 98, 104,
        110, 112, 115, 117–120, 123–125, 128, 134,
        136, 138, 140, 142, 143, 152, 162, 164, 167,
        170–172, 174, 175, 177, 180, 188, 190, 191,
        193–196, 201, 243, 246, 247, 253, 254,
        263–265, 267, 269
discrimination   10, 19, 20, 22, 43, 51, 56, 60,
        70, 73, 79, 85, 86, 115, 117, 121, 127, 132,
        133, 144, 161, 184, 197, 231, 253
disease   7, 63, 102, 110, 136, 152, 252, 256
disengaged   14, 235, 255, 259
disrupt   44, 86, 135, 138, 141, 144, 188, 192, 212,
        246
distance   7, 31, 35, 53, 93, 165, 182, 244, 254
diverse   21, 24, 33–35, 43, 45, 58, 64, 67, 69,
        72, 75, 96, 98, 100, 103, 107 108, 110, 118,
        119, 121, 191, 196, 203, 231, 232, 236, 237,
        239, 250, 253–255, 267
diversity   4, 12, 17, 20–23, 25, 26, 28, 33, 34,
        42, 45, 46, 50, 51, 53, 54, 57, 57–59, 61,
        63, 70, 80, 81, 86, 97, 98, 110, 111, 121, 124,
        125, 139, 143, 149, 175, 183, 236, 240, 249,
        253, 256, 259, 266, 267
drawings   25, 27, 49, 67, 76, 80, 91, 95, 136,
        177, 185, 231, 256

ecological   43, 47, 48, 98, 128, 148, 167, 182,
        183, 186, 193, 195, 197, 207–210, 222, 242,
        245–247, 254, 258, 264
economic   2, 3, 6, 9, 18, 24, 26, 30, 34, 37, 42,
        43, 46–48, 50, 55, 66, 73, 79, 87, 91, 93,
        105, 109, 114, 116, 117, 119, 121, 133, 143,
        161, 168, 173, 176, 201, 207, 226, 229, 233,
        237, 255
economy   3, 5, 6, 11, 25, 28, 37, 45, 47, 63, 89,
        92, 98, 110, 113, 122, 128, 138, 154, 176, 185,
        208–210, 213, 217, 218, 221, 244, 245, 250,
        256, 262, 263, 267

312   INDEX

ecosystem   9, 24, 33, 44, 45, 74, 100, 140, 147,
     170, 190, 208, 209, 218
education   1, 4–6, 12, 18, 19, 22, 34–38, 42–48,
     51–53, 57, 58, 64–67, 70, 97–101, 105, 108,
     109, 130, 141, 143, 170, 173, 174, 180, 191–209,
     211–214, 231, 234, 255, 260, 262, 264
educationalization   154, 167, 174, 188
efficiency   14, 17, 28, 37, 38, 50, 53, 61, 92, 137,
     162, 169, 200, 205, 215
emails   116, 123, 181, 233
embed   42, 44, 48, 100, 115, 116, 141, 173, 234,
     237
emotions   41, 53, 62, 132, 156, 161, 187, 261
employability   14, 37, 41, 89, 128, 183, 196, 197,
     211, 231, 245
environmental   6, 42, 124, 193, 221, 223, 225,
     229, 240, 246, 249, 266, 267
epistemology   202
equality   3, 4, 6, 12, 17, 19, 21–23, 34, 42, 50, 51,
     54, 56, 70, 86, 97, 98, 110, 111, 115, 119, 121,
     139, 145, 159, 190, 212, 254, 259–261
equality act   19, 139, 254, 260
error   88, 117, 121
essential   13, 82, 87, 133, 176, 203, 207, 224,
     236
ethics   13, 18, 22, 33, 39, 40, 43, 57, 62, 65, 74,
     110, 124, 127, 128, 137, 147, 219, 221, 233
ethnic   81, 121, 137, 144, 261
ethnicity   34, 67, 68, 76, 153, 161, 221
excellence   44, 47, 53, 65, 66, 107, 140, 141,
     143, 169, 190–196, 204–207, 215–217, 219,
     220, 232, 235
exchange   15, 24, 37, 39, 125, 140, 244, 258
exclude   16, 20, 48, 49, 54, 87, 111, 196, 212
experience   6, 24, 27, 33, 35, 39, 44, 46, 57–59,
     63, 68, 72, 76, 78, 100, 128, 134, 143, 153,
     161–175, 177, 179–187, 189, 191, 192, 212,
     213, 245, 251, 254, 263
exploitation   49, 231, 267
extremism   256
evolution   9, 238, 267

Facebook   7, 18, 39, 58, 73, 99, 133, 151, 242,
     257
face masks   35, 53, 54, 252, 268
fair   180
flawed   4, 139, 140, 170, 190, 201, 210
flesh electric   58, 68, 70, 76, 98, 183
fluid   2, 8, 10, 11, 21, 25, 44, 46, 49, 57, 58, 67,
     70, 76, 78, 88, 104, 134, 164, 168, 169, 172,
     183, 192, 196, 197, 201, 259

frameworks   15, 18, 22–24, 34, 38, 42, 46, 65,
     100, 114, 137, 139–142, 182, 193, 194, 206,
     213, 217, 220, 221, 223, 232, 241, 245, 249
fraud   26, 264
freedom   121, 154, 155, 205, 215, 216, 247, 248,
     256
fuel   268
futures   6, 18, 25, 39, 41, 47, 52, 75, 110, 123,
     128, 177, 209, 214, 246, 250, 251, 252, 256,
     260, 266

gender   10, 11, 13, 19, 22, 34, 41, 59, 60, 62, 67,
     68, 73, 76, 78, 121, 134, 144, 146–148, 153,
     161, 172, 185, 194, 202, 221, 222, 233, 234,
     236, 253, 261
generation   78, 146, 158, 170, 187, 247, 254
generic   34, 44, 74, 118, 134, 145, 169, 174, 177,
     181, 182, 196, 231
genomics   11, 192, 203
geographical   161, 22
gig economy   36, 92, 176
global   3, 7, 13, 14, 16, 18–20, 28, 35, 37, 43, 47,
     50, 52, 58, 63, 69, 70, 86, 87, 89, 91–93,
     98–100, 104, 105, 107, 114, 115, 120, 123,
     124, 144, 146, 152, 153, 168, 169, 189, 191,
     193, 200, 208, 209, 211, 220, 232, 233,
     237, 242–246, 252 254, 263, 266
Google   18, 113, 138, 147, 151, 242, 244, 261
government   7, 17, 29, 39, 41, 47, 62, 65, 69,
     88, 103, 106, 109, 113, 118, 120, 125, 140,
     154, 157, 171, 175, 179, 215, 216, 220, 225,
     227, 228, 231, 248, 252, 253, 257, 264

health   6, 13, 20, 28, 33–35, 50, 53, 54, 62, 71,
     90, 92, 93, 96–99, 101, 102, 105–107, 117,
     136, 144, 153–155, 158, 166, 174, 176, 177,
     197, 215, 229, 252, 254–256, 258, 266
higher education   1, 13, 36, 37, 41, 44, 62, 66,
     70, 108, 109, 130, 141, 143, 170, 173, 174, 180,
     191, 193, 205–207, 209, 211, 214, 231, 234
history   64, 85–87, 96, 97, 117, 122, 124, 153,
     200, 207, 208
home   2, 17, 28, 29, 33, 34, 36, 61, 79, 82, 83,
     91–93, 97, 103, 107, 120, 121, 126, 144, 152,
     166, 167, 177, 264, 268
homogenise   180
human computer interaction (HCI)   51, 134,
     137, 142, 147
human data interaction   16, 86
human rights   12, 14–19, 30, 49, 60, 61, 121,
     124, 139, 152, 190, 232, 259, 265, 266

INDEX 313

humanities 50, 51, 53, 87, 96, 111, 136, 138, 139, 141–143, 211, 247, 248, 250, 258, 263, 265, 269

humanity 5, 45, 103, 105, 112, 209, 221, 246

humans 12, 14–19, 30, 49, 51, 60, 61, 86, 121, 124, 134, 137, 139, 142, 147, 152, 190, 232, 259, 265, 266

hybrid 63, 65, 126, 203, 227, 229, 257, 258, 266

iconography 128, 130, 166, 205

identities 4, 8, 12, 13, 25, 40, 41, 49, 57–59, 62, 66–68, 70, 76, 107, 119, 137, 145, 148, 233, 235–237, 253, 261

identity 3, 4, 10, 11, 14, 16, 20, 21, 25, 27, 41, 44, 46, 50, 55, 60, 61, 63, 66–71, 73, 74, 76, 77, 84, 87, 88, 91, 111, 120, 121, 126, 127, 133–135, 143, 144, 156, 169, 184, 185, 219, 240, 259, 264, 265

image 14, 102, 120, 146, 147, 163, 221, 235, 236

inclusive practice 13, 21, 40, 44, 70, 74, 115, 125, 141, 199, 233, 236

inclusivity 1–4, 6, 7, 10, 12–25, 28, 30, 33, 34, 36–38, 45, 46, 51, 52, 54, 56–59, 61, 62, 65, 67–70, 72, 74–76, 86, 87, 89, 99, 100, 104, 105, 107, 110, 116–118, 122, 125, 126, 133–137, 141–144, 148, 153, 159, 162, 164, 170, 173, 175, 180, 183, 185, 188, 194, 212, 213, 219, 227, 231–239, 245, 249–251, 253, 256–258, 261, 263, 265

inclusion 3, 11–13, 15, 17, 21, 22, 24, 34, 42, 51, 53, 54, 153, 171, 231, 254

inclusive 13, 15, 16, 22, 24, 25, 28, 35, 40, 44, 48, 52, 57, 59, 63, 67, 70, 74, 100, 115, 120, 125, 131, 137, 139, 141, 149, 159, 167, 184, 186, 188, 189, 193, 194, 199, 210, 213, 214, 219, 227, 233, 236, 244, 247, 250, 255, 257, 258, 261, 264, 269

individual 5, 6, 10–12, 18–21, 23–25, 30, 31, 33, 39, 42–44, 46, 49, 53, 56, 58, 63, 68, 74, 76, 77, 80, 93, 96, 97, 100, 114, 116, 121–124, 126, 133, 134, 139, 143, 239, 244, 252, 253, 260, 261, 264

inequality 12, 16, 20, 115, 145, 146, 202, 229, 231, 260

inequities 33, 46, 55, 80, 108, 112, 114–116, 126, 139, 182, 207, 212, 214, 227, 228, 254

influence 10, 42, 48, 67, 78, 103, 135, 141, 148, 183, 200, 216, 237, 240, 251

infrastructure 42, 146, 148, 150, 170, 206, 229, 254, 261, 268

injustice 20, 70, 77, 144, 180, 221, 222

innovative 138, 206, 207, 220

Instagram 61, 80, 152, 159, 186

institutions 6, 12, 14, 15, 21–25, 32, 48, 72, 76, 80, 85, 86, 100, 105, 106, 114, 115, 119, 122, 123, 125, 140–142, 149, 152, 154, 159, 162, 164, 168, 173, 174, 185, 228, 232, 238, 239, 244, 247, 248, 267

intelligence 5, 11, 22, 46, 51, 63, 65, 110–112, 120, 133, 140, 167, 188, 257, 259

interconnections 19, 98, 118, 169, 213, 231

interdisciplinary 6, 47, 134, 189, 197, 199, 202, 203, 209–211, 218, 252, 253, 262

interface 185

internet 2–6, 9, 10, 12, 15–17, 30, 49, 54, 69, 70, 84, 88, 112–116, 127, 130, 132, 135, 143–146, 151, 161, 221, 227, 228, 232, 255, 257, 264, 266

Internet of Things (IoT) 15, 112, 148, 256, 257

intersect 14, 23, 47, 56, 60, 68, 74–76, 117, 118, 121, 126, 183, 197, 202, 255, 259, 260

intersection 7, 19, 46, 87, 115, 133, 162, 238, 246, 260

intimate 3, 9, 10, 15, 19, 46, 50, 70, 71, 98, 102, 139, 161, 186, 258, 269

irrationality 84, 92, 98, 109, 116, 123, 141, 155, 164, 200, 231, 246

isolate 23, 35, 152, 165, 222, 244

justice 11, 44, 46, 80, 104, 118, 124, 125, 134, 137, 139, 145, 152, 170, 202, 222, 231, 232, 266

key workers 27, 34, 82, 84, 85, 93, 176, 177

knowledge

knowledge-based economy 45, 47, 191, 211

Knowledge Exchange Framework (KEF) 140

labour 8, 13, 14, 18, 30, 33–36, 38, 39, 41, 44, 47, 51, 58, 64, 66, 70, 71, 73, 87–89, 98, 103, 108, 109, 120, 128, 138, 152, 163, 170, 171, 175, 176, 191, 204, 211, 214, 216, 220, 231, 239, 241, 242, 254

language 4, 7–10, 12, 14, 33, 41, 51, 58, 59, 71–74, 77, 78, 88, 92, 98, 102, 108, 110, 113, 118, 124, 128, 134, 139, 145, 153, 165, 183, 185, 191, 193, 198, 203, 210, 212, 221, 223, 224, 232, 234, 241, 242, 252, 259

laptop 10, 76, 151, 185

leaders 28, 66, 127, 164, 229, 233–237, 242, 243, 245, 251

learning 13–15, 22, 28, 34, 35, 37–39, 41–44, 46, 47, 51, 58, 61, 63–66, 69, 77, 85, 87, 90, 97, 98, 100, 107, 108, 114, 115, 122, 123, 125, 135, 143, 148, 149, 156, 161–164, 167–169, 171, 172, 175, 184, 185, 187, 203, 204, 209, 212, 229, 232, 234, 244, 254, 264

lecturers 108, 142, 181, 194, 206

legibility 40, 57, 126, 231

LGBTQ+ 78

liberal 47, 213, 215

lifelong learning 15, 47, 85, 122, 167, 184

linguistically 58, 89, 118, 128, 254

literacy 18, 159, 163, 203, 229

lived experience 33, 57, 63, 68, 78, 153, 244

local 8, 24, 35, 37, 48, 58, 68, 69, 96, 107, 117, 148, 156, 181, 192, 202, 205, 207, 208, 222, 225, 227, 228, 240, 243–245, 248, 249, 252

lockdown 9, 13, 25, 29, 31, 34, 36, 53, 64, 71, 82, 89, 90, 93, 94, 97, 99, 105–107, 119, 144, 152, 158, 174, 177, 228, 259, 264

machines 22, 29, 39, 111, 147, 148, 256, 266

marginalised 20, 26, 35, 68, 115, 134, 137, 189, 194, 213, 222, 236, 244

marketized 48, 61, 62, 65, 128, 167, 185, 188, 194, 237

Massive Open Online Course (MOOC) 234

material 53, 72, 85, 86, 97, 102, 128, 133, 146, 213, 218, 221–224, 232, 243, 254, 256,

McDonaldisation 14, 17, 20, 28, 29, 37, 50–52, 89, 92, 98, 109, 114, 119, 125, 194, 200, 204, 208, 231, 264, 272

McPolicy 13, 16, 21, 34, 37, 39, 44–48, 51, 52, 70, 72, 108–111, 114, 115, 123, 125, 128, 139, 141, 142, 159, 162–164, 169, 170, 172, 186, 189–192, 197, 198, 204, 205, 208–214, 218, 231, 232, 234, 235, 239–241, 247, 253, 254, 259, 263, 264

meaning 20, 38, 51–53, 66, 67, 80, 88, 102, 124, 131, 147, 164, 187, 209, 223, 239, 249, 257

measuring 20, 21, 44, 66, 74, 107, 111, 168, 170, 191, 192, 194, 196, 197, 199, 205, 208, 219

media 2, 6, 18, 20, 24, 25, 54, 60, 64, 71, 74, 77, 79, 82, 88, 90, 93, 100, 102, 118, 127, 131, 135, 140, 144, 147, 159, 170, 190, 209, 220, 227, 254–257

mental health 20, 28, 35, 62, 107, 153, 158, 166, 174, 177, 229, 254

menu 14, 41, 168, 170, 196, 197

minority 28, 81, 119, 121, 144, 147, 148, 244

narratives 20, 25, 76, 124, 158, 163, 262

negotiability 16, 40, 57, 126, 231

neoliberal 25, 28, 30, 41, 47, 48, 52, 63, 66, 89, 104, 105, 122, 123, 141, 142, 192, 198, 211, 213–215, 217, 218, 238, 242, 245, 246, 250, 254, 263, 264

neoliberalism 42, 123, 208, 211, 215, 235

networks 3, 5, 18, 25, 33, 36, 60, 113, 170, 188, 225, 265

nominalisation 14, 109

non-human 11, 49, 57, 70, 98, 111, 183, 208, 213, 219, 221, 222, 255, 265

online 2–4, 6, 7, 9–13, 16–18, 26, 29, 32–36, 43–47, 49, 55, 56, 58–61, 63–65, 70, 73, 81, 88, 120, 121, 126–128, 131, 146, 151, 152, 156, 159, 165, 167, 177, 180, 181, 183, 189, 190, 194, 201, 227–231, 233, 234, 238, 241, 242, 244, 245, 252, 254, 256, 258, 265

oppression 62, 88, 144, 185

organic 5, 42, 45, 203, 207, 214, 225, 258

organisations 12, 14, 18, 19, 53, 55, 56, 78, 87, 96, 99, 109, 14, 155, 196, 225, 235, 238, 249

outcomes 14, 16, 21, 22, 51, 67, 74, 140, 141, 147, 164, 170, 192, 196, 203, 204, 206, 212

pandemic 7, 13, 16–18, 25, 28–37, 41, 43–50, 53, 54, 57, 63, 64, 82, 89, 90, 101–103, 105, 106, 108, 114–116, 118, 126, 129, 133, 143, 152, 155, 156, 164, 168, 170, 173, 176, 177, 182, 187, 194, 195, 200, 202, 207, 220, 227, 229, 232, 235, 237, 241–243, 248, 250–256, 259, 260, 264

participation 14, 11, 24, 46, 48, 82, 99, 100, 109, 110, 118, 122, 135–137, 148, 169, 187–189, 203, 212, 227, 231, 240

partners 38, 127, 142, 193, 221, 225, 237

pedagogy 138, 159, 172, 189, 199

people 2, 4, 6, 10, 11, 13–22, 24, 25, 27, 28, 31, 33, 34, 36, 38, 39, 45, 49, 51, 54–61, 63, 65, 67–74, 76–79, 81–83, 86–93, 96–98, 100, 101, 103, 104, 106, 108, 110, 112, 113, 116, 123, 126, 132, 136, 140, 141, 143, 145–147, 152, 161, 163, 164, 167, 182, 183, 187, 211, 224, 227, 232, 236, 266

INDEX 315

performance   30, 39, 47, 49, 51, 76, 77, 80, 81,
    87, 111, 121, 123, 132, 133, 162, 170, 196, 201,
    214, 215, 234, 241
personal   2, 3, 9, 15, 16, 20, 22, 24, 25, 33, 36,
    39, 44, 46, 54, 60, 62, 63, 66, 69–71, 73,
    74, 77, 78, 81, 85, 88, 89, 91, 93, 96, 99,
    100, 103, 104, 108, 110, 118, 123, 126–128,
    130, 134, 135, 140, 145, 148, 149, 152–154,
    159, 161, 163, 164, 166, 168, 169, 173, 177,
    180, 183–187, 194, 196, 197, 202, 204, 205,
    210–213, 223, 233, 235, 237–239, 243, 256
personalised   47, 168, 184, 188, 189, 204
pivot   194, 240, 241, 255
platforms   2, 3, 5, 9, 12, 18, 22, 24, 30, 32, 33,
    43–47, 49, 55, 56, 58, 60, 61, 64, 77–80,
    82, 85, 88, 90–93, 98, 99, 101, 107, 112,
    114, 116–118, 120, 121, 126–128, 131, 146,
    151, 152, 156, 159, 165, 167, 177, 180, 181,
    183, 189, 190, 194, 201, 227–231, 233, 234,
    238, 241, 242, 244, 245, 252, 254, 256,
    258, 265
policies   1, 12–14, 22, 23, 25, 26, 32–38, 41,
    43, 49–51, 53–55, 58, 59, 61, 62, 65, 66,
    71, 76, 90, 98, 99, 109, 114–116, 118, 119,
    124, 134, 135, 137, 141, 145, 152, 158, 164,
    167–169, 171, 172, 175, 177, 188, 190, 194,
    196–198, 202, 206, 207, 211, 212, 214, 232,
    234, 237, 239, 243–247, 253, 254, 257
policy   5–7, 12–16, 19, 25, 28, 42, 43, 46, 48,
    51, 57, 58, 70, 112, 117–120, 125, 140, 143,
    152, 170, 171, 174, 177, 180, 188, 191, 195,
    196, 211, 212, 216, 227, 235, 239, 242, 243,
    264, 269
policy discourse   5–7, 12–16, 19, 25, 28, 42, 43,
    46, 48, 51, 57, 58, 70, 112, 117–120, 125,
    140, 143, 152, 170, 171, 174, 177, 180, 188,
    191, 195, 196, 211, 212, 216, 227, 235, 239,
    242, 243, 264, 269
policy texts   13, 25, 125, 128, 245
political   2, 5, 10, 24, 39, 40, 41, 46–48, 57, 59,
    62, 65, 66, 69, 73, 77, 78, 86, 88, 103–105,
    116, 122, 128, 133, 144, 155, 189, 203, 223,
    225, 233
political economy   3, 6, 9, 11, 25, 37, 47, 48,
    50, 66, 87, 89, 98, 109, 113, 114, 117, 119,
    121, 122, 128, 130, 133, 136, 143, 162, 168,
    185, 207, 208, 217–219, 232, 262–264,
    267, 272
positionality   10, 15, 23, 24, 36, 43, 44, 48, 49,
    52, 53, 56, 57, 59, 60, 63, 65–67, 70, 74,
    76, 77, 86, 89–91, 100, 107, 117, 120, 122,

143, 145, 161, 162, 168, 169, 182, 186, 201,
    213, 214, 219, 235, 238, 262, 267
post   4, 10, 44, 88, 94, 183, 186, 246, 263, 265,
    266
postdigital   10, 15, 23, 24, 36, 43, 44, 48, 49, 52,
    53, 56, 57, 59, 60, 63, 65–67, 70, 74, 76,
    77, 86, 89–91, 100, 107, 117, 120, 122, 143,
    145, 161, 162, 168, 169, 182, 186, 201, 213,
    214, 219, 235, 238, 262, 267
postdigital positionality   10, 15, 23, 24, 36,
    43, 44, 48, 49, 52, 53, 56, 57, 59, 60, 63,
    65–67, 70, 74, 76, 77, 86, 89–91, 100,
    107, 117, 120, 122, 143, 145, 161, 162, 168,
    169, 182, 186, 201, 213, 214, 219, 235, 238,
    262, 267
posthuman   3, 49, 64, 213, 222, 223, 266
posthumanism   221
power relations   25, 68–70, 76, 77, 88, 112,
    164, 169, 183, 185, 192, 196, 201
powerful   13, 15, 37, 44, 58, 59, 64, 95, 99,
    114, 121, 126, 131, 136, 138, 139, 142, 161,
    184–186, 192, 194, 200, 202, 213, 217,
    228, 233, 238, 245, 246, 252, 254, 255,
    263
precision   46, 203, 262, 265
predictability   14, 28, 37, 92, 137, 200
predicted grades   75, 173, 179, 180, 260
predigital   6, 35, 51, 59, 63, 64, 66, 219
prejudice   20, 55, 56, 80, 121
privacy   17, 18, 60, 61, 146, 156, 158, 237, 256,
    266
private   17, 24, 32, 33, 36, 38, 71, 98, 114, 126,
    133, 149, 206, 215, 216, 228, 234, 237,
    265, 267
privilege   26, 82, 86, 142, 185, 221, 223
production   4, 22, 51, 52, 93, 108, 138, 139, 168,
    195, 206, 218, 226, 245, 255, 260
professional   14, 33, 36, 80, 161, 192, 216,
    256
programming   3, 18, 39, 55, 62, 70, 77, 80, 120,
    126, 139, 147, 148, 170
protests   53, 79, 112, 144, 179, 180, 216, 267
psychology   261
public   2, 18, 19, 24, 32–34, 36, 39, 50, 79, 93,
    98, 101–103, 118, 126, 140, 209, 212, 214,
    216, 218, 220, 225, 232, 252, 254, 266

quality   15, 48, 65, 66, 69, 120, 123, 141, 159,
    164, 179, 181, 188, 192, 197, 206, 209, 211,
    214, 216, 219, 220, 226, 241, 264
queer   141–143

race   10, 11, 13, 19, 22, 34, 41, 59, 60, 67, 68, 76,
       80, 127, 134, 144, 146–148, 152, 172, 185,
       202, 221, 222, 233, 234, 236, 253
racism   20, 34, 56, 79, 80, 82, 121, 134, 144, 158
rainbow   93, 95, 102, 176–178
rational   14, 20, 21, 25, 26, 28, 30, 37, 39,
       42–44, 47–51, 53, 54, 62, 69, 70, 74, 85,
       87, 98, 100, 108, 109, 111, 112, 114–117,
       119, 123–125, 134, 136–139, 141, 143, 155,
       161–164, 169, 171, 174, 180, 192, 194, 206,
       209, 212, 232, 237, 239, 242, 245, 256
rationalisation   20, 35, 36, 50–52, 109, 122,
       200, 272
rationality   28, 30, 37, 41, 42, 51, 71, 82, 84, 87,
       92, 104, 105, 109–111, 120, 145, 162, 163,
       200, 205, 208, 240, 245–247, 259, 262
reality   4, 7, 15, 44, 89, 114, 146, 208, 219, 252,
       268
reflexivity   10, 46, 68, 69, 71, 72, 89, 99, 105,
       140, 168, 196, 197, 212, 237
regional   63, 206, 207, 229, 245, 257
relations   10, 12, 19, 21, 23, 25, 40, 43–45, 58,
       68–70, 76, 77, 88, 93, 102, 112, 115, 121,
       139, 164, 169, 183, 185, 188, 192, 196, 201,
       208, 222, 235, 239, 255, 266
relationships   6, 11, 31, 33, 41–43, 50, 57, 59,
       77, 101, 138, 141, 150, 155, 169, 183, 184,
       188, 189, 194, 199, 206, 208, 214, 218, 221,
       236, 252, 264, 267, 269
renewal   6, 220, 267
research   3–5, 14, 17, 20, 27, 28, 33–36,
       41–44, 46, 47, 57, 59, 62, 63, 67–69, 74,
       86, 96–100, 107, 113, 119, 133, 134, 137,
       140–142, 146–148, 156, 171, 183, 185, 188,
       189, 191, 196, 197, 200, 202, 203, 206,
       211–214, 216–224, 226, 228, 232, 234, 238,
       240, 243–245, 258, 260, 262, 268
Research Excellence Framework (REF)   140,
       216
resistance   10, 37, 110, 134, 142, 146, 185, 247
restrictions   29, 64, 156, 166, 171, 220, 254,
       259
retention   4, 43, 66, 118, 203, 212, 231, 240
rhetoric   4, 48, 59, 111, 141, 167, 169, 171, 172,
       174, 180, 182, 183, 210, 213, 235, 236, 238,
       240
rules   26, 62, 103, 120, 156, 157, 177, 185, 187,
       213, 215, 224, 239, 243

safe   17, 31, 66, 94, 154, 177, 178
sanitiser   27, 102, 200, 201, 259

science   4, 5, 7, 9, 11, 22, 45, 48, 50, 52, 97, 99,
       101, 111, 122, 124, 138, 148, 153, 177, 186,
       193, 198, 201, 203, 205, 208, 209, 214,
       218–221, 223–226, 258, 262
scientific   3, 5, 22, 43, 45–47, 62, 96, 99, 102,
       113, 193, 195, 197, 201, 203, 206, 211, 212,
       214, 218–221, 224, 242, 246, 250, 252,
       254, 259, 263, 266
secrets   2, 9, 126
sector   15, 19, 33, 37, 62, 96, 133, 139, 143, 148,
       168, 170, 171, 176, 189, 193, 206, 210,
       213–215, 234, 236, 238, 246–253, 258,
       265–267
security   17, 88, 116, 140, 146, 151, 215, 254,
       256, 266
self-isolate   35, 165, 244
selfie   53
separation   14, 46, 93, 171, 175, 187, 194, 206,
       217, 233
sexuality   10, 68, 136, 221, 253
sheets   1–3, 11, 79, 80, 82, 126, 149, 150, 266
situated   188, 212, 213
skills   13, 17, 23, 35, 37, 47, 53, 90, 98, 126, 144,
       147, 148, 155, 167, 186, 194, 198, 203, 227,
       229, 231, 238, 264
social construction   93
social distancing   18, 29, 31, 35, 61, 91–93, 103,
       177, 259
social justice   11, 44, 46, 104, 118, 124, 125, 134,
       137, 139, 145, 152, 170, 202, 231, 232, 266
social media   2, 6, 18, 20, 47, 54, 58, 60, 61, 82,
       88–90, 93, 112, 126, 127, 131, 135, 140, 146,
       147, 170, 209, 220, 255–257
social mobility   46, 107, 118
society   5, 6, 9–13, 15, 16, 24, 25, 35, 42–44, 46,
       48, 50, 51, 53, 57, 58, 60, 63, 67, 68, 75,
       82, 83, 90–92, 96, 98, 100, 101, 105–107,
       114, 115, 118, 122–124, 126, 128, 134, 139,
       143, 145, 152, 155, 158, 167, 168, 170, 173,
       175, 182, 184, 185, 192–194, 198, 203,
       212–214, 216, 218, 221, 223–225, 229, 232,
       237, 238, 243, 249, 255, 256, 262, 263,
       266, 267
sociology   78, 252, 262
software   3, 12, 60, 61, 112, 114, 117, 120, 123, 133,
       138, 140, 141, 146, 156, 239
space   5, 6, 9, 20, 39, 59, 68, 71, 72, 111, 122, 134,
       136, 156, 162, 163, 182, 184, 185, 207, 210,
       238, 256, 257, 259
species   59, 223, 267
statues   79, 85

INDEX   317

standardised   14, 187, 202
stories   2, 18, 20, 62, 77, 86, 100, 107, 137
strategies   3, 6, 14, 16, 21, 30, 33, 35, 37, 44, 46,
      53, 107, 111, 115, 116, 118, 136, 139, 148, 158,
      159, 163, 175, 197, 215, 220, 241, 242, 253,
      255, 265
strategy   18, 21, 23, 39, 42, 46, 49, 63, 109, 115,
      123, 173, 197, 211, 249
stressful   181
structure   113, 127, 163, 168, 185, 198, 216, 238,
      239, 253, 254, 261
students   17, 20–23, 33–37, 42, 43, 45–48, 58,
      65, 67, 71, 74–77, 82, 86, 98, 99, 106–108,
      114–116, 118–120, 124, 125, 128, 132, 141–143,
      148, 149, 154, 158, 159, 161–177, 179–191,
      194, 196–199, 201–207, 209, 210, 212, 228,
      231–233, 235, 239, 243, 245, 254, 267
subjectivities   33, 52, 58, 71, 72, 75, 100, 114,
      184, 186, 216
subjectivity   25, 68, 70–72, 76, 89, 119, 145,
      175, 184, 195, 216, 218, 261
surveillance   5, 18, 54, 58, 60, 61, 72, 92, 127,
      215, 218, 239, 254, 256
sustainable   6, 47, 48, 52, 106, 193, 194, 202,
      208–210, 214, 218, 219, 227, 243, 246,
      249, 254, 263, 264
symbols   93, 94, 177
symptoms   27, 29, 123, 222
systemic bias   56, 159, 160
systems   2–4, 6, 11, 13, 16–22, 32, 38, 43, 46,
      48, 57, 62, 63, 66, 70–72, 87, 89, 90, 101,
      106, 111, 112, 116–122, 126, 133, 138–140,
      145–147, 149, 152, 156, 158, 161, 164, 170,
      183–185, 191, 193, 196, 199, 200, 209, 212,
      219, 221, 231–233, 236, 237, 240, 241, 243,
      244, 247, 249

targets   23, 47, 136, 154, 162, 196, 197, 214, 215,
      226, 233, 234, 235
teaching   14, 32–36, 42, 47, 50, 62, 65, 66, 68,
      69, 97, 99, 100, 102, 107, 119, 122, 133, 135,
      139–141, 147, 154, 155, 169, 196, 197, 204,
      206, 209, 211, 217, 218, 223, 240, 244, 262
techniques   17, 53, 77, 104, 140, 186, 199, 200,
      202, 203, 215
technoscience   14, 16, 235
technologies   3, 6, 12–14, 16, 22, 30, 32, 35,
      42, 44, 48, 50–52, 57–61, 63, 70, 76, 80,
      81, 87, 93, 98, 99, 101, 107, 110–112, 116,
      119, 121, 123, 125–127, 133, 135, 138, 139,
      145–147, 153, 159, 185, 188, 214, 221, 224,

      225, 234, 237, 244, 249, 250, 253, 259,
      261–263, 267
technology   4–6, 9, 14–16, 18, 23, 24, 31,
      33–38, 41, 42, 46–48, 50, 51, 54, 55,
      57–59, 64, 70–72, 75, 90, 91, 97, 98, 109,
      110, 112, 114–120, 123–126, 137–139, 143,
      146, 153, 155, 156, 158, 161, 167, 188, 190,
      200, 201, 203, 204, 209, 218, 224–229,
      231, 232, 237, 242, 247, 261–264
technology enhanced learning   34, 41, 46,
      115, 158
Teaching Excellence Framework (TEF)   140–
      142, 170, 175, 241
testimonies   97, 106, 107, 177, 232
therapeutic   53, 66, 127, 162, 171, 172, 174, 175,
      254
the student experience   44, 46, 58, 108, 128,
      161, 166–175, 177, 180–184, 186, 189, 191,
      198, 200, 212, 213, 232, 245
TikTok   88, 257
Tools   51, 60, 66, 115, 117, 131, 193, 202, 210
tracking   60, 90
transparency   38, 40, 65, 75, 76, 190, 196
travel   2, 9, 34–36, 64, 77, 81, 91, 184, 195, 266
trust   62, 85, 86, 92, 97, 140, 170, 179, 229, 233,
      249, 266,
tweet   2, 102, 112
Twitter   7, 39, 55, 103, 104, 164, 227, 228,
      255–257, 261

unconscious   54–56, 142
universities   3, 6, 7, 12, 14–24, 28, 32, 33, 35, 36,
      38, 41–45, 47, 48, 52, 56, 61–67, 75, 86,
      87, 97–100, 106–111, 114–116, 119–123, 125,
      128, 129, 133, 137, 139–143, 149, 152, 154,
      155, 158, 159, 162, 166–171, 173–177, 180,
      182, 185, 187, 188, 191, 195, 196, 200–203,
      205–208, 212–214, 216, 217, 227, 229,
      233–250, 252–256, 259, 264, 265
university   3, 4, 12, 14–17, 21–23, 30, 33, 35,
      37–42, 45, 48, 62, 63, 65–67, 74, 76, 78,
      88, 106–109, 115, 116, 119, 120, 122, 123,
      128–130, 133, 134, 139, 141, 143, 148, 149,
      152, 153, 155, 158, 163, 165–177, 180, 183,
      184, 186, 195, 197, 203, 205–209, 211, 214,
      217, 218, 225–228, 231–235, 237–243,
      245–251, 256, 258, 267–269

vaccine   7, 19, 46, 104, 105
values   2, 7, 9, 10, 12, 21, 33, 34, 38, 39, 42, 46,
      48, 49, 50, 57, 63, 65–68, 77, 130, 136,

138, 145, 153, 155, 164, 170, 173, 184, 192, 195, 199–201, 204, 205, 211, 212, 219, 225, 234, 237, 253, 254, 256

victimisation   175

viral   7, 9, 11, 17, 46, 69, 97, 100, 101, 139, 177, 191, 227

virtual   2–7, 9–12, 15, 17, 20, 38, 39, 41, 44, 49, 54–56, 63, 66, 70, 73, 76, 80–82, 86, 88, 102, 104, 114, 115, 116, 118, 152, 156, 158, 176, 187, 190, 200, 206, 214, 227, 228, 232, 238, 255, 257, 266, 267

virus   7, 9, 17, 25, 28, 29, 34, 36, 71, 93, 102, 103, 105, 117, 123, 139, 144, 152, 159, 164, 165, 200, 222, 235, 235, 252, 259, 266

visual   90, 128, 130, 166

vulnerability   71, 171, 175, 176, 264, 266

wave   106

websites   37, 56, 82, 84, 120, 255

wellbeing   11, 47, 53, 66, 105, 162, 167, 169, 172–174, 181, 190, 197, 205, 229, 267

wifi   126, 149, 151, 185, 229

work   13, 16, 17, 22, 31, 34, 36, 37, 40, 43, 47, 52, 53, 55, 68, 71, 74, 76, 80, 82, 91, 98, 105, 110, 117, 121, 122, 126, 137, 141, 148, 167, 176, 180, 185, 187, 216, 236, 237, 241, 243, 246, 256, 263, 265

working   16, 17, 36, 47, 54, 61, 64, 73, 80, 92, 96, 99, 107, 112, 128, 143, 176–178, 192, 214, 220, 224, 229, 244, 256, 261, 264

Zoom   91, 227

Printed in the United States
by Baker & Taylor Publisher Services